The Theory and Practice of Constitutional Change in America

American University Studies

Series X
Political Science

Vol. 42

PETER LANG
New York • San Francisco • Bern • Baltimore
Frankfurt am Main • Berlin • Wien • Paris

The Theory and Practice of Constitutional Change in America

A Collection of Original Source Materials

John R. Vile, Editor

PETER LANG
New York • San Francisco • Bern • Baltimore
Frankfurt am Main • Berlin • Wien • Paris

Library of Congress Cataloging-in-Publication Data

The Theory and practice of constitutional change in America: a collection of original source materials/ [edited by] John R. Vile.
p. cm. — (American university studies. Series X, Political science; vol. 42)
Includes bibliographical references and index.
1. United States—Constitutional law—Amendments—History—Sources. 2. Constitutional amendments—History—Sources. 3. Political science—History—Sources. I. Vile, John R. II. Series.
KF4555.T47 1993 342.73′029—dc20 93-2514
[347.30229] CIP
ISBN 0-8204-2193-6
ISSN 0740-0470

Die Deutsche Bibliothek-CIP-Einheitsaufnahme

Vile, John R.:
The theory and practice of constitutional change in America: a collection of original source materials/ John R. Vile. - New York; San Francisco; Bern; Frankfurt am Main; Berlin; Wien; Paris: Lang, 1993
(American university studies: Ser. 10, Political science; Vol. 42)
ISBN 0-8204-2193-6
NE: American university studies / 10

The paper in this book meets the guidelines for permanence and durability of the Committee on Production Guidelines for Book Longevity of the Council on Library Resources.

Printed in the United States of America.

To the memory of my grandparents,

Arthur and Lucina Vile

and

Albert and Grace Griffith

Contents

Preface

While recent bicentennial celebrations would indicate that many Americans revere their Constitution, most Americans must surely also take it for granted that constitutions are subject to change. At the state level, constitutions are amended, and even replaced, fairly often. While more than 10,000 changes—albeit many of them redundant—have been offered to the United States Constitution, it has been amended less frequently. Moreover, of the twenty-seven amendments which have been proposed and ratified to date, the first ten were adopted as a group while the Twenty-First repealed the imposition of alcoholic prohibition which was imposed by the Eighteenth. Still, it is common to hear calls for amendments to remedy perceived defects in the Constitution or to modify or overturn recent judicial decisions as to its meaning.

Although the mechanisms for constitutional change appear to be a New World invention, the topic of constitutional change has been a recurrent theme in political thought. Some voices in this debate are fairly well known, but others have been muffled or ignored. This book attempts to provide a forum for both kinds of sources. Selections include readings from political and legal theorists, from judicial decisions, from speeches, and from important documents. While no such readings can be exhaustive, this selection should significantly expand the scope of contemporary discussion.

The readings are presented in rough chronological sequence. While the time periods chosen are necessarily somewhat arbitrary, the readings are grouped within parameters that are not wholly of the author's own making. The first chapter is a discussion of antecedents and influences. It accordingly deals with theorists who were known to, and might therefore have exerted influence on or reflected ideas that were familiar to, the American Founding Fathers. Chapter 2 follows up with a focus on the period roughly from the beginning of the American Revolution through the end of Washington's administration. Chapter 3 continues the debate through the first half of the nineteenth century, while Chapter 4 focuses on the Civil War period and its aftermath. Chapter 5 recounts analyses and critiques of the amending process, mostly negative, by leading Progressive spokesmen while Chapter 6 indicates some of the reactions that Progressive Era amendments spawned among conservative opponents and in the courts. Finally, Chapter 7 carries this debate forward by focusing on a number of recent amending controversies.

The author believes the selections in this book are fairly representative of the range of debates that have surrounded the processes of constitutional change. Whenever possible, readings have been paired to emphasize the dialogues that have surrounded key amending issues. For the most part, footnotes within readings have been omitted to facilitate easy reading, and some headings have been added to identify the topics of discussion. Although the author has views on many of the subjects discussed here, he sees this as a forum for giving voice to a wide range of opinions rather than an occasion to grind partisan axes. The author will be pleased if these readings give insights into the uniqueness, the importance, and the range of issues surrounding the processes of constitutional change.

Acknowledgments

The author would like to acknowledge the continuing support he has received from his former teachers, family members, colleagues, and friends, many of whom have been cited by name in former books. The author is particularly appreciative to Middle Tennessee State University, and especially to members of the Faculty Research Committee and the Patent and Copyright Committees, for their support of this book without which this volume could not have been published. He would also like to thank Christopher S. Myers and Christine Marra of Peter Lang Publishing and Kevin McMahon and Maureen Conway of Laserset.

Chapter 1

Historical and Philosophical Antecedents to the Amending Process

When they were established, both the American form of government and its amending mechanisms were unique, but neither constitutional provisions nor forms of government spring full-blown into existence. The readings in this chapter establish that the subjects of legal continuity and change which amending processes address were a perennial object of serious political thought from the time of the Old Testament, through Greek and Roman history, and on through more contemporary political and philosophical writings with which the American Founders were familiar. At the able hands of William Penn, these theories had even been crystalized into a rudimentary amending mechanism long before the former American colonies would declare their independence. Other ideas were clearly present which would pave the way for such mechanisms as the constitutional convention, entrenchment clauses, and the use of extraordinary amending majorities, which would receive fuller articulation in the American Revolutionary period.

1.1 Daniel in the Lion's Den and the Danger of Unalterable Laws*

At least two passages (found in Esther and Daniel) from the Hebrew Scriptures, or Old Testament, refer to the unalterable

* Daniel 6:3-23. KJV. Verse numbers omitted.

laws of the Medes and Persians. The familiar story of Daniel in the lion's den has special significance when it is recognized that King Darius was forced to risk his servant's life because of the unalterability of the law which was then in place in Babylon, the city of exile for Daniel and his Jewish compatriots. Only God's direct intervention saved Daniel from the terrible consequences of this unalterability. The passage below is taken from the version of the Bible most familiar to the American Founders.

Daniel in the Lion's Den

Then this Daniel was preferred above the presidents and princes, because an excellent spirit was in him; and the king thought to set him over the whole realm.

Then the presidents and princes sought to find occasion against Daniel concerning the kingdom; but they could find none occasion nor fault; forasmuch as he was faithful, neither was there any error or fault found in him.

Then said these men, We shall not find any occasion against this Daniel, except we find it against him concerning the law of his God.

Then these presidents and princes assembled together to the king, and said thus unto him, King Darius, live for ever.

All the presidents of the kingdom, the governors, and the princes, the counsellors, and the captains, have consulted together to establish a royal statute, and to make a firm decree, that whosoever shall ask a petition of any God or man for thirty days, save of thee, O king, he shall be cast into the den of lions.

Now, O king, establish the decree, and sign the writing, that it be not changed, according to the law of the Medes and Persians, which altereth not.

Wherefore king Darius signed the writing and the decree.

Now when Daniel knew that the writing was signed, he went into his house; and his windows being open in his chamber toward Jerusalem, he kneeled upon his knees three times a day, and prayed, and gave thanks before his God, as he did aforetime.

Then these men assembled, and found Daniel praying and making supplication before his God.

Then they came near, and spake before the king concerning the king's decree; Hast thou not signed a decree, that every man that shall ask a petition of any God or man within thirty days, save of thee, O king, shall be cast into the den of lions? The king answered and said, The thing is true, according to the law of the Medes and Persians, which altereth not.

Then answered they and said before the king, That Daniel, which is of the children of the captivity of Judah, regardeth not thee, O king, nor the decree that thou hast signed, but maketh his petition three times a day.

Then the king, when he heard these words, was sore displeased with himself, and set his heart on Daniel to deliver him: and he laboured till the going down of the sun to deliver him.

Then these men assembled unto the king, and said unto the king, Know, O king, that the law of the Medes and Persians is, That no decree nor statute which the king established may be changed.

Then the king commanded, and they brought Daniel, and cast him into the den of lions. Now the king spake and said unto Daniel, Thy God whom thou servest continually, he will deliver thee.

And a stone was brought, and laid upon the mouth of the den; and the king sealed it with his own signet, and with the signet of his lords; that the purpose might not be changed concerning Daniel.

Then the king went to his palace, and passed the night fasting: neither were instruments of musick brought before him: and his sleep went from him.

Then the king arose very early in the morning, and went in haste unto the den of lions.

And when he came to the den, he cried with a lamentable voice unto Daniel: and the king spake and said to Daniel, O Daniel, servant of the living God, is thy God, whom thou servest continually, able to deliver them from the lions?

Then said Daniel unto the king, O king, live for ever.

My God hath sent his angel, and hath shut the lions' mouths, and they have not hurt me: forasmuch as before him innocency was found in me; and also before them, O king, have I done no hurt.

Then was the king exceeding glad for him, and commanded that they should take Daniel up out of the den. So Daniel was taken up out of the den, and no manner of hurt was found upon him, because he believed in his God.

1.2 Plutarch Discusses a Lawgiver Who Strove for Permanence*

The American Founders were quite familiar with Greek and Roman history, and they often modeled their own actions after those of classical statesmen and attempted to draw contemporary lessons from a study of their history. Both Greece and Rome had a number of well-known law-givers, some of whom James Madison would later cite in *Federalist* No. 38 (found in reading 2.7 of this book). One of the most interesting of these law-givers was Lycurgus, who was credited with having created the long-lasting constitution of Sparta. As the example from Plutarch (42-102 A.D.) excerpted below indicates, Lycurgus took some rather extraordinary means to ensure the durability of his laws, measures which may not, however have proven completely successful, as the reference to events in the reign of King Agis indicate.

The Example of Lycurgus

When he perceived that his more important institutions had taken root in the minds of his countrymen, that custom had rendered them familiar and easy, that his commonwealth was now grown up and able to go alone, then, as Plato somewhere tells us, the Maker of the world, when first he saw it existing and beginning its motion, felt joy, even so Lycurgus, viewing with joy and satisfaction the greatness and beauty of his politi-

---

* Plutarch, *Plutarch's Lives of Illustrious Men*, trans. by John Dryden and others (New York: Hurst and Company, Publishers, 1900; reprint of 1859 edition), vol. 1, pp. 111-12; 114.

cal structure, now fairly at work and in motion, conceived the thought to make it immortal too, and, as far as human forecast could reach, to deliver it down unchangeable to posterity. He called an extraordinary assembly of all the people, and told them that he now thought everything reasonably well established, both for the happiness and the virtue of the state; but that there was one thing still behind, of the greatest importance, which he thought not fit to impart until he had consulted the oracle; in the meantime, his desire was that they would observe the laws without any the least alteration until his return, and then he would do as the god should direct him. They all consented readily, and bade him hasten his journey; but, before he departed, he administered an oath to the two kings, the senate, and the whole commons, to abide by and maintain the established form of polity until Lycurgus should be come back. This done, he set out for Delphi, and, having sacrificed to Apollo, asked him whether the laws he had established were good, and sufficient for a people's happiness and virtue. The oracle answered that the laws were excellent, and that the people, while it observed them, should live in the height of renown. Lycurgus took the oracle in writing, and sent it over to Sparta; and, having sacrificed the second time to Apollo, and taken leave of his friends and his son, he resolved that the Spartans should not be released from the oath they had taken, and that he would, of his own act, close his life where he was. He was now about that age in which life was still tolerable, and yet might be quitted without regret. Everything, moreover, about him was in a sufficiently prosperous condition. He, therefore, made an end of himself by a total abstinence from food, thinking it a statesman's duty to make his very death, if possible, an act of service to the state, and even in the end of his life to give some example of virtue and effect some useful purpose. He would, on the one hand, crown and consummate his own happiness by a death suitable to so honorable a life, and, on the other, would secure to his countrymen the enjoyment of the advantages he had spent his life in obtaining for them, since they had solemnly sworn the maintenance of his institutions until his return. Nor was he deceived in his expectations for the city of

Lacedaemon continued the chief city of all Greece for the space of five hundred years, in strict observance of Lycurgus's laws, in all which time there was no manner of alteration made, during the reign of fourteen kings down to the time of Agis, the son of Archidamus. For the new creation of the ephori, though thought to be in favor of the people, was so far from diminishing, that it very much heightened, the aristocratical character of the government.

In the time of Agis, gold and silver first flowed into Sparta, and with them all those mischiefs which attend the immoderate desire of riches. Lysander promoted this order; for by bringing in rich spoils from the wars, although himself incorrupt, he yet by this means filled his country with avarice and luxury, and subverted the laws and ordinances of Lycurgus; so long as which were in force, the aspect presented by Sparta was rather that of a rule of life followed by one wise and temperate man, than of the political government of a nation. . . .

Aristocrates, the son of Hipparchus, says that he died in Crete, and that his Cretan friends, in accordance with his own request when they had burned his body, scattered the ashes into the sea; for fear lest, if his relics should be transported to Lacedaemon, the people might pretend to be released from their oaths, and made innovations in the government. Thus much may suffice for the life and actions of Lycurgus.

1.3 Plato Councils Against Change But Provides a Mechanism for It*

Plato (427-327 B.C..) one of the earliest Greek philosophers, is still regarded as among the greatest thinkers of all times. A student of Socrates, whom he immortalized in a number of his dialogues, Plato wrote a number of works on political thought. Prior to Plato, the philosopher Heraclitus had argued that the world was in constant flux while the philosopher Parmenides had argued that change was illusory and that all things remained fundamentally the same. In Plato's own works, he

---

* Plato, *The Laws*, trans. B. Jowett, vol. 5 of *The Dialogues of Plato*, 2nd ed. (Oxford: The Clarendon Press, 1875), pp. 366-8; 533-4.

attempted to stress the need for regimes to be founded on stable principles that were beyond the flux of ordinary politics.

One of Plato's later and most mature works was entitled, *The Laws* where the primary character is an Athenian Stranger. Plato's stress on permanency is indicated in his discussion of children's games. His acceptance of a Nocturnal Council to give stability to the state but to revise the laws when necessary also indicates his understanding of the need for legal change.

Discussion of Children's Games and Change

ATHENIAN: I say that in states generally no one has observed that the plays of childhood have a great deal to do with the permanence or want of permanence in legislation. For when plays are ordered with a view to children having the same plays and amusing themselves after the same manner, and finding delight in the same playthings, the more solemn institutions of the state are allowed to remain undisturbed. Whereas if sports are disturbed and innovations are made in them, and they constantly change, and the young never speak of their having the same likings, or the same established notions of good and bad taste, either in the bearing of their bodies or in their dress, but he who devises something new and out the way in figures and colours and the like is held in special honour, we may truly say that no greater evil can happen in a state; for he who changes the sports is secretly changing the manners of the young, and making the old to be dishonoured among them and the new to be honoured. And I affirm that there is nothing which is a greater injury to all states than saying or thinking thus. Will you hear me tell how great I deem it to be?

CLEINIAS: You mean the evil of blaming antiquity in states?

ATHENIAN: Exactly.

CLEINIAS: If you are speaking of that, you will find in us hearers who are disposed to receive what you say not unfavourably but most favourably.

ATHENIAN: I should expect so.

CLEINIAS: Proceed.

ATHENIAN: Well, then, let us give all the greater heed to one another's words. The argument says that to change from anything except the bad is the most dangerous of all things; this is true in the case of the seasons and of the winds, in the management of our bodies and the habits of our minds—true of all things except, as I said before, of the bad. He who looks at the constitution of individuals accustomed to eat any sort of meat or drink any drink or do any work which they could get, may see that they are at first disordered, but afterwards, as time goes on, their bodies grow adapted to them, and they learn to know and like variety, and have good health and enjoyment of life; and if ever afterwards they are confined again to a superior diet, at first they are troubled with disorders, and with difficulty become habituated to their new food. A similar principle we may imagine to hold good about the minds of men and the nature of their souls. For when they have been brought up in certain laws, which by some Divine Providence have remained unchanged during long ages, so that no one has any memory or tradition of their ever having been otherwise than they are, then every one is afraid and ashamed to change that which is established. The legislator must somehow find a way of implanting this reverence for antiquity, and I would propose the following way:—People are apt to fancy, as I was saying before, that when the plays of children are altered they are merely plays, not seeing that the most serious and detrimental consequences arise out of the change; and they readily comply with the child's wishes instead of deterring him, not considering that these children who make innovations in their games, when they grow up to be men will be different from the last generation of children, and, being different, will desire a different sort of life, and under the influence of this desire will want other institutions and laws; and no one ever apprehends that there will follow what I just now called the greatest of evils to states. Changes in bodily fashions are no such serious evils, but frequent changes in the praise and censure of manners are the greatest of evils, and require the utmost prevision.

CLEINIAS: To be sure.

ATHENIAN: And now do we still hold to our former assertion, that rhythms and music in general are imitations of good and evil characters in men? What say you?

CLEINIAS: This is the only doctrine which I can admit.

ATHENIAN: Must we not, then, try in every possible way to prevent our youth desiring imitations and novelties either in dance or song? nor must any one be allowed to offer them varieties of pleasures..

CLEINIAS: Most true.

The Nocturnal Council

ATHENIAN: Were we not saying that there must be in our city a council which was to be of this sort: Ten of the oldest guardians of the law, and all those who have obtained prizes of virtue, were to meet, and the council was also to include those who had visited foreign countries in the hope of hearing something that might be of use in the preservation of the laws, and who, having come safely home, and having been tested in these same matter, had proved themselves to be worthy to take part in the meeting;—each of the members was to select some young man of not less than thirty years of age, he himself judging in the first instance whether the young man is worthy by nature and education, and then introducing him to the others, and if he seem to them also to be worthy he was to be adopted by them; but if not, they are forbidden to elect him, and still more is he forbidden to accept their nomination. The meeting of the council was to be held early in the morning, when everybody was at leisure from all other business, whether public or private,—something of that sort was said by us before.

CLEINIAS: True.

ATHENIAN: Then now returning to the council, I would say further,—that this institution having all the required conditions, might save us all, and be the anchor of the state, if let down into the sea.

1.4 Aristotle Discusses the Value of Legal Innovation*

Aristotle (384-322 B.C.) was a student of Plato and another of the most significant Greek philosophers whose thought virtually encompassed all the knowledge of his day from biology through metaphysics. Aristotle's political thought is chiefly found in his *Ethics* and his *Politics*. Book II of *The Politics* explores actual and ideal states. The following selection which focuses on a suggestion made by an exotic thinker named Hippodamus, demonstrates that while, like Plato, Aristotle recognized the need for some changes, Aristotle's central emphasis was on legal stability.

Should Innovators Be Honored?

To honor those who discover anything which is useful to the state is a proposal which has a specious sound, but cannot safely be enacted by law, for it may encourage reformers, and perhaps even lead to political commotions. This question involves another. It has been doubted whether it is or is not expedient to make any changes in the laws of a country, even if another law be better. Now, if all changes are inexpedient, we can hardly assent to the proposal of Hippodamus; for, under pretense of doing a public service, a man may introduce measures which are really destructive to the laws or to the constitution. But, since we have touched upon this subject, perhaps we had better go a little into detail, for, as I was saying, there is a difference of opinion, and it may sometimes seem desirable to make changes. Such changes in the other arts and sciences have certainly been beneficial; medicine, for example, and gymnastic, and every other art and craft have departed from traditional usage. And, if politics be an art, change must be necessary in this as in any other art. That improvement has occurred is shown by the fact that old customs are exceedingly simple and barbarous. For the ancient Hellenes went about armed and bought their brides of each other. The remains of ancient laws which have come down to us are quite absurd; for

* Aristotle, *Politics & Poetics*, trans. by Benjamin Jowett and S. H. Butcher, intro. by Horace M. Kallen (New York: The Heritage Press, 1964), Book II, Chapter 8, pp. 57-8.

example, at Cumae there is a law about murder, to the effect that if the accuser produce a certain number of witnesses from among his own kinsmen, the accused shall be held guilty. Again, men in general desire the good, and not merely what their fathers had. But the primeval inhabitants, whether they were born of the earth or were the survivors of some destruction, may be supposed to have been no better than ordinary or even foolish people among ourselves (such is certainly the tradition concerning the earth-born men); and it would be ridiculous to rest contented with their notions. Even when laws have been written down, they ought not always to remain unaltered. As in other sciences, so in politics, it is impossible that all things should be precisely set down in writing; for enactments must be universal, but actions are concerned with particulars. Hence we infer that sometimes and in certain cases laws may be changed; but when we look at the matter from another point of view, great caution would seem to be required. For the habit of lightly changing the laws is an evil, and, when the advantage is small, some errors both of lawgivers and rulers had better be left; the citizen will not gain so much by making the change as he will lose by the habit of disobedience. The analogy of the arts is false; a change in a law is a very different thing from a change in an art. For the law has no power to command obedience except that of habit, which can only be given by time, so that a readiness to change from old to new laws enfeebles the power of the law. Even if we admit that the laws are to be changed, are they all to be changed, and in every state? And are they to be changed by anybody who likes, or only by certain persons? These are very important questions. . . .

1.5 Machiavelli Points to the Need for Constitutional Renewal*

Best known for his candid and sometimes shocking advice in *The Prince*, Niccolo Machiavelli's (1469-1527) more compre-

* Niccolo Machiavelli, *Discourses on the First Decade of Titus Livius*, trans. Ninian Hill Thomson (London: Kegan Paul, Trench & Co., 1883), Book I, Chapter 2, pp. 11-2; Book III, Chapter 1, pp. 327-9.

hensive political teaching is found in *The Discourses* where he indicated his preference for republican governments where people participated in the defense and governance of the polity. While some view Machiavelli as the first among the moderns, he almost always had an eye to historical experience. He was particularly concerned about the desirability for periodic renewal within states, as in religions, and the need for great men who could bring about reforms. These concerns were reflected in the following passages from *The Discourses*.

Different Kinds of Republics

These [cities] as they have had different origins, so likewise have had different laws and institutions. For to some at their very first commencement, or not long after, laws have been given by a single legislator, and all at one time; like those given by Lycurgus to the Spartans; while to others they have been given at different times, as need rose or accident determined; as in the case of Rome. That republic, indeed, may be called happy, whose lot has been to have a founder so prudent as to provide for it laws under which it can continue to live securely, without need to amend them; as we find Sparta preserving hers for eight hundred years, without deterioration and without any dangerous disturbance. On the other hand, some measure of unhappiness attaches to the State which, not having yielded itself once for all into the hands of a single wise legislator, is obliged to recast its institutions for itself; and of such States, by far the most unhappy is that which is furthest removed from a sound system of government, by which I mean that its institutions lie wholly outside the path which might lead it to a true and perfect end. For it is scarcely possible that a State in this position can ever, by any chance, set itself to rights; whereas another whose institutions are imperfect, if it have made a good beginning and such as admits of its amendment, may in the course of events arrive at perfection. It is certain, however, that such States can never be reformed without great risk; for, as a rule, men will accept no new law altering the institutions of their State, unless the necessity for such a change be demonstrated; and since this necessity cannot arise without danger, the State may easily be overthrown before the new order of things is established. . . .

For a Sect or Commonwealth to last long, it must often be brought back to its Beginnings

Doubtless, all the things of this world have a limit set to their duration; yet those of them the bodies whereof have not been suffered to grow disordered, but have been so cared for that either no change at all has been wrought in them, or, if any, a change for the better and nor for the worse, will run that course which Heaven has in a general way appointed them. And since I am now speaking of mixed bodies, for States and Sects are so to be regarded, I say that for them these are wholesome changes which bring them back to their first beginnings.

Those States consequently stand surest and endure longest which, either by the operation of their institutions can renew themselves, or come to be renewed by accident apart from any design. Nothing, however, can be clearer than that unless thus renewed these bodies do not last. Now the way to renew them is, as I have said, to bring them back to their beginnings, since all beginnings of sects, commonwealths, or kingdoms must needs have in them a certain excellence, by virtue of which they gain their first reputation and make their first growth. But because in progress of time this excellence becomes corrupted, unless something be done to restore it to what it was at first, these bodies necessarily decay: for as the physicians tell us in speaking of the human body, "Something or other is daily added which sooner or later will require treatment."

As regards commonwealths, this return to the point of departure is brought about either by extrinsic accident or by intrinsic foresight. As to the first, we have seen how it was necessary that Rome should be taken by the Gauls, that being thus in a manner reborn, she might recover life and vigour, and resume the observances of religion and justice which she had suffered to grow rusted by neglect. . . .

It is necessary then, as I have said already, that where men dwell together in a regulated society, they be often reminded of those ordinances in conformity with which they ought to live, either by something inherent in these, or else by some external accident. A reminder is given in the former of these two ways, either by the passing of some law whereby the members of the society are brought to an account; or else by some man of rare worth arising among them, whose virtuous life and example have the same effect as a law. In a Commonwealth, accordingly, this end is served either by the virtues of some one of its citizens, or by the operation of its institutions.

The institutions whereby the Roman Commonwealth was led back to its starting point, were the tribuneship of the people and the censorship, together with all those laws which were passed to check the insolence and ambition of its citizens. Such institutions, however, require fresh life to be infused into them by the worth of some one man who fearlessly devotes himself to give them effect in opposition to the power of those who set them at defiance.

1.6 Sir Richard Hooker Distinguishes Among Three Types of Old Testament Laws*

Richard Hooker (1554-1600) was a defender of the organization and doctrine of the Church of England against Puritan reformers who desired still further changes along the lines of the Protestant Reformation. The passage below defending the Church of England has much wider implications for political change because it shows how Christian theorists with great regard for Holy Scripture might recognize that not all parts of such Scripture were equally applicable in modern context.

The Mutability of Divine Law

In a word, we plainly perceive by the difference of those three laws which the Jews received at the hands of God, the moral, ceremonial, and judicial, that if the end for which and the matter according whereunto God maketh his laws continue always one and the same, his laws also do the like; for which

---

* Richard Hooker, *Of the Laws of Ecclesiastical Polity*, (New York: Everyman's Library, 1969), Book 3, pp. 331-334.

cause the moral law cannot be altered: secondly, that whether the matter whereon laws are made continue or continue not, if their end have once ceased, they cease also to be of force; as in the law ceremonial it fareth: finally, that albeit the end continue, as in that law of theft specified and in a great part of those ancient judicials it doth; yet forasmuch as there is not in all respects the same subject or matter remaining for which they were first instituted, even this is sufficient cause of change: and therefore laws, though both ordained of God himself, and the end for which they were ordained continuing, may notwithstanding cease, if by alterations of persons or times they be found insufficient to attain unto that end. In which respect why may we not presume that God doth even call for such change or alteration as the very condition of things themselves doth make necessary? . . .

Touching points of doctrine, as for example, the Unity of God, the Trinity of Persons, salvation by Christ, the resurrection of the body, life everlasting, the judgment to come, and such like, they have been since the first hour that there was a Church in the world, and till the last they must be believed. But as for matters of regiment, they are for the most part of another nature. To make new articles of faith and doctrine no man thinketh it lawful; new laws of government what commonwealth or church is there which maketh not either at one time or another? "The rule of faith," said Tertullian, "is but one, and that alone immoveable and impossible to be framed or cast anew." The law of outward order and polity not so. There is no reason in the world wherefore we should esteem it as necessary always to do, as always to believe, the same things; seeing every man knoweth that the matter of faith is constant, the matter contrariwise of action daily changeable, especially the matter of action belonging unto church polity. Neither can I find that men of soundest judgment have any otherwise taught, than that articles of belief, and things which all men must of necessity do to that end that they may be saved, are either expressly set down in Scripture or else plainly thereby to be gathered. But touching things which belong to discipline and outward polity, the Church hath authority to make canons, laws, and decrees, even as we read that in the Apostles' times it did. Which kind of laws (forasmuch as they are not in themselves necessary to salvation) may after they are made be also changed as the difference of times or places shall require. Yea, it is not denied I am sure by themselves, that certain things in discipline are of that nature, as they may be varied by times, places, persons, and other the like circumstances. Whereupon I demand, are those changeable points of discipline commanded in the word of God or no? If they be not commanded and yet may be received in the Church, how can their former position stand, condemning all things in the Church which in the word are not commanded? If they be commanded and yet may suffer change, how can this latter stand, affirming all things immutable which are commanded of God? Their distinction touching matters of substance and of circumstance, though true, will not serve. For be they great things or be they small, if God have commanded them in the Gospel, and his commanding them in the Gospel do make them unchangeable, there is no reason we should more change the one than we may the other. If the authority of the maker do prove unchangeableness in the laws which God hath made, then must all laws which he hath made be necessarily for every permanent, though they be but of circumstance only and not of substance. I therefore conclude, that neither God's being author of laws for government of his Church, nor his committing them unto Scripture, is any reason sufficient wherefore all churches should for ever be bound to keep them without change.

1.7 Sir Matthew Hale Discusses the Amendment of Laws*

Many of the American Founders were lawyers, and almost all of them were roughly familiar with developments in the

---

* Sir Matthew Hale, *The History of the Common Law of England*, ed. Charles M. Gray (Chicago: The University of Chicago Press, 1971), p. 40.

Sir Matthew Hale, "Considerations Touching the Amendment or Alteration of Lawes," *A Collection of Tracts Relative to the Laws of England From Manuscripts*, ed. Francis Hargrave (Dublin: Printed for E. Lynch et. al., 1787), pp. 253-60; 262-66; 268-74. Spellings have been modernized.

English system of common law. Sir Matthew Hale was among those English jurists about whom Americans would have known. Hale (1609-76) lived through a tempestuous time of British history and served as Lord Chief Justice from 1671-76. Below are two excerpts. The first, the shorter, is from Hale's *History of the Common Law of England* and is an analogy which at once demonstrated the role of continuity and change in English law. The longer essay, from a collection of tracts printed in the same year as the writing of the U.S. Constitution, analyzes in great detail the appropriateness of rewriting constitutions.

The Analogy of the Argonauts' Ship

So that Use and Custom, and Judicial Decisions and Resolutions, and Acts of Parliament, tho' not now extant, might introduce some *New* Laws, and alter some *Old*, which we now take to be the very Common Law itself, tho' the Times and precise Periods of such Alterations are not explicitly or clear known: But tho' those particular Variations and Accessions have happened in the Laws, yet they being only partial and successive, we may with just Reason say, They are the same English Laws now, that they were 600 Years since in the general. As the Argonauts Ship was the same when it returned home, as it was when it went out, tho' in that long Voyage it had successive Amendments, and scarce came back with any of its former Materials; and as Titius is the same Man he was 40 Years since, tho' Physicians tells us, That in a Tract of seven Years, the Body has scarce any of the same Material Substance it had before.

Amendment or Alteration of Laws

Chapter I

The business of amendment or alteration of laws is a choice and tender business, neither wholly to be omitted when the necessity requires, and yet very cautiously and warily to be undertaken, though the necessity may, or, at least, may seem to require it.

And that I may the more evenly guide myself in this discourse, I shall begin with the consideration of both those extremes, viz.

I. The error in the excess, the over busy and hasty and violent attempt in mutation of laws under pretence of reformation.

And, II. the error in the defect, a willful and over-strict adhering in every particular to the continuance of the laws in the state we find them, though the reformation of them be never so necessary, safe and easy.

Touching the first of these, the offence or error in the excess: and therein I will first consider the dangerousness of this temper in men to be over facile in the change or alteration of the laws; and then I will examine, upon what reasons or pretences, or indeed infirmities, men are usually carried to this fickleness and unsteadiness in relation to laws.

Touching the danger and inconvenience of over much hastiness in changing of old laws, and introducing of new, there be these considerations, that render such dispositions and such attempts very dangerous.

1. Every law that is old hath this advantage over any new law, in that it is better known already to the people who are concerned in it, than any new law possibly can be without some length of time; by means whereof it must needs come to pass, that though a new law be possibly as good, and it may be in some degree better than the old, yet many great inconveniences happen in that interval, which will occur between the promulgation of the new law, and the full and perfect knowledge thereof, in those who are concerned in that law: and if there were no other advantage of the continuance of old laws above the introducing of new but this, yet it should make people very shy and careful in changes, and most perfectly to demonstrate, that the advantage of the change would be so great, that it would preponderate this very single consideration, viz. the notoriety of the old and the novelty of the new.

2. It is most certain, that time and long experience is much more ingenious, facile and judicious, than all the wisest and acutest wits in the world co-existing can be. It discovers such varieties of emergencies and cases, that no man could ever

otherwise have imagined. It discovers such inconveniences in things, that no man would otherwise have imagined. And on the other side, in every thing that is new, or at least in most things, especially relating to laws, there are thousands of new occurrences and intanglements, and coincidences, and complications, that would not possibly be at first foreseen. And the reason is apparent; because laws concern such multitudes, and those of various dispositions, passions, wits, interests, concerns, that it is not possible for any human foresight to discover at once, or to provide expedients against, in the first constitution of a law.— Now a law, that hath abidden the test of time, hath met with most of these varieties and complications; and experience hath in all that process of time discovered these complications and emergencies, and so has applied suitable remedies and cures for these various emergencies. So that in truth ancient laws, especially, that have a common concern, are not the issues of the prudence of this or that council or senate, but they are the production of the various experiences and applications of the wisest thing in the inferior world; to wit, time, which as it discovers day after day new inconveniences, so it doth successively apply new remedies: and indeed it is a kind of aggregation of the discoveries, results and applications of ages and events; so that it is a great adventure to go about to alter it, without very great necessity, and under the greatest demonstration of safety and convenience imaginable.

3. An overbusy meddling with the alteration of laws, though under the plausible name and pretence of reformation, doth necessarily introduce a great fluidness, lubricity and unsteadiness in the laws, and renders it upon every little occasion subject to perpetual fluxes, vicissitudes and mutations. When once this law in changed, why may not that which is introduced be changed, and so onwards in perpetual motion? So that possibly in the period of an age or two, the law of a kingdom, and with it it's government, may have as many shapes as a silkworm hath in the period of a year; so that they that now live, cannot project under what laws their children shall live, nor the child or grandchild understand by what laws the kingdom was governed in the time of the father or grandfather; and thereby the constitution of the government, the rules of

property, and all things that are concerned to have the greatest fixedness that may be, shall become as lax and unstable, as if every age underwent a conquest from a foreign state. And therefore in all times, the wisest lawgivers and counsellors have been every careful to keep the settled laws of a kingdom, as steady and fast as might be; and hence it was, that, not so much to gain observance as firmness to their laws, they were always stiled sacred, and the people induced into a venerable esteem of them, by a pretence that their laws were given from heaven, and therefore not to be changed by any inferior authority.

4. Overmuch tampering with, and changing of laws, which have obtained by long use and custom, is commonly very ungrateful and unacceptable to the people, into whom their ancient laws and customs are twisted and woven as a part of their nature, and introduceth jealousies and suspicious of designs upon them, and gives a handle to busy and turbulent spirits, to insinuate unto them the bad consequences that may ensue upon such change, and oftentimes begets seditious rebellions and tumults, and prepares people's minds for distempers. And though possibly at the first changes may be ushered in with plausible pretences and quiet, and possibly please the multitude with wonderful expectations of good and benefit thereby; yet, when they find themselves disappointed, and possibly some unexpected inconvenience emergeth upon the change, then presently the mouths of people are opened against innovation, and the higher their expectation is raised upon the pretence and promise of benefit, the more they are enraged by any though inconsiderable disappointment therein.

Upon these, and many more weighty considerations, the wisest men in all times have been very tender and jealous of changes of laws. And upon this account, though when William the first came in, he introduced here in England many parts of the Norman customs and laws, yet when things began to settle, he found it not only convenient but necessary to restore unto the people their old laws, especially those that obtained upon the account and reverence of Edward the Confessor. And when in the time of H. 3. the clergy endeavoured, but in one point, viz. that of bastardy, to introduce the ecclesiastical laws, the nobility stoutly and resolutely answered, *Nolumus leges Anglice mutari.*

Therefore it is of great importance upon any alteration of the laws to be sure,

1. That the change be demonstrable to be for the better, and such as cannot introduce any considerable inconvenience in the other end of the wallet.

2. That the change, though most clearly for the better, be not in foundations or principles, but in such things as may consist with the general frame and basis of the government or law.

3. That the changes be gradual, and not too much at once, or at least more than the exigence of things requires.

Chapter. II

I have in the precedent chapter considered the first extreme, and the danger and inconvenience of it. I shall now examine, what are those humours in men, that commonly breed this disease and instability in men in relation to the change of laws. And upon a due consideration thereof, we shall the better see what persons, what tempers and dispositions, and what times are least unseasonable and unfit for such proposals; and gather thereby a prudent jealousy, when we see changes ushered in by such persons or dispositions, or at such seasons or times, though the pretensions may be plausible.

(1.) As the nature of man generally is affected with novelty, so there are some persons and dispositions, that are wonderfully fond of it, and rather than want it will have it even in those things which are most ordinarily perniciously hurt by it. Such are the form of government and ancient municipal laws. The very same itch of novelty and innovation, that carries some dispositions to novelty in garbs and gestures, or to new fashions in clothes, carries such when they happen to be in place to innovations and new fashions in laws; a certain restlessness and nauseousness in what they have, and a giddy humour after something what which is new, and possibly upon no other account but because it is new, or possibly upon some over expectations of the benefits of such change, though they have no full nor perfect notion of what is to be introduced in the place of what they nauseate.

(2.) A second ground of it is possibly some personal mischief, that they in their own particular have received by the present constitution of laws. For there is in mankind a passionate self-law, which makes men think, that whatsoever crosseth them in their interest or concern is unjust and fit to be altered. And upon this account it will be impossible for any law to be stable; for laws are not fitted for persons, but for things, and must of necessity displease or prejudice the interest of one party. That, which may be preserves the right and property of one may, may and must of necessity cross and thwart that upon which another man mistakenly thinks or calls his right: and if upon a peevish, discontented humour, every man that is crossed by a law must be studying of alterations, there must be no law at all; for possibly that very new law, that such a discontented person would introduce, will one time or other do him mischief; or if it do not, yet it may do another man a mischief in his concern, and will as much justify him in a new innovation as it could the other in the last.

(3.) A third ground of precipitate and inconsiderate innovation in laws, is the want of a due consideration of the true state and nature of all human affairs, especially in that of laws and government, viz. a conceit of a possibility of framing such laws and constitutions, as might be faultless, and exquisitely accommodate to the concerns of the whole community, and of every member of it. And hence if there once occur any inconvenience in a law, presently away with it, and a new frame or model must be excogitated and introduced, and then all will be well. But this is a great error; for it is most certain, that when all the wisdom and prudence and forecast in the world is used, all human things will still be imperfect. There is no wisdom or counsel perfect, but the wisdom and counsel of Almighty God, who hath infinite knowledge to foresee all possible emergencies, and hath infinite wisdom to accommodate and fit every thing according to its necessity and conveniency, and infinite power to bow and bend every thing to the determination of his own most wise counsel and will. And if it could be supposed that any human contrivance could be perfect and faultless (as possibly some may be very accurate, as we see in mechanical works); yet it is not possible, that any human law can be perfect and faultless. No. Time itself, that as we have said is wiser than all the coexisting wits in the world, is not able to foresee a perfect law that will be absolutely faultless. And the reason is apparent; because it concerns the manners of many men, which are so various, uncertain and complicated, both in themselves and the circumstances adhering to them, that they are not possibly to be exactly fitted. We see in the concerns of one man, how various his actions, his passions, his concerns are; how they change every moment; what new circumstances adhere to them to-day that did not yesterday: and if the state of things be so various and complicated in one man, how various, intricated and perplexed will they be with a multitude of men! And if they are various in respect of a multitude of men, how various will they be with a multitude in various successions of ages, and the occurrences or emergencies thereof! And laws are made in relation to such multitudes in such successions, to which it is impossible that it should perfectly be fit and accommodate. If it be squared, so that it fit *ut plurimum*, and doth more good, though it possibly *pro bocue et nunc* may do some harm, yet it is a good law. And besides, according to new emergencies, if they are of moment and importance, there may be some new appendications put to it without a total alteration of the law; such alterations, as do not so much constitute a new law, as amend the old; so that it still morally continues the same law, notwithstanding these appendications, as the Argonauts' ship was the same ship at the end of their voyage as it was at the beginning, though there remained little of the old materials but the chine and ribs of it.

And now possibly some may say, that since all human laws are imperfect, and only the counsels and determinations of Almighty God are perfect, why then may we not take a short compendious course, and take in the judicials given by God by the hand of Moses, and so avoid that inconvenience of the imperfection of human laws, the positive judicial law of

Almighty God being substituted in the place of all other human laws, and all human laws abrogated and exterminated?

To this I say, that most certainly the judicial law given by Moses was the law of God, and consequently a most perfect law according to the use and end for which it was designed; a law of perfect wisdom, as being the production of an infinite wisdom. But yet this must be observed in relation to the perfection of things of this kind. That is in truth perfect, that is perfect in relation to its use and end, *cui nihil deeſt* that may be useful and apposite to that end. . . .

(4.) A fourth ground of, or rather temptation to, a precipitate alteration of laws already made, is the ignorance of the laws that are so intended to be altered, in these that are fond of such alteration; and this ignorance of the laws, provokes an alteration upon these occasions. . . .

(5.) A fifth occasion or temptation to be changing of the laws is somewhat akin to the former, viz. an over-weening esteem and valuation, that a man many times hath of some pretty new expedient, that his own fancy or the fancy of others has suggested for the reformation of something per-chance at least seemingly amiss in the law, without a due deep attentive consideration of what inconveniences would attend such substitution. Indeed oftentimes men are in love with the product of their own heads; and as they have not the patience or impartiality to examine it, so they are not willing to hear of anything that might interrupt the pleasure of their fancy, or contradict or disparage it, tho' upon never so clear and pregnant a reason and evidence. And by this means men, having their minds intent upon what they would be at in this kind, seldom discover the inconveniences till they feel them; like boys, that blow a bubble out of a walnut-shell, which when it is up, run after it with their eyes fixed only upon their bubble, and never consider what ditches they fall into or what breaches they run into in their pursuit, till they feel the damage which they had not prudence or patience to foresee. The truth is, if upon the discovery of some inconvenience in laws the business were only to provide a plaster for that sore, the reformation of any law were very easy. But the great business of a reformer is, not only to see that his remedy be apposite, but that it doth not introduce some other considerable inconvenience, or at least with the inconvenience that it remedies takes not away some other considerable convenience, which the former constitution before the alteration brought with it. For as I before said, the estimate that is to be made, is to be made not upon those single inconveniences that are remedied, but upon the whole account of profit and loss, upon the whole cargo, not upon this or that particular commodity; for full we may remember, that the wisdom and prudence of a long tract of time and experience hath made a kind of aggregation and contignation in the fabric of laws. One piece is for the most part subservient unto and mortified in another, as the frame of a ship or house is, at least when principals are concerned. And therefore there must be a great knowledge and a vast circumspection in every considerable alteration of the law.

(6.) A sixth occasion or temptation to alter the law are certain passions in men; and because they are of several kinds, but yet all reducible to the same head, I shall enumerate the most considerable, and so conclude this chapter.

1. Vain glory.—Men are fond to be enrolled in the number of legislators with Solon, Lycurgus, Huma, and others; and would be tampering upon that account to get a name.

2. Ambition.—Commonly the first step of ambitious men, and one of the most popular and taking to lift themselves up to place and power, is with Absolom to be reforming the constitution or administration of the laws.

3. Fear.—When men have achieved great power by usurpations or other undue means, the first thing they ordinarily attempt is reformation of laws; partly *ad faciendum populum*; partly to remove such laws as fit too hard and uneasy upon their usurped power; but principally to engage the generality of men in the acting under new laws, and holding their interest and properties under them, and thereby they may be engaged in a common defence against the true and just power, left upon return of things into their ancient channel the repeal of such acts and interests derived under such laws may ensue.

4. Envy and malice at the professors and profession of the law; and that upon these accounts, upon the account of their

wealth, power, number, wisdom, and the necessary use of them. Men hate those either they fear, or that have a great advantage either of esteem for wisdom and knowledge above themselves: and this very envy at the professors many times discover itself against the law they profess, in contriving new systems and models to put their hands out that they think at present in; though this attempt commonly succeeds to the authors with the like disadvantage, as the conspiracy of the limbs against the stomach; they weaken and sometimes destroy themselves in the attempt.

Chapter III

By what hath been said in the two preceding chapters, a man would suppose, that all alterations, amendments, or reformations, of municipal laws, were wholly to be interdicted; and no room left for it with safety or prudence; but what hath been once settled for law must stand everlastingly without any reformation or alteration; and that men were better to live under the inconveniences of an old law, than undergo that hazard and inconvenience, which may incur by any amendment or superinduction of any new laws.

And accordingly many wise and excellent men have labored, and still do labor under this extreme; and the motives, reasons or temptations to the extreme seem to be such as these:

1. By long use and custom men, especially that are aged and have been long educated in the profession and practice of the law, contract a kind of superstitious veneration of it beyond what is just and reasonable. And it happens to them as it doth to the Romanists in point of religion, in relation to ancient rites and ceremonies transmitted to them from their ancestors, that, though they become overburdensome by their multitude, or ridiculous by their vanity or impertinency, or antiquated by the alteration of the ends and uses for which they were at first instituted or introduced, yet they are zealously retained, though to the apparent detriment and oppression of religion itself. And accordingly it happens to these men in point of laws. They tenaciously and rigorously maintain these very forms and proceedings and practices, which, tho' possibly at first they were seasonable and useful, yet by the very change of

matters they become not only useless and impertinent, but burdensome and inconvenient and prejudicial to the common justice and the common good of mankind: not considering the forms and prescripts of laws were not introduced for their own sakes, but for the use of public justice; and therefore, when they become insipid, useless, impertinent, and possibly derogatory to the end, they may and must be removed.

2. An over-jealous fear, that it may be possible, that some unthought-of inconvenience may emerge, which may introduce some unexpected mischief to the community, and with it a disparagement to the judgment of those that are undertakers in it. And this lion in the way chokes all industrious application to this most necessary business. Indeed this very fear must make men that have to do in this important affair the more considerate and circumspect, the more advising and deliberating, the more solicitous and careful, and the more mature and to take the longer time in their results, but must not wholly obstruct the work itself, when the public necessity and good calls for it.

3. A timorousness to displease and disoblige great officers and ministers of justice, especially such as have paid dear for places of this nature (one of the greatest banes to justice and necessary reformation); for it must needs follow upon a due reformation of what is amiss, that some offices must be laid aside as needless, other pared from their redundancy. And it is true, those that are concerned in point of interest in such reformation, will be sprightfully watchful to see if any thing of inconvenience may emerge upon such alterations; and they will be ready to inculcate it with disadvantage enough to such as shall be instrumental therein. And if they find the least imaginable default (as it is impossible but some such thing may evene) they will industriously magnify and aggravate it beyond the bounds of truth or prudence. It is a little petty revenge they please themselves withall. But I shall not need to decry such a pitiful pusillanimity or narrowness of mind, that will neglect a public important good, either because it may create some advantage to themselves in point of profit, or to those who hold places of advantage in courts of justice or relating thereunto.

4. A jealousy, lest any thing offered for the amendment of what is amiss in the law may give a handle to others to ravel into the whole frame of it, and to be tampering with it to the public detriment; and so that which is intended to perfect and advance the law shall be used like a little wedge put into a great piece of timber, which shall give opportunity to violent persons to drive greater after them, and cleave the whole in pieces.

And indeed this often falls out in great assemblies, especially if times be not very sedate when any thing of this nature is offered. Perchance one grafts upon it some thing else, and a second a second thing, and a third a third; whereby the sole design at first is lost, and something, or it may be many things, produced, pernicious both to the law and government. But this may be with care and vigilence prevented, especially as our legislative constitution is established. There be several halts and stops before a law of this nature be perfected, whereby at any of which such an inundation, if it should happen, may be obstructed; and that which is good and necessary be carried on, as I shall have occasion to mention hereafter.

5. Exemplary miscarriages, in the late times, of such as have undertaken reformation both in matters civil and ecclesiastical, hath brought a disrepute upon the undertaking of any reformation in either; so that the very name of reformation and a reformer begins to be a style or name of contempt or obloquy; so that men are as fearful to be under the imputation of a reformer of the law, as they would be of the name of knave or fool, or hypocrite. . . .

But notwithstanding all these difficulties and obstructions, I think good and wise men may and ought to make some prudent essay even in this great business, and with very good success both to their own reputation and the public benefit. And in order to the encouragement therein, I shall propound these considerations:

1. We are not without excellent and happy examples or reformation in this kind to the general good and advantage of mankind; yea, and for the very preservation of the laws themselves, which without due husbandry of them will die of themselves, like trees that want pruning. . . .

The second consideration is that, as all sublumary things are subject to corruption and putrefaction, to diseases and rust, so even laws themselves, by long tract of time gather certain diseases and excrescences; certain abuses and corruptions grow into the law, as close as the ivy unto the tree, or the rust to the iron, and in a little tract of time gain the reputation of being part of the law. So that a great and considerable part of that reformation, that is pleased for, is not so much of the law, as of abuses and corruptions, and wens and excrescences, and delays and formalities and exactions, that do adhere to the law, and will in time strangle and stifle it with it close adherence to it. And when these dear and profitable exuberances, and ulcers are looked after, presently those, that are concerned in the profit thereof, or do not duly distinguish between the law and its abuses and diseases, cry out upon destroying the law, and altering of the law, when in truth it is the rescuing of the law from those encroachments or abuses that are made upon or brought into it.

3. And yet farther, I do not think, that the only things fit to be reformed in the law are the abuses and corruptions of it; but there are some things, that are really and truly parts of the law as necessary to be reformed as the errors or abuses of it.

And we must remember, that laws were not made for their own sakes, but for the sake of those who were to be guided by them; and though it is true they are and ought to be sacred, yet, if they be or are become unuseful for their end, they must either be amended if it may be, or new laws be substituted, and the old repealed, so it be do done regularly, deliberately, and so far forth only as the exigence or convenience justly demands it.—And in this respect the saying is true, *salus populi suprema lex esto*.

Now laws become or are unuseful to their end upon two accounts. 1. When in their very constitution and fabric they are rotten and faulty, and unjust, and impossible to be born without remarkable and common inconvenience. I shall not apply this part to the thing in question.—But 2dly, when a law tho' never so good in its first institution, yet by reason of some accidental emergencies that do most usually happen in tract of time, either becomes obsolete and out of use, or weak and unprofitable to its end, or inconsistent with some new superinduction that time and variety of occasions have introduced. And as this is most clear in all laws, so in our English laws we shall find, what was in use, and possibly very effectual in its time, is now deserted and antiquated, and utterly unapplicable to the present state of administration in England. Glanville wrote a system of our English laws in the time of H. 2. Bracton in the time of H. 3. Britton in the time of E. 2. Let any man read them, and see, whether he can by any means accommodate that administration to the present state of things, or the present regiment or order of things to that. Nay, if we come to the year-books of the time of E. 3. any man, that knows any thing in this kind, will most certainly find, that it cannot fit us; for where is there now one assise or real action brought, unless when they have no other remedy? So that the stream of things have, as it were, left that channel, and taken a new one; and he, that thinks a state can be exactly steered by the same laws in every kind, as it was two or three hundred years since, may as well imagine, that the clothes that fitted him when he was a child should serve him when he is grown a man. The matter changeth the custom; the contracts the commerce; the dispositions, educations and tempers of men and societies change in a long tract of time; and so much their laws in some measure be changed, or they will not be useful for their state and condition. And besides all this, as I before said, time is the wiseth under heaven. These very laws, which at first seemed the wiseth constitution under heaven, have some flaws and defects discovered in them by time. As manufactures, mercantile arts, architecture and building, and philosophy itself, receive new advantages and discoveries by time and experience; so much more do laws, which concern the manners and customs of men.

All that, which I contend for in the first and second chapter, is, not to render laws of men like laws of nature fixed and unalterable, but that it be done with great prudence, advice, care, and upon a full and clear prospect of the whole business.

4. But yet further, by length of time and continuance laws are so multiplied and grown to that excessive variety, that there is a necessity of reduction of them, or otherwise it is not

manageable; as we have before observed touching the Roman laws, which in a tract of 1300 years grew to 2000 great volumes. And the reason is, because this age for the purpose received from the last a body of laws, and they add more and transmit the whole to the next age, and they add to what they had received and transmit the whole stock to the next age. Thus as the rolling of a snow-ball, it increaseth in bulk in every age, till it become utterly unmanageable. And hence it is, that even in the laws of England we have so many varieties of forms of conveyances, feoffment, fines, release, confirmation, grant, attornment, common recovery, deeds, enrolled, &c., because the use coming in at several times, every age did retain somewhat of what was past, and added somewhat of it's own, and so carried over the whole product to the quotient. And this produceth mistakes. A man perchance useth one sort of conveyance, where he should have used another. It breeds uncertainty and contradiction of opinion, and that begets suits and expense. It must necessarily cause ignorance in the professors and profession itself; because the volumes of the law are not easily to be mastered.

5. There be in the law to this day somethings continuing, which, though possibly of ordinary use or occurrence, yet are mischievous when they come to be used, and would not at all be missed if taken away, and which I shall in the pursuit of particulars evidence to the satisfaction I believe of every knowing, considering and unprejudiced mind.

6. I shall add but this one thing more, that it may justly be feared, that if something considerable for the reformation of this amiss in the law be not done by knowing and judicious persons, too much may some time or other be done by some, either out of envy at the professors, or mistaken apprehensions or popular humors. The amendment of things amiss timely, by knowing, able and judicious men that understand their business, may do very much good, and prevent very much evil that may otherwise ensue; and when the business is begun by such hands, it may possibly be too late to allay it. And although it be true, that as the legislative power is established there be many reserves to prevent or stop such an inundation, yet we know not how high the public necessities of supplies

may arise, considering our many great undertakings in the kingdom: and it is no new thing to observe very hard and unreasonable terms granted as the price and purchase of supplies, when they cannot be had upon easier terms. And it will have this plausible pretence, that the judges and lawyers will do nothing to the laws, and therefore it shall be done by other hands. Such a humor would be more easily prevented by a wise and seasonable undertaking in this kind, which would not be so easily diverted or allayed, if once it should be flying. And thus much shall serve for this chapter.

Chapter IV

Upon what hath been said in precedent chapters, it seems apparent, that, as on the one side some things may be fit to be done in relation to the amendment of the laws, yet on the other side it is necessary, that exceeding caution be used as well touching the matter, as the matter how, and the persons by whom, and the season wherein such a reformation may be made.

There are two extremes before observed; and he, that can steer his course herein between them both, hath attained the magistery; only with this caution, that if there must be an error, let it be rather in the defect than in the excess. We know already the world of what is. We know not the world of what may be in an excess. And therefore, before I come to particulars, I will premise some general cautions in reference to the matter, manner, persons, and time or season or such an undertaking.

I. For the matter, that may or may not bear an amendment or alteration, these things must be observed.

(1.) That nothing tend to the alteration of the government in any measure; for that were to introduce ruin and confusion, not reformation; as late and sad experience hath abundantly evidenced.

(2.) That nothing be altered that is a foundation or principal integral of the law; for these are very sound, and ought not to be touched, lest the whole fabric should be endangered. We must do herein, as a wise builder doth with an house that hath some inconveniences or is under some decays. Possibly here or there a door or a window may be altered, or a partition made; but as long as the foundations or principals of the house be found, they must not be tampered with. The inconveniences in the law are of such a nature, as may be easily remedied without unsettling the frame itself; and such amendments, though they seem small and inconsiderable, will render the whole fabric much more safe and useful. But of the particulars in their season.

II. Touching the manner and persons, these things are to be observed.

(1.) That it be done deliberately and leisurely. An attentive consideration will every day ripen the judgement of those that shall be employed in such a service farther than they can at first imagine.

(2.) Let every point be fully debated and impartially examined, before it fix into a resolution.

(2.[sic]) What can be done by the power and authority of the court and judges [should be done by them], without troubling a parliament for such things. And truly this would go a very great way in the reformation of things amiss in the law, and such as are of this nature shall be observed in the particulars hereafter mentioned. For sometimes it falls out that an unnecessary application to parliament, in things that are otherwise curable, breeds unexpected inconveniences. What the poet saith of miracles I may say in this case:

Nec Deus intersit, nisi dignus vindice nodus Inciderit.

(4.) In these remedies, that are given by parliament, let it be particular, and as little left *arbitrio judicis* as may be. Upon such a remission, forward men will do too much when much is left to their power; but wise and cautious men will do too little. Such a remedy therefore will be hurtful, not useful. But wise and honest men desire to understand their rule; though some things are of such a nature, as must in the particular application or exercise be left to the judges and officers of courts, as the forming and modelling of writs, process, pleadings, and other proceedings, in conformity and subservience of what is to be settled by parliament in this behalf.

(5.) Let no laws of this nature have a retrospect; but let the time that they shall be put in execution, have such a prospect, as men may not be surprized by the change of things, but may be fitted and prepared for and conusant of it.

(6.) In the preparing and passing of these laws, I would wish these methods were observed, viz.—1. That it would please the king, with the advice of both houses of parliament, to require the judges and other sages of the law to prepare bills, that may be fit for the reformation of the law against the next session. For as I would not have any man intermeddle in so great business without a most authentic injunction by the king and his supreme council, lest he should come under the prejudice of a busy body or an undertaker; so on the other side, I think no persons are so fit to be employed in the first digestion of such a business, but such as know what best belongs unto it, and how far may be gone with safety and convenience: and as it were an unworthy thing, especially in a judge, to prefer his own interest or profit, or the interest of the courts or officers of courts, above the public benefit, so it were an unworthy thing to suspect such a business in those, who are interested with the lives, liberties and estates of the people in their judicial employments. 2. Such bills so prepared should be presented to the house of commons in the first place; because they represent in a more special manner the common interest of the people. 3. When such bills are twice read and committed, and have been one or twice particularly debated at the committee, it may be very fit to call the judges to a solemn debate at the committee of the house of commons; where they may give the reasons, why they go so far, and why no further; and that their opinion be asked touching any alterations or amendments offered, and the reasons in relation thereunto; for it many times falls out, that a very good and profitable bill is suddenly spoiled with a word inserted or a word expunged, which would be prevented, if the contrivers of the bill were first heard to it; and thus many a good law is lost, or not retrieved again without many messages and conferences between the houses. 4. When the bill comes to the lords and is twice read and committed, it were fit, that all the judges attend the committee for the reasons above given. —Bills thus prepared and hammered would have fewer flaws, and necessity of supplemental or explanatory laws, than hath of late times happened.

III. Touching the time or season for such a business, it must be observed, that it is not every parliament that is fit for such a business. When either the times are turbulent or busy, or when other occasions of state are many, great or important, that is not a season for such an undertaking; for it is not possible among such hurries of business, there can be that attendance upon and attention unto a business of this nature, as in truth it requires. It must be at such a time, when there is a great tranquility and home and little engagement abroad, that the parliament may resolvedly, patiently, attentively, and constantly apply itself to the work. Otherwise it will not be all done, or not half done, or perchance over done, which is worse than if not done at all. . . .

1.8 John Locke Proposes a Moderate Theory of Revolution*

John Locke (1632-1704) is generally credited with being one of the most influential English theorists on the thought of later American revolutionaries. Locke had argued that government was based upon consent (although tacit consent played a major role in his thought) and was created for the purpose of securing men's lives, liberties, and estates. Accordingly, when government failed in these purposes, he argued that the people had a right to establish a new government. Little concerned with institutional mechanisms, Locke rested such a right on an "appeal to heaven," or revolution. In the following passage

* John Locke, *Two Treatises of Government*, (J.M. Dent & Sons, Ltd.: London, 1982), pp. 228-235.

from Locke's famous *Second Treatise*, he argued that recognizing a right of revolution would not unduly destabilize existing governments, and he attempted to broaden the traditional understanding of rebellion to include rulers who violated the trust of their people.

The Purposes of Government

The reason why men enter into society is the preservation of their property; and the end while they choose and authorise a legislative is that there may be laws made, and rules set, as guards and fences to the properties of all the society, to limit the power and moderate the dominion of every part and member of the society. For since it can never be supposed to be the will of the society that the legislative should have a power to destroy that which every one designs to secure by entering into society, and for which the people submitted themselves to legislators of their own making: whenever the legislators endeavour to take away and destroy the property of the people, or to reduce them to slavery under arbitrary power, they put themselves into a state of war with the people, who are thereupon absolved from any farther obedience, and are left to the common refuge which God hath provided for all men against force and violence. Whensoever, therefore, the legislative shall transgress this fundamental rule of society, and either by ambition, fear, folly, or corruption, endeavour to grasp themselves, or put into the hands of any other, an absolute power over the lives, liberties, and estates of the people, by this breach of trust they forfeit the power the people had put into their hands for quite contrary ends, and it devolves to the people, who have a right to resume their original liberty, and by the establishment of a new legislative (such as they shall think fit), provide for their own safety and security, which is the end for which they are in society. What I have said here concerning the legislative in general holds true also concerning the supreme executor, who having a double trust put in him, both to have a part in the legislative and the supreme execution of the law, acts against both, when he goes about to set up his own arbitrary will as the law of the society. He acts also contrary to his trust when he employs the force, treasure, and offices of the society to corrupt the representatives and gain them to his purposes, when he openly pre-engages the electors, and prescribes, to their choice, such whom he has, by solicitation, threats, promises, or otherwise, won to his designs, and employs them to bring in such who have promised beforehand what to vote and what to enact. Thus to regulate candidates and electors, and new model the ways of election, what is it but to cut up the government by the roots, and poison the very fountain of public security? For the people having reserved to themselves the choice of their representatives as the fence to their properties, could do it for no other end but that they might always be freely chosen, and so chosen, freely act and advise as the necessity of the commonwealth and the public good should, upon examination and mature debate, be judged to require. This, those who give their votes before they hear the debate, and have weighed the reasons on all sides, are not capable of doing. To prepare such an assembly as this, and endeavour to set up the declared abettors of his own will, for the true society, is certainly as great a breach of trust, and as perfect a declaration of a design to subvert the government, as is possible to be met with. To which, if one shall add rewards and punishments visibly employed to the same end, and all the arts of perverted law made use of to take off and destroy all that stand in the way of such a design, and will not comply and consent to betray the liberties of their country, it will be past doubt what is doing. What power they ought to have in the society who thus employ it contrary to the trust went along with it in its first institution, is easy to determine; and one cannot but see that he who has once attempted any such thing as this cannot any longer be trusted.

To this, perhaps, it will be said that the people being ignorant and always discontented, to lay the foundation of government in the unsteady opinion and uncertain humour of the people, is to expose it to certain ruin; and no government will be able long to subsist if the people may set up a new legislative whenever they take offence at the old one. To this I answer, quite the contrary. People are not so easily got out of their old forms as some are apt to suggest. They are hardly to be prevailed with to amend the acknowledged faults in the frame they have been accustomed to. And if there be any original defects, or adventitious ones introduced by time or corruption, it is not an easy thing to get them changed, even when all the world sees there is an opportunity for it. This slowness and aversion in the people to quit their old constitutions has in the many revolutions have been seen in this kingdom, in this and former ages, still kept us to, or after some interval of fruitless attempts, still brought us back again to our old legislative of king, lords and commons; and whatever provocations have made the crown be taken from some of our princes' heads, they never carried the people so far as to place it in another line.

But it will be said this hypothesis lays a ferment for frequent rebellion. To which I answer:

First: no more than any other hypothesis. For when the people are made miserable, and find themselves exposed to the ill usage of arbitrary power, cry up their governors as much as you will for sons of Jupiter, let them be sacred and divine, descended or authorised from Heaven; given them out for whom or what you please, the same will happen. The people generally ill treated, and contrary to right, will be ready upon any occasion to ease themselves of a burden that sits heavy upon them. They will wish and seek for the opportunity, which in the change, weakness, and accidents of human affairs, seldom delays long to offer itself. He must have lived but a little while in the world, who has not seen examples of this in his time; and he must have read very little who cannot produce examples of it in all sorts of governments in the world.

Secondly: I answer, such revolutions happen not upon every little mismanagement in public affairs. Great mistakes in the ruling part, many wrong and inconvenient laws, and all the slips of human frailty will be borne by the people without mutiny or murmur. But if a long train of abuses, prevarications, and artifices, all tending the same way, make the design visible to the people, and they cannot but feel what they lie under, and see whither they are going, it is not to be wondered that they should then rouse themselves, and endeavour to put the rule into such hands which may secure to them the ends for which government was at first erected, and without which, ancient names and specious forms are so far from being better, that they are much worse than the state of Nature or pure anarchy; the inconveniencies being all as great and as near, but the remedy farther off and more difficult.

Thirdly: I answer, that this power in the people of providing for their safety anew by a new legislative when their legislators have acted contrary to their trust by invading their property, is the best fence against rebellion, and the probablest means to hinder it. For rebellion being an opposition, not to persons, but authority, which is founded only in the constitutions and laws of the government: those, whoever they be, who, by force, break through, and, by force, justify their violation of them, are truly and properly rebels. For when men, by entering into society and civil government, have excluded force, and introduced laws for the preservation of property, peace, and unity amongst themselves, those who set up force again in opposition to the laws, do *rebellare*—that is, bring back again the state of war, and are properly rebels, which they who are in power, by the pretence they have to authority, the temptation of force they have in their hands, and the flattery of those about them being likeliest to do, the properest way to prevent the evil is to show them the danger and injustice of it who are under the greatest temptation to run into it.

In both the forementioned cases, when either the legislative is changed, or the legislators act contrary to the end for which they were constituted, those who are guilty are guilty of rebellion. For if any one by force takes away the established legislative of any society, and the laws by them made, pursuant to their trust, he thereby takes away the umpirage which every one had consented to for a peaceable decision of all their controversies, and a bar to the state of war amongst them. They who remove or change the legislative take away this decisive power, which nobody can have but by the appointment and consent of the people, and so destroying the authority which the people did, and nobody else can set up, and introducing a power which the people hath not authorised, actually introduce a state of war, which is that of force without authority; and thus by removing the legislative established by the society, in whose decisions the people acquiesced and united as to that of their own will, they untie the knot, and expose the people anew to the state of war. And if those, who by force take away the legislative, are rebels, the legislators themselves, as has been shown, can be no less esteemed so, when they who were set up for the protection and preservation of the people, their liberties and properties shall by force invade and endeavour to take them away; and so they putting themselves into a state of war with those who made them the protectors and guardians of their peace, are properly, and with the greatest aggravation, *rebellantes*, rebels.

But if they who say it lays a foundation for rebellion mean that it may occasion civil wars or intestine broils to tell the people they are absolved from obedience when illegal attempts are made upon their liberties or properties, and may oppose the unlawful violence of those who were their magistrates when they invade their properties, and may oppose the unlawful violence of those who were their magistrates when they invade their properties, contrary to the trust put in them, and that, therefore, this doctrine is not to be allowed, being so destructive to the peace of the world; they may as well say, upon the same ground, that honest men may not oppose robbers or pirates, because this may occasion disorder or bloodshed. If any mischief come in such cases, it is not to be charged upon him who defends his own right, but on him that invades his neighbour's. If the innocent honest man must quietly quit all he has for peace sake to him who will lay violent hands upon it, I desire it may be considered what a kind of peace there will be in the world which consists only in violence and rapine, and which is to be maintained only for the benefit of robbers and oppressors. Who would not think it an admirable peace betwixt the mighty and the mean, when the lamb, without resistance, yielded his throat to be torn by the imperious wolf? Polyphemus's den gives us a perfect pattern of such a peace. Such a government wherein Ulysses and his companions had nothing to do but quietly to suffer themselves to be devoured. And no doubt Ulysses, who was a prudent man, preached up passive obedience, and exhorted them to a quiet submission by representing to them of what concernment peace was to mankind, and by showing the inconveniencies might happen if they should offer to resist Polyphemus, who had now the power over them.

The end of government is the good of mankind; and which is best for mankind, that the people should be always exposed to the boundless will of tyranny, or that the rulers should be sometimes liable to be opposed when they grow exorbitant in the use of their power, and employ it for the destruction, and not the preservation, of the properties of their people?

Nor let any one say that mischief can arise from hence as often as it shall please a busy head or turbulent spirit to desire the alteration of the government. It is true such men may stir whenever they please, but it will be only to their own just ruin and perdition. For till the mischief be grown general, and the ill designs of the rulers become visible, or their attempts sensible to the greater part, the people, who are more disposed to suffer than right themselves by resistance, are not apt to stir. The examples of particular injustice or oppression of here and there an unfortunate man moves them not. But if they universally have a persuasion grounded upon manifest evidence that designs are carrying on against their liberties, and the general course and tendency of things cannot but give them strong suspicions of the evil intention of their governors, who is to be blamed for it? Who can help it if they, who might avoid it, bring themselves into this suspicion? Are the people to be blamed if they have the sense of rational creatures, and can think of things no otherwise than as they find and feel them? And is it not rather their fault who put things in such a posture that they would not have them thought as they are? I grant that the pride, ambition, and turbulency of private men have sometimes caused great disorders in commonwealths, and factions have been fatal to states and kingdoms. But whether the mischief hath oftener begun in the people's wantonness, and a desire to cast off the lawful authority of their rulers, or in the rulers' insolence and endeavours to get and exercise an arbitrary power over the people, whether oppression or disobedience gave the first rise to the disorder, I leave it to impartial history to determine. This I am sure, whoever, either ruler or subject, by force goes about to invade the rights of either prince or people, and lays the foundation for overturning the constitution and frame of any just government, he is guilty of the greatest crime I think a man is capable of, being to answer for all those mischiefs of blood, rapine, and desolation, which the breaking to pieces of governments bring on a country; and he who does it is justly to be esteemed the common enemy and pest of mankind, and is to be treated accordingly.

That subjects or foreigners attempting by force on the properties of any people may be resisted with force is agreed on all hands; but that magistrates doing the same thing may be resisted, hath of late been denied; as if those who had the greatest privileges and advantages by the law had thereby a power to break those laws by which alone they were set in a better place than their brethren; whereas their offence is thereby the greater, both as being ungrateful for the greater share they have by the law, and breaking also that trust which is put into their hands by their brethren.

Whosoever uses force without right—as every one does in society who does it without law—puts himself into a state of war with those against whom he so uses it, and in that state all former ties are cancelled, all other rights cease, and every one has a right to defend himself, and to resist the aggressor. . . .

1.9 William Penn Crystallizes a Mechanism for Constitutional Change*

William Penn (1644-1718), an English Quaker, was granted a charter by the British King to settle in America. Unlike some others who had also come to America to practice religious liberty, Penn not only wanted liberty for himself but was willing to grant it to others as well. Penn appears to have been the first to include a provision for amendment in the charters which he formulated for his colonies, the first appearing in a charter for Pennsylvania of 1682-3. By 1701 Penn had for-

* *The Federal and State Constitutions Colonial Charters and Other Organic Laws of the States, Territories, and Colonies now or heretofore forming the United States of America*, Francis N. Thorpe (Washington: Government Printing Office, 1909), pp. 560-1.

malized both an amending mechanism and a reservation to protect individual rights, as is evident in the following selection from the Charter he issued to Delaware in 1701.

Amending Process for Delaware

And no Act, Law or Ordinance whatsoever, shall at any Time hereafter, be made or done, to alter, change or diminish the Form or Effect of this Charter, or any Part of Clause therein, contrary to the true Intent and Meaning thereof, without the Consent of the Governor for the Time being and *Six* Parts of *Seven* of the Assembly met.

BUT, because the Happiness of Mankind depends so much upon the Enjoying of Liberty of their Consciences, as aforesaid, I do hereby solemnly declare, promise and grant, for me, my Heirs and Assigns, That the *First* Article of this Charter relating to Liberty of Conscience, and every Part and Clause therein, according to the true Intent and Meaning thereof, shall be kept and remain, without any Alteration, inviolably for ever.

1.10 David Hume Warns Against Pursuit of a Perfect Commonwealth*

David Hume (1711-1776) was one of the greatest of the English empiricists. In arguing for the U.S. Constitution, leading Federalists, including James Madison the author of *Federalist* No. 10, utilized Hume's argument in "Idea of a Perfect Commonwealth," that it was possible to have republican government in a government that covered a large land area; Anti-Federalists, following the Baron de Montesquieu's arguments in *The Spirit of the Laws*, had argued that republican government was only possible within smaller areas, i.e. the states.

The following selection from Hume's essay shows his reluctance to tamper with existing constitutions—a reluctance shared by Hume's compatriot, Edmund Burke, that seems to be reflected in Madison's writings which are included in Chap-

---

* David Hume, *Hume's Moral and Political Philosophy* (New York: Hafner Publishing Co., 1948), pp. 373-4, pp. 362-5.

ter 2 of this book. The selection from Hume's second essay, "Of the Original Contract," shows his hesitancy to condition the existence of government on consent alone. While this notion may contradict certain sentiments in Locke's writings which were later echoed in America, Hume's emphasis on the role of habit and of implicit consent again reflect some themes Madison would later develop in his later correspondence with Thomas Jefferson.

Experiments in Governments

It is not with forms of government as with other artificial contrivances, where an old engine may be rejected if we can discover another more accurate and commodious, or where trials may safely be made even though the success be doubtful. An established government has an infinite advantage by that very circumstance of its being established, the bulk of mankind being governed by authority, not reason, and never attributing authority to anything that has not the recommendation of antiquity.

To tamper, therefore, in this affair, or try experiments merely upon the credit of supposed argument and philosophy, can never be the part of a wise magistrate, who will bear a reverence to what carries the marks of age; and though he may attempt some improvements for the public good, yet will he adjust his innovations as much as possible to the ancient fabric, and preserve entire the chief pillars and supports of the constitution.

The mathematicians in Europe have been much divided concerning that figure of a ship which is the most commodious for sailing; and Huygens, who at last determined the controversy, is justly thought to have obliged the learned as well as commercial world, though Columbus had sailed to America and Sir Francis Drake made the tour of the world without any such discovery. As one form of government must be allowed more perfect than another, independent of the manners and humours of particular men, why may we not inquire what is the most perfect of all, though the common botched and inaccurate governments seem to serve the purposes of society, and though it be not so easy to establish a new system of government as to build a vessel upon a new construction? The subject is surely the most worthy of curiousity of any the wit of man can possibly devise. And who knows, if this controversy were fixed by the universal consent of the wise and learned, but, in some future age, an opportunity might be afforded of reducing the theory to practice, either by a dissolution of some old government or by the combination of men to form a new one in some distant part of the world? In all cases, it must be advantageous to know what is the most perfect in the kind, that we may be able to bring any real constitution or form of government as near it as possible by such gentle alterations and innovations as may not give too great disturbance to society.

The Role of Consent

My intention here is not to exclude the consent of the people from being one just foundation of government. Where it has a place, it is surely the best and most sacred of any. I only contend that it has very seldom had place in any degree, and never almost in its full extent; and that, therefore, some other foundation of government must also be admitted.

Were all men possessed of so inflexible a regard to justice that of themselves they would totally abstain from the properties of others, they had for ever remained in a state of absolute liberty, without subjection to any magistrate or political society. But this is a state of perfection of which human nature is justly deemed incapable. Again, were all men possessed of so perfect an understanding as always to know their own interests, no form of government had ever been submitted to but what was established on consent, and was fully canvassed by every member of the society. But this state of perfection is likewise much superior to human nature. Reason, history, and experience show us that all political societies have had an origin much less accurate and regular; and were one to choose a period of time when the people's consent was the least regarded in public transactions, it would be precisely on the establishment of a new government. In a settled constitution their inclinations are often consulted; but during the fury of revolutions, conquests, and public convulsions, military force or political craft usually decides the controversy.

When a new government is established, by whatever means, the people are commonly dissatisfied with it, and pay obedience more from fear and necessity than from any idea of allegiance or of moral obligation. The prince is watchful and jealous, and must carefully guard against every beginning or appearance of insurrection. Time, by degrees, removes all these difficulties, and accustoms the nation to regard as their lawful or native princes that family which at first they considered as usurpers or foreign conquerors. In order to found this opinion, they have no recourse to any notion of voluntary consent or promise which, they know, never was in this case either expected or demanded. The original establishment was formed by violence and submitted to from necessity. The subsequent administration is also supported by power, and acquiesced in by the people, not as a matter of choice, but of obligation. They imagine not that their consent gives their prince a title. But they willingly consent, because they think that, from long possession, he has acquired a title independent of their choice or inclination.

Would it be said that, by living under the dominion of a prince which one might leave, every individual has given a *tacit* consent to his authority and promised him obedience, it may be answered that such an implied consent can only have place where a man imagines that the matter depends on his choice. But where he thinks—as all mankind do who are born under established governments—that by his birth he owes allegiance to a certain prince or certain form of government, it would be absurd to infer a consent or choice, which he expressly in this case renounces and disclaims.

Can we seriously say that a poor peasant or artisan has a free choice to leave his country, when he knows no foreign language or manners, and lives from day to day by the small wages which he acquires? We may as well assert that a man, by remaining in a vessel, freely consents to the dominion of the master, though he was carried on board while asleep, and must leap into the ocean and perish the moment he leaves her.

What if the prince forbid his subjects to quit his dominions, as in Tiberius' time it was regarded as a crime in a Roman knight that he had attempted to fly to the Parthians, in order to escape the tyranny of that emperor? Or as the ancient Muscovites prohibited all traveling under pain of death? And did a prince observe that many of his subjects were seized with the frenzy of migrating to foreign countries, he would, doubtless, with great reason and justice restrain them in order to prevent the depopulation of his own kingdom. Would he forfeit the allegiance of all his subjects by so wise and reasonable a Law? Yet the freedom of their choice is surely, in that case, ravished from them.

A company of men, who should leave their native country in order to people some uninhabited region, might dream of recovering their native freedom, but they would soon find that their prince still laid claim to them, and called them his subjects even in their new settlement. And in this he would but act conformably to the common ideas of mankind.

The truest *tacit* consent of this kind that is ever observed is when a foreigner settles in any country, and is beforehand acquainted with the prince, and government, and laws, to which he must submit; yet is his allegiance, though more voluntary, much less expected or depended on than that of a natural-born subject. On the contrary, his native prince still asserts a claim to him. And if he punish not the renegade when he seizes him in war with his new prince's commission, this clemency is not founded on the municipal law, which in all countries condemns the prisoner, but on the consent of princes, who have agreed to this indulgence in order to prevent reprisals.

Did one generation of men go off the stage at once, and another succeed, as is the case with silk worms and butterflies, the new race, if they had sense enough to choose their government, which surely is never the case with men, might voluntarily and by general consent establish their own form of civil polity without any regard to the laws or precedents which prevailed among their ancestors. But as human society is in perpetual flux, one man every hour going out of the world, another coming into it, it is necessary in order to preserve stability in government that the new brood should conform themselves to their established constitution, and nearly follow the path which their fathers, treading in the footsteps of theirs, had marked out to them. Some innovations must necessarily have place in every human institution; and it is happy where the enlightened genius of the age give these a direction to the side of reason, liberty, and justice. But violent innovations no individual is entitled to make. They are even dangerous to be attempted by the legislature. More ill than good is ever to be expected from them. And if history affords examples to the contrary, they are not to be drawn into precedent, and are only to be regarded as proofs that the science of politics affords few rules which will not admit of some exception, and which may not sometimes be controlled by fortune and accident. The violent innovations in the reign of Henry VIII proceeded from an imperious monarch, seconded by the appearance of legislative authority; those in the reign of Charles I were derived from faction and fanaticism; and both of them have proved happy in the issue. But even the former were long the source of many disorders, and still more dangers; and if the measures of allegiance were to be taken from the latter, a total anarchy must have place in human society, and a final period at once be put to every government.

1.11 Jean-Jacques Rousseau Outlines a Plan for Constitutional Renewal*

The French philosopher, Jean-Jacques Rousseau (1712-78), while not as influential in the New World as Locke and Montesquieu, would certainly have been familiar to many of America's Founders. His work in the *Social Contract* excerpted below would certainly have suggested to American readers the mechanism of a constitutional convention, which many states would begin to call during the American Revolutionary period which is documented in the next chapter.

---

* Jean Jacques Rousseau, *The Social Contract and Discourses*, trans. by G.D.H. Cole (New York E.P. Dutton and Company, Inc., 1950).

Fixed Assemblies

It is not enough for the assembled people to have once fixed the constitution of the State by giving it sanction to a body of law; it is not enough for it to have set up a perpetual government, or provided once for all for the election of magistrates. Besides the extraordinary assemblies unforeseen circumstances may demand, there must be fixed periodical assemblies which cannot be abrogated or prorogued so that on the proper day the people is legitimately called together by law, without need of any formal summoning. . . .

The moment the people [are] legitimately assembled as a sovereign body, the jurisdiction of the government wholly lapses, the executive power is suspended, and the person of the meanest citizen is as sacred and inviolable as that of the first magistrate; for in the presence of the person represented, representatives no longer exist. . . .

The periodical assemblies of which I have already spoken are designed to prevent or postpone this calamity [usurpation of sovereignty by the government], above all when they need no formal summoning; for in that case, the prince cannot stop them without openly declaring himself a law-breaker and an enemy of the State.

The opening of these assemblies, whose sole object is the maintenance of the social treaty, should always take the form of putting two propositions that may not be suppressed, which should be voted on separately.

The first is: "Does it please the Sovereign to preserve the present form of government?"

The second is; "does it please the people to leave its administration in the hands of those who are actually in charge of it?"

1.12 Edmund Burke Opposes Revolutionary Change*

Edmund Burke (1729-97), whose philosophy is akin in many ways to that of David Hume, is often cited as the father of

---

* Edmund Burke, *Reflections on the Revolution in France*, (London: J.M. Dent & Sons Ltd. 1910; reprint 1960), pp. 19-20; 31-3; 164-66.

modern political conservatism. An English member of parliament and philosopher who was sympathetic to the American grievances that led up to the Revolutionary War, Burke was much less tolerant of the French Revolutionaries of 1789. He believed they were waging a war, not on behalf of concrete rights, but rather for unrealizable, abstract ideals that would eventually force the revolutionaries to turn on one another—a near prophetic insight into the actual course the Revolution would take.

In the passages below, from Burke's famed *Reflections on the Revolution in France*, he contrasts his ideal of orderly change which he associated with Great Britain with what he saw in France. While Americans would not have accepted all the specific British institutions Burke defended nor the organic unwritten constitution behind them, and while Americans would be split on how supportive the United States should be of the French Revolution, many no doubt viewed their own Lockean inspired Revolution as a wholesome alternative to the bloodletting that was associated with the changes in France.

The Need for Change

A state without the means of some change is without the means of its conservation. Without such means it might even risk the loss of that part of the constitution which it wished the most religiously to preserve. The two principles of conservation and correction operated strongly at the two critical periods of the Restoration and Revolution, when England found itself without a king. At both those periods the nation had lost the bond of union in their ancient edifice; they did not, however, dissolve the whole fabric. On the contrary, in both cases they regenerated the deficient part of the old constitution through the parts which were not impaired. They kept these old parts exactly as they were, that the part recovered might be suited to them. They acted by the ancient organized states in the shape of their old organization, and not by the organic *moleculoe* of a disbanded people. At no time, perhaps, did the sovereign legislature manifest a more tender regard to that fundamental principle of British constitutional policy, than at the time of the Revolution, when it deviated from the direct line of hereditary succession. The crown was carried somewhat out of the line in which it had before moved; but the new line was derived from the same stock. It was still a line of hereditary descent; still an hereditary descent in the same blood, though an hereditary descent qualified with Protestantism. When the legislature altered the direction, but kept the principle, they showed that they held it inviolable.

Change, like generations, should proceed gradually

You will observe, that from Magna Charta to the Declaration of Right, it has been the uniform policy of our constitution to claim and assert our liberties, as an *entailed inheritance* derived to us from our forefathers, and to be transmitted to our posterity; as an estate specially belonging to the people of this kingdom, without any reference whatever to any other more general or prior right. By this means our constitution preserves a unity in so great a diversity of its parts. We have an inheritable crown; an inheritable peerage; and a House of Commons and a people inheriting privileges, franchises, and liberties, from a long line of ancestors.

This policy appears to me to be the result of profound reflection; or rather the happy effect of following nature, which is wisdom without reflection, and above it. A spirit of innovation is generally the result of a selfish temper and confined views. People will not look forward to posterity, who never look backward to their ancestors. Besides, the people of England well know, that the idea of inheritance furnishes a sure principle of conservation and a sure principle of transmission; without at all excluding a principle of improvement. It leaves acquisition free; but it secures what it acquires. Whatever advantages are obtained by a state proceeding on these maxims, are locked fast as in a sort of family settlement; grasped as in a king of mortmain for ever. By a constitutional policy, working after the pattern of nature, we receive, we hold, we transmit our government and our privileges, in the same manner in which we enjoy and transmit our property and our lives. The institutions of policy, the goods of fortune, the gifts of providence, are handed down to us, and from us, in the same course and order. Our political system is placed in a just correspondence and symmetry with the order of the world, and with the mode of existence decreed to a permanent body composed of transitory parts; wherein, by the disposition of a stupendous wisdom, moulding together the great mysterious incorporation of the human race, the whole, at one time, is never old, or middle-aged, or young, but, in a condition of unchangeable constancy, moves on through the varied tenor of perpetual decay, fall, renovation, and progression. Thus, by preserving the method of nature in the conduct of the state, in what we improve, we are never wholly new; in what we retain, we are never wholly obsolete. By adhering in this manner and on those principles to our forefathers, we are guided not by the superstition of antiquarians, but by the spirit of philosophic analogy. In this the image of a relation in blood; binding up the constitution of our country with our dearest domestic ties; adopting our fundamental laws into the bosom of our family affections; keeping inseparable, and cherishing with the warmth of all their combined and mutually reflected charities, our state, our hearths, our sepulchres, and our altars.

Through the same plan of a conformity to nature in our artificial institutions, and by calling in the aid of her unerring and powerful instincts, to fortify the fallible and feeble contrivances of our reason, we have derived several other, and those no small benefits, from considering our liberties in the light of an inheritance. Always acting as if in the presence of canonized forefathers, the spirit of freedom, leading in itself to misrule and excess, is tempered with an awful gravity. This idea of a liberal descent inspires us with a sense of habitual native dignity, which prevents that upstart insolence almost inevitably adhering to and disgracing those who are the first acquirers of any distinction. By this means our liberty becomes a noble freedom. It carries an imposing and majestic aspect. It has a pedigree and illustrating ancestors. It has its bearings, and its ensigns armorial. It has its gallery of portraits; its monumental inscriptions; its records, evidences, and titles. We procure reverence to our civil institutions on the principle upon which nature teaches us to revere individual men; on account of their age, and on account of those from whom they are descended. All your sophisters cannot produce anything better adapted to preserve a rational and manly freedom than the course that we have pursued, who have chosen our nature rather than our speculations, our breasts rather than our inventions, for the great conservatories and magazines of our rights and privileges.

Reform Differs From Abolition

It is this inability to wrestle with difficulty which has obliged the arbitrary Assembly of France to commence their schemes of reform with abolition and total destruction. But is it in destroying and pulling down that skill is displayed? Your mob can do this as well at least as your assemblies. The shallowest understanding, the rudest hand, is more than equal to that task. Rage and phrensy will pull down more in half an hour, than prudence, deliberation, and foresight can build up in a hundred years. The errors and defects of old establishments are visible and palpable. It calls for little ability to point them out; and where absolute power is given, it requires but a word wholly to abolish the vice and the establishment together. The same lazy but reckless disposition, which loves sloth and hates quiet, directs the politicians, when they come to work for supplying the place of what they have destroyed. To make everything the reverse of what they have seen is quite as easy as to destroy. No difficulties occur in what has never been tried. Criticism is almost baffled in discovering the defects of what has not existed; and eager enthusiasm and cheating hope have all the wide field of imagination, in which they may expatiate with little or no opposition.

At once to preserve and to reform is quite another thing. When the useful parts of an old establishment are kept, and what is superadded is to be fitted to what is retained, a vigorous mind, steady, persevering attention, various powers of comparison and combination, and the resources of an understanding fruitful in expedients, are to be exercised; they are to be exercised in a continued conflict with the combined force of opposite vices, with the obstinacy that rejects all improvement, and the levity that is fatigued and disgusted with everything of which it is in possession. But you may object—"A process of this kind is slow. It is not fit for an assembly, which glories in performing in a few months the work of ages. Such a mode of reforming, possibly, might take up many years." Without question it might; and it ought. It is one of the excellencies of a method in which time is amongst the assistants, that its operation is slow, and in some cases almost imperceptible. If circumspection and caution are a part of wisdom, when we work only upon inanimate matter, surely they become a part of duty too, when the subject of our demolition and construction is not brick and timber, but sentient beings, by the sudden alteration of whose state, condition, and habits, multitudes may be rendered miserable. But it seems as if it were the prevalent opinion in Paris, that an unfeeling heart, and an undoubting confidence, are the sole qualifications for a perfect legislator. Far different are my ideas of that high office. The true lawgiver ought to have a heart full of sensibility. He ought to love and respect his kind, and to fear himself. It may be allowed to his temperament to catch his ultimate object with an intuitive glance; but his movements towards it ought to be deliberate. Political arrangement, as it is a work for social ends, is to be only wrought by social means. There mind must conspire with mind. Time is required to produce that union of minds which alone can produce all the good we aim at. Our patience will achieve more than our force. If I might venture to appeal to what is so much out of fashion in Paris, I mean to experience, I should tell you, that in my course I have known, and, according to my measure, have co-operated with great men; and I have never yet seen any plan which has not been mended by the observations of those who were much inferior in understanding to the person who took the lead in the business. By a slow but well-sustained progress, the effect of each step is watched; the good or ill success of the first gives light to us in the second; and so, from light to light, we are conducted with safety through the whole series. We see that the parts or the system do not clash. The evils latent in the most promising contrivances are provided for as they arise. One advantage is at little as possible sacrificed to another. We compensate, we reconcile, we balance. We are enabled to unite into a consistent whole the various anomalies and contending principles that are found in the minds and affairs of men. From hence arises, not an excellence in simplicity, but one far superior, an excellence in composition. Where the great interests of mankind are concerned through a long succession of generations, that succession ought to be admitted into some share in the councils which are so deeply to affect them. If justice requires this, the work itself requires the aid of more minds than one age can furnish. It is from this view of things that the best legislators have been often satisfied with the establishment of some sure, solid, and ruling principle in government; a power like that which some of the philosophers have called a plastic nature; and having fixed the principle, they have left if afterwards to its own operation.

To proceed in this manner, that is, to proceed with a presiding principle, and a prolific energy, is with me the criterion of profound wisdom. What your politicians think the marks of a bold, hardy genius, are only proofs of a deplorable want of ability. By their violent haste and their defiance of the process of nature, they are delivered overly blindly to every projector and adventurer, to every alchymist and empiric. They despair of turning to account anything that is common. Diet is nothing in their system of remedy. The worst of it is, that this their despair of curing common distempers by regular methods, arises not only from defect of comprehension, but, I fear, from some malignity of disposition. . . .

Chapter 2

The American Founding Period

Few if any periods in American political history have been more important or creative than that of the American Founding. Inaugurated by a Declaration of Independence intended to justify the right of revolution, the period forced Americans to formulate their own institutions and to provide for change in these institutions in a less violent and more regularized fashion. The initial attempt at continental union proved inadequate, in part because of an inadequate method of change. Debates raged over the desirability of periodic change and over the adequacy of the proposed amending mechanism in the new Constitution, a mechanism put to the test in meeting demands for a bill of rights and for an amendment to reverse an unpopular Supreme Court decision. By the end of his administration, Washington could commend the mechanism for change in the Constitution while warning that the Constitution could be subverted if this mechanism were bypassed.

2.1 The Declaration of Independence Proclaims the Right of Revolution*

Of all public documents in American history, few are as important or as lyrical as the Declaration of Independence, authored by Thomas Jefferson and later revised and adopted by the Second Continental Congress. Much of the document consists of a series of indictments against the King of England. The opening two paragraphs, however, sought to justify the deci-

---

* *The Federal Convention and the Formation of the Union of the American States*, ed. Winton U. Solberg (Indianapolis: The Bobbs-Merrill Company, Inc., 1958), pp. 34-5.

sion of the American colonies to declare their independence in broader philosophic terms. In the process, Jefferson indicated that, since government was based on consent and instituted for the protection of certain rights, the people have the right to alter such governments when they no longer accomplish the objects for which they were established.

The Rights of the People

WHEN in the course of human events, it becomes necessary for one people to dissolve the political bands which have connected them with another, and to assume among the powers of the earth, the separate and equal station to which the Laws of Nature and of Nature's God entitle them, a decent respect to the opinions of mankind requires that they should declare the causes which impel them to the separation.—We hold these truths to be self-evident, that all men are created equal, that they are endowed by their Creator with certain unalienable Rights; that among these are Life, Liberty, and the pursuit of Happiness.—That to secure these rights, Governments are instituted among Men, deriving their just powers from the consent of the governed,—That whenever any Form of Government becomes destructive of these ends, it is the Right of the People to alter or to abolish it, and to institute new Government, laying its foundation on such principles, and organizing its powers in such form, as to them shall seem most likely to effect their Safety and Happiness. Prudence, indeed, will dictate that Governments long established should not be changed for light and transient causes; and accordingly all experience hath shown that mankind are more disposed to suffer, while evils are sufferable, than to right themselves by abolishing the forms to which they are accustomed. But when a long train of abuses and usurpations, pursuing invariably the same Object, evinces a design to reduce them under absolute Despotism, it is their right, it is their duty, to throw off such Government, and to provide new Guards for their future security.—Such has been the patient sufferance of these Colonies; and such is now the necessity which constrains them to alter their former Systems of government. The history of the present King of Great Britain is a history of repeated injuries and usurpations, all having in direct object the establishment of an absolute Tyranny over these States.

2.2 State Constitutions Provide for Constitutional Change*

At the time of the writing of the Declaration of Independence, many states had already begun replacing their old charters with new constitutions. Not all state constitutions contained provisions for amendments. Those that did tended to fall into three types—those which permitted amendment by legislative action, those which provided for amendment by constitutional convention, and those that provided for periodic meetings of a Council of Censors to review the laws. Examples of these three types of provisions are provided below.

Constitution of Georgia, 1777

No alteration shall be made in this constitution without petitions from a majority of the counties, and the petitions from each county to be signed by a majority of voters in each county within this State; at which time the assembly shall order a convention to be called for that purpose, specifying the alterations to be made, according to the petitions preferred to the assembly by the majorities of the counties as aforesaid.

Constitution of Maryland, 1776

That this Form of Government, and the Declaration of Rights, and no part thereof, shall be altered, changed, or abolished, unless a bill so to alter, change or abolish the same shall pass the General Assembly, and be published at least three months before a new election, and shall be confirmed by the General Assembly, after a new election of Delegates, in the first session after such new election; providing that nothing in this form of government, which relates to the eastern shore particularly, shall at any time hereafter be altered, unless for the alteration

* *The Federal and State Constitutions Colonial Charters and Other Organic Laws of the States, Territories, and Colonies now or heretofore forming the United States of America*, Francis N. Thorpe (Washington: Government Printing Office, 1909), vol. 2, p. 789; vol. 3, p. 1701; vol. 5, p. 3092.

and confirmation thereof at least two-thirds of all the members of each branch of the General Assembly shall concur.

Constitution of Pennsylvania, 1776

The said council of censors shall also have power to call a convention, to meet within two years after their sitting, if there appear to them an absolute necessity of amending any article of the constitution which may be defective, explaining such as may be thought not clearly expressed, and of adding such as are necessary for the preservtion of the rights and happiness of the people: But the articles to be amended, and the amendments proposed, and such articles as are proposed to be added or abolished, shall be promulgated at least six months before the day appointed for the election of such convention, for the previous consideration of the people, that they may have opportunity of instructing their delegates on the subject.

2.3. Thomas Jefferson Argues for a Constitution Superior to the Legislature*

In Thomas Jefferson's only full-length book, he devoted many pages to describing and critiquing the constitution of the state of which he had been governor. Jefferson clearly believed that if a constitution was to be superior to ordinary acts of legislation, then it needed to have a source of authority independent of the state legislature. This view would explain the increasing popularity of constitutional conventions such as would eventually be used to propose the United States Constitution in place of the Articles of Confederation.

Jefferson included the proposed draft of a new state constitution in his book. Among the provisions of this constitution was a proposal for calling a new convention at the request of two of the three branches of government. It was this proposal that James Madison would later criticize in readings from *The Federalist* which are included later in this chapter.

---

* Thomas Jefferson, *Notes on the State of Virginia* (New York: Harper & Row, Publishers, 1964), pp. 111-2; 115-19; 194; 204-5.

Altering the State Constitution

This constitution was formed when we were new and unexperienced in the science of government. It was the first, too, which was formed in the whole United States. No wonder then that time and trial have discovered very capital defects in it. . . .

That the ordinary legislature may alter the constitution itself. On the discontinuance of assemblies, it became necessary to substitute in their place some other body, competent to the ordinary business of government, and to the calling forth the powers of the State for the maintenance of our opposition to Great Britain. Conventions were therefore introduced, consisting of two delegates from each county, meeting together and forming one house, on the plan of the former house of burgesses, to whose places they succeeded. These were at first chosen anew for every particular session. But in March 1775, they recommended to the people to choose a convention, which should continue in office a year. This was done, accordingly, in April 1775, and in the July following that convention passed an ordinance for the election of delegates in the month of April annually. It is well known, that in July 1775, a separation from Great Britain and establishment of republican government, had never yet entered into any person's mind. A convention, therefore, chosen under that ordinance, cannot be said to have been chosen for the purposes which certainly did not exist in the minds of those who passed it. Under this ordinance, at the annual election in April 1776, a convention for the year was chosen. Independence, and the establishment of a new form of government, were not even yet the objects of the people at large. One extract from the pamphlet called Common Sense had appeared in the Virginia papers in February, and copies of the pamphlet itself had got in a few hands. But the idea had not been opened to the mass of the people in April, much less can it be said that they had made up their minds in its favor.

So that the electors of April 1776, no more than the legislators of July 1775, not thinking of independence and a permanent republic, could not mean to vest in these delegates powers of establishing them, or any authorities other than those of the ordinary legislature. So far as a temporary organization of government was necessary to render our opposition energetic, so far their organization was valid. But they received in their creation no power but what were given to every legislature before and since. They could not, therefore, pass an act transcendent to the powers of other legislatures. If the present assembly pass an act, and declare it shall be irrevocable by subsequent assemblies, the declaration is merely void, and the act repealable, as other acts are. So far, and no farther authorized, they organized the government by the ordinance entitled a constitution or form of government. It pretends to no higher authority than the other ordinances of the same session; it does not say that it shall be perpetual; that it shall be unalterable by other legislatures; that it shall be transcendent above the powers of those who they knew would have equal power with themselves. Not only the silence of the instrument is a proof they thought it would be alterable, but their own practice also; for this very convention, meeting as a house of delegates in general assembly with the Senate in the autumn of that year, passed acts of assembly in contradiction to their ordinance of government; and every assembly from that time to this has done the same. I am safe, therefore, in the position that the constitution itself is alterable by the ordinary legislature. Though this opinion seems founded on the first elements of common sense, yet is the contrary maintained by some persons. 1. Because, say they, the conventions were vested with every power necessary to make effectual opposition to Great Britain. But to complete this argument, they must go on, and say further, that effectual opposition could not be made to Great Britain without establishing a form of government perpetual and unalterable by the legislature; which is not true. An opposition which at some time or other was to come to an end, could not need a perpetual institution to carry it on; and a government amendable as its defects should be discovered, was as likely to make effectual resistance, as one that should be unalterably wrong. Besides, the assemblies were as much vested with all powers requisite for resistance as the conventions were. If, therefore, these powers included that of modelling the form of government in the one case, they did so in the other. The assemblies then as well as the conventions may model the government; that is, they may alter the ordinance of government. 2. They urge, that if the convention had meant that this instrument should be alterable, as their other ordinances were, they would have called it an ordinance; but they have called it a *constitution*, which, ex vi termini, means "an act above the power of the ordinary legislature." I answer that *constitutio, constitutium, statum, lex,* are convertible terms. "*Constitutio* dictur jus quod a principle conditure." "*Constitutium*, quod ab imperatoribus rescriptum statutumve est." "*Statutum*, idem quod lex." Calvini Lexicon juridicum. *Constitution* and *statute* were originally terms of the civil law, and from thence introduced by ecclesiastics into the English law. Thus in the statute 25 Hen. VIII. c. 19, . 1, "*Constitutions* and *ordinances*" are used as synonymous. The term *constitution* has many other significations in physics and politics; but in jurisprudence, whenever it is applied to any act of the legislature, it invariably means a statute, law, or ordinance, which is the present case. No inference then of a different meaning can be drawn from the adoption of this title; on the contrary, we might conclude that, by their affixing to it a term synonymous with ordinance or statute. But of what consequence is their meaning, where their power is denied? If they meant to do more than they had power to do, did this give them power? It is not the name, but the authority that renders an act obligation. Lord Coke says, "an article of the statute, 11 F. II. c. 5, that no person should attempt to revoke any ordinance then made, is repealed, for that such restraint is against the jurisdiction and power of the parliament." 4 Inst. 42. And again, "though divers parliaments have attempted to restrain subsequent parliaments, yet could they never effect it; for the latter parliament hath ever power to abrogate, suspend, qualify, explain, or make void the former in the whole or in any part thereof, notwithstanding any words of restraint, prohibition, or penalty, in the former; for it is a maxim in the laws of the parliament, quod leges posteriores priores contrarias abrogant." 4 Inst. 43. To get rid of the magic supposed to be in the word *constitution*, let us translate it into its definition as given by those who think it above the power of the law;

and let us suppose the convention, instead of saying, "We the ordinary legislature, establish a *constitution*," had said, "We the ordinary legislature, establish an act *above the power of the ordinary legislature*." Does not this expose the absurdity of the attempt? 3. But, say they, the people have acquiesced, and this has given it an authority superior to the laws. It is true that the people did not rebel against it; and was that a time for the people to rise in rebellion? Should a prudent acquiescence, at a critical time, be construed into a confirmation of every illegal thing done during that period? Besides, why should they rebel? At an annual election they had chosen delegates for the year, to exercise the ordinary powers of legislation, and to manage the great contest in which they were engaged. These delegates thought the contest would be best managed by an organized government. They therefore, among others, passed an ordinance of government. They did not presume to call it perpetual and unalterable. They well knew they had no power to make it so; that our choice of them had been for no such purpose, and at a time when we could have no such purpose in contemplation. Had an unalterable form of government been meditated, perhaps we should have chosen a different set of people. There was no cause then for the people to rise in rebellion. But to what dangerous lengths will this argument lead? Did the acquiescence of the colonies under the various acts of power exercised by Great Britain in our infant State, confirm these acts, and so far invest them with the authority of the people as to render them unalterable, and our present resistance wrong? On every unauthoritative exercise of power by the legislature must the people rise in rebellion, or their silence be construed into a surrender of that power to them? If so, how many rebellions should we have had already? One certainly for every session of assembly. The other States in the union have been of opinion that to render a form of government unalterable by ordinary acts of assembly, the people must delegate persons with special powers. They have accordingly chosen special conventions to form and fix their governments. The individuals then who maintain the contrary opinion in this country, should have the modesty to suppose it possible that they may be wrong, and the rest of America right. But if there be only a possibility of their being wrong, if only a plausible doubt remains of the validity of the ordinance of government, is it not better to remove that doubt by placing it on a bottom which none will dispute? If they be right we shall only have the unnecessary trouble of meeting once in convention. If they be wrong, they expose us to the hazard of having no fundamental rights at all. True it is, this is no time for deliberating on forms of government. While an enemy is within our bowels, the first object is to expel him. But when this shall be done, when peace shall be established, and leisure give us for intrenching within good forms, the rights for which we have bled, let no man be found indolent enough to decline a little more trouble for placing them beyond the reach of question. . . .

Jefferson's draft of a Constitution for Virginia

During the progress of that war [the Revolutionary War], through which we had to labor for the establishment of our rights, the legislature of the commonwealth of Virginia found it necessary to make a temporary organization of government for preventing anarchy, and pointing our efforts to the two important objects of war against our invaders, and peace and happiness among ourselves. But this, like all other acts of legislation, being subject to change by subsequent legislatures, possessing equal powers with themselves; it has been thought expedient, that it should receive those amendments which time and trial have suggested, and be rendered permanent by a power superior to that of the ordinary legislature. The general assembly therefore of this State recommend it to the good people thereof, to choose delegates to meet in general convention, with powers to form a constitution of government for them, and to declare those fundamentals to which all our laws present and future shall be subordinate; and, in compliance with this recommendation, they have thought proper to make choice of us, and to vest us with powers for this purpose. . . .

Any two of the three branches of government concurring in opinion, each by the voice of two-thirds of their whole existing number, that a convention is necessary for altering this constitution, or correcting breaches of it, they shall be authorized to issue writs to every county for the election of so many delegates as they are authorized to send to the general assembly, which elections shall be held, and writs returned, as the laws shall have provided in the case of elections of delegates of assembly, *mutatis mutandis*, and the said delegates shall meet at the usual place of holding assemblies, three months after date of such writs, and shall be acknowledged to have equal powers with this present convention. The said writs shall be signed by all the members approving the same.

2.4 The Articles of Confederation Defer to State Sovereignty*

Written by John Dickinson and modified and adopted by the Continental Congress in 1777, the Articles of Confederation, the nation's first experiment in formal continental union, was not officially ratified until 1781. Two provisions, or articles, of the Articles of Confederation are especially important for understanding its ultimate failure. Article 2 indicates that the Articles were planted on the shifting sands of individual state sovereignty; national authority, exercised by a unicameral legislature, was nonexistent in such vital areas as coining money, taxation, raising armies, and controlling interstate commerce. In few places was state sovereignty more evident than in Article XIII of the Articles which provided that the Articles could not be amended without unanimous consent. This wooden requirement ultimately led those gathered at the Constitutional Convention in 1787 to bypass the amending mechanism of the Articles altogether in proposing a new Document.

ART. 2. Each State retains its sovereignty, freedom and independence, and every power, jurisdiction, and right, which is not by this confederation expressly delegated to the United States, in Congress assembled.

ART. 13. Every State shall abide by the determinations of the United States, in Congress assembled, on all questions which,

---

* Merrill Jensen, *The Articles of Confederation* (Madison: The University of Wisconsin Press, 1966), pp. 263, 270.

by this confederation, are submitted to them. And the articles of this confederation shall be inviolably observed by every State, and the union shall be perpetual; nor shall any alteration any any time hereafter be made in any of them, unless such alteration be agreed to in a Congress of the United States, and be afterwards confirmed by the legislatures of every State.

2.5. Debates at the Constitutional Convention*

Few events in American history were more important than the writing of the U.S. Constitution in Philadelphia in the summer of 1787. The weakness of the Articles of Confederation and its inability to deal with crises like Shay's Rebellion which broke out in Massachusetts in the winter of 1786-7, led many to believe that the only solution was a new constitution. The Annapolis Convention of the previous September (a follow-up to an earlier meeting between Maryland and Virginia at Mt. Vernon) had called on the states to send delegates to a meeting to consider such a possibility.

The Constitutional Convention began meeting in May, 1787. All states except Rhode Island were represented, and a total of fifty-five delegates attended. The first plan proposed at the convention and generally attributed to James Madison, the Virginia Plan, took the approach that it was necessary to introduce such a new document rather than simply patch up the Articles of Confederation. The authors of the Virginia Plan also had the foresight to recognize the need for an amending process.

James Madison and others kept notes at the Constitutional Convention which are quite helpful in understanding the intentions of those who drafted the Document. While debate at the Convention on the amending issue was not extensive, it showed a general recognition of the need for an effective

---

* *Journal of the Constitutional Convention Kept by James Madison*, ed. E.H. Scott (Chicago: Scott, Foresman and Company, 1893, pp. 63, 110, 149, 692-94, and 736-39. Pinckney letter from *The Records of the Federal Convention of 1787*, ed. Max Farrand (New Haven: Yale University Press, 1911), vol. 3, pp. 120-21.

amending mechanism as well as concern as to whether amendments should be proposed by the Congress or by the states. Delegates were also concerned that certain constitutional provisions would be unamendable. The mechanism in Article V was written with these objects in view. Charles Pinckney's observations during the convention also bring into view the way that the new amending process was crafted to differ from that within the Articles of Confederation.

Resolution in the Virginia Plan, May 29

13. Resd. that provision ought to be made for the amendment of the Articles of Union whensoever it shall seem necessary, and that the assent of the National Legislature ought not to be required thereto.

June 5

[In reference to article 15] Mr. Pinkney doubted the propriety or necessity of it.

Mr. Gerry favored it. The novelty & difficulty of the experiment requires periodical revision. The prospect of such a revision would also give intermediate stability to the government. Nothing had yet happened in the States where this provision existed to prove its impropriety.

June 11

Col. Mason urged the necessity of such a provision. The plan now to be formed will certainly be defective, as the Confederation has been found on trial to be. Amendments therefore will be necessary, and it will be better to provide for them, in an easy, regular and Constitutional way than to trust to chance and violence. It would be improper to require the consent of the National. Legislature, because they may abuse their power, and refuse their assent on that very account. The opportunity for such an abuse, may be the fault of the Constitution calling for amendmt.

Mr. Randolph enforced these arguments.

The words, "without requiring the consent of the Natl. Legislature" were postponed. The other provision in the clause passed *nem. con.*

August 6
On the application of the Legislatures of two thirds of the States in the Union, for an amendment of this Constitution, the Legislature of the United States shall call a convention for that purpose.

August 30
Mr. GOUVERNEUR MORRIS suggested, that the Legislature should be left at liberty to call a Convention whenever they pleased.

Concerns Over the Convention Mechanism, September 10
Mr. Gerry moved to reconsider Article 19. viz, "On the application of the Legislatures of two thirds of the States of the Union, for an amendment of this Constitution, the Legislature of the United States shall call a Convention for that purpose."

This Constitution, he said, is to be paramount to the State Constitutions. It follows, hence, from this article that two thirds of the States may obtain a Convention, a majority of which can bind the Union to innovations that may subvert the State-Constitutions altogether. He asked whether this was a situation proper to be run into.

Mr. Hamilton seconded. the motion, but, he said, with a different view from Mr. GERRY—He did not object to the consequences stated by Mr. GERRY—There was no greater evil in subjecting the people of the United States to the major voice than the people of a particular State. It had been wished by many, and was much to have been desired, that an easier mode for introducing amendments had been provided by the Articles of Confederation. It was equally desirable now, that an easy mode should be established for supplying defects which will probably appear in the new System. The mode proposed was not adequate. The State Legislatures will not apply for alterations; but with a view to increase their own powers. The National Legislature will be the first to perceive, and will be most sensible to, the necessity of amendments; and ought also to be empowered, whenever two-thirds of each branch should concur, to call a Convention. There could be no danger in giving this power, as the people would finally decide in the case.

Mr. MADISON remarked on the vagueness of the terms, "call a Convention for the purpose," as sufficient reason for reconsidering the article. How was a Convention to be formed?—By what rule decide?—what the force of its acts?

On the motion of Mr. GERRY to reconsider,—

Massachusetts, Connecticut, Pennsylvania, Delaware, Maryland, Virginia, North Carolina, South Carolina, Georgia, aye —9; New Jersey, no—1; New Hampshire, divided.

Mr. SHERMAN moved to add to the article "or the Legislature may propose amendments to the several States for their approbation; but no amendments shall be binding until consented to by the several States"

Mr. GERRY seconded the motion.

Mr. WILSON moved to insert "two thirds of," before the words, "several States;" on which amendment to the motion of Mr. Sherman.

New Hampshire, Pennsylvania, Delaware, Maryland, Virginia, aye—5; Massachusetts, Connecticut, New Jersey, North Carolina, South Carolina, Georgia, no—6.

Mr. WILSON then moved to insert "three fourths of," before "the several States," which was agreed to *nem: con:*

Mr. MADISON moved to postpone the consideration of the amended proposition in order to take up the following.

"The Legislature of the United States, whenever two thirds of both Houses shall deem necessary, or on the application of two thirds of the Legislatures of the several States, shall propose amendments to this Constitution, which shall be valid to all intents and purposes as part thereof, when the same shall have been ratified by three fourths, at least, of the Legislatures of the several States, or by conventions in three fourths thereof, as one or the other mode of ratification may be proposed by the Legislature of the United States"

Mr. HAMILTON seconded. the motion.

Mr. RUTLEDGE said he never could agree to give a power by which the articles relating to slaves might be altered by the States not interested in that property and prejudiced against it. In order to obviate this objection, these words were added to the proposition: "provided that no amendments, which may be made prior to the year 1808. shall in any manner affect the fourth and fifth sections of the seventh article" The postponement being agred to,—

On the question On the proposition of Mr. MADISON and Mr. HAMILTON as amended—

Massachusetts, Connecticut, New Jersey, Pennsylvania, Maryland, Virginia, North Carolina, South Carolina, Georgia, aye—9; Delaware, no—1; New Hampshire, divided.

Further Concerns, September 15

Article V. "The Congress, whenever two thirds of both Houses shall deem necessary, or on the application of two thirds of the Legislatures of the several States shall propose amendments to this Constitution, which shall be valid to all intents and purposes as part thereof, when the same shall have been ratified by three fourths at least of the Legislatures of the several States, or by Conventions in three fourths thereof, as the one or the other mode of ratification may be proposed by the Congress: provided that no amendment which may be made prior to the year 1808 shall in any manner affect the first and fourth clauses in the ninth section of Article I."

Mr. SHERMAN expressed his fears that three fourths of the States might be brought to do things fatal to particular States; as abolishing them altogether, or depriving them of their equality in the Senate. He thought it reasonable that the proviso in favor of the States importing slaves should be extended so as to provide that no State should be affected in its internal police, or deprived of its equality in the Senate.

Colonel MASON thought the plan of amending the Constitution exceptionable and dangerous. As the proposing of amendments is in both the modes to depend, in the first immediately, and in the second ultimately, on Congress, no amendments of the proper kind, would ever be obtained by the people, if the Government should become oppressive, as he verily believed would be the case.

Mr. GOUVERNEUR MORRIS and Mr. GERRY moved to amend the Article, so as to require a Convention on application of two-thirds of the States.

Mr. MADISON did not see why Congress would not be as much bound to propose amendments applied for by two thirds of the States, as to call a call a Convention on the like application. He saw no objection, however, against providing for a Convention for the purpose of amendments, except only that difficulties might arise as to the form, the quorum &c. which in constitutional regulations ought to be as much as possible avoided.

The Motion of Mr. GOUVERNEUR MORRIS and Mr. GERRY was agreed to *nem: con.*

Mr SHERMAN moved to strike out of Article 5, after "legislatures," the words, "of three fourths," and so after the word "Conventions," leaving future Conventions to act in this matter like the present Conventions according to circumstances.

On this motion,—

Massachusetts, Connectiuct, New Jersey, aye—3; Pennsylvania, Delaware, Maryland, Virginia, North Carolina, South Carolina, Georgia, no—7; New Hampshire, divided.

Mr. GERRY moved to strike out the words, "or by Conventions in three fourths thereof." On which motion,—

Connecticut, aye—1; New Hampshire, Massachusetts, New Jersey, Pennsylvania, Delaware, Maryland, Virginia, North Carolina, South Carolina, Georgia, no—10.

Mr. SHERMAN moved, according to his idea above expressed, to annex to the end of the Article a further proviso "that no State shall, without its consent, be affected in its internal police, or deprived of its equal suffrage in the Senate",

Mr. MADISON. Begin with these special provisos, and every State will insist on them, for their boundaries, exports &c.

On the motion of Mr. SHERMAN,—

Connecticut, New Jersey, Delaware, aye—3; New Hampshire, Massachusetts, Pennsylvania, Maryland, Virginia, North Carolina, South Carolina, Georgia, no—8.

Mr. GOUVERNEUR MORRIS moved to annex a further proviso—"that no State, without its consent shall be deprived of its equal suffrage in the Senate"

This motion being dictated by the circulating murmurs of the small States was agreed to without debate, no one opposing it, or on the question saying no.

Observations of Charles Pinckney on Abolition of Unanimity Requirement

[The provisions of Article V] both go to destroy that unanimity which upon these occasions the present System has unfortunately made necessary—the propriety of this alteration has been so frequently suggested, that I shall only observe that it is to this unanimous consent, the depressed situation of the Union is undoubtedly owing. Had the measures recommended by Congress and assented to, some of them by eleven and others by twelve of the States, been carried into execution, how different would have been the complexion of Public Affairs? To this weak, this absurd part of the Government, may all our distresses be fairly attributed.

If the States were equal in size and importance, a majority of the Legislatures might be sufficient for the grant of any new Powers; but disproportioned as they are and must continue for a time; a larger number may now in prudence be required—but I trust no Government will ever again be adopted in this Country, whose Alteration cannot be effected but by the assent of all its Members. The hazardous situation the United Netherlands are frequently placed in on this account, as well as our own mortifying experience, are sufficient to warn us from a danger which has already nearly proved fatal. It is difficult to form a Government so perfect as to render alterations unnecessary; we must expect and provide for them:—But difficult as the forming a perfect Government would be, it is scarcely more so, than to induce Thirteen separate Legislatures, to think and act alike upon one subject—the alterations that nine think necessary, ought not to be impeded by four—a minority so inconsiderable should be obliged to yield.

2.6 The U.S. Constitution Provides an Amending Process

Article V of the U.S. Constitution embodies the compromises at the Convention on the amending process. At least two other constitutional provisions relate to constitutional revision. In seeing that states are guaranteed a republican form of government, but not specifying the details of such governments, Article IV allows for constitutional changes—which have subsequently been frequent—at the state level. Finally, Article VII provides that the new Constitution would be adopted, not unanimously by the state legislatures as the Articles of Confederation required, but by the consent of specially called conventions in nine or more states.

Article V

The Congress, whenever two thirds of both Houses shall deem it necessary, shall propose Amendments to this Constitution, or, on the Application of the Legislatures of two thirds of the several States, shall call a Convention for proposing Amendments, which, in either Case, shall be valid to all Intents and Purposes, as Part of this Constitution, when ratified by the Legislatures of three fourths of the several States, or by Conventions in three fourths thereof, as the one or the other Mode of Ratification may be proposed by the Congress; Provided that no Amendment which may be made prior to the Year One thousand eight hundred and eight shall in any Manner affect the first and fourth Clauses in the Ninth Section of the first Article; and that no State, without its Consent, shall be deprived of it's equal Suffrage in the Senate.

Article IV, Section 4

The United States shall guarantee to every State in this Union a Republican Form of Government, and shall protect each of them against Invasion; and on Application of the Legislature, or of the Executive (when the Legislature cannot be convened) against domestic Violence.

Article VII

The Ratification of the Conventions of nine States, shall be sufficient for the Establishment of this Constitution between the States so ratifying the Same.

2-7. Publius Explains and Defends the Amending Process*

Among the most effective pieces of advocacy on behalf of the new Constitution, *The Federalist Papers* originally started out as a series of essays in the New York newspapers and were later collected into a book. Written under the pen name of Publius, a Roman statesman, the essays were authored by Alexander Hamilton, James Madison, and John Jay, the first two of whom had been participants in the Constitutional Convention. The essays reprinted below attempted to classify the new government in a way that readers could understand, to emphasize the democratic nature of the convention mechanism, to support the authors of the Constitution against charges that they usurped their powers, to defend the amending mechanism against those who favored more liberal or restrictive measures, and to argue against a second constitutional convention by showing that necessary amendments could be readily adopted once the Constitution was in place.

The U.S. Constitution Contrasted to Others, Fed. No. 38 (Madison)

It is not a little remarkable that in every case reported by ancient history, in which government has been established with deliberation and consent, the task of framing it has not been committed to an assembly of men, but has been performed by some individual citizen of pre-eminent wisdom and approved integrity.

Minor, we learn, was the primitive founder of the government of Crete, as Zaleucus was of that of the Locrians. Theseus first, and after him Draco and Solon, instituted the government of Athens. Lycurgus was the lawgiver of Sparta. The foundation of the original government of Rome was laid by Romulus, and the work completed by two of his elective successors, Numa and Tullius Hostilius. On the abolition of royalty the consular administration was substituted by Brutus, who stepped forward with a project for such a reform, which,

---

* *The Federalist*, ed. Paul L. Ford (New York: Henry Holt and Company, 1898), pp. 237-42; 251-2; 252-9: 291-2; 334-42; and 583-88.

he alleged, had been prepared by Tullius Hostilius, and to which his address obtained the assent and ratification of the senate and people. This remark is applicable to confederate governments also. Amphictyon, we are told, was the author of that which bore his name. The Achaean league received its first birth from Achaeus, and its second from Aratus.

What degree of agency these reputed lawgivers might have in their respective establishments, or how far they might be clothed with the legitimate authority of the people, cannot in every instance be ascertained. In some, however, the proceeding was strictly regular. Draco appears to have been intrusted by the people of Athens with indefinite powers to reform its government and laws. And Solon, according to Plutarch, was in a manner compelled, by the universal suffrage of his fellow-citizens, to take upon him the sole and absolute power of new-modeling the constitution. The proceedings under Lycurgus were less regular; but as far as the advocates for a regular reform could prevail, they all turned their eyes toward the single efforts of that celebrated patriot and sage, instead of seeking to bring about a revolution by the intervention of a deliberative body of citizens.

Whence could it have proceeded that a people, jealous as the Greeks were of their liberty, should so far abandon the rules of caution as to place their destiny in the hands of a single citizen? Whence could it have proceeded that the Athenians, a people who would not suffer an army to be commanded by fewer than ten generals, and who required no other proof of danger to their liberties than the illustrious merit of a fellow-citizen, should consider one illustrious citizen as a more eligible depositary of the fortunes of themselves and their posterity than a select body of citizens, from whose common deliberations more wisdom, as well as more safety, might have been expected? These questions cannot be fully answered without supposing that the fears of discord and disunion among a number of counselors exceeded the apprehension of treachery or incapacity in a single individual. History informs us, likewise, of the difficulties with which these celebrated reformers had to contend, as well as the expedients which they were obliged to employ in order to carry their reforms into effect. Solon, who seems to have indulged a more temporizing policy, confessed that he had not given to his countrymen the government best suited to their happiness but most tolerable to their prejudices. And Lycurgus, more true to his object, was under the necessity of mixing a portion of violence with the authority of superstition, and of securing his final success by a voluntary renunciation, first of his country, and then of his life. If these lessons teach us, on one hand, to admire the improvement made by America on the ancient mode of preparing and establishing regular plans of government, they serve not less, on the other, to admonish us of the hazards and difficulties incident to such experiments and of the great imprudence of unnecessarily multiplying them.

Is it an unreasonable conjecture that the errors which may be contained in the plan of the convention are such as have resulted rather from the defect of antecedent experience on this complicated and difficult subject than from a want of accuracy or care in the investigation of it; and, consequently, such as will not be ascertained until an actual trial shall have pointed them out? This conjecture is rendered probable, not only by many considerations of a general nature, but by the particular case of the Articles of Confederation. It is observable that among the numerous objections and amendments suggested by the several States, when these articles were submitted for their ratification, not one is found which alludes to the great and radical error which on actual trial has discovered itself. And if we except the observations which New Jersey was led to make, rather by her local situation than by her peculiar foresight, it may be questioned whether a single suggestion was of sufficient moment to justify a revision of the system. . . .

A patient who finds his disorder daily growing worse, and that an efficacious remedy can no longer be delayed without extreme danger, after coolly revolving his situation and the characters of different physicians, selects and calls in such of them as he judges most capable of administering relief and best entitled to his confidence. The physicians attend; the case of the patient is carefully examined; a consultation is held; they are unanimously agreed that the symptoms are critical, but that the case, with proper and timely relief, is so far from being desperate that it may be made to issue in an improvement of his constitution. They are equally unanimous in prescribing the remedy by which this happy effect is to be produced. The prescription is no sooner made known, however, than a number of persons interpose, and, without denying the reality or danger of the disorder, assure the patient that the prescription will be poison to this constitution, and forbid him, under pain of certain death, to make use of it. Might not the patient reasonably demand, before he ventured to follow this advice, that the authors of it should at least agree among themselves on some other remedy to be substituted? And if he found them differing as much from one another as from his first counselors, would he not act prudently in trying the experiment unanimously recommended by the latter, rather than be hearkening to those who could neither deny the necessity of a speedy remedy nor agree in proposing one?

Such a patient and in such a situation is America at the moment. She has been sensible of her malady. She has obtained a regular and unanimous advice from men of her own deliberate choice. And she is warned by others against following this advice under pain of the most fatal consequences. Do the monitors deny the reality of her danger? No. Do they deny the necessity of some speedy and powerful remedy? No. Are they agreed, are any two of them agreed, in their objections to the remedy proposed, or in the proper one to be substituted? . . .

As it can give no umbrage to the writers against the plan of the federal Constitution, let us suppose that, as they are the most zealous, so they are also the most sagacious, of those who think the late convention were unequal to the task assigned them, and that a wiser and better plan might and ought to be substituted. Let us further suppose that their country should concur, both in this favorable opinion of their merits, and in their unfavorable opinion of the convention; and should accordingly proceed to form them into a second convention, with full powers, and for the express purpose of revising and remolding the work of the first. Were the experiment to be seriously made, though it required some effort to view it seriously even in fiction, I leave it to be decided by the sample of opinions just exhibited, whether, with all their enmity to their predecessors, they would, in any one point, depart so widely from their example as in the discord and ferment that would mark their own deliberations; and whether the Constitution now before the public would not stand as fair a chance for immortality as Lycurgus gave to that of Sparta, by making its change to depend on his own return from exile and death, if it were to be immediately adopted, and were to continue in force, not until a BETTER, but until ANOTHER should be agreed upon by this new assembly of lawgivers.

It is a matter both of wonder and regret that those who raise so many objections against the new Constitution should never call to mind the defects of that which is to be exchanged for it. It is not necessary that the former should be perfect: it is sufficient that the latter is more imperfect. No man would refuse to give brass for silver or gold, because the latter had some alloy in it. No man would refuse to quit a shattered and tottering habitation for a firm and commodious building, because the latter had not a porch to it, or because some of the rooms might be a little larger or smaller, or the ceiling a little higher or lower, than his fancy would have planned them. . . .

The Amending Mechanism: Neither wholly national nor Federal, Federalist No. 39 (Madison)

If we try the Constitution by its last relation to the authority by which amendments are to be made, we find it neither wholly *national* nor wholly *federal*. Were it wholly national, the supreme and ultimate authority would reside in the *majority* of the people of the Union; and this authority would be competent at all times, like that of a majority of every national society, to alter or abolish its established government. Were it wholly federal, on the other hand, the concurrence of each State in the Union would be essential to every alteration that would be binding on all. The mode provided by the plan of the convention is not founded on either of these principles. In requiring more than a majority, and particularly in computing the proportion by *States*, not by *citizens*, it departs from the *national* and advances towards the *federal* character; in rendering the concurrence of less than the whole number of States sufficient, it loses again the *federal* and partakes of the *national* character.

The Propriety of Convention Actions, Federalist No. 40, (Madison)

The *second* point to be examined is, whether the convention were authorized to frame and propose this mixed Constitution.

The powers of the convention ought, in strictness, to be determined by an inspection of the commissions given to the members by their respective constituents. As all of these, however, had reference, either to the recommendation from the meeting at Annapolis, in September, 1786, or to that from Congress, in February, 1787, it will be sufficient to recur to these particular acts.

The act from Annapolis recommends the "appointment of commissioners to take into consideration the situation of the United States; to devise *such further provisions* as shall appear to them necessary to render the Constitution of the federal government *adequate to the exigencies of the Union*; and to report such an act for that purpose, to the United States in Congress assembled, as when agreed to by them, and afterwards confirmed by the legislature of every State, will effectually provide for the same."

The recommendatory act of Congress is in the words following: "Whereas, there is provision in the articles of Confederation and perpetual Union, for making alterations therein, by the assent of a Congress of the United States, and of the legislatures of the several States; and whereas experience hath evinced, that there are defects in the present Confederation; as a mean to remedy which, several of the States, and *particularly the State of New York*, by express instructions to their delegates in Congress, have suggested a convention for the purposes expressed in the following resolution; and such convention appearing to be the most probable mean of establishing in these States *a firm national government*:

"*Resolved.*—That in the opinion of Congress it is expedient, that on the second Monday of May next a convention of delegates, who shall have been appointed by the several States, be held at Philadelphia for the sole and express purpose *of revising the articles of Confederation*, and reporting to Congress and the several legislatures such *alterations and provisions therein*, as shall, when agreed to in Congress and confirmed by the States, render the federal Constitution *adequate to the exigencies of government* and *the preservation of the Union*."

From these two acts, it appears, 1st, that the object of the convention was to establish, in these States, *a firm national government*; 2d, that this government was to be such as would be *adequate to the exigencies of government and the preservation of the Union*; 3d, that these purposes were to be effected by *alterations and provisions in the articles of Confederation*, as it is expressed in the act of Congress, or by *such further provisions as should appear necessary*, as it stands in the recommendatory act from Annapolis; 4th, that the alterations and provisions were to be reported to Congress, and to the States, in order to be agreed to by the former and confirmed by the latter.

From a comparison and fair construction of these several modes of expression is to be deduced the authority under which the convention acted. They were to frame a *national government*, adequate to the *exigencies of government*, and *of the Union*; and to reduce the articles of Confederation into such form as to accomplish these purposes.

There are two rules of construction, dictated by plain reason, as well as founded on legal axioms. The one is that every part of the expression ought, if possible, to be allowed some meaning, and be made to conspire to some common end. The other is that where the several parts cannot be made to coincide, the less important should give way to the more important part; the means should be sacrificed to the end rather than the end to the means.

Suppose, then, that the expressions defining the authority of the convention were irreconcilably at variance with each other; that a *national* and *adequate government* could not possibly, in the judgment of the convention, be effected by *alterations* and *provisions* in the *articles of Confederation*; which part of the definition ought to have been embraced, and which rejected? Which was the more important, which the less important part? Which the end; which the means? Let the most scrupulous expositors of delegated powers; let the most inveterate objectors against those exercised by the convention, answer these questions. Let them declare whether it was of most importance to the happiness of the people of America that the articles of Confederation should be disregarded, and an adequate government be provided, and the Union preserved; or that an adequate government should be omitted, and the articles of Confederation preserved. Let them declare whether the preservation of these articles was the end for securing which a reform of the government was to be introduced as the means; or whether the establishment of a government, adequate to the national happiness, was the end at which these articles themselves originally aimed, and to which they ought, as insufficient means, to have been sacrificed.

But is it necessary to suppose that these expressions are absolutely irreconcilable to each other; that no *alterations* or *provisions* in *the articles of the Confederation* could possibly mold them into a national and adequate government; into such a government as has been proposed by the convention?

No stress, it is presumed, will, in this case, be laid on the *title*; a change of that could never be deemed an exercise of ungranted power. *Alterations* in the body of the instrument are expressly authorized. *New provisions* therein are also expressly authorized. Here then is a power to change the title; to insert new articles; to alter old ones. Must it of necessity be admitted that this power is infringed, so long as a part of the old articles remain? Those who maintain the affirmative ought at least to mark the boundary between authorized and usurped innovations; between that degree of change which lies within the compass of *alterations and further provisions*, and that which amounts to a *transmutation* of the government. Will it be said that the alterations ought not to have touched the substance of the Confederation? The States would never have appointed a convention with so much solemnity, nor described its objects with so much latitude, if some *substantial* reform had not been in contemplation. Will it be said that the *fundamental principles* of the Confederation were not within the purview of the convention, and ought not to have been varied? I ask, What are these principles? Do they require that, in the establishment of the Constitution, the States should be regarded as distinct and independent sovereigns? They are so regarded by the Constitution proposed. Do they require that the members of the government should derive their appointment from the legislatures, not from the people of the States? One branch of the new government is to be appointed by these legislatures; and under the Confederation, the delegates to Congress *may all* be appointed immediately by the people, and in two States are actually so appointed. Do they require that the powers of the government should act on the States, and not immediately on individuals? In some instances, as has been shown, the powers of the new government will act on the States in their collective characters. In some instances, also, those of the existing government act immediately on individuals. In cases of capture; of piracy; of the post office; of coins, weights, and measures; of trade with the Indians; of claims under grants of land by different States; and, above all, in the case of trials by courts-martial in the army and navy, by which death may be inflicted without the intervention of a jury, or even of a civil magistrate—in all these cases the powers of the Confederation operate immediately on the persons and interests of individual citizens. Do these fundamental principles require, particularly, that no tax should be levied without the intermediate agency of the States? The Confederation itself authorized a direct tax, to a certain extent, on the post office. The power of coinage has been so construed by Congress as to levy a tribute immediately from that source also. But pretermitting these instances, was it not an acknowledged object of the convention, and the universal expectation of the people, that the regulation of trade should be submitted to the general government in such a form as would render it an immediate source of general revenue? Had not Congress repeatedly recommended this measure as not inconsistent with the fundamental principles of the Confederation? Had not every State but one, had not New York herself, so far complied with the plan of Congress as to recognize the *principle* of the innovation? Do these principles, in fine, require that the powers of the general government should be limited, and that, beyond this limit, the States should be left in possession of their sovereignty and independence? We have seen that in the new government, as in the old, the general powers are limited; and that the States, in all unenumerated cases, are left in the enjoyment of their sovereign and independent jurisdiction.

The truth is that the great principles of the Constitution proposed by the convention may be considered less as absolutely new than as the expansion of principles which are found in the articles of Confederation. The misfortune under the latter system has been that these principles are so feeble and confined as to justify all the charges of inefficiency which have been urged against it, and to require a degree of enlargement which gives to the new system the aspect of an entire transformation of the old.

In one particular it is admitted that the convention have departed from the tenor of their commission. Instead of reporting a plan requiring the confirmation *of the legislatures of all the States*, they have reported a plan which is to be confirmed by the *people*, and may be carried into effect by *nine States only*. It is worthy of remark that this objection, though the most plausible, has been the least urged in the publications which have swarmed against the convention. The forbearance can only have proceeded from an irresistible conviction of the absurdity of subjecting the fate of twelve States to the perverseness or corruption of a thirteenth; from the example of inflexible opposition given by a *majority* of one sixtieth of the people of America to a measure approved and called for by the voice of twelve States, comprising fifty-nine sixtieths of the people—an example still fresh in the memory and indignation of every citizen who has felt for the wounded honor and prosperity of his country. As this objection, therefore, has been in a manner waived by those who have criticized the powers of the convention, I dismiss it without further observation.

The *third* point to be inquired into is, how far considerations of duty arising out of the case itself could have supplied any defect of regular authority.

In the preceding inquiries the powers of the convention have been analyzed and tried with the same rigor, and by the same rules, as if they had been real and final powers for the establishment of a Constitution for the United States. We have seen in what manner they have borne the trial even on that supposition. It is time now to recollect that the powers were merely advisory and recommendatory; that they were so meant by the States and so understood by the convention; and that the latter have accordingly planned and proposed a Constitution which is to be of no more consequence than the paper on which it is written, unless it be stamped with the approbation of those to whom it is addressed. This reflection places the subject in a point of view altogether different, and will enable us to judge with propriety of the course taken by the convention.

Let us view the ground on which the convention stood. It may be collected from their proceedings that they were deeply and unanimously impressed with the crisis which had led their country almost with one voice to make so singular and solemn an experiment for correcting the errors of a system by which this crisis had been produced; that they were no less deeply and unanimously convinced that such a reform as they have proposed was absolutely necessary to effect the purposes of their appointment. It could not be unknown to them that the hopes and expectations of the great body of citizens throughout this great empire were turned with the keenest anxiety to the event of their deliberations. They had every reason to believe that the contrary sentiments agitated the minds and bosoms of every external and internal foe to the liberty and prosperity of the United States. They had seen, in the origin and progress of the experiment, the alacrity with which the *proposition* made by a single State (Virginia) toward a partial amendment of the Confederation had been attended to and promoted. They had seen the *liberty assumed* by a very *few deputies* from a *very few* States, convened at Annapolis, of recommending a great and critical object, wholly foreign to their commission, not only justified by the public opinion but actually carried into effect by twelve out of the thirteen States. They had seen, in a variety of instances, assumptions by Congress, not only of recommendatory, but of operative powers, warranted, in the public estimation, by occasions and objects infinitely less urgent than those by which their conduct was to be governed. They must have reflected that, in all great changes of established governments, forms ought to give way to substance; that a rigid adherence in such cases to the former would render nominal and nugatory the transcendent and precious right of the people to "abolish or alter their governments as to them shall seem most likely to effect their safety and happiness," since it is impossible for the people spontaneously and universally to move in concert toward their object; and it is therefore essential that such changes be instituted by some *informal and unauthorized propositions*, made by some patriotic and respectable citizen or number of citizens. They must have recollected that it was by this irregular and assumed privilege of proposing to the people plans for their safety and happiness that the States were first united against the danger with which they were threatened by their ancient government; that committees and congresses were formed for concentrating their efforts and defending their rights; and that *conventions* were *elected* in *the several States* for establishing the constitutions under which they are now governed; nor could it have been forgotten that no little ill-timed scruples, no zeal for adhering to ordinary forms were anywhere seen, except in those who wished to indulge, under these masks, their secret enmity to the substance contended for. They must have borne in mind that, as the plan to be framed and proposed was to be submitted *to the people themselves*, the disapprobation of this supreme authority would destroy it forever; its approbation blot out antecedent errors and irregularities. It might even have occurred to them that, where a disposition to cavil prevailed, their neglect to execute the degree of power vested in them, and still more their recommendation of any measure whatever, not warranted by their commission, would not less excite animadversion, than a recommendation at once of a measure fully commensurate to the national exigencies.

Had the convention, under all these impressions and in the midst of all these considerations, instead of exercising a manly confidence in their country, by whose confidence they had been so peculiarly distinguished, and of pointing out a system capable, in their judgment, of securing its happiness, taken the cold and sullen resolution of disappointing its ardent hopes, of sacrificing substance to forms, of committing the dearest interests of their country to the uncertainties of delay and the hazard of events, let me ask the man who can raise his mind to one elevated conception, who can awaken in his bosom one patriotic emotion, what judgment ought to have been pronounced by the impartial world, by the friends of mankind, by every virtuous citizen, on the conduct and character of this assembly? Or if there be a man whose propensity to condemn is susceptible of no control, let me then ask what sentence he has in reserve for the twelve States who *usurped the power* of sending deputies to the convention, a body utterly unknown to their constitutions; for Congress, who recommended the appointment of this body, equally unknown to the Confederation; and for the State of New York, in particular, which first urged and then complied with this unauthorized interposition?

But that the objectors may be disarmed of every pretext, it shall be granted for a moment that the convention were neither authorized by their commission, nor justified by circumstances in proposing a Constitution for their country: does it follow that the Constitution ought, for that reason alone, to be rejected? If, according to the noble precept, it be lawful to accept good advice even from an enemy, shall we set the ignoble example of refusing such advice even when it is offered by our friends? The prudent inquiry, in all cases, ought surely to be, not so much *from whom* the advice comes, as whether the advice be *good*.

The sum of what has been here advanced and proved is that the charge against the convention of exceeding their powers, except in one instance little urged by the objectors, has no foundation to support it; that if they had exceeded their powers, they were not only warranted, but required, as the confidential servants of their country, by the circumstances in which they were placed, to exercise the liberty which they assumed; and that finally, if they had violated both their powers and their obligations, in proposing a Constitution, this ought nevertheless to be embraced, if it be calculated to accomplish the views and happiness of the people of America. How far this character is due to the Constitution is the subject under investigation.

The Propriety of the Amending Process, Federalist No. 43, (Madison)

8. "To provide for amendments to be ratified by three-fourths of the States, under two exceptions only."

That useful alterations will be suggested by experience could not but be foreseen. It was requisite, therefore, that a mode for introducing them should be provided. The mode preferred by the convention seems to be stamped with every mark of propriety. It guards equally against that extreme facility which would render the Constitution too mutable, and that extreme difficulty which might perpetuate its discovered faults. It, moreover, equally enables the general and the State governments to originate the amendment of errors, as they may be pointed out by the experience on one side or on the other. The exception in favor of the equality of suffrage in the Senate was probably meant as a palladium to the residuary sovereignty of the States, implied and secured by that principle of representation in one branch of the legislature; and was probably insisted on by the States particularly attached to that equality. The other exception must have been admitted on the same considerations which produced the privilege defended by it.

9. "The ratification of the convention of nine States shall be sufficient for the establishment of this Constitution between the States, ratifying the same."

This article speaks for itself. The express authority of the people alone could give due validity to the Constitution. To have required the unanimous ratification of the thirteen States would have subjected the essential interests of the whole to the caprice or corruption of a single member. It would have marked a want of foresight in the convention which our own experience would have rendered inexcusable.

Discussion of Jefferson's Proposal for Constitutional Revision, Federalist No. 49 (Madison)

The author of the "Notes on the State of Virginia," quoted in the last paper, has subjoined to that valuable work the draught of a constitution which had been prepared in order to be laid before a convention expected to be called in 1783, by the legislature, for the establishment of a constitution for that commonwealth. The plan, like everything from the same pen, marks a turn of thinking, original, comprehensive, and accurate; and is the more worthy of attention as it equally displays a fervent attachment to republican government and an enlightened view of the dangerous propensities against which it ought to be guarded. One of the precautions which he proposes, and on which he appears ultimately to rely as a palladium to the weaker departments of power against the invasions of the stronger, is perhaps altogether his own, and, as it immediately relates to the subject of our present inquiry, ought not to be overlooked.

His proposition is "that whenever any two of the three branches of government shall concur in opinion, each by the voices of two-thirds of their whole number, that a convention is necessary for altering the constitution, or *correcting breaches of it*, a convention shall be called for the purpose."

As the people are the only legitimate fountain of power, and it is from them that the constitutional charter, under which the several branches of government hold their power, is derived, it seems strictly consonant to the republican theory to recur to the same original authority not only whenever it may be necessary to enlarge, diminish, or new-model the powers of the government, but also whenever any one of the departments may commit encroachments on the chartered authorities of the others. The several departments being perfectly coordinate by the terms of their common commission, none of them, it is evident, can pretend to an exclusive or superior right of settling the boundaries between their respective powers; and how are the encroachments of the stronger to be prevented, or the wrongs of the weaker to be redressed, without an appeal to the people themselves, who, as the grantors of the commission, can alone declare its true meaning and enforce its observance?

There is certainly great force in this reasoning, and it must be allowed to prove that a constitutional road to the decision of the people ought to be marked out and kept open for certain great and extraordinary occasions. But there appear to be insuperable objections against the proposed recurrence to the people as a provision, in all cases, for keeping the several departments of power within their constitutional limits.

In the first place, the provision does not reach the case of a combination of two of the departments against the third. If the legislative authority, which possesses so many means of operating on the motives of the other departments, should be able to gain to its interest either of the others, or even one-third of its members, the remaining department could derive no advantage from its remedial provision. I do not dwell, however, on this objection, because it may be thought to be rather against the modification of the principle than against the principle itself.

In the next place, it may be considered as an objection inherent in the principle that, as every appeal to the people would carry an implication of some defect in the government, frequent appeals would in a great measure deprive the government of that veneration which time bestows on everything, and without which perhaps the wisest and freest governments would not possess the requisite stability. If it be true that all governments rest on opinion, it is no less true that the strength of opinion in each individual, and its practical influence on his conduct, depend much on the number which he supposes to have entertained the same opinion. The reason of man, like man himself, is timid and cautious when left alone, and acquires firmness and confidence in proportion to the number with which it is associated. When the examples which fortify opinion are *ancient* as well as *numerous*, they are known to have a double effect. In a nation of philosophers, this consideration ought to be disregarded. A reverence for the laws would be sufficiently inculcated by the voice of an enlightened reason. But a nation of philosophers is as little to be expected as the philosophical race of kings wished for by Plato. And in every other nation the most rational government will not find it a superfluous advantage to have the prejudices of the community on its side.

The danger of disturbing the public tranquillity by interesting too strongly the public passions is a still more serious objection against a frequent reference of constitutional questions to the decision of the whole society. Notwithstanding the success which has attended the revisions of our established forms of government, and which does so much honor to the virtue and intelligence of the people of America, it must be confessed that the experiments are of too ticklish a nature to be unnecessarily multiplied. We are to recollect that all the existing constitutions were formed in the midst of a danger which repressed the passions most unfriendly to order and concord; of an enthusiastic confidence of the people in their patriotic leaders which stifled the ordinary diversity of opinions on great national questions; of a universal ardor for new and opposite forms, produced by a universal resentment and indignation against the ancient government; and whilst no spirit of party connected with the changes to be made, or the abuses to be reformed, could mingle its leaven in the operation. The future situations in which we must expect to be usually placed, do not present any equivalent security against the danger which is apprehended.

But the greatest objection of all is that the decisions which would probably result from such appeals would not answer the purpose of maintaining the constitutional equilibrium of the government. We have seen that the tendency of republican governments is to an aggrandizement of the legislative at the expense of the other departments. The appeals to the people, therefore, would usually be made by the executive and judiciary departments. But whether made by one side or the other, would each side enjoy equal advantages on the trial? Let us view their different situations. The members of the executive and judiciary departments are few in number, and can be personally known to a small part only of the people. The latter, by the mode of their appointment, as well as by the nature and permanency of it, are too far removed from the people to share much in their prepossessions. The former are generally the objects of jealousy, and their administration is always liable to be discolored and rendered unpopular. The members of the legislative department, on the other hand, are numerous. They are distributed and dwell among the people at large. Their connections of blood, of friendship, and of acquaintance embrace a great proportion of the most influential part of the society. The nature of their public trust implies a personal influence among the people, and that they are more immediately the confidential guardians of the rights and liberties of the people. With these advantages, it can hardly be supposed that the adverse party would have an equal chance for a favorable issue.

But the legislative party would not only be able to plead their cause most successfully with the people. They would probably be constituted themselves the judges. The same influence which had gained them an election into the legislature, would gain them a seat in the convention. If this should not be the case with all, it would probably be the case with many, and pretty certainly with those leading characters on whom everything depends in such bodies. The convention, in short, would be composed chiefly of men who had been, who actually were, or who expected to be, members of the department whose conduct was arraigned. They would consequently be parties to the very question to be decided by them.

It might, however, sometimes happen that appeals would be made under circumstances less adverse to the executive and judiciary departments. The usurpations of the legislature might be so flagrant and so sudden as to admit of no specious coloring. A strong party among themselves might take side with the other branches. The executive power might be in the hands of a peculiar favorite of the people. In such a posture of things, the public decision might be less swayed by prepossessions in favor of the legislative party. But still it could never be expected to turn on the true merits of the question. It would inevitably be connected with the spirit of preexisting parties, or of parties springing out of the question itself. It would be connected with persons of distinguished character and extensive influence in the community. It would be pronounced by the very men who had been agents in, or opponents of, the measures to which the decision would relate. The *passions*, therefore, not the *reason*, of the public would sit in judgment. But it is the reason, alone, of the public, that ought to control and regulate the government. The passions ought to be controlled and regulated by the government.

We found in the last paper, that mere declarations in the written constitution are not sufficient to restrain the several departments within their legal rights. It appears in this that occasional appeals to the people would be neither a proper nor an effectual provision for that purpose. How far the provisions of a different nature contained in the plan above quoted might be adequate, I do not examine. Some of them are unquestionably founded on sound political principles, and all of them are framed with singular ingenuity and precision.

Periodic Constitutional Revision, Fed. No. 50 (Madison)

It may be contended, perhaps, that instead of *occasional* appeals to the people, which are liable to the objections urged against them, *periodical* appeals are the proper and adequate means of *preventing and correcting infractions of the Constitution*.

It will be attended to that, in the examination of these expedients, I confine myself to their aptitude for *enforcing* the Constitution, by keeping the several departments of power within their due bounds, without particularly considering them as provisions for *altering* the Constitution itself. In the first view, appeals to the people at fixed periods appear to be nearly as ineligible as appeals on particular occasions as they emerge. If the periods be separated by short intervals, the measures to be reviewed and rectified will have been of recent date, and will be connected with all the circumstances which tend to vitiate and pervert the result of occasional revisions. If the periods be distant from each other, the same remark will be applicable to all recent measures; and in proportion as the remoteness of the others may favor a dispassionate review of them, this advantage is inseparable from inconveniences which seem to counterbalance it. In the first place, a distant prospect of public censure would be a very feeble restraint on power from those excesses to which it might be urged by the force of present motives. Is it to be imagined that a legislative assembly, consisting of a hundred or two hundred members, eagerly bent on some favorite object, and breaking through the restraints of the Constitution in pursuit of it, would be arrested in their career, by considerations drawn from a censorial revision of their conduct at the future distance of ten, fifteen, or twenty years? In the next place, the abuses would often have completed their mischievous effects before the remedial provision would be applied. And in the last place, where this might not be the case, they would be of long standing, would have taken deep root, and would not easily be extirpated.

The scheme of revising the constitution, in order to correct recent breaches of it, as well as for other purposes, has been actually tried in one of the States. One of the objects of the Council of Censors which met in Pennsylvania in 1783 and 1784, was, as we have seen, to inquire "whether the constitution had been violated, and whether the legislative and executive department had encroached on each other." This important and novel experiment in politics merits in several points of view, very particular attention. In some of them it may, perhaps, as a single experiment, made under circumstances somewhat peculiar, be thought to be not absolutely conclusive. But as applied to the case under consideration, it involves some facts, which I venture to remark, as a complete and satisfactory illustration of the reasoning which I have employed.

First. It appears, from the names of the gentlemen who composed the council, that some, at least, of its most active and leading members had also been active and leading characters in the parties which pre-existed in the State.

Secondly. It appears that the same active and leading members of the council had been active and influential members of the legislative and executive branches, within the period to be reviewed, and even patrons or opponents of the very measures to be thus brought to the test of the Constitution. Two of the members had been vice presidents of the State, and several others members of the executive council, within the seven preceding years. One of them had been speaker, and a number of others distinguished members, of the legislative assembly within the same period.

Thirdly. Every page of their proceedings witnesses the effect of all these circumstances on the temper of their deliberations. Throughout the continuance of the council, it was split into two fixed and violent parties. The fact is acknowledged and lamented by themselves. Had this not been the case, the face of their proceedings exhibits a proof equally satisfactory. In all questions, however unimportant in themselves, or unconnected with each other, the same names invariably contrasted on the opposite columns. Every unbiased observer may infer, without danger of mistake, and at the same time without meaning to reflect on either party, or any individuals of either party, that, unfortunately, *passion*, not *reason*, must have presided over their decisions. When men exercise their reasons coolly and freely on a variety of distinct questions, they inevitably fall into different opinions on some of them. When they are governed by a common passion, their opinions, if they are so to be called, will be the same.

Fourthly. It is at least problematical whether the decisions of this body do not, in several instances, misconstrue the limits prescribed for the legislative and executive departments, instead of reducing and limiting them within their constitutional places.

Fifthly. I have never understood that the decisions of the council on constitutional questions, whether rightly or erroneously formed, have any effect in varying the practice founded on legislative constructions. It even appears, if I mistake not, that in one instance the contemporary legislature denied the constructions of the council, and actually prevailed in the contest.

This censorial body, therefore, proves at the same time, by its researches, the existence of the disease, and, by its example, the inefficacy of the remedy.

This conclusion cannot be invalidated by alleging that the State in which the experiment was made was at that crisis, and had been for a long time before, violently heated and distracted by the rage of party. Is it to be presumed that, at any future septennial epoch, the same State will be free from parties? Is it to be presumed that any other State, at the same or any other given period, will be exempt from them? Such an event ought to be neither presumed nor desired; because an extinction of parties necessarily implies either a universal alarm for the public safety, or an absolute extinction of liberty.

Were the precaution taken of excluding from the assemblies elected by the people to revise the preceding administration of the government, all persons who should have been concerned with the government within the given period, the difficulties would not be obviated. The important task would probably devolve on men, who, with inferior capacities, would in other respects be little better qualified. Although they might not have been personally concerned in the administration, and therefore not immediately agents in the measures to be examined, they would probably have been involved in the parties connected with these measures, and have been elected under their auspices.

The Adequacy of the Amending Process, Fed. No. 85 (Hamilton)

Concessions of the part of friends of the plan, that it has not a claim to absolute perfection, have afforded matter of no small triumph to its enemies. "Why," say they, "should we adopt an imperfect thing? Why not amend it and make it perfect before it is irrevocably established?" This may be plausible enough, but it is only plausible. In the first place, I remark that the extent of these concessions has been greatly exaggerated. They have been stated as amounting to an admission that the plan is radically defective, and that without material alterations the rights and the interests of the community cannot be safely confided to it. This, as far as I have understood the meaning of those who make the concessions, is an entire perversion of their sense. No advocate of the measure can be found who will not declare as his sentiment that the system, though it may not be perfect in every part, is, upon the whole, a good one; is the best that the present views and circumstances of the country will permit; and is such an one as promises every species of security which a reasonable people can desire.

I answer, in the next place, that I should esteem it the extreme of imprudence to prolong the precarious state of our national affairs, and to expose the Union to the jeopardy of successive experiments, in the chimerical pursuit of a perfect plan. I never expect to see a perfect work from imperfect man. The result of the deliberations of all collective bodies must necessarily be a compound, as well of the errors and prejudices, as of the good sense and wisdom of the individuals of whom they are composed. The compacts which are to embrace the thirteen distinct States in a common bond of amity and union must as necessarily be a compromise of as many dissimilar interests and inclinations. How can perfection spring from such materials?

The reasons assigned in an excellent little pamphlet lately published in this city, are unanswerable to show the utter improbability of assembling a new convention under circumstances in any degree so favorable to a happy issue as those in which the late convention met, deliberated, and concluded. I will not repeat the arguments there used, as I presume the production itself has had an extensive circulation. It is certainly well worthy the perusal of every friend to his country. There is, however, one point of light in which the subject of amendments still remains to be considered, and in which it has not yet been exhibited to public view. I cannot resolve to conclude without first taking a survey of it in this aspect.

It appears to me susceptible of absolute demonstration that it will be far more easy to obtain subsequent than previous amendments to the Constitution. The moment an alteration is made in the present plan, it becomes, to the purpose of adoption, a new one, and must undergo a new decision of each State. To its complete establishment throughout the Union, it will therefore require the concurrence of thirteen States. If, on the contrary, the Constitution proposed should once be ratified by all the States as its stands, alterations in it may at any time be effected by nine States. Here, then, the chances are as thirteen to nine in favor of subsequent amendment, rather than of the original adoption of an entire system.

That is not all. Every Constitution for the United States must inevitably consist of a great variety of particulars, in which thirteen independent States are to be accommodated in their interests or opinions of interest. We may of course expect to see, in any body of men charged with its original formulation, very different combinations of the parts upon different points. Many of those who form a majority on one question may become the minority on a second, and as association dissimilar to either may constitute the majority on a third. Hence the necessity of molding and arranging all the particulars which are to compose the whole in such a manner as to satisfy all the parties to the compact; and hence, also, an immense multiplication of difficulties and casualties in obtaining the collective assent to a final act. The degree of that multiplication must evidently be in a ratio to the number of particulars and the number of parties.

But every amendment to the Constitution, if once established, would be a single proposition, and might be brought forward singly. There would then be no necessity for management or compromise, in relation to any other point—no giving nor taking. The will of the requisite number would at once bring the matter to a decisive issue. And consequently, whenever nine, or rather ten States, were united in the desire of a particular amendment, that amendment must infallibly take place. There can, therefore, be no comparison between the facility of effecting an amendment, and that of establishing in the first instance a complete Constitution.

In opposition to the probability of subsequent amendments, it has been urged that the persons delegated to the administration of the national government will always be disinclined to yield up any portion of the authority of which they were once possessed. For my own part, I acknowledge a thorough conviction that any amendments which may, upon mature consideration, be thought useful, will be applicable to the organization of the government, not to the mass of its powers; and on this account alone, I think there is weight in the observation just stated. I also think there is little weight in it on another account. The intrinsic difficulty of governing thirteen States at any rate, independent of calculations upon an ordinary degree of public spirit and integrity, will, in my opinion, constantly impose on the national rulers the necessity of a spirit of accommodation to the reasonable expectations of their constituents. But there is yet a further consideration, which proves beyond the possibility of a doubt that the observation is futile. It is this, that the national rulers, whenever nine States concur, will have no option upon the subject. By the fifth article of the plan, the Congress will be obliged "on the application of the legislatures of two-thirds of the States (which at present amount to nine), to call a convention for proposing amendments, which shall be valid, to all intents and purposes, as part of the Constitution, when ratified by the legislatures of three-fourths of the States, or by conventions in three-fourths thereof." The words of this article are peremptory. The Congress "shall call a convention." Nothing in this particular is left to the discretion of that body. And of consequence all the declamation about the disinclination to a change vanishes in air. Nor, however difficult it may be supposed to unite two-thirds or three-fourths of the State legislatures, in amendments which may affect local interests, can there be any room to apprehend any such difficulty in a union on points which are merely relative to the general liberty or security of the people. We may safely rely on the disposition of the State legislatures to erect barriers against the encroachments of the national authority.

If the foregoing argument is a fallacy, certain it is that I am myself deceived by it, for it is, in my conception, one of those rare instances in which a political truth can be brought to the test of a mathematical demonstration. Those who see the matter in the same light with me, however zealous they may be for amendments, must agree in the propriety of a previous adoption as the most direct road to their own object.

The zeal for attempts to amend, prior to the establishment of the Constitution, must abate in every man who is ready to accede to the truth of the following observations of a writer equally solid and ingenious: "To balance a large state or society (says he), whether monarchical or republican, on general laws, is a work of so great difficulty that no human genius, however comprehensive, is able, by the mere dint of reason and reflection, to effect it. The judgments of many must unite in the work; experience must guide their labor; time must bring it to perfection, and the feeling of inconveniences must correct the mistakes which they *inevitably* fall into in their first trials and experiments." [Hume] These judicious reflections contain a lesson of moderation to all the sincere lovers of the Union, and ought to put them upon their guard against hazarding anarchy, civil war, a perpetual alienation of the States from each other, and perhaps the military despotism of a victorious demagogue, in the pursuit of what they are not likely to obtain but from time and experience. It may be in me a defect of political fortitude, but I acknowledge that I cannot entertain an equal tranquillity with those who affect to treat the dangers of a longer continuance in our present situation as imaginary. A nation without a national government is in my view an awful spectacle. The establishment of a Constitution, in time of profound peace, by the voluntary consent of a whole people, is a prodigy, to the completion of which I look forward with trembling anxiety. I can reconcile it to no rules of prudence to let go the hold we now have, in so arduous an enterprise, upon seven out of the thirteen States, and, after having passed over so considerable a part of the ground, to recommence the course. I dread the more the consequences of new attempts because I know that powerful individuals, in this and in other States, are enemies to a general national government in every possible shape.

2.8. Federalists and Anti-Federalists Debate the Amending Process at the State Ratifying Conventions*

As Article VII of the U.S. Constitution indicates, the Constitution was reported to the states to be ratified or rejected by special conventions called for this purpose. Debate was often vigorous, Federalists defending the new document and Anti-Federalists raising every real and imagined objection. Below are some of the arguments made for and against the amending process.

---

* *The Debates in the Several State Conventions on the Adoption of the Federal Constitution*, 5 vols. ed. Jonathan Elliot (New York: Burt Franklin reprint: From 1888 edition), vol. 2, pp. 116-7; vol. 3, pp. 48-51; vol. 4, pp. 176-8 and 212-3.

From the Massachusetts Convention

After the 5th article was read at the table,—

The Hon. Mr. KING observed, that he believed gentlemen had not, in their objections to the Constitution, recollected that this article was a part of it; for many of the arguments of gentlemen were founded on the idea of future amendments being impracticable. The honorable gentleman observed on the superior excellence of the proposed Constitution in this particular, and called upon gentlemen to produce an instance, in any other national constitution, where the people had so fair an opportunity to correct any abuse which might take place in the future administration of the government under it.

Dr. JARVIS. Mr President, I cannot suffer the present article to be passed, without rising to express my entire and perfect approbation of it. Whatever may have been my private opinion of any other part, or whatever faults or imperfections I have remarked, or fancied I have seen, in any other instance, here, sir, I have found complete satisfaction: this has been a resting place, on which I have reposed myself in the fullest security, whenever a doubt has occurred, in considering any other passage in the proposed Constitution. The honorable gentleman last speaking has called upon those persons who are opposed to our receiving the present system, to show another government, in which such a wise precaution has been taken to secure to the people the right of making such alterations and amendments, in a peaceable way, as experience shall have proved to be necessary. Allow me to say, sir, as far as the narrow limits of my own information extend, I know of no such example. In other countries, sir,—unhappily for mankind,—the history of their respective revolutions has been written in blood; and it is in this only that any great or important change in our political situation has been effected, without public commotions. When we shall have adopted the Constitution before us, we shall have in this article an adequate provision for all the purposes of political reformation. If, in the course of its operation, this government shall appear to be too severe, here are the means by which this severity may be assuaged and corrected. If, on the other hand, it shall become too languid in its movement, here, again, we have a method designated, by which a new portion of health and spirit may be infused into the Constitution.

There is, sir, another view, which I have long since taken of this subject, which has produced the fullest conviction, in my own mind, in favor of our receiving the government which we have now in contemplation. Should it be rejected, I beg gentlemen would observe, that a concurrence of all the states must be had before a new convention can be called to form another Constitution; but the present article provides, upon nine states' concurring in any alteration or amendment to be proposed either by Congress or any future convention, that this alteration shall be a part of the Constitution, equally powerful and obligatory with any other part. If it be alleged that this union is not likely to happen, will it be more likely that a union of a greater number of concurring sentiments may be had, as must be, in case we reject the Constitution in hopes of a better? But that this is practicable, we may safely appeal to the history of this country as a proof, in the last twenty years. We have united against the British; we have united in calling the late federal Convention; and we may certainly unite again in such alterations as in reason shall appear to be important for the peace and happiness of America.

In the constitution of this state, the article providing for alterations is limited in its operation to a given time; but in the present Constitution, the article is perfectly at large, unconfined to any period, and may admit of measures being taken in any moment after it is adopted. In this point is has undoubtedly the advantage. I shall not sit down, sir, without repeating, that, as it is clearly more difficult for twelve states to agree to another convention, than for nine to unite in favor of amendments, so it is certainly better to receive the present Constitution, in the hope of its being amended, than it would be to reject it altogether, with, perhaps, the vain expectation of obtaining another more agreeable than the present.

From the Virginia Convention, Patrick Henry

To encourage us to adopt it, they tell us that there is a plain, easy way of getting amendments. When I come to contemplate this part, I suppose that I am mad, or that my countrymen are so. The way to amendment is, in my conception, shut. Let us consider this plain, easy way. [Henry procedes to quote from Article V]

Hence it appears that three fourths of the states must ultimately agree to any amendment that may be necessary. Let us consider the consequence of this. However uncharitable it may appear, yet I must tell my opinion—that the most unworthy characters may get into power, and prevent the introduction of amendments. Let us suppose—for the case is supposable, possible, and probable—that you happen to deal those powers to unworthy hands; will they relinquish powers already in their possession, or agree to amendments? Two thirds of the Congress, or of the state legislatures, are necessary even to propose amendments. If one third of these be unworthy men, they may prevent the application for amendments; but what is destructive and mischievous, is, that three fourths of the state legislatures, or of the state conventions, must concur in the amendments when proposed! In such numerous bodies, there must necessarily be some designing, bad men. To suppose that so large a number as three fourths of the states will concur, is to suppose that they will possess genius, intelligence, and integrity, approaching to miraculous. It would indeed be miraculous that they should concur in the same amendments, or even in such as would bear some likeness to one another; for four of the smallest states, that do not collectively contain one tenth part of the population of the United States, may obstruct the most salutary and necessary amendments. Nay, in these four states, six tenths of the people may reject these amendments; and suppose that amendments shall be opposed to amendments, which is highly probable,—is it possible that three fourths can ever agree to the same amendments? A bare majority in these four small states may hinder the adoption of amendments; so that we may fairly and justly conclude that one twentieth part of the American people may prevent the removal of the most grievous inconveniences and oppression, by refusing to accede to amendments. A trifling minority may reject the most salutary amendments. Is this an easy mode of securing the public liberty? It is, sir, a most fearful situation, when the most contemptible minority can prevent the alteration of the most oppressive government; for it may, in many respects, prove to be such. Is this the spirit of republicanism?

What, sir, is the genius of democracy? Let me read that clause of the bill of rights of Virginia which relates to this: 3d clause:—that government is, or ought to be, instituted for the common benefit, protection, and security of the people, nation, or community. Of all the various modes and forms of government, that is best, which is capable of producing the greatest degree of happiness and safety, and is most effectually secured against the danger of mal-administration; and that whenever any government shall be found inadequate, or contrary to those purposes, a majority of the community hath an indubitable, unalienable, and indefeasible right to reform, alter, or abolish it, in such manner as shall be judged most conducive to the public weal.

This, sir, is the language of democracy—that a majority of the community have a right to alter government when found to be oppressive. But how different is the genius of your new Constitution from this! How different from the sentiments of freemen, that a contemptible minority can prevent the good of the majority! If, then, gentlemen, standing on this ground, are come to that point, that they are willing to bind themselves and their posterity to be oppressed, I am amazed and inexpressibly astonished. If this be the opinion of the majority, I must submit; but to me, sir, it appears perilous and destructive. I cannot help thinking so. Perhaps it may be the result of my age. These may be feelings natural to a man of my years, when the American spirit has left him, and his mental powers, like the members of the body, are decayed. If, sir, amendments are left to the twentieth, or tenth part of the people of America, your liberty is gone forever. We have heard that there is a great deal of bribery practised in the House of Commons, in England, and that many of the members raise themselves to preferments by selling the rights of the whole of the people. But, sir, the tenth part of that body cannot continue oppressions on the rest of the people. English liberty is, in this case, on a firmer foundation than American liberty. It will be easily contrived to procure the opposition of one tenth of the people to any alteration, however judicious. The honorable gentleman who presides told us that, to prevent abuses in our government, we will assemble in Convention, recall our delegates powers, and punish our servants for abusing the trust reposed in them. O sir, we should have fine times, indeed, if, to punish tyrants, it were only sufficient to assemble the people! Your arms, wherewith you could defend yourselves, are gone; and you have no longer an aristocratical, no longer a democratical spirit. Did you ever read of any revolution in a nation, brought about by the punishment of those in power, inflicted by those who had no power at all? You read of a riot act in a country which is called one of the freest in the world, where a few neighbors cannot assemble without the risk of being shot by a hired soldiery, the engines of despotism. We may see such an act in America.

The North Carolina Convention, Mr. Iredell, Mr. Lancaster
Article 5th.

Mr. IREDELL. Mr. Chairman, this is a very important clause. In every other constitution of government that I have ever heard or read of, no provision is made for necessary amendments. The misfortune attending most constitutions which have been deliberately formed, has been, that those who formed them thought their wisdom equal to all possible contingencies, and that there could be no error in what they did. The gentlemen who framed this Constitution thought with much more diffidence of their capacities; and, undoubtedly, without a provision for amendment it would have been more justly liable to objection, and the characters of its framers would have appeared much less meritorious. This, indeed, is one of the greatest beauties of the system, and should strongly recommend it to every candid mind. The Constitution of any government which cannot be regularly amended when its defects are experienced, reduces the people to this dilemma—they must either submit to its oppressions, or bring about amendments, more or less, by a civil war. Happy this, the country we live in! The Constitution before us, if it be adopted, can be altered with as much regularity, and as little confusion, as any act of Assembly; not, indeed, quite so easily, which would be extremely impolitic; but it is a most happy circumstance, that there is a remedy in the system itself for its own fallibility, so that alterations can without difficulty be made, agreeable to the general sense of the people. Let us attend to the manner in which amendments may be made. The proposition for amendments may arise from Congress itself, when two thirds of both houses shall deem it necessary. If they should not, and yet amendments be generally wished for by the people, two thirds of the legislatures of the different states may require a general convention for the purpose, in which case Congress are under the necessity of convening one. Any amendments which either Congress shall propose, or which shall be proposed by such general convention, are afterwards to be submitted to the legislatures of the different states, or conventions called for that purpose, as Congress shall think proper, and, upon the ratification of three fourths of the states, will become a part of the Constitution. By referring this business to the legislatures, expense would be saved; and in general, it may be presumed, they would speak the genuine sense of the people. It may, however, on some occasions, be better to consult an immediate delegation for that special purpose. This is therefore left discretionary. It is highly probable that amendments agreed to in either of these methods would be conducive to the public welfare, when so large a majority of the states consented to them. And in one of these modes, amendments that are now wished for may, in a short time, be made to this Constitution by the states adopting it.

It is, however, to be observed, that the 1st and 4th clauses in the 9th section of the 1st article are protected from any alteration till the year 1808; and in order that no consolidation should take place, it is provided that no state shall, by any amendment or alteration, be ever deprived of an equal suffrage in the Senate without its own consent. The first two prohibitions are with respect to the census, (according to which direct taxes are imposed,) and with respect to the importation of slaves. As to the first, it must be observed, that there is a material difference between the Northern and Southern States. The Northern States have been much longer settled, and are much fuller of people, than the Southern, but have not land in equal proportion, nor scarcely any slaves. The subject of this article was regulated with great difficulty, and by a spirit of concession which it would not be prudent to disturb for a good many years. In twenty years, there will probably be a great alteration, and then the subject may be reconsidered with less difficulty and greater coolness. In the mean time, the compromise was upon the best footing that could be obtained. A compromise likewise took place in regard to the importation of slaves. It is probable that all the members reprobated this inhuman traffic; but those of South Carolina and Georgia would not consent to an immediate prohibition of it—one reason of which was, that, during the last war, they lost a vast number of negroes, which loss they wish to supply. In the mean time it is left to the states to admit or prohibit the importation, and Congress may impose a limited duty upon it.

Mr. BASS observed, that it was plain that the introduction of amendments depended altogether on Congress.

Mr. IREDELL replied, that it was very evident that it did not depend on the will of Congress; for that the legislatures of two thirds of the states were authorized to make application for calling a convention to propose amendments, and, on such application, it is provided that Congress *shall* call such convention, so that they will have no option. . . .

Mr. LANCASTER

We find that the ratification of nine states shall be sufficient for its establishment between the states so ratifying the same. This, as has been already taken notice of, is a violation of the Confederation. We find that, by that system, no alteration was to take place, except it was ratified by every state in the Union. Now, by comparing this last article of the Constitution to that part of the Confederation, we find a most flagrant violation. The Articles of Confederation were sent out with all solemnity on so solemn an occasion, and were to be always binding on the states; but, to our astonishment, we see that nine states may do away the force of the whole. I think, without exaggeration, that it will be looked upon, by foreign nations, as a serious and alarming change.

How do we know that, if we propose amendments, they shall be obtained after actual ratification? May not these amendments be proposed with equal propriety, and more safety, as the condition of our adoption? If they violate the 13th article of the Confederation in this manner, may they not, with equal propriety, refuse to adopt amendments, although agreed to and wished for by two thirds of the states? This violation of the old system is a precedent for such proceedings as these. That would be a violation destructive to our felicity. We are now determining a question deeply affecting the happiness of millions yet unborn. It is the policy of freemen to guard their privileges. Let us, then, as far as we can, exclude the possibility of tyranny. . . .

2.9 Jefferson and Madison Discuss Generational Rights*

The readings in this chapter should already demonstrate that, although they would later be close political allies and co-founders of the Democratic-Republican Party, Jefferson and Madison emphasized different aspects of constitutional change; Jefferson was more willing to institute such change and Madison was reluctant to do so. In few places is this contrast more evident than in a pair of letters that the two exchanged in 1789-80 when Jefferson was in Paris. Jefferson perceptively raised the question of whether one generation had the power to bind another, and Madison showed both his depth and independence of thought in responding.

Jefferson's Letter to Madison, September 6, 1789

DEAR SIR,—I sit down to write to you without knowing by what occasion I shall send my letter. I do it because a subject comes into my head which I would wish to develope a little

---

* *The Works of Thomas Jefferson*, Paul L. Ford ed. (New York: C.P. Putnam's Sons: The Knickerbocker Press, 1905), Vol. 6, pp. 3-11. *The Writings of James Madison*, ed. Gaillard Hunt 9 vols.(New York: G.P. Putnam's Sons, The Knickerbocker Press, 1904), vol. 5, pp. 437-441.

more than is practicable in the hurry of the moment of making up general dispatches.

The question Whether one generation of men has a right to bind another, seems never to have been started either on this or our side of the water. Yet it is a question of such consequences as not only to merit decision, but place also, among the fundamental principles of every government. The course of reflection in which we are immersed here on the elementary principles of society has presented this question to my mind; and that no such obligation can be transmitted I think very capable of proof. I set out on this ground which I suppose to be self evident, "*that the earth belongs in usufruct to the living*," that the dead have neither powers nor rights over it. The portion occupied by any individual ceases to be his when himself ceases to be, and reverts to the society. If the society has formed no rules for the appropriation of its lands in severalty, it will be taken by the first occupants. These will generally be the wife and children of the decedent. If they have formed rules of appropriation, those rules may give it to the wife and children, or to some one of them, or to the legatee of the deceased. So they may give it to his creditor. But the child, the legatee or creditor takes it, not by any natural right, but by a law of the society of which they are members, and to which they are subject. Then no man can by *natural right* oblige the lands he occupied, or the persons who succeed him in that occupation, to the paiment of debts contracted by him. For if he could, he might during his own life, eat up the usufruct of the lands for several generations to come, and then the lands would belong to the dead, and not to the living, which would be reverse of our principle. What is true of every member of the society individually, is true of them all collectively, since the rights of the whole can be no more than the sum of the rights of individuals. To keep our ideas clear when applying them to a multitude, let us suppose a whole generation of men to be born on the same day, to attain mature age on the same day, and to die on the same day, leaving a succeeding generation in the moment of attaining their mature age all together. Let the ripe age be supposed of 21. years, and their period of life 34. years more, that being the average term given by the bills of mortality to persons who have already attainded 21. years of age. Each successive generation would, in this way, come on and go off the stage at a fixed moment, as individuals do not. Then I say the earth belongs to each of these generations during it's course, fully, and in their own right. The 2d. generation receives it clear of the debts and incumbrances of the 1st., the 3d. of the 2d. and so on. For if the 1st could charge it with a debt, then the earth would belong to the dead and not the living generation. Then no generation can contract debts greater than may be paid during the course of it's own existence. At 21. years of age they may bind themselves and their land for 34. years to come: at 22. for 33: at 23 for 32. and at 54 for one year only; because these are the terms of life which remain to them at those respective epochs. But a material difference must be noted between the succession of an individual and that of a whole generation. Individuals are parts only of a society, subject to the laws of a whole. These laws may appropriate the portion of land occupied by a decedent to his creditor rather than to any other, or to his child, on condition he satisfied his creditor. But when a whole generation, that is, the whole society dies, as in the case we have supposed, and another generation or society succeeds, this forms a whole, and there is no superior who can give their territory to a third society, who may have lent money to their predecessors beyond their faculty of paying.

What is true of a generation all arriving to self-government on the same day, and dying all on the same day, is true of those on a constant course of decay and renewal, with this only difference. A generation coming in and going out entire, as in the first case, would have a right in the 1st year of their self dominion to contract a debt for 33. years, in the 10th. for 24. in the 20th. for 14. in the 30th. for 4. whereas generations changing daily, by daily deaths and births, have one constant term beginning at the date of their contract, and ending when a majority of those of full age at that date shall be dead. The length of that term may be estimated from the tables of mortality, corrected by the circumstances of climate, occupation &c. peculiar to the country of the contractors. Take, for instance, the table of M. de Buffon wherein he states 23,994 deaths, and the ages at which they happened. Suppose a society in which 23,994 persons are born every year and live to the ages stated in this table. The conditions of that society will be as follows. 1st. it will consist constantly of 617,703 persons of all ages. 2nly. of those living at any one instant of time, one half will be dead in 24. year 8. months. 3dly. 10,675 will arrive every year at the age of 21. years complete. 4thly. it will constantly have 348,417 persons of all ages above 21. years. 5ly. and the half of those of 21. years and upwards living at any one instant of time will be dead in 18. years 8. months, or say 19. years as the nearest integral number. Then 19. years is the term beyond which neither the representatives of a nation, nor even the whole nation itself assembled, can validly extend a debt.

To render this conclusion palpable by example, suppose that Louis XIV. and XV. had contracted debts in the name of the French nation to the amount of 10.000 milliards of livres and that the whole had been contracted in Genoa. The interest of this sum would be 500 milliards, which is said to be the whole rent-roll, or nett proceeds of the territory of France. Must the present generation of men have retired from the territory in which nature produced them, and ceded it to the Genoese creditors? No. They have the same rights over the soil on which they were produced, as the preceding generations had. They derive these rights not from their predecessors, but from nature. They then and their soil are by nature clear of the debts of their predecessors. Again suppose Louis XV. and his contemporary generation had said to the money lenders of Genoa, give us money that we may eat, drink, and be merry in our day; and on condition you will demand no interest till the end of 19. years, you shall then forever after receive an annual interest of 12 per cent. The money is lent on these conditions, is divided among the living, eaten, drank, and squandered. Would the present generation be obliged to apply the produce of the earth and of their labour to replace their dissipations? Not at all.

I suppose that the received opinion, that the public debts of one generation devolve on the next, has been suggested by our seeing habitually in private life that he who succeeds to lands is required to pay the debts of his ancestor or testator, without considering that this requisition is municipal only, not moral, flowing from the will of the society which has found it convenient to appropriate the lands become vacant by the death of their occupant on the condition of a paiment of his debts; but that between society and society, or generation and generation there is no municipal obligation, no umpire but the law of nature. We seem not to have perceived that, by the law of nature, one generation is to another as one independant nation to another.

The interest of the national debt of France being in fact but a two thousandth part of it's rent-roll, the paiment of it is practicable enough; and so becomes a question merely of honor or expediency. But with respect to future debts; would it not be wise and just for that nation to declare in the constitution they are forming that neither the legislature, nor the nation itself can validly contract more debt, than they may pay within their own age, or within the term of 19. years? And that all future contracts shall be deemed void as to what shall remain unpaid at the end of 19. years from their date? This would put the lenders and the borrowers also, on their guard. By reducing too the faculty of borrowing within its natural limits, it would bridle the spirit of war, to which too free a course has been procured by the inattention of money lenders to this law of nature, that succeeding generations are not responsible for the preceding.

On similar ground it may be proved that no society can make a perpetual constitution, or even a perpetual law. The earth belongs always to the living generation. They may manage it then, and what proceeds from it, as they please, during their usufruct. They are masters too of their own persons, and consequently may govern them as they please. But persons and property make the sum of the objects of government. The constitution and the laws of their predecessors extinguished them, in their natural course, with those whose will gave them being. This could preserve that being till it ceased to be itself, and no longer. Every constitution, then, and every law, naturally expires at the end of 19. years. If it be enforced longer, it is an act of force and not of right.

It may be said that the succeeding generation exercising in fact the power of repeal, this leaves them as free as if the constitution or law had been expressly limited to 19. years only. In the first place, this objection admits the right, in proposing an equivalent. But the power of repeal is not an equivalent. It might be indeed if every form of government were so perfectly contrived that the will of the majority could always be obtained fairly and without impediment. But this is true of no form. The people cannot assemble themselves; their representation is unequal and vicious. Various checks are opposed to every legislative proposition. Factions get possession of the public councils. Bribery corrupts them. Personal interests lead them astray from the general interests of their constituents; and other impediments arise so as to prove to every practical man that a law of limited duration is much more manageable than one which needs a repeal.

This principle that the earth belongs to the living and not to the dead is of very extensive application and consequences in every country, and most especially in France. It enters into the resolution of the questions Whether the nation may change the descent of lands holden in tail? Whether they may change the appropriate of lands given antiently to the church, to hospitals, colleges, orders of chivalry, and otherwise in perpetuity? whether they may abolish the charges and privileges attached on lands, including the whole catalogue ecclesiastical and feudal? it goes to hereditary orders, distinctions and appellations; to perpetual monopolies in commerce, the arts or sciences; with a long trail of *et ceteras*: and it renders the question of reimbursement a question of generosity and not of right. In all these cases the legislature of the day could authorize such appropriations and establishments for their own time, but no longer; and the present holders, even where they or their ancestors have purchased, are in the case of *bona fide* purchasers of what the seller had no right to convey.

Turn this subject in your mind, my Dear Sir, and particularly as to the power of contracting debts, and develope it with that perspicuity and cogent logic which is so peculiarly yours.

Your station in the councils of our country gives you an opportunity of producing it to public consideration, of forcing it into discussion. At first blush it may be rallied as a theoretical speculation; but examination will prove it to be solid and salutary. It would furnish matter for a fine preamble to our first law for appropriating the public revenue; and it will exclude, at the threshold of our new government the contagious and ruinous errors of this quarter of the globe, which have armed despots with means not sanctioned by nature for binding in chains their fellow-men. We have already given, in example, one effectual check to the Dog of war, by transferring the power of letting him loose from the executive to the Legislative body, from those who are to spend to those who are to pay. I should be pleased to see this second obstacle held out by us also in the first instance. No nation can make a declaration against the validity of long-contracted debts so disinterestedly as we, since we do not owe a shilling which may not be paid with ease principal and interest, within the time of our own lives. Establish the principle also in the new law to be passed for protecting copy rights and new inventions, by securing the exclusive right for 19. instead of 14 years. . .

Madison's reply, February 4, 1790

DEAR SIR, –

Your favor of Jany 9, inclosing one of Sepr last did not get to hand till a few days ago. The idea which the latter evolves is a great one; and suggests many interesting reflections to Legislators; particularly when contracting and providing for public debts. Whether it can be received in the extent to which your reasonings carry it, is a question which I ought to turn more in my thoughts than I have yet been able to do, before I should be justified in making up a full opinion on it. My first thoughts lead me to view the doctrine as not *in all respects* compatible with the course of human affairs. I will endeavour to sketch the grounds of my skepticism. "as the Earth belongs to the living, not to the dead, a living generation can bind itself only; in every Society the will of the majority binds the whole; according to the laws of mortality, a majority of those ripe for the exercise of their will do not live beyond the term of 19 years; to this term then is limited the validity of every act of the Society, nor can any act be continued beyond this term without an *express* declaration of the public will." This I understand to be the outline of the argument.

The Acts of a political society may be divided into three classes:

1. the fundamental constitution of the Government.

2. laws involving some stipulation, which renders them irrevocable at the will of the Legislature.

3. laws involving no such irrevocable quality.

1. However applicable in theory the doctrine may be to a Constitution, it seems liable in practice to some weighty objections.

Would not a Government ceasing of necessity at the end of a given term, unless prolonged by some Constitutional Act, previous to its expiration, be too subject to the casualty and consequences of an interregnum?

Would not a Government so often revised become too mutable & novel to retain that share of prejudice in its favor which is a salutary aid to the most rational Government?

Would not such a periodical revision engender pernicious factions that might not otherwise come into existence; and agitate the public mind more frequently and more violently than might be expedient?

2. In the second class of acts involving stipulations, must not exceptions at least to the doctrine, be admitted?

If the earth be the gift of *nature* to the living, their title can extend to the earth in its natural state only. The *improvements* made by the dead form a debt against the living, who take the benefit of them. This debt cannot be otherwise discharged than by a proportionate obedience to the will of the Authors of the improvements.

But a case less liable to be controverted may perhaps be stated. Debts may be incurred with a direct view to the interests of the unborn as well as of the living. Such are debts for repelling a Conquest, the evils of which descend through many generations. Debts may even be incurred principally for the benefit of posterity: Such perhaps is the debt incurred by the U. States. In these instances the debts might not be dischargeable within the term of 19 years.

There seems, then, to be some foundation in the nature of things; in the relation which one generation bears to another, for the *descent* of obligations from one to another. Equity may require it. Mutual good may be promoted by it. And all that seems indispensable in stating the account between the dead and the living, is to see that the debts against the latter do not exceed the advances made by the former. Few of the incumbrances entailed on nations by their predecessors would bear a liquidation even on this principle.

3. Objections to the doctrine, as applied to the third class of Acts must be merely practical. But in that view alone they appear to be material.

Unless such temporary laws should be kept in force by acts regularly anticipating their expiration, all the rights depending on positive laws, that is most of the rights of property would become absolutely defunct, and the most violent struggles ensue between the parties interested in reviving & those interested in reforming the antecedent state of property. Nor does it seem improbable that such an event might be suffered to take place. The checks & difficulties opposed to the passage of laws which render the power of repeal inferior to an opportunity to reject, as a security against oppression, would here render the latter an insecure provision against anarchy. Add to this that the very possibility of an event so hazardous to the rights of property could not but depreciate its value; that the approach of the crisis w^d increase the effect; that the frequent return of periods superseding all the obligations dependent on antecedent laws & usages, must by weakening the sense of them, co-operate with motives to licenciousness already too powerful; and that the general uncertainty & vicissitudes of such a state of things would, on one side, discourage every useful effort of steady industry pursued under the sanction of existing laws, and on the other, give an immediate advantage to the more sagacious over the less sagacious part of the Society.

I can find no relief from such embarrassments, but in the received doctrine that a *tacit* assent may be given to established Governments & laws, and that this assent is to be inferred from the omission of an express revocation. It seems more practicable to remedy by well-constituted Governments the pestilent operation of this doctrine, in the unlimited sense in which it is at present rec[d], than it is to find a remedy for the evils necessarily springing from an unlimited admission of the contrary doctrine.

It is not doubtful whether it be possible to exclude wholly the idea of an implied or tacit assent, without subverting the very foundation of Civil Society?

On what principle is it that the voice of the majority binds the minority? It does not result I conceive from a law of nature but from compact founded on utility. A greater proportion might be required by the fundamental Constitution of Society, if under any praticular [sic] circumstances it were judged eligible. Prior therefore to the establishment of this principle, *unanimity* was necessary; and rigid Theory, accordingly presupposes the assent of every individual to the rule, which subjects the minority to the will of the majority. If this assent cannot be given tacitly, or be not implied where no positive evidence forbids, no person born in Society, could on attaining ripe age, be bound by any acts of the majority, and either a unanimous renewal of every law would be necessary, as often as a new member should be added to the Society, or the express consent of every new member be obtained to the rule by which the majority decides for the whole.

If these observations be not misapplied, it follows that a limitation of the validity of all Acts to the computed life of the generation establishing them, is in some cases not required by theory, and in others not consistent with practice. They are not meant however to impeach either the utility of the principle as applied to the cases you have particularly in view, or the general importance of it in the eye of the Philosophical Legislator. On the contrary it would give me singular pleasure to see it first announced to the world in a law of the U. States, and always kept in view as a salutary restraint on living generations from *unjust & unnecessary* burdens on their successors.

This is a pleasure however which I have no hope of enjoying. The spirit of Philosophical legislation has not prevailed at all in some parts of America and is by no means the fashion of this part, or of the present Representative Body. The evils suffered or feared weakness in Government and licenciousness in the people, have turned the attention more towards the means of strengthening the powers of the former, than of narrowing their extent in the minds of the latter. Besides this it is so much easier to decry the little difficulties immediately incident to every great plan, than to comprehend its general & remote benefits, that further light must be added to the Councils of our Country before many truths which are seen through the medium of Philosophy, become visible to the naked eye of the ordinary politician.

2.10. Noah Webster Questions Perpetual Constitutions*

Although his writings do not often attract the same attention as those of his contemporaries, the writings of Noah Webster—later to be recognized as a great American lexicographer—at the time of the writing of the U.S. Constitution are as fascinating as any. What is particularly fascinating about Webster's essays, published in *American Magazine* under the pen name Giles Hickory, are the way they combine arguments like Jefferson's against perpetual constitutions with arguments against the very notion of bill of rights which Jefferson and others so cherished.

No Need for a Bill of Rights

One of the principal objections to the new Federal Constitution is, that it contains no *Bill of Rights*. This objection, I presume to assert, is founded on ideas of government that are totally false. Men seem determined to adhere to old prejudices, and reason *wrong*, because our ancestors reasoned *right*. A Bill of Rights against the encroachments of Kings and Barons, or against any power independent of the people, is

* Noah Webster, *American Magazine* 1 (1787-88), 13-15, 75-80, 137-45, 402-10. Spellings have been modernized.

perfectly intelligible; but a Bill of Rights against the encroachments of an elective Legislature, that is, against our *own* encroachments on *ourselves*, is a curiosity in government.

One half the people who read books, have so little ability to apply what they read to their own practice, that they had better not read at all. The English nation, from which we descended have been gaining their liberties, inch by inch, by forcing concessions from the crown and the Barons, during the course of six centuries. *Magna Charta*, which is called the palladium of English liberty, was dated in 1215, and the people of England were not represented in Parliament till the year 1265. Magna Charta established the rights of the Barons and the clergy against the encroachments of royal prerogative; but the commons or people were hardly noticed in that deed. There was but one clause in their favor, which stipulated that, "No villain or rustic should, by any fine, be bereaved of his carts, plows and instruments of husbandry." As for the rest, they were considered as a part of the property belonging to an estate, and were transferred, as other moveables, at the will of their owners. In the succeeding reign, they were permitted to send Representatives to Parliament; and from that time have been gradually assuming their proper degree of consequence in the British Legislature. In such a nation, every law or statute that defines the powers of the crown, and circumscribes them within determinate limits, must be considered as a barrier to guard popular liberty. Every acquisition of freedom must be established as a *right*, and solemnly recognized by the supreme power of the nation; lest it should be again resumed by the crown under pretence of ancient prerogative; For this reason, the habeas corpus act passed in the reign of Charles 2d, the statute of the 2d of William and Mary, and many others which are declaratory of certain privileges, are justly considered as the pillars of English freedom.

These statutes are however not esteemed because they are unalterable; for the same power that enacted them, can at any moment repeal them; but they are esteemed, because they are barriers erected by the Representatives of the nation, against a power that exists independent of their own choice. But the same reasons for such declaratory constitutions do not exist in

America, where the supreme power is *the people in their Representatives*. The *Bills of Rights*, prefixed to several of the constitutions of the United States, if considered as assigning the reasons of our separation from a foreign government, or as solemn declarations of right against the encroachments of a foreign jurisdiction, are perfectly rational, and were doubtless necessary. But if they are considered as barriers against the encroachments of our own Legislatures, or as constitutions unalterable by posterity, I venture to pronounce them nugatory, and to the last degree absurd.

In our governments, there is no power of legislation, independent of the people; no power that has an interest detached from that of the public; consequently there is no power existing against which it is necessary to guard. While our Legislatures therefore remain elective, and the rulers have the same interest in the laws, as the subjects have, the rights of the people will be perfectly secure without any declaration in their favor.

But this is not the principal point. I undertake to prove that a standing *Bill of Rights* is *absurd*, because no constitutions, in a free government, can be unalterable. The present generation have indeed a right to declare what *they* deem a *privilege*; but they have no right to say what the *next* generation shall deem a privilege. A State is a supreme corporation that never dies. Its powers, when it acts for itself, are at all times, equally extensive; and it has the same right to *repeal* a law this year, as it had to *make* it the last. If therefore our posterity are found by our constitutions, and can neither amend nor annul them, they are to all intents and purposes our slaves.

But it will be enquired, have we then no right to say, that trial by jury, the liberty of the press, the habeas corpus writ and other invaluable privileges, shall never be infringed nor destroyed? By no means. We have the same right to say that lands shall descend in a particular mode to the heirs of the deceased proprietor, and that such a mode shall never be altered by future generations, as we have to pass a law that the trial by jury shall never be abridged. The right of Jury-trial, which we deem invaluable, may in future cease to be a privilege; or other modes of trial more satisfactory to the people, may be devised. Such an event is neither impossible nor improbable. Have we then a right to say that our posterity shall not be judges of their own circumstances? The very attempt to make *perpetual* constitutions, is the assumption of a right to control the opinions of future generations; and the legislate for those over whom we have as little authority as we have over a nation in Asia. Nay we have as little right to say that trial by jury shall be perpetual, as the English, in the reign of Edward the Confessor, had, to bind their posterity forever to decide causes by fiery Ordeal, or single combat. There are perhaps many laws and regulations, which from their consonance to the eternal rules of justice, will always be good and conformable to the sense of a nation. But most institutions in society, by reason of an unceasing change of circumstances, either become altogether improper or require amendment; and every nation has at all times, the right of judging of its circumstances and determining on the propriety of changing its laws.

The English writers talk much of the omnipotence of Parliament; and yet they seem to entertain some scruples about their right to change particular parts of their constitution. I question much whether Parliament would not hesitate to change, on any occasion, an article of Magna Charta. Mr. Pitt, a few years ago, attempted to reform the mode of representation in Parliament. Immediately an uproar was raised against the measure, as *unconstitutional*. The representation of the kingdom, when first established, was doubtless equal and wise; but by the increase of some cities and boroughs and the depopulation of others, it has become extremely *unequal*. In some boroughs there is scarcely an elector left to enjoy its privileges. If the nation feels no great inconvenience from this change of circumstances, under the old mode of representation, a reform is unnecessary. But if such a change has produced any national evils of magnitude enough to be felt, the present form of electing the Representatives of the nation, however *constitutional*, and venerable for its antiquity, may at any time be amended, if it should be the sense of Parliament. The *expediency* of the alteration must always be a matter of opinion; but all scruples as to the *right* of making it are totally groundless.

Magna Charta may be considered as a contract between two parties, the King and the Barons, and no contract can be altered but by the consent of both parties. But whenever any article of that deed or contract shall become inconvenient or oppressive, the King, Lords and Commons may either amend or annul it at pleasure.

The same reasoning applies to each of the United States, and to the Federal Republic in general. But an important question will arise from the foregoing remarks, which must be the subject of another paper.

The Power of the Legislature to Write a Constitution

The important question I proposed to discuss in this number is this—"Whether, in a free State, there ought to be any distinction between the powers of the people or electors, and the powers of the Representatives in the Legislature." Or in other words, "whether the legislative body is not or ought not to be a standing convention, invested with the whole power of their constituents."

In supporting the affirmative of this question, I must face the opinions and prejudices of my countrymen; yet if we attend closely to the merits of the question, stripped of all its specious covering, we shall perhaps find more arguments in favor of this side, than we at first suspect.

In the first place, a Legislature must be the supreme power, whose decisions are laws, binding upon the whole State. Unless the Legislature is the supreme power, and invested with *all* the authority of the State, its acts are not laws, obligatory upon the whole State, I am sensible that it is a favorite idea in this country, bandied about from one demagogue to another, that *rulers are the servants of the people*. So far as their business is *laborious* and *embarrassing*, it implies a degree of servitude; but in any other view, the opinion is totally false. The people ought at least to place their rulers, who are generally men of the first abilities and integrity, on a level with themselves; for that is an odd kind of government indeed, in which, *servants* govern their *masters*. The truth is, a Representative, as an individual, is on a footing with other people; as a Representative of a State, he is invested with a share of the sovereign authority, and is so far a *Governor* of the people. In short, the collective body of Representatives is the collective sense and authority of the people; and so far are the members from being the *servants* of the people, that they are just as much *masters, rulers, governors,* whatever appellation we give them, as the people would be themselves in a convention of the whole State. But in the second place, the public good or safety requires that the powers of a Legislature should be co-extensive with those of the people. That a Legislature should be competent to pass any law that the public safety and interest may require, is a position that no man will controvert. If therefore it can be proved that the reservation of any power in the hands of the people, may at times interfere with the power of the Legislature to consult the public interest, and prevent its exercise, it must be acknowledged that such reservation is not only impolitic, but unjust. That a Legislature should have unlimited power to do *right,* is unquestionable; but such a power they cannot have, unless they have all the power of the State; which implies an unlimited power to do *wrong*. For instance, suppose the constitution of any state to declare, that no standing army shall be kept up in time of peace; then the Legislature can not raise and maintain a single soldier to guard our frontiers, without violating the constitution. To say that new enlistments every year will save the constitution, is idle; for if a body of troops raised for thirty years is a standing army, then a body raised for twenty years, or for six months is a standing army; and the power to raise troops for a year, is a power to raise them at any time and maintain them for ever; but with the addition of much trouble and a load of expense. Since therefore there never was, and probably never will be a time, till the millennium shall arrive, when troops will not be necessary to guard the frontiers of States, a clause in a constitution, restricting a Legislature from maintaining troops in time of peace, will unavoidably disable them from guarding the public interest. That a power to raise and equip troops at pleasure, may be abused is certain; but that the public safety cannot be established without that power, is equally certain.

The liberty of a people does not rest on any reservation of power in their hands aside of their Legislature; it rests singly on this principle, *a union of interests between the governors and governed*. While a Legislator himself, his family and his property are all liable to the consequences of the laws which he makes for the State, the rights of the people are so safe from the invasion of power, as they can be on this side heaven. This union of interest depends partly on the laws of property; but mostly on the *freedom of election*. The right of electing rulers is the people's prerogative; and while this remains unabridged, it is a sufficient barrier to guard all their other rights. This prerogative should be kept sacred; and if the people ever suffer any abridgment of this privilege, it must be their own folly and an irrecoverable loss.

Still further, I maintain that a people have no right to say, that any civil or political regulation shall be perpetual, because they have no right to make laws for those who are not in existence. This will be admitted; but still the people contend that they have a right to prescribe rules for their Legislature—rules which shall not be changed but by the people in a convention. But what is a convention? Why a body of men chosen by the people in the manner they choose the members of the Legislature, and commonly composed of the same men; but at any rate they are neither wiser nor better. The sense of the people is no better known in a convention, than in the Legislature.

But admit the right of establishing certain rules or principles which an ordinary Legislature cannot change, and what is the consequence? It is this, a change of circumstances may supersede the propriety of such rules, or render alterations necessary to the safety of freedom of the State; yet there is no power existing, but in the people at large, to make the necessary alterations. A convention then must be called to transact a business, which an ordinary Legislature can transact just as well—a convention differing from the Legislature merely in name and in a few formalities of their proceedings. But when people have enjoyed a tolerable share of happiness under a government, they will not readily step out of the common road of proceeding, and evils insensibly increase to an enormous degree, before the people can be persuaded to a change. The reservation therefore of certain powers may, by an imperceptible change of circumstances, prove highly pernicious to a State. For example, When the commons of England were first admitted to a share in the legislation of that kingdom, which was probably in the reign of Henry III, in 1265, the representation was tolerably equal. But the changes in the population of different parts of the kingdom have destroyed all equality. The mode of election therefore should be reformed. But how shall it be done? If there is a constitution in that kingdom, which settles the mode of election, and that constitution is an act of the people, paramount to the power of the Parliament, and unchangeable by them, a convention of the people must be called to make an alteration which would be as well made in Parliament. This would occasion infinite trouble and expense.

But the danger is, that as an evil of this kind increases, so will the lethargy of the people, and their habits of vice and negligence. Thus the disease acquires force, for want of an early remedy, and a dissolution ensues. But a Legislature, which is always watching the public safety, will more early discover the approaches of disorders, and more speedily apply a remedy. This is not precisely the case with the British constitution, for it was not committed at once to parchment and ratified by the people. It consists rather of practice, or common law, with some statutes of Parliament. But the English have been too jealous of changing their practice, even for the better. The idea of an *unalterable constitution* has had too much influence in preventing a reform in their representation.

But we have an example nearer home directly in point. The charter of Connecticut declares that each town shall have liberty to send *one* or *two* deputies to the General Court, and the constant practice has been to send *two*. While the towns were few, the number of Representatives was not inconvenient; but since the complete settlement of the State, and the multiplication of the towns, the number has swelled the Legislature to an unwieldly and expansive size. The house of Representatives consists of about 170 members.—An attempt has been made, as several sessions, to lesson the representation by limiting each town to one Deputy. A question arises, have the Assembly a right to lessen the representation? In most States, it would be decided in the negative. Yet in that State it is no question at all: for there is a standing law expressly delegating the *whole* power of *all* the freemen to the Legislature. But I bring this instance to prove the possibility of changes in any system of government, which will require material alterations in its fundamental principles; and the Legislature should always be competent to make the necessary amendments, or they have not an unlimited power to do right.

The distinction between the *Legislature* and a *convention* is, for the first time, introduced into Connecticut by the recommendation of the late convention of States, in order to adopt the new constitution. The Legislature of the State, without adverting to laws or practice, immediately recommended a convention for that purpose. Yet a distinction between a *Convention* and a *Legislature* is, in that State, a palpable absurdity, even by their own laws; for there is no constitution in the State, except its laws which are always repealable by an ordinary Legislature; and the laws and uniform practice, from the first organization of the government, declare that *the Legislature has all the power of all the people*. A convention therefore can have no more power, and differs no more from an ordinary Legislature, than one Legislature does from another. Or rather it is no more than a Legislature chosen for *one particular purpose* of supremacy whereas an ordinary Legislature is competent to *all* purposes of supremacy. But had the Legislature of that State ratified or rejected the new constitution without consulting their constituents, their act would have been valid and binding. This is the excellence of the constitution of Connecticut, that the *Legislature* is considered *as the body of the people*; and the people have not been taught to make a distinction which should never exist, and consider themselves as *masters* of their *rulers*, and their power as paramount to the laws. To this excellence in her frame of government, that State is indebted for uniformity and stability in public measures, during a period of one hundred and fifty years—a period of unparalleled tranquility, never once disturbed by a violent obstruction of justice or any popular commotion or rebellion. Wretched indeed would be the people of that State, should they adopt the vulgar maxim, that their rulers are their *servants*. We then may expect that the *laws* of those *servants* will be treated with the same contempt, as they are in some other States.

But from the manner in which government is constituted, it is evident that there is no power residing in the State at large, which does not reside in the legislature. I know it is said that government originates in *compact*; but I am very confident, that if this is true, the *compact* is different from any other kind of compact that is known among men. In all other *compacts*, *agreements* or *covenants*, the assent of every person concerned, or who is to be bound by the compact, is requisite to render it valid and obligatory upon such person. But I very much question whether this ever takes place in any constitution of government.

Perhaps so far their [sic] is an *implied compact* in government, that every man consents to be bound by the opinion of a majority; but this is all a *supposition*, for the consent of a hundredth part of a society is never obtained.

The truth is, government originates in *necessity* and *utility*; and whether their is an implied compact or not, the opinions of the *few* must be overruled, and submit to the opinions of the *many*. But the opinions of a majority cannot be known, but in an Assembly of the whole society; and no *part* of the society has a right to decide upon a measure which equally affect the *whole*, without a consultation with the whole, to hear their arguments and objections. It is said that *all* power resides in the *people*; but it must be remembered, that let the supreme power be where it will, it can be exercised only in an *assembly of the whole State*, or in an *assembly of the representatives of the whole State*.

Suppose the power to reside in the people, yet they can not, and they have no right to exercise it in their scattered districts —and the reason is very obvious—it is impossible that the propriety of a measure can be ascertained, without the best general information, and a full knowledge of the opinions of the men on whom it is to operate.

By opinions here I would not be understood to mean the various opinions formed on a view of a particular interest, for these opinions may be obtained by sending to each district and collecting instructions; but I mean the *opinions* of the *whole society*, formed on the *information* and *debates* of the *whole society*. These opinions can be formed no where but in a convention of the *whole state* or of their *representatives*. So far therefore are the people from having a power paramount to that of their representatives in Convention, that they can exercise no act of supremacy or legislation at all, but in a convention of the whole State by representatives. Unless therefore, it can be proved that a *convention* so called, which is composed mostly of the same men as a Legislature, possesses some wisdom, power, or qualifications which a legislature *does not* and *cannot*, then the distinction is useless and trifling. A legislature is supposed to consist of men whom the people judge best qualified to superintend their interests—a convention cannot be composed of better men—and in fact we find it generally composed of the *same men*. If therefore no act of sovereignty can be exercised but in an Assembly of representatives, of what consequence is it whether we call it a *Convention* or a *Legislature*?

To me it appears that a distinction is made without a difference; but a distinction that will often prevent good measures, perpetuate evils in government, and by creating a pretended power paramount to the legislature, tend to bring laws into contempt.

Unalterable Constitutions

The constitution of Virginia, like that of Connecticut, stands of the true principles of a Republican Representative Government. It is not shackled with a Bill of Rights, and every part of it, is at any time, alterable by an ordinary legislature. When I say *every part* of the constitution is alterable, I would except the right of elections, for the representatives have not power to prolong the period of their own delegation. This is not numbered among the rights of legislation, and deserves a separate consideration. This right is not vested in the legislature—it is in the people at large—it cannot be alienated without changing the form of government. Nay the right of election is not only the *basis*, but the *whole frame* or essence of a republican constitution—it is not merely *one*, but it is the *only* legislative or constitutional act, which the people at large can with propriety exercise.

The simple principle for which I contend is this—"That in a representative democracy, the delegates chosen for legislators ought, at all times, to be competent to every possible act of legislation *under that form of government*; but not to *change that form*. Besides it is contrary to all our ideas of *deputation* or *agency for others*, that the person acting should have the power of extending the period of agency beyond the time specified in his commission. The representative of a people is, as to his own powers, in the situation of an Attorney, whose letters commission him to do every thing which his constituent could do, where [sic] he on the spot; but for a limited time only. At the expiration of that time his powers cease; and a representative has no more right to extend that period, than a plenipotentiary has to renew his commission. The British Parliament, by prolonging the period of their existence from one to three, and from three to seven years, committed an unjust act—an act however which has been confirmed by the acquiescence of the nation, and thus received the highest constitutional sanction. I am sensible that the Americans are much concerned for the liberties of the British nation, and the act for making Parliaments sequential is often mentioned as an arbitrary oppressive act, destructive of English liberty. The English are doubtless obliged to us for our tender concern for their happiness—yet for myself I entertain no such ideas—The English have generally understood and advocated their rights as well as any nation, and I am confident that the nation enjoys as much happiness and freedom, and much more tranquility, under sequential Parliaments, than they would with annual elections. Corruption to obtain offices will every attend wealth; it is generated with it—grows up with it—and will, always fill a country with violent factions and illegal practices. Such are the habits of the people, that money will have a principal influence in carrying elections; and such vast sums are necessary for the purpose, that if elections were annual, none but a few of the wealthiest men could defray the expense—the land-holders of moderate estates would not offer themselves as candidates—and thus in fact annual elections, with the present habits of the people, would actually diminish the influence of the commons, by throwing the advantage into the hands of a corrupt ministry, and a few overgrown nabobs. Before annual election would be a blessing to the English, their habits must be changed—but this cannot be effected by human force. I wish my countrymen would believe that other nations understand and can guard their privileges, without any lamentable outcries from this side of the Atlantic. Government will always take its complexion from the habits of the people—habits are continually changing from age to age—a body of legislators taken from the people, will generally represent these habits at the time when they are chosen—hence these two important conclusions, 1st That a legislative body should be frequently renewed and always taken from the people—2d That a government which is perpetual, or incapable of being accommodated to every change of national habits, must in time become a *bad* government.

With this view of the subject, I cannot suppress my surprise at the reasoning of Mr. Jefferson on this very point. [Note cites *Notes on Virginia*] He considers it as a defect in the constitution of Virginia, that *it can be altered by an ordinary legislature.* He observes that the Convention which framed the present Constitution of that State" received no powers in their creation which were not given to every legislature before and since. . . .

But suppose the framers of this ordinance had said, that it should be *perpetual* and *unalterable*; such a declaration would have been void. Nay altho the people themselves had individually and unanimously declared the ordinance perpetual, the declaration would have been invalid. One Assembly cannot pass an act, binding upon a subsequent Assembly of equal authority; [a note exempts contracts from this reasoning] and the people in 1776 had no authority, and consequently could delegate none, to pass a single act which the people in 1777 could not repeal and annul. And Mr Jefferson himself in the very next sentence assigns a reason, which is an unanswerable argument in favor of my position, and a complete refutation of his own. These are his words. "Not only the silence of the instrument is a proof they thought it would be alterable, but their own practice also: for this very convention, meeting as a House of Delegates in General Assembly with the new Senate in the autumn of that year, passed acts of Assembly in contradiction to their ordinance of government; *and every Assembly from that time to this has done the same.*

Did Mr. Jefferson reflect upon the inference that would be justly drawn from these facts? Did he not consider that he was furnishing his opponents with the most effectual weapons against himself? The acts passed by *every subsequent Assembly in contradiction to the first ordinance*, prove that all the Assemblies were *fallible* men; and consequently not competent to make *perpetual Constitutions* for future generations. To give Mr Jefferson, and the other advocates for *unchangeable Constitutions*, the fullest latitude in their argument, I will suppose every freeman in Virginia could have been assembled to deliberate upon a form of government, and that the present form, or even one more perfect, had been the result of their Councils —and that they had declared it unalterable. What would have been the consequence? Experience would probably have discovered, what is the fact—and what forever will be the case —that *Conventions* are not possessed of *infinite wisdom*—that the wisest men cannot devise a perfect system of government. Suppose then that after all this solemn national transaction, and a formal declaration that their proceedings should be unalterable, a single article of the constitution should be found to interfere with some national benefit—some material advantage; where would be the power to change or reform that article? In the same general Assembly of all the people, and in no other body. But must a State be put to this inconvenience, to find a remedy for every defect of constitution?

Suppose, however, the *Convention* had been empowered to declare the form of government *unalterable*: What would have been the consequence. Mr. Jefferson himself has related the consequence. Every succeeding Assembly has found errors or defects in that frame of government, and has happily applied a remedy. But had not every Legislature had power to make these alterations, Virginia must have gone thro the farce and the trouble of calling an *extraordinary* Legislature, to do that which an *ordinary* Legislature could do just as well, in their annual session; or those errors must have remained in the constitution, to the injury of the State.

The whole argument for bills of rights and unalterable constitutions rests on two suppositions, viz. that the Convention which frames the government, is *infallible*; and that future Legislatures will be *less honest—less wise—and less attentive to the interest of the State*, than a present Convention: The first supposition is *always false*, and the last is *generally* so. A declaration of perpetuity, annexed to a form of government, implies a supposition of *perfect wisdom and probity* in the framers; which is both arrogant and impudent—and it implies a supposed power in them, to abridge the power of a succeeding Convention and of the future state or body of people. The last supposition is, in every possible instance of legislation *false*; and an attempt to exercise such a power, a high handed act of tyranny. But setting aside the argument, grounded on a want of power in one Assembly to abridge the power of another, what occasion have we to be so jealous of future Legislatures? Why should we be so anxious to guard the future rights of a nation? Why should we not distrust the people and the Representatives of the present age, as well as those of future ages, in whose acts we have not the smallest interest? For my part, I believe that the people and their Representatives, two or three centuries hence, will be as honest, as wise, as faithful to themselves, and will understand their rights as well, and be as able to defend them, as the people are at this period. The contrary supposition is absurd.

I know it is said that other nations have lost their liberties by the ambitious designs of their rulers, and we may do the same. The experience of other nations furnishes the ground of all the arguments used in favor of an unalterable constitution. The advocates seem determined that posterity shall not lose their liberty, even if they should be willing and desirous to surrender it. If a few declarations on parchment will secure a single blessing to posterity, which they would otherwise lose, I resign the argument and will receive a thousand declarations. Yet so thoroughly convinced am I of the opposite tendency and effect of such unalterable declarations, that, were it possible to render them valid, I should deem every article an infringement of civil and political liberty. I should consider every article as a restriction which might impose some duty which in time might cease to be useful and necessary, while the obligation of performing it might remain; or which in its operation might prove pernicious, by producing effects which were not expected, and could not be foreseen. There is no one single right, no privilege which is commonly deemed fundamental, which may not, by an unalterable establishment, preclude some amendment, some improvement in the future administration of government. And unless the advocates for unalterable constitutions of government, can prevent all changes in the wants, the inclinations, the habits and circumstances of people, they will find it difficult, even with all their declarations of unalterable rights, to prevent changes in government. A paper declaration is a very feeble barrier against the force of national habits, and inclinations.

The loss of liberty, as it is called, in the kingdoms of Europe, has, in several instances, been a mere change of government, effected by a change of habits, and in some instances this change has been favorable to liberty. The government of Denmark was changed from a mixed form, like that of England, to an absolute monarchy, by a solemn deliberate act of the people, or States. Was this a loss of liberty? So far from it, that the change removed the oppressions of faction, restored liberty to the subject and tranquility to the kingdom. The change was a blessing to the people. It indeed lodged a power in the Prince to dispose of life and property; but at the same time it lodged in him a *power to defend both*—a power which before was lodged *no where*—and it is infinitely better that such a power should be vested in a *single hand*, than that it should *not exist at all*. The monarchy of France has grown out of a number of petty States and lordships; yet it is a fact, proved by history and experience, that the subjects of that kingdom have acquired liberty, peace and happiness in proportion to the diminution of the powers of the petty sovereignties, and the extension of the prerogatives of the Monarch. It is said that Spain lost her liberties under the reign of Charles Vth; but I question the truth of the assertion; it is probable that the subject has gained as much by an abridgement of the powers of the nobility, as he lost by an annihilation of the Cortez. The United Netherlands fought with more bravery and perseverance to preserve their rights, than any other people, since the days of Leonidas; and yet no sooner established a government, so jealously guarded as to defeat its own designs, and prevent the good effects of government, than they neglected its principles—the freemen resigned the privilege of election, and committed their liberties to a rich aristocracy.

There was no compulsion—no external force in producing this revolution; but the form of government, which had been established on paper, and solemnly ratified, was not suited to the genius of the subjects. The burghers had a right of electing their rulers; but they voluntarily neglected it; and *a bill of rights*, a *perpetual constitution* on parchment guaranteeing that right, was a useless form of words, because opposed to the temper of the people. The government assumed a complexion, more correspondent to their habits, and tho in theory no constitution is more cautiously guarded against an infringement of popular privileges, yet in practice it is a real aristocracy.

The progress of government in England has been the reverse—The people have been gaining freedom by intrenching upon the powers of the nobles and the royal prerogatives. These changes in government do not proceed from *bills of rights, unalterable forms* and *perpetual establishments*— liberty is never secured by such paper declarations; nor lost for want of them.—The truth is Government originates in necessity, and takes its form and structure from the genius and habits of the people; and if on paper a form is not accommodated to those habits, it will assume a new form, in spite of all the formal sanctions of the supreme authority of a State. Were the monarchy of France to be dissolved, and the wisest system of republican government ever invented, solemnly declared, by the King and his council, to be the constitution of the kingdom; the people, with their present habits, would refuse to receive it; and resign their privileges to their beloved sovereign. But so opposite are the habits of the Americans, that an attempt to erect a monarchy or an aristocracy over the United States, would expose the authors to the loss of their heads. The truth is, the people of Europe, since they became civilized, have, in no kingdom, possessed the true principles of liberty. The [sic] could not therefore lose what they never possessed. There has been, from time immemorial, some rights of government—some prerogatives vested in some man or body of men, independent of the suffrages of the body of the subjects. This circumstances distinguishes the governments of Europe and of all the world, from those of America. There has been in the free nations of Europe an incessant struggle between freedom or national rights, and hereditary prerogatives. The contest has ended variously in different kingdoms; but generally in depressing the power of the nobility; ascertaining and limiting the prerogatives of the crown, and extending the privileges of the people. The Americans have seen the records of their struggles; and without considering that the objects of the context *do not exist in this country*; they are laboring to guard rights which there is no party to attack. They are as jealous of their rights, as if there existed here a King's prerogatives or the powers of nobles, independent of their own will and choice, and ever eager to swallow up their liberties. But there is *no man* in America, who claims any rights but what are common *to every man*—there is no man who has an interest in invading popular privileges, because his attempt to curtain another's rights, would expose his own to the same abridgement. The jealousy of people in this country has no proper object against which it can rationally arm them—it is therefore directed against themselves, or against an invasion they *imagine* may happen in future ages. The context for *perpetual bills of rights* against a future tyranny, resembles Don Quixotes fighting windmills; and I never can reflect on the declamation about an *unalterable constitution* to guard certain rights, without wishing to add another article, as necessary as those that are generally mentioned; viz, "that no future Convention or Legislature shall cut their own throats, or those of their constituents." While the habits of the Americans remain as they are, the people will choose their Legislature from their own body—that Legislature will have an interest inseperable from that of the people—and therefore an act to restrain their power in any article of legislation, is as unnecessary as an act to prevent them from committing suicide.

Mr Jefferson, in answer to those who maintain that the form of government in Virginia is unalterable, because it is called a *constitution*, which, ex vi termini, means an act above the power of the ordinary Legislature, asserts that *constitution*, *statute*, *law* and *ordinance* are synonymous terms and convertible, as they are used by writers on government: Constitutio dicitur jus quod a principle conditur. Constitutum, quot ab imperatoribus rescriptum statutumve est. Statutum, idem quod lex. Here the words *constitution*, *statute* and *law* are defined by each other—They were used as convertible terms by all former writers whether Roman or British; and before the terms of the civil law were introduced, our Saxon ancestors used the correspondent English words, *bid* and *fet*. From hence he concludes that no inference can be drawn from the meaning of the word, that a *constitution* has a higher authority than a law or statute. This conclusion of Mr. Jefferson is just.

He quotes Lord Coke also to prove than any Parliament can abridge, suspend or qualify the acts of a preceding Parliament. It is a maxim in their laws, that "Leges posteriorer priores contrarias abrogant." After having fully proved that *constitution*, *statute*, *law* and *ordinance* are words of similar import, and that the constitution of Virginia is at any time alterable by the ordinary Legislature, he proceeds to prove the danger to which the rights of the people are exposed for want of an *unalterable form of government*. The first proof of this danger he mentions, is, the power which the Assembly exercises of determining its own quorum. The British Parliament fixes its own quorum—The former Assemblies of Virginia did the same. During the war the Legislature determined that *forty* members should be a quorum to proceed to business, altho not a fourth part of the whole house. The danger of delay, it was judged, would warrant the measure. This precedent, our writer supposes, is subversive of the principles of the government, and dangerous to liberty.

It is a dictate of natural law that a *majority should govern*; and the principles is universally received and established in all societies, where no other mode has been arbitarily fixed. This natural right cannot be alienated *in pereptuum*; for altho a Legislature, or even the body of the people may resign the powers of government to forty or to four men, when they please, yet they may likewise resume them at pleasure. . . .

The danger therefore arising from a power in the Assembly to determine their own quorum, is merely ideal; for no law can be perpetual—the authority of a majority of the people or of their Representatives, is always competent to repeal any act that it found unjust or inconvenient. The acquiescence however of the people of the States mentioned, and that in one of them for a long course of years, under an oligarchy; or their submission to the power of a minority, is an incontestable proof of what I have before observed, that theories and *forms of government* are *empty things*—that the spirit of a government springs immediately from the temper of the people—and the exercise of it will generally take its tone from their feelings. It proves likewise that a *union of interests* between the rulers and the people, which union will always coexist with free elections, is not only the *best*, but the *only* security for their liberties which they can wish for and demand. . . .

2.11. The First Congress Debates the Bill of Rights*

Among the most contentious issues dividing the Federalist supporters of the new Constitution and their Anti-Federalist opponents was the issue of whether a Bill of Rights was necessary. Although the issue had been mentioned at the Constitutional Convention, it had not been extensively debated there. Most delegates believed that since the new national government was a government of delegated powers, it simply would have no authority to legislate in areas like freedom of speech or religion that Anti-Federalists would later come to argue

* Taken from *Annals* of the U.S. House of Representatives, June-August 1789, Vol. 1, pp. 424-433; 436-440; 442; 444-5; 447-8; 450; 707-123; and 719.

could be impaired. Some further argued that a Bill of Rights that omitted some rights could provide justification for annulling such rights.

While he was not an Anti-Federalist, Thomas Jefferson corresponded from Paris with his friend James Madison to let him know that he too favored a Bill of Rights. This counsel, together with election pressure in his own congressional district where Madison was squaring off against Anti-Federalist James Monroe, led Madison to change his mind. Madison feared that, if no Bill of Rights were promised, the new Constitution would never be adopted, and he and other leading Federalists accordingly indicated that they would support a Bill of Rights once the Constitution was adopted.

True to his word, Madison introduced and defended the Bill of Rights in the first Congress and pushed for quick action. The record of the debates below give insights into Madison's motives for introducing the Bill of Rights and indicate that not all congressmen were as anxious as Madison to adopt the first ten amendments, many arguing that changes were premature until defects actually revealed themselves in practice. There was also extensive debate as to whether alterations should be incorporated into the body of the Constitution or be added as supplementary amendments to it.

Debates in the First Congress

Mr. MADISON rose, and reminded the House that this was the day that he had heretofore named for bringing forward amendments to the Constitution, as contemplated in the fifth article of the Constitution. He then addressed the Speaker as follows: This day, Mr. Speaker, is the day assigned for taking into consideration the subject of amendments to the Constitution. As I considered myself bound in honor and in duty to do what I have done on this subject, I shall proceed to bring the amendments before you as soon as possible, and advocate them until they shall be finally adopted or rejected by a Constitutional majority of this House. With a view of drawing your attention to this important object, I shall move that this House do now resolve itself into a Committee of the Whole on the state of the Union; by which an opportunity will be given, to bring forward some propositions, which I have strong hopes will meet with the unanimous approbation of this House, after the fullest discussion and most serious regard. I therefore move you, that the House now go into a committee on this business.

Mr. SMITH was not inclined to interrupt the measures which the public were so anxiously expecting, by going into a Committee of the Whole at this time . . . For, said he, it must appear extremely impolitic to go into the consideration of amending the Government, before it is organized, before it has begun to operate. Certainly, upon reflection, it must appear to be premature. I wish, therefore, gentlemen would consent to the delay: for the business which lies in an unfinished state—I mean particularly the collection bill—is necessary to be passed; else all we have hitherto done is of no effect. . . .

Mr. JACKSON.—I am of opinion we ought not to be in a hurry with respect to altering the Constitution. For my part, I have no idea of speculating in this serious manner on theory. If I agree to alterations in the mode of administering this Government, I shall like to stand on the sure ground of experience, and not be treading air. What experience have we had of the good or bad qualities of this Constitution? Can any gentleman affirm to me one proposition that is a certain and absolute amendment? I deny that he can. Our Constitution, sir, is like a vessel just launched, and lying at the wharf; she is untried, you can hardly discover any one of her properties. It is not known how she will answer her helm, or lay her course; whether she will bear with safety the precious freight to be deposited in her hold. But, in this state, will the prudent merchant attempt alterations? Will he employ workmen to tear off the planking and take asunder the frame? He certainly will not. Let us, gentlemen, fit out our vessel, set up her masts, and expand her sails, and be guided by the experiment in our alterations. If she sails upon an uneven keel, let us right her by adding weight where it is wanting. In this way, we may remedy her defects to the satisfaction of all concerned; but if we proceed now to make alterations, we may deface a beauty, or deform a well proportioned piece of workmanship.

In short, Mr. Speaker, I am not for amendments at this time; but if gentlemen should think it is a subject deserving of attention, they will surely not neglect the more important business which is now unfinished before them. Without we pass the collection bill we can get no revenue, and without revenue the wheels of Government cannot move. I am against taking up the subject at present, and shall therefore be totally against the amendments, if the Government is not organized, that I may see whether it is grievous or not.

When the propriety of making amendments shall be obvious from experience, I trust there will be virtue enough in my country to make them. . . .

Let the Constitution have a fair trial; let it be examined by experience, discover by that test what its errors are, and then talk of amending; but to attempt it now is doing it at a risk, which is certainly imprudent. . . .

Mr. GOODHUE.—I believe it would be perfectly right in the gentleman who spoke last, to move a postponement to the time he has mentioned; because he is opposed to the consideration of amendments altogether. But I believe it will be proper to attend to the subject earlier; because it is the wish of many of our constituents, that something should be added to the Constitution, to secure in a stronger manner their liberties from the inroads of power. Yet I think the present time premature; inasmuch as we have other business before us, which is incomplete, but essential to the public interest. When that is finished, I shall concur in taking up the subject of amendments.

Mr. BURKE thought amendments to the Constitution necessary, but this was not the proper time to bring them forward. He wished the Government completely organized before they entered upon this ground. . . .

Mr. MADISON.—The gentleman from Georgia (Mr. JACKSON) is certainly right in his opposition to my motion for going into a Committee of the Whole, because he is unfriendly to the object I have in contemplation; but I cannot see that the gentlemen who wish for amendments to be proposed at the present session, stand on good ground when they object to the House going into committee on this businesss.

When I first hinted to the House my intention of calling their deliberations to this object, I mentioned the pressure of other important subjects, and submitted the propriety of postponing this till the more urgent business was despatched; but finding that business not despatched, when the order of the day for considering amendments arrived, I thought it a good reason for a farther delay; I move the postponement accordingly. I am sorry the same reason still exists in some degree, but it operates with less force, when it is considered that it is not now proposed to enter into a full and minute discussion of every part of the subject, but merely to bring it before the House, that our constituents may see we pay a proper attention to a subject they have much at heart; and if it does not give that full gratification which is to be wished, they will discover that it proceeds from the urgency of business of a very important nature. But if we continue to postpone from time to time, and refuse to let the subject come into view, it may occasion suspicions, which, though not well founded, may tend to inflame or prejudice the public mind against our decisions. They may think we are not sincere in our desire to incorporate such amendments in the Constitution as will secure those rights, which they consider as not sufficiently guarded. The applications for amendments come from a very respectable number of our constituents, and it is certainly proper for Congress to consider the subject, in order to quiet that anxiety which prevails in the public mind. Indeed, I think it would have been of advantage to the Government if it had been practicable to have made some propositions for amendments the first business we entered upon; it would have stifled the voice of complaint, and made friends of many who doubted the merits of the Constitution. Our future measures would then have been more generally agreeably supported; but the justifiable anxiety to put the Government into operation prevented that; it therefore remains for us to take it up as soon as possible. I wish then to commence the consideration at the present moment. . . .

Mr. SHERMAN.—I am willing that this matter should be brought before the House at a proper time. I suppose a number of gentlemen think it their duty to bring it forward; so that there is no apprehension it will be passed over in silence. Other gentlemen may be disposed to let the subject rest until the more important objects of Government are attended to; and I should conclude, from the nature of the case, that the people expect the latter from us in preference to altering the Constitution, because they have ratified that instrument, in order that the Government may begin to operate. . . .

Mr. WHITE.—I hope the House will not spend much time on this subject, till the more pressing business is despatched; but, at the same time, I hope we shall not dismiss it altogether, because I think a majority of the people who have ratified the Constitution, did it under the expectation that Congress would, at some convenient time, examine its texture and point out where it was defective, in order that it might be judiciously amended. Whether, while we are without experience, amendments can be digested in such a manner as to give satisfaction to a Constitutional majority of this House, I will not pretend to say; but I hope the subject may be considered with all convenient speed. I think it would tend to tranquilize the public mind. . . .

Mr. PAGE.—My colleague tells you he is ready to submit to the Committee of the Whole his ideas on the subject. If no objection had been made to his motion, the whole business might have been finished before this. He has done me the honor of showing me certain propositions which he has drawn up; they are very important, and I sincerely wish the House may receive them. After they are published, I think the people will wait with patience till we are at leisure to resume them. But it must be very disagreeable to them to have it postponed from time to time, in the manner it has been for six weeks past; they will be tired out by a fruitless expectation. Putting myself into the place of those who favor amendments, I should suspect Congress did not mean seriously to enter upon the subject; that it was vain to expect redress from them. I should begin to turn my attention to the alternative contained in the fifth article, and think of joining the Legislatures of those States which have applied for calling a new convention. How dangerous such an expedient could be I need not mention; but I venture to affirm, that unless you take early notice of this subject, you will not have power to deliberate. The people will clamor for a new convention; they will not trust the House any longer. Those, therefore, who dread the assembling of a convention, will do well to acquiesce in the present motion, and lay the foundation of a most important work. . . .

Mr. VINING.—I hope the House will not go into a Committee of the Whole. . . . But I have two other reasons for opposing this motion; the first is, the uncertainty with which we must decide on questions of amendment, founded merely on speculative theory; the second is the previous question, how far it is proper to take the subject of amendments into consideration, without the consent of two-thirds of both Houses? I will submit it to gentlemen, whether the words of the Constitution," The Congress, whenever two-thirds of both Houses shall deem it necessary, shall propose amendments," do not bear my construction, that it is as requisite for two-thirds to sanction the expediency of going into the measure at present, as it will be to determine the necessity of amending at all. I take it that the fifth article admits of this construction, and think that two-thirds of the Senate and House of Representatives must concur in the expediency as to the time and manner of amendments, before we can proceed to the consideration of the amendments themselves. For my part, I do not see the expediency of proposing amendments. I think, sir, the most likely way to quiet the perturbation of the public mind, will be to pass salutary laws; to give permanency and stability to Constitutional regulations, founded on principles of equity and adjusted by wisdom. Although hitherto we have done nothing to tranquilize that agitation which the adoption of the Constitution threw some people into, yet the storm has abated and a calm succeeds. The people are not afraid of leaving the question of amendments to the discussion of their representatives; but is this the juncture for discussing it? What have Congress done towards completing the business of their appointment? . . .

Mr. MADISON.—I am sorry to be accessary to the loss of a single moment of time by the House. . . .

I will state my reasons why I think it proper to propose amendments, and state the amendments themselves so far as I think they ought to be proposed. If I thought I could fulfil the duty which I owe to myself and my constituents, to let the subject pass over in silence, I most certainly should not trespass upon the indulgence of this House. But I cannot do this, and am therefore compelled to beg a patient hearing to what I have to lay before you. And I do most sincerely believe, that if Congress will devote but one day to this subject, so far as to satisfy the public that we do not disregard their wishes, it will have a salutary influence on the public councils, and prepare the way for a favorable reception of our future measures. It appears to me that this House is bound by every motive of prudence, not to let the first session pass over without proposing to the State Legislatures, some things to be incorporated into the Constitution, that will render it as acceptable to the whole people of the United States, as it has been found acceptable to a majority of them. I wish, among other reasons why something should be done, that those who had been friendly to the adoption of this Constitution may have the opportunity of proving to those who were opposed to it that they were as sincerely devoted to liberty and a Republican Government, as those who charged them with wishing the adoption of the Constitution in order to lay the foundation of an aristocracy or despotism. It will be a desirable thing to extinguish from the bosom of every member of the community, any apprehensions that there are those among his countrymen who wish to deprive them of the liberty for which they valiantly fought and honorably bled. And if there are amendments desired of such a nature as will not injure the Constitution, and they can be ingrafted so as to give satisfaction to the doubting part of our fellow-citizens, the friends of the Federal Government will evince that spirit of deference and concession for which they have hitherto been distinguished.

It cannot be a secret to the gentlemen in this House, that, notwithstanding the ratification of this system of Government by eleven of the thirteen United State[s], in some cases unanimously, in others by large majorities; yet still there is a great number of our constituents who are dissatisfied with it; among whom are many respectable for their talents and patriotism, and respectable for the jealousy they have for their liberty, which, though mistaken in its object, is laudable in its motive. There is a great body of the people falling under this description, who at present feel much inclined to join their support to the cause of Federalism, if they were satisfied on this one point. We ought not to disregard their inclination, but, on principles of amity and moderation, conform to their wishes, and expressly declare the great rights of mankind secured under this Constitution. The acquiescence which our fellow-citizens show under the Government, calls upon us for a like return of moderation. But perhaps there is a stronger motive than this for our going into a consideration of the subject. It is to provide those securities for liberty which are required by a part of the community; I allude in a particular manner to those two States that have not thought fit to throw themselves into the bosom of the Confederacy. It is a desirable thing, on our part as well as theirs, that a re-union should take place as soon as possible. I have no doubt, if we proceed to take those steps which would be prudent and requisite at this juncture, that in a short time we should see that disposition prevailing in those States which have not come in, that we have seen prevailing in those States which have embraced the Constitution.

But I will candidly acknowledge, that, over and above all these considerations, I do conceive that the Constitution may be amended; that is to say, if all power is subject to abuse, that then it is possible the abuse of the powers of the General Government may be guarded against in a more secure manner than is now done, while no one advantage arising from the exercise of that power shall be damaged or endangered by it. We have in this way something to gain, and, if we proceed with caution, nothing to lose. And in this case it is necessary to proceed with caution; for while we feel all these inducements to go into a revisal of the Constitution, we must feel for the Constitution itself, and make that revisal a moderate one. I should be unwilling to see a door opened for a reconsideration of the whole structure of the Government—for a re-consideration of the principles and the substance of the powers given;

because I doubt, if such a door were opened, we should be very likely to stop at that point which would be safe to the Government itself. But I do wish to see a door opened to consider, so far as to incorporate those provisions for the security of rights, against which I believe no serious objection has been made by any class of our constituents: such as would be likely to meet with the concurrence of two-thirds of both Houses, and the approbation of three-fourths of the State Legislatures. I will not propose a single alteration which I do not wish to see take place, as intrinsically proper in itself, or proper because it is wished for by a respectable number of my fellow-citizens; and therefore I shall not propose a single alteration but is likely to meet the concurrence required by the Constitution. There have been objections of various kinds made against the Constitution. Some were levelled against its structure because the President was without a council; because the Senate, which is a legislative body, had judicial powers in trials on impeachments; and because the powers of that body were compounded in other respects, in a manner that did not correspond with a particular theory; because it grants more power than is supposed to be necessary for every good purpose, and controls the ordinary powers of the State Governments. I know some respectable characters who opposed this Government on these grounds; but I believe that the great mass of the people who opposed it, disliked it because it did not contain effectual provisions against the encroachments on particular rights, and those safeguards which they have been long accustomed to have interposed between them and the magistrate who exercises the sovereign power; nor ought we to consider them safe, while a great number of our fellow-citizens think these securities necessary.

It is a fortunate thing that the objection to the Government has been made on the ground I stated; because it will be practicable, on that ground, to obviate the objection, so far as to satisfy the public mind that their liberties will be perpetual, and this without endangering any part of the Constitution, which is considered as essential to the existence of the Government by those who promoted its adoption. [Madison proceeds to list the amendments he favors.]

The first of these amendments relates to what may be called a bill of rights. I will own that I never considered this provision so essential to the Federal Constitution as to make it improper to ratify, until such an amendment was added; at the same time, I always conceived, that in a certain form, and to a certain extent, such a provision was neither improper nor altogether useless. I am aware that a great number of the most respectable friends to the Government, and champions for republican liberty, have thought such a provision not only unnecessary, but even improper; nay, I believe some have gone so far as to think it even dangerous. Some policy has been made use of, perhaps, by gentlemen on both sides of the question: I acknowledge the ingenuity of those arguments which were drawn against the Constitution by a comparison with the policy of Great Britain, in establishing a declaration of rights; but there is too great a difference in the case to warrant the comparison: therefore, the arguments drawn from that source were in a great measure inapplicable. In the declaration of rights which that country has established, the truth is, they have gone no farther than to raise a barrier against the power of the Crown; the power of the Legislature is left altogether indefinite. Although I know wherever the great rights, the trial by jury, freedom of the press, or liberty of conscience, come in question in that body, the invasion of them is resisted by able advocates, yet their Magna Charta does not contain any one provision for the security of those rights, respecting which the people of America are most alarmed. The freedom of the press and rights of conscience, those choicest privileges of the people, are unguarded in the British Constitution.

But although the case may be widely different, and it may not be thought necessary to provide limits for the legislative power in that country, yet a different opinion prevails in the United States. The people of many States have thought it necessary to raise barriers against power in all forms and departments of Government, and I am inclined to believe, if once bills of rights are established in all the States as well as the Federal Constitution, we shall find, that, although some of them are rather unimportant, yet, upon the whole, they will have a salutary tendency. It may be said, in some instances, they do no more than state the perfect equality of mankind. This, to be sure, is an absolute truth, yet it is not absolutely necessary to be inserted at the head of a Constitution.

In some instances they assert those rights which are exercised by the people in forming and establishing a plan of Government. In other instances, they specify those rights which are retained when particular powers are given up to be exercised by the Legislature. In other instances, they specify positive rights, which may seem to result from the nature of the compact. Trial by jury cannot be considered as a natural right, but a right resulting from a social compact, which regulates the action of the community, but it is essential to secure the liberty of the people as any one of the pre-existent rights of nature. In other instances, they lay down dogmatic maxims with respect to the construction of the Government; declaring that the Legislative, Executive, and Judicial branches, shall be kept separate and distinct. Perhaps the best way of securing this in practice is, to provide such checks as will prevent the encroachment of the one upon the other.

But, whatever may be the form which the several States have adopted in making declarations in favor of particular rights, the great object in view is to limit and qualify the powers of Government, by excepting out of the grant of power those cases in which the Government ought not to act, or to act only in a particular mode. They point these exceptions sometimes against the abuse of the Executive power, sometimes against the Legislative, and, in some cases, against the community itself; or, in other words, against the majority in favor of the minority.

In our Government it is, perhaps, less necessary to guard against the abuse in the Executive Department than any other; because it is not the stronger branch of the system, but the weaker. It therefore must be levelled against the Legislative, for it is the most powerful, and most likely to be abused, because it is under the least control. Hence, so far as a declaration of rights can tend to prevent the exercise of undue power, it cannot be doubted but such declaration is proper. But I confess that I do conceive, that in a Government modified like this of the United States, the great danger lies rather in the abuse of the community than in the Legislative body. The prescriptions in favor of liberty ought to be levelled against that quarter where the greatest danger lies, namely, that which possesses the highest prerogative of power. But this is not found in either the Executive or Legislative departments of Government, but in the body of the people operating by the majority against the minority.

It may be thought that all paper barriers against the power of the community are too weak to be worthy of attention. I am sensible they are not so strong as to satisfy gentlemen of every description who have seen and examined thoroughly the texture of such a defence; yet, as they have a tendency to impress some degree of respect for them, to establish the public opinion in their favor, and rouse the attention of the whole community, it may be one means to control the majority from those acts to which they might be otherwise inclined.

It has been said, by way of objection to a bill of rights, by many respectable gentlemen out of doors, and I find opposition on the same principles likely to be made by gentlemen on this floor, that they are unnecessary articles of a Republican Government, upon the presumption that the people have those rights in their own hands, and that is the proper place for them to rest. It would be a sufficient answer to say, that this objection lies against such provisions under the State Governments, as well as under the General Government; and there are, I believe, but few gentlemen who are inclined to push their theory so far as to say that a declaration of rights in those cases is either ineffectual or improper. It has been said, that in the Federal Government they are unnecessary, because the powers are enumerated, and it follows, that all that are not granted by the Constitution are retained; that the Constitution is a bill of powers, the great residuum being the rights of the people; and, therefore, a bill of rights cannot be so necessary as if the residuum was thrown into the hands of the Government. I admit that these arguments are not entirely without foundation; but they are not conclusive to the extent which has been supposed. It is true, the powers of the General Government are circumscribed, they are directed to particular objects; but even if Government keeps within those limits, it has certain discretionary powers with respect to the means, which may admit of abuse to a certain extent, in the same manner as the powers of the State Governments under their constitutions may to an indefinite extent; because in the Constitution of the United States, there is a clause granting to Congress the power to make all laws which shall be necessary and proper for carrying into execution all the powers vested in the Government of the United States, or in any department or officer thereof; this enables them to fulfil every purpose for which the Government was established. Now, may not laws be considered necessary and proper by Congress, (for it is for them to judge of the necessity and propriety to accomplish those special purposes which they may have in contemplation,) which laws in themselves are neither necessary nor proper; as well as improper laws could be enacted by the State Legislatures, for fulfilling the more extended objects of those Governments? . . .

It may be said, indeed it has been said, that a bill of rights is not necessary, because the establishment of this Government has not repealed those declarations of rights which are added to the several State constitutions; that those rights of the people which had been established by the most solemn act, could not be annihilated by a subsequent act of that people, who meant and declared at the head of the instrument, that they ordained and established a new system, for the express purpose of securing to themselves and posterity the liberties they had gained by an arduous conflict.

I admit the force of this observation, but I do not look upon it as conclusive. In the first place, it is too uncertain ground to leave this provision upon, if a provision is at all necessary to secure rights so important as many of those I have mentioned are conceived to be, by the public in general, as well as those in particular who opposed the adoption of this Constitution. Besides, some States have no bills of rights, there are others provided with very defective ones, and there are others whose bills of rights are not only defective, but absolutely improper; instead of securing some in the full extent which republican principles would require, they limit them too much to agree with the common ideas of liberty.

It has been objected also against a bill of rights, that, by enumerating particular exceptions to the grant of power, it would disparage those rights which were not placed in that enumeration; and it might follow by implication, that those rights which were not singled out, were intended to be assigned into the hands of the General Government, and were consequently insecure. This is one of the most plausible arguments I have ever heard urged against the admission of a bill of rights into this system; but, I conceive, that it may be guarded against. I have attempted it, as gentlemen may see by turning to the last clause of the fourth resolution. [Reference is to the clause that eventually became the Ninth Amendment.]

It has been said that it is unnecessary to load the Constitution with this provision, because it was not found effectual in the constitution of the particular States. It is true, there are a few particular States in which some of the most valuable articles have not, at one time or other, been violated; but it does not follow but they may have, to a certain degree, a salutary effect against the abuse of power. If they are incorporated into the Constitution, independent tribunals of justice will consider themselves in a peculiar manner the guardians of those rights; they will be an impenetrable bulwark against every assumption of power in the Legislative or Executive; they will be naturally led to resist every encroachment upon rights expressly stipulated for in the Constitution by the declaration of rights. Besides this security, there is a great probability that such a declaration in the federal system would be enforced; because the State Legislatures will jealously and closely watch the operations of this Government, and be able to resist with more effect every assumption of power, than any other power on earth can do; and the greatest opponents to a Federal Government admit the State Legislatures to be sure guardians of the people's liberty. I conclude, from this view of the subject, that it will be proper in itself, and highly politic, for the tranquillity of the public mind, and the stability of the Government, that we should offer something, in the form I have proposed, to be incorporated in the system of Government, as a declaration of the rights of the people.

[Madison proceeds to elaborate on other changes he would like to see in the Constitution.]

Mr. JACKSON.—The more I consider the subject of amendments, the more I am convinced it is improper. I revere the rights of my constituents as much as any gentleman in Congress, yet I am against inserting a declaration of rights in the Constitution, and that for some of the reasons referred to by the gentleman last up. If such an addition is not dangerous or improper, it is at least unnecessary: that is a sufficient reason for not entering into the subject at a time when there are urgent calls for our attention to important business. Let me ask gentlemen, what reason there is for the suspicions which are to be removed by this measure? Who are Congress, that such apprehensions should be entertained of them? Do we not belong to the mass of the people? Is there a single right that, if infringed, will not affect us and our connexions as much as any other person? Do we not return at the expiration of two years into private life, and is not this a security against encroachments? Are we not sent here to guard those rights which might be endangered, if the Government was an aristocracy or a despotism? View for a moment the situation of Rhode Island, and say whether the people's rights are more safe under State Legislatures than under a Government of limited powers. Their liberty is changed to licentiousness. But do gentlemen suppose bills of rights necessary to secure liberty? If they do, let them look at New York, New Jersey, Virginia, South Carolina, and Georgia. Those States have no bills of rights, and is the liberty of the citizens less safe in those States, than in the other of the United States? I believe it is not.

There is a maxim in law, and it will apply to bills of rights, that when you enumerate exceptions, the exceptions operate to the exclusion of all circumstances that are omitted; consequently, unless you except every right from the grant of power, those omitted are inferred to be resigned to the discretion of the Government.

The gentleman endeavors to secure the liberty of the press; pray how is this in danger? There is no power given to Congress to regulate this subject as they can commerce, or peace, or war. Has any transaction taken place to make us suppose such an amendment necessary? . . .

If we actually find the Constitution had upon experience, or the rights and privileges of the people in danger, I here pledge myself to step forward among the first friends of liberty to prevent the evil; and if nothing else will avail, I will draw my sword in the defence of freedom, and cheerfully immolate at that shrine my property and my life. But how are we now proceeding? Why, on nothing more than theoretical speculation, pursuing a mere *ignis fatuus*, which may lead us into serious embarrassments. The imperfections of the Government are now unknown; let it have a fair trial, and I will be bound they show themselves; then we can tell where to apply the remedy, so as to secure the great object we are aiming at. . . .

Mr. GERRY.—I do not rise to go into the merits or demerits of the subject of amendments; nor shall I make any other observations on the motion for going into a Committee of the Whole on the state of the Union, which is now withdrawn, than merely to say, that, referring the subject to that committee, is treating it with the dignity its importance requires. But I consider it improper to take up this business, when our attention is occupied by other important objects. We should despatch the subjects now on the table, and let this lie over until a period of more leisure for discussion and attention. The gentleman from Virginia says it is necessary to go into a consideration of this subject, in order to satisfy the people. For my part, I cannot be of his opinion. The people know we are employed in the organization of the Government, and cannot expect that we should forego this business for any other. But I would not have it understood, that I am against entering upon amendments when the proper time arrives. I shall be glad to set about it as soon as possible, but I would not stay the operations of the Government on this account. I think with the gentleman from Delaware, (Mr. VINING) that the great wheels of the political machine should first be set in motion; and with the gentleman from Georgia, (Mr. JACKSON,) that the vessel ought to be got under way, lest she lie by the wharf till she beat off her rudder, and run herself a wreck ashore.

I say I wish as early a day as possible may be assigned for taking up this business, in order to prevent the necessity which the States may think themselves under of calling a new convention. For I am not, sir, one of those blind admirers of this system, who think it all perfection; nor am I so blind as not to see its beauties. The truth is, it partakes of humanity; in it is blended virtue and vice, errors and excellence. But I think if it is referred to a new convention, we run the risk of losing some of its best properties; this is a case I never wish to see. Whatever might have been my sentiments of the ratification of the Constitution without amendments, my sense now is, that the salvation of America depends upon the establishment of this Government, whether amended or not. If the Constitution which is now ratified should not be supported, I despair of ever having a Government of these United States. . . .

Mr. SHERMAN.—I do not suppose the Constitution to be perfect, nor do I imagine if Congress and all the Legislatures on the continent were to revise it, that their united labors would make it perfect. I do not expect any perfection on this side the grave in the works of man; but my opinion is, that we are not at present in circumstances to make it better. It is a wonder that there has been such unanimity in adopting it, considering the ordeal it had to undergo; and the unanimity which prevailed at its formation is equally astonishing; amidst all the members from the twelve States present at the Federal Convention, there were only three who did not sign the instrument to attest their opinion of its goodness. Of the eleven States who have received it, the majority have ratified it without proposing a single amendment. This circumstance leads me to suppose that we shall not be able to propose any alterations that are likely to be adopted by nine States; and gentlemen know, before the alterations take effect, they must be agreed to by the Legislatures of three-fourths of the States in the Union. Those States which have not recommended alterations, will hardly adopt them, unless it is clear that they tend to make the Constitution better. Now, how this can be made out to their satisfaction I am yet to learn; they know of no defect from experience. It seems to be the opinion of gentlemen generally that this is not the time for entering upon the discussion of amendments: our only question therefore is, how to get rid of the subject. Now, for my own part, I would prefer to have it referred to a Committee of the Whole, rather than a special committee, and therefore shall not agree to the motion now before the House. . . .

At length Mr. LAWRENCE'S motion was agreed to, and Mr. MADISON's Propositions were ordered to be referred to the Committee of the Whole.

Thursday, August 13

The House then resolved itself into a Committee of the Whole, Mr. BOUDINOT in the Chair, and took the amendments under consideration. The first article ran thus: "In the introductory paragraph of the Constitution, before the words 'We the people,' add 'Government being intended for the benefit of the people and the rightful establishment thereof being derived from their authority alone.'"

Mr. SHERMAN.—I believe, Mr. Chairman, this is not the proper mode of amending the Constitution. We ought not to interweave our propositions into the work itself, because it will be destructive of the whole fabric. We might as well endeavor to mix brass, iron, and clay, as to incorporate such heterogeneous articles, the one contradictory to the other. Its absurdity will be discovered by comparing it with a law. Would any Legislature endeavor to introduce into a former set a subsequent amendment, and let them stand so connected? When an alteration is made in an act, it is done by way of supplement; the latter act always repealing the former in every specified case of difference.

Besides this, sir, it is questionable whether we have the right to propose amendments in this way. The Constitution is the act of the people, and ought to remain entire. But the amendments will be the act of the State Governments. Again, all the authority we possess is derived from that instrument; if we mean to destroy the whole, and establish a new Constitution, we remove the basis on which we mean to build. . . .

Mr. MADISON.—Form, sir, is always of less importance than the substance; but on this occasion I admit that form is of some consequence, and it will be well for the House to pursue that which upon reflection, shall appear to be the most eligible. Now it appears to me, that there is a neatness and propriety in incorporating the amendments into the Constitution itself; in that case, the system will remain uniform and entire; it will certainly be more simple when the amendments are interwoven into those parts to which they naturally belong, than it will if they consist of separate and distinct parts. We shall then be able to determine its meaning without references or comparison; whereas, if they are supplementary, its meaning can only be ascertained by a comparison of the two instruments, which will be a very considerable embarrassment. It will be difficult to ascertain to what parts of the instrument the amendments particularly refer; they will create unfavorable comparisons; whereas, if they are placed upon the footing here proposed, they will stand upon as good foundation as the original work. Nor is it so uncommon a think as gentlemen suppose; systematic men frequently take up the whole law, and, with its amendments and alterations, reduce it into one act. I am not, however, very solicitous about the form, provided the business is but well completed.

Mr. SMITH did not think the amendment proposed by the honorable gentlemen from Connecticut was compatible with the Constitution, which declared, that the amendments recommended by Congress, and ratified by the Legislatures of three-fourths of the several States, should be part of this Constitution; in which case it would form one complete system; but according to the idea of the amendment, the instrument is to have five or six suits of improvements. Such a mode seems more calculated to embarrass the people than any thing else, while nothing in his opinion was a juster cause of complaint than the difficulties of knowing the law, arising from Legislative obscurities that might easily be avoided. He said, that it had certainly been the custom in several of the State Governments to amend their laws by way of supplement. But South Carolina had been an instance of the contrary practice, in revising the old code; instead of making acts in addition to acts, which is always attended with perplexity, she has incorporated them, and brought them forward as a complete system, repealing the old. This is what he understood was intended to be done by the committee; the present copy of the Constitution was to be done away, and a new one substituted in its stead. . . .

Mr. LIVERMORE was clearly of opinion, that whatever amendments were made to the Constitution, they ought to stand separate from the original instrument. We have no right, said he, to alter a clause any otherwise than by a new proposition. We have well-established precedents for such a mode of procedure in the practice of the British Parliament and the State Legislatures throughout America. I do not mean, however, to assert that there has been no instance of a repeal of the whole law on enacting another; but this has generally taken place on account of the complexity of the original, with its supplements. Were we a mere Legislative body, no doubt it might be warrantable in us to pursue a similar method; but it is questionable whether it is possible for us, consistent with the oath we have taken, to attempt a repeal of the Constitution of the United States, by making a new one to substitute in its place; the reason of this is grounded on a very simple consideration. It is by virtue of the present Constitution, I presume, that we attempt to make another; now, if we proceed to the repeal of this, I cannot see upon what authority we shall erect another; if we destroy the base, the superstructure falls of course. At some future day it may be asked upon what authority we proceeded to raise and appropriate public moneys. We suppose we do it in virtue of the present Constitution; but it may be doubted whether we have a right to exercise any of its authorities while it is suspended, as it will certainly be from the time that two-thirds of both Houses have agreed to submit it to the State Legislatures; so that, unless we mean to destroy the whole Constitution, we ought to be careful how we attempt to amend it in the way proposed by the committee. From hence, I presume it will be more prudent to adopt the mode proposed by the gentleman from Connecticut, than it will be to risk the destruction of the whole by proposing amendments in the manner recommended by the committee. . . .

Mr. STONE.—It is not a matter of much consequence, with respect to the preservation of the original instrument, whether the amendments are incorporated or made distinct; because the records will always show the original form in which it stood. But, in my opinion, we ought to mark its progress with truth in every step we take. If the amendments are incorporated in the body of the work, it will appear, unless we refer to the archives of Congress, that GEORGE WASHINGTON, and the other worthy characters who composed the convention, signed an instrument which they never had in contemplation. The one to which he affixed his signature purports to be adopted by the unanimous consent of the delegates from every State there assembled. Now if we incorporate these amendments, we must undoubtedly go further, and say that the Constitution so formed was defective, and had need of alteration; we therefore propose to repeal the old and substitute a new one in its place. From this consideration alone, I think we ought not to pursue the line of conduct drawn for us by the committee. This perhaps is not the last amendment the Constitution may receive; we ought therefore to be careful how we set a precedent which, in dangerous and turbulent times, may unhinge the whole.

With respect to the observations of the gentleman from South Carolina, I shall just remark, that we have no authority to repeal the whole Constitution. The words referred to in that instrument only authorize us to propose amendment to it, which, when properly ratified, are to become valid, as a part of the same; but these can never be construed to empower us to make a new Constitution. . . .

Mr GERRY asked, if the mode could make any possible difference, provided the sanction was the same; or whether it would operate differently in any one instance? If it will not, we are disputing about form, and the question will turn on the expediency. Now one gentleman tells you, that he is so attached to this instrument, that he is unwilling to lose any part of it; therefore, to gratify him, we may throw it into a supplementary form. But let me ask, will not this as effectually destroy some parts, as if the correction had been made by way of incorporation? or will posterity have a more favorable opinion of the original, because it has been amended by distinct acts? For my part, I cannot see what advantage can accrue from adopting the motion of the honorable gentleman from Connecticut, unless it be to give every one the trouble of erasing out of his copy certain words and sentences, and inserting others. But, perhaps, in our great veneration for the original composition, we may go further, and pass an act to prohibit these interpolations, as it may injure the text.

All this, sir, I take to be trifling about matters of little consequence. The Constitution has undoubtedly provided that the amendments shall be incorporated, if I understand the import of the words "and shall be valid to all intents and purposes, as part of the Constitution." If it had said that the present form should be preserved, then it would be proper to propose the alterations by way of a supplement. One gentleman has said, we shall lose the names that are now annexed to the instrument. They are names, sir, I admit, of high respect; but I would ask that gentleman, if they would give validity to the Constitution, if it were not ratified by the several States? or if their names were struck out, whether it would be of less force than at present? If he answer these questions in the negative, I shall consider it of no consequence whether the names are appended to it or not. But it will be time enough to discuss this point, when a motion is made for striking them out.

If we proceed in the way proposed by the honorable gentleman from Connecticut, I presume the title of our first amendment will be, a supplement to the Constitution of the United States; the next a supplement to the supplement, and so on, until we have supplements annexed five times in five years, wrapping up the Constitution in a maze of perplexity; and as great an adept as that honorable gentleman is at finding out the truth, it will take him, I apprehend, a week or a fortnight's study to ascertain the true meaning of the Constitution.

It is said, if the amendments are incorporated, it will be a virtual repeal of the Constitution. I say the effect will be the same in a supplementary way; consequently the objection goes for nothing, or it goes against making any amendment whatever.

It is said that the present form of the amendments is contrary to the 5th article. I will not undertake to define the extent of the word amendment, as it stands in the fifth article; but I suppose if we proposed to change the division of the powers given to the three branches of the Government, and that proposition is accepted and ratified by three-fourths of the State Legislatures, it will become as valid, to all intents and purposes, as any part of the Constitution; but if it is the opinion of gentlemen that the original is to be kept sacred, amendments will be of no use, and had better be omitted; whereas, on the other hand, if they are to be received as equal in authority, we shall have five or six constitutions, perhaps differing in material points from each other, but all equally valid; so that they may require a man of science to determine what is or is not the Constitution. This will certainly be attended with great inconvenience, as the several States are bound not to make laws contradictory thereto, and all officers are sworn to support it, without knowing precisely what it is. . . .

Mr. JACKSON.—I do not like to differ with gentlemen about form; but as so much has been said, I wish to give my opinion; it is this: that the original Constitution ought to remain inviolate, and not be patched up, from time to time, with various stuffs resembling Joseph's coat of many colors. . . .

The Constitution of the Union has been ratified and established by the people; let their act remain inviolable; if any thing we can do has a tendency to improve it, let it be done, but without mutilating and defacing the original. . . .

2.12 The Bill of Rights Expresses the Nation's Commitment to Liberty

Altogether twelve amendments were submitted by Congress for adoption as the Bill of Rights. Of these, ten were ratified, all in 1791. Under Madison's supervision, none of these amendments altered the form of government, but, contrary to Madison's hopes, these amendments limited only the national government, a point that was reinforced in a decision written by Chief Justice John Marshall in *Barron v. Baltimore* (1833). Moreover, the Bill of Rights, like subsequent amendments, was added to the end of the Constitution rather than integrated into the text of the document. The ratification of the Bill of Rights so soon after adoption of the Constitution must have done much to convince Americans that the amending process in Article V was adequate to the nation's needs.

Amendment I
Congress shall make no law respecting an establishment of religion, or prohibiting the free exercise thereof, or abridging the freedom of speech, or of the press; or the right of the people peaceably to assemble and to petition the Government for a redress of grievances.

Amendment II
A well regulated Militia, being necessary to the security of a free State, the right of the people to keep and bear Arms, shall not be infringed.

Amendment III
No soldier shall, in time of peace be quartered in any house, without the consent of the Owner, nor in time of war, but in a manner to be prescribed by Law.

Amendment IV
The right of the people to be secure in their persons, houses, papers, and effects, against unreasonable searches and seizures, shall not be violated, and no Warrants shall issue, but upon probable cause, supported by Oath or affirmation, and particularly describing the place to be searched, and the persons or things to be seized.

Amendment V
No person shall be held to answer for a capital, or otherwise infamous crime, unless on a presentment or indictment of a Grand Jury, except in cases arising in the land or naval forces, or in the Militia, when in actual service in time of war or public danger; nor shall any person be subject for the same

offence to be twice put in jeopardy of life or limb; nor shall be compelled in any criminal case to be a witness against himself, nor be deprived of life, liberty, or property, without due process of law; nor shall private property be taken for public use, without just compensation.

Amendment VI
In all criminal prosecutions, the accused shall enjoy the right to a speedy and public trial, by an impartial jury of the State and district wherein the crime shall have been committed, which district shall have been previously ascertained by law, and to be informed of the nature and cause of the accusation; to be confronted with the witnesses against him; to have compulsory process for obtaining witnesses in his favor, and to have the Assistance of Counsel for his defence.

Amendment VII
In suits at common law, where the value in controversy shall exceed twenty dollars, the right of trial by jury shall be preserved, and no fact tried by jury, shall be otherwise reexamined in any Court of the United States, than according to the rules of the common law.

Amendment VIII
Excessive bail shall not be required, nor excessive fines imposed, nor cruel and unusual punishments inflicted.

Amendment IX
The enumeration in the Constitution, of certain rights, shall not be construed to deny or disparage others retained by the people.

Amendment X
The powers not delegated to the United States by the Constitution, nor prohibited by it to the states, are reserved to the States respectively, or to the people.

2.13. The Eleventh Amendment Reverses a Supreme Court Decision and is in Turn Questioned in Court*

In one of its earliest rulings, the U.S. Supreme Court decided in *Chisholm v. Georgia* (1793) that a state could be sued by a citizen of another state. Although this decision was arguably in accord with the language in Article III which dealt with the jurisdiction of the Supreme Court, it was contrary to assurances that some Federalists have given in their debates with Anti-Federalists as to how the new Constitution would be interpreted. It may not therefore be surprising that the Court's decision was overturned by the adoption and ratification, in 1798, of the Eleventh Amendment. This amendment thus both recognized the power of the Court to interpret the Constitution and indicated that such power was subject to reversal by the people exercising their power under authority of Article V.

A 1798 case further complicated the picture, indicating that the Supreme Court would have to interpret the new amendment. At issue were two questions—the retrospective effect, if any, of the amendment and whether the President's signature was necessary for its ratification. Although the Court's decision was a short one, the arguments of counsel enable modern readers both to grasp the central issues in dispute and the judicial disposition of these matters.

Amendment XI

The Judicial power of the United States shall not be construed to extend to any suit in law or equity, commenced or prosecuted against one of the United States by Citizens of another State, or by Citizens or Subjects of any Foreign State.

Hollingsworth v. Virginia

The proposition [the Eleventh Amendment] being now adopted by the constitutional number of States, *Lee* Attorney-General, submitted this question to the court,—Whether the Amendment did, or did not, supersede all suits depending, as

---

* *Hollingsworth v. Virginia,* 3 U.S. 378 (1789).

well as prevent the institution of new suits against any one of the United States, by citizens of another State?

W. Tilghman and *Rawle*, argued in the negative, contending, that the jurisdiction of the Court was unimpaired, in relation to all suits instituted, previously to the adoption of the amendment. They premised, that it would be a great hardship, that persons legally suing, should be deprived of a right of action, or be condemned to the payment of costs, by an amendment of the Constitution *ex post facto*; 4 *Bac. Abr. 636. 7. pl. 5.* And that the jurisdiction being before regularly established, the amendment notwithstanding the words *"shall not be construed,"* *&c.* must be considered, in fact, as introductory of a new system of judicial authority. There are, however, two objections to be discussed: 1st. The amendment has not been proposed in the form prescribed by the Constitution, and, therefore, it is void. Upon an inspection of the original roll, it appears that the amendment was never submitted to the President for his approbation. The Constitution, declares that "every order, resolution, or vote, to which the concurrence of the Senate and House of Representatives may be necessary (except on a question of adjournment) shall be presented to the President of the *United States*; and before the same shall take effect, shall be approved by him, or being disapproved by him, shall be repassed by two thirds of the Senate and House of Representatives, &c." *Art. 1. s.7.* Now, the Constitution, likewise declares, that the concurrence of both Houses shall be necessary to a proposition for amendments. *Art. 5.* And it is no answer to the objection, to observe, that as two thirds of both Houses are required to originate the proposition, it would be nugatory to return it with the President's negative, to be repassed by the same number; since the reasons assigned for his disapprobation might be so satisfactory as to reduce the majority below the constitutional proportion. The concurrence of the President is required in matters of infinitely less importance; and whether on subjects of ordinary legislation, or of constitutional amendments, the expression is the same, and equally applied to the act of both Houses of Congress.

2d. The second objection arises from the terms of the amendment itself. The words "commenced or prosecuted," are properly in the past time; but, it is clear, that they ought not to be so gramatically restricted; for, then, a citizen need only discontinue his present suit, and commence another, in order to give the court cognizance of the cause. To avoid this evident absurdity, the words must be construed to apply only to suits *to be* "commenced and prosecuted. The spirit of the constitution is opposed to every thing in the nature of an *ex post facto* law, or retrospective regulation. No *ex post facto* law can be passed by Congress. *Const. Art. 1. s. 9.* No *ex post facto* law can be passed by the Legislature of any individual state. *Ibid. s. 10.* It is true, than an amendment to the Constitution cannot be controuled by those provisions; and if the words were explicit and positive, to produce the retrospective effect, contended for, they must prevail. But the words are doubtful; and, therefore, they ought to be so construed, as to conform to the general principles of the Constitution. . . .

Lee, Attorney General. The case before the court, is that of a suit against a state, in which the defendant has never entered an appearance: but the amendment is equally operative in all the cases against states, where there has been an appearance, or even where there have been a trial and judgment. An amendment of the constitution, and the repeal of a law, are not, manifestly, on the same footing: Nor can an explanatory law be expounded by foreign matter. The amendment in the present instance, is merely explanatory, in substance, as well as language. From the moment those who gave the power to sue a state, revoked and annulled it, the power ceased to be a part of the constitution; and if it does not exist there, it cannot in any degree be found, or exercised, elsewhere. The policy and rules, which, in relation to ordinary acts of legislation, declare that no *ex post facto* law shall be passed, do not apply to the formation, or amendment, of a constitution. The people limit and restrain the power of the legislature, acting under a delegated authority; but they impose no restraint on themselves. They could have said by an amendment to the constitution, that no judicial authority should be exercised, in any case, under the *United States*; and, if they had said so, could a court be held, or a judge proceed, on any judicial business, past or future from the moment of adopting the amendment? On general ground, then, it was in the power of the people to annihilate the whole, and the question is, whether they have annihilated a part of the judicial authority of the *United States*? Two objections are made: 1st, That the amendment has not been proposed in due form. But has not the same course been pursued relative to all the other amendments, that have been adopted? [A footnote notes—CHASE, Justice. There can, surely, be no necessity to answer that argument. The negative of the President applies only to the ordinary cases of legislation. He has nothing to do with the proposition, or adoption, of amendments to the Constitution.] And the case of amendments is evidently a substantive act, unconnected with the ordinary business of legislation, and not within the policy, or terms, of investing the President with a qualified negative on the acts and resolutions of Congress. 2d, That the amendment itself only applies to future suits. But whatever force there may be in the rules for construing statutes, they cannot be applied to the present case. It was the policy of the people to cut off that branch of the judicial power, which had been supposed to authorized suits by individuals against states; and the words being so extended as to support that policy, will equally apply to the past and to the future. A law, however, cannot be denominated retrospective, or *ex post facto*, which merely changes the remedy, but does not affect the right: In all the states, in some form or other, a remedy is furnished for the fair claims of individuals against the respective governments. The amendment is paramount to all the laws of the union; and if any part of the judicial act is in opposition to it, that part must be expunged. There can be no amendment of the constitution, indeed, which may not in some respect, be called *ex post facto*; but the moment it is adopted, the power that it gives, or takes away, begins to operate, or cease to exist.

THE COURT, on the day succeeding the argument, delivered an unanimous opinion, that the amendment being constitutionally adopted, there could not be exercised any jurisdiction, in any case, past or future, in which a state was sued by the citizens of another state, or by citizens, or subjects, of any foreign state.

2.14 George Washington Praises the Amending Process and Warns Against Bypassing It*

Although his views are not cited as frequently as those of Madison, Jefferson, Adams, and other more philosophical participants in the American Revolution, few, if any individuals, were as important as George Washington who is appropriately designated father of his country. Washington had led the revolutionary forces during the war, chaired the Constitutional Convention, and served as the nation's first President.

Below are two selections from Washington's writings which are used to round out the views of the American Founders. This first is a short excerpt from a letter dated February 7, 1788 to the Marquis de Lafayette. During the time when the Constitution was being debated, Washington indicated, as he was many times to do, his faith in the efficacy of the amending process to correct any woes. The second, better known selection, is taken from Washington's Farewell Address. Again, Washington professed his faith in the process and warned—in apparent reference to an attempt by the U.S. House of Representatives in his second term to void the Jay Treaty—against attempts to change the Constitution by other means. This address was appropriately dated, September 17, 1796, nine years from the signing of the U.S. Constitution in Philadelphia.

A Constitutional Door to Amendment

It will at least be a recommendation to the proposed Constitution that it is provided with more checks and barriers against the introduction of Tyranny, and those of a nature less liable to be surmounted, than any Government hitherto instituted among mortals, hath possessed. We are not to expect perfection in this world; but mankind, in modern times, have apparently made some progress in the science of government.

---

* *The Writings of George Washington*, John C. Fitzpatrick, ed. 39 vols. (Washington: U.S. Government Printing Office, 1931-44), vol. 29, p. 410-11.

A Compilation of the Messages and Papers of the Presidents, 1789-1908, by James D. Richardson, Vol. I (n.p.: Bureau of National Literature and Art, 1908), pp. 217, 219-20.

Should that which is now offered to the People of America, be found on experiment less perfect than it can be made, a Constitutional door is left open for its amelioration.

Some respectable characters have wished, that the States, after having pointed out whatever alterations and amendments may be necessary, would appoint another federal Convention to modify it upon those documents. For myself, I have wondered that sensible men should not see the impracticality of the scheme. The members would go fortified with such Instructions that nothing but discordant ideas could prevail.

Selections From The Farewell Address

To the efficacy and permanency of your union a government for the whole is indispensable. No alliances, however strict, between the parts can be an adequate substitute. They must inevitably experience the infractions and interruptions which all alliances in all times have experienced. Sensible of this momentous truth, you have improved upon your first essay by the adoption of a Constitution of Government better calculated than your former for an intimate union and for the efficacious management of your common concerns. This Government, the offspring of our own choice, uninfluenced and unawed, adopted upon full investigation and mature deliberation, completely free in its principles, in the distribution of its powers, uniting security with energy and containing within itself a provision for its own amendment, has a just claim to your confidence and your support. Respect for its authority, compliance with its laws, acquiescence in its measures, are duties enjoined by the fundamental maxims of true liberty. The basis of our political systems is the right of the people to make and to alter their constitutions of government. But the constitution which at any time exists till changed by an explicit and authentic act of the whole people is sacredly obligatory upon all. The very idea of the power and the right of the people to establish government presupposes the duty of every individual to obey the established government. . . .

It is important, likewise, that the habits of thinking in a free country should inspire caution in those intrusted with its administration to confine themselves within their respective constitutional spheres, avoiding in the exercise of the powers of one department to encroach upon another. The spirit of encroachment tends to consolidate the powers of all the departments in one, and thus to create, whatever the form of government, a real despotism. A just estimate of that love of power and proneness to abuse it which predominates in the human heart is sufficient to satisfy us of the truth of this position. The necessity of reciprocal checks in the exercise of political power, by dividing and distributing it into different depositories, and constituting each the guardian of the public weal against invasions by the others, has been evinced by experiments ancient and modern, some of them in our country and under our own eyes. To preserve them must be as necessary as to institute them. If in the opinion of the people the distribution or modification of the constitutional powers be in any particular wrong, let it be corrected by an amendment in the way which the Constitution designates. But let there be no change by usurpation; for though this in one instance may be the instrument of good, it is the customary weapon by which free governments are destroyed. The precedent must always greatly overbalance in permanent evil any partial or transient benefit which the use can at any time yield.

Chapter 3

The Early Nineteenth Century

Throughout the early nineteenth century, most commentary on the Article V amending process continued to be favorable, but it was increasingly clear that the Constitution could be changed not only by formal amendment but also by presidential initiatives, congressional practices, and judicial interpretations. In addition, some sectional spokesmen asserted that states should have the authority to interpret the Constitution. Many states revised their constitutions in the early nineteenth century. Near mid-century, the nation was reminded by a dispute in Rhode Island that, in states without the means of formal amendment, some people would assert their claims through revolutionary means.

3.1 The Twelfth Amendment Remedies a Defect in the Electoral College

There can be little doubt that one of the purposes of Article V was to provide for unforeseen contingencies which developed in the operation of government. One such unanticipated exigency was caused by the rise of political parties which were not specifically mentioned in the U.S. Constitution. As a result, those running for President and Vice-President now ran on a ticket. Under the original electoral college scheme, each electoral delegate was required to cast two votes; the person then getting the highest number of votes became President, and the person getting the second highest became Vice-president. In the election of 1800, all electors casting their vote for the Democratic Republican candidate, Thomas Jefferson, also cast their votes for Aaron Burr, who, it was assumed, would serve as Vice-President. The result was a tie in the electoral votes that threw the election to the House of Representatives where Jefferson's election was eventually decided by his opponents, the Federalists, who, it seemed, trusted Burr even less than Jefferson.

It is interesting that Jefferson claimed in letters that he threatened to call a constitutional convention if his election, which had clearly been intended by the people, had not been confirmed. Subsequently, the Twelfth Amendment was adopted to prevent future electoral problems; its wordiness suggests that its Framers had recognized a number of ways that the electoral college mechanism could malfunction.

Amendment XII (1804)

The electors shall meet in their respective states and vote by ballot for President and Vice-President, one of whom, at least, shall not be an inhabitant of the same state with themselves; they shall name in their ballots the person voted for as President, and in distinct ballots the person voted for as Vice-President, and they shall make distinct lists of all persons voted for as President, and of all persons voted for as Vice-President, and of the number of votes for each, which lists they shall sign and certify, and transmit sealed to the seat of the government of the United States, directed to the President of the Senate;—The President of the Senate shall, in presence of the Senate and House of Representatives, open all the certificates and the votes shall then be counted;—The person having the greatest number of votes for President, shall be the President, if such number be a majority of the whole number of Electors appointed; and if no person have such majority, then from the persons having the highest numbers not exceeding three on the list of those voted for as President, the House of Representatives shall choose immediately, by ballot, the President. But in choosing the President, the votes shall be taken by states, the representatives from each state having one vote; a quorum for this purpose shall consist of a member or members from two-thirds of the states, and a majority of all the states shall be necessary to a choice. And if the House of Representatives shall not choose a President whenever the right of choice shall devolve upon them, before the fourth day of March next following, then the Vice-President shall act as President, as in the case of the death or other constitutional disability of the President.—The person having the greatest number of votes as Vice-President, shall be the Vice-President, if such number be a majority of the whole number of Electors appointed, and if no person have a majority, then from the two highest numbers on the list, the Senate shall choose the Vice-President; a quorum for the purpose shall consist of two-thirds of the whole number of Senators, and a majority of the whole number shall be necessary to a choice. But no person constitutionally ineligible to the office of President shall be eligible to that of Vice-President of the United States.

3.2 The Supreme Court Affirms the Power of Judicial Review*

One of the most critical cases in the early history of the U.S. Supreme Court was *Marbury v. Madison.* Marbury had been appointed as a justice of the peace by the outgoing President John Adams, a Federalist, who was carrying out a Federalist plan to stack the judiciary prior to the Republicans' arrival. When Thomas Jefferson's new secretary of State, James Madison, arrived at his office, he found that, while signed and sealed, Marbury's commission had never been delivered. As Democratic Republicans, neither Jefferson nor Madison had an incentive to deliver Marbury's commission. Marbury subsequently sued, going directly to the Supreme Court for a writ of mandamus commanding Madison to give him his commission.

In deciding his case, the Supreme Court, led by its Federalist Chief Justice John Marshall, established the principle of judicial review, that is, the principle that the courts in America have the power to declare a federal law to be void because it is unconstitutional (such review had previously been exercised over state laws). In this case, Marshall decided that the Supreme Court had no authority to issue the writ Marbury requested because the law appearing to confer such authority

---

* *Marbury v. Madison*, 5 U.S. 137 (1803), 176-180.

in the present case, that is, in a case of original jurisdiction before the Supreme Court, was unconstitutional.

This decision has tremendous implications for the constitutional amending process. Consistent with the language of Article V, Marshall's decision indicated that the written Constitution was superior to ordinary laws and could not be changed by them. At the same time, by making the courts the authoritative interpreters of the Constitution, judicial review opened up the possibility that understandings of the Constitution could be changed through judicial interpretations rather than by, or in addition to, Article V processes. Many subsequent cases in this book will demonstrate the complex relationship that has emerged between judicial review and constitutional amendment.

The Force of Unconstitutional Legislation

The authority, therefore, given to the Supreme Court, by the act establishing the judicial courts of the United States, to issue writs of mandamus to public officers, appears not to be warranted by the constitution; and it becomes necessary to inquire whether a jurisdiction so conferred can be exercised.

The question, whether an act, repugnant to the constitution, can become the law of the land, is a question deeply interesting to the United States; but, happily, not of an intricacy proportioned to its interest. It seems only necessary to recognize certain principles, supposed to have been long and well established, to decide it.

That the people have an original right to establish, for their future government, such principles, as, in their opinion, shall most conduce to their own happiness is the basis on which the whole American fabric has been erected. The exercise of this original right is a very great exertion; nor can it, nor ought it, to be frequently repeated. The principles, therefore, so established, are deemed fundamental. And as the authority from which they proceed is supreme, and can seldom act, they are designed to be permanent.

This original and supreme will organizes the government, and assigns to different departments their respective powers.

It may either stop here, or establish certain limits not to be transcended by those departments.

The government of the United States is of the latter description. The powers of the legislature are defined and limited; and that those limits may not be mistaken, or forgotten, the constitution is written. To what purpose are powers limited, and to what purpose is that limitation committed to writing, if these limits may, at any time, be passed by those intended to be restrained? The distinction between a government with limited and unlimited powers is abolished, if those limits do not confine the persons on whom they are imposed, and if acts prohibited and acts allowed, are of equal obligation. It is a proposition too plain to be contested, that the constitution controls any legislative act repugnant to it; or, that the legislature may alter the constitution by an ordinary act.

Between these alternatives there is no middle ground. The constitution is either a superior paramount law, unchangeable by ordinary means, or it is on a level with ordinary legislative acts, and, like other acts, is alterable when the legislature shall please to alter it.

If the former part of the alternative be true, then a legislative act contrary to the constitution is not law: if the latter part be true, then written constitutions are absurd attempts, on the part of the people, to limit a power in its own nature illimitable.

Certainly all those who have framed written constitutions contemplate them as forming the fundamental and paramount law of the nation, and, consequently, the theory of every such government must be, that an act of the legislature, repugnant to the constitution, is void.

This theory is essentially attached to a written constitution, and, is consequently, to be considered, by this court, as one of the fundamental principles of our society. It is not therefore to be lost sight of in the further consideration of this subject.

If an act of the legislature, repugnant to the constitution, is void, does it, notwithstanding its invalidity, bind the courts, and oblige them to give it effect? Or, in other words, though it be not law, does it constitute a rule as operative as if it was a law? This would be to overthrow in fact what was established in theory; and would seem, at first view, an absurdity too gross to be insisted on. It shall, however, receive a more attentive consideration.

It is emphatically the province and duty of the judicial department to say what the law is. Those who apply the rule to particular cases, must of necessity expound and interpret that rule. If two laws conflict with each other, the courts must decide on the operation of each.

So if a law be in opposition to the constitution; if both the law and the constitution apply to a particular case, so that the court must either decide that case conformably to the law, disregarding the constitution; or conformably to the constitution, disregarding the law; the court must determine which of these conflicting rules governs the case. This is of the very essence of judicial duty.

If, then, the courts are to regard the constitution, and the constitution is superior to any ordinary act of the legislature, the constitution, and not such ordinary act, must govern the case to which they both apply.

Those, then, who controvert the principle that the constitution is to be considered, in court, as a paramount law, are reduced to the necessity of maintaining that courts must close their eyes on the constitution, and see only the law.

This doctrine would subvert the very foundation of all written constitutions. It would declare that an act which, according to the principles and theory of our government, is entirely void, is yet, in practice, completely obligatory. It would declare that if the legislature shall do what is expressly forbidden, such act, notwithstanding the express prohibition, is in reality effectual. It would be given [sic] to the legislature a practical and real omnipotence, with the same breath which professes to restrict their powers within narrow limits. It is prescribing limits, and declaring that those limits may be passed at pleasure.

That it thus reduces to nothing what we have deemed the greatest improvement on political institutions, a written constitution, would of itself be sufficient, in America, where written constitutions have been viewed with so much reverence, for rejecting the construction. But the peculiar expressions of the constitution of the United States furnish additional arguments in favour of its rejection.

The judicial power of the United States is extended to all cases arising under the constitution.

Could it be the intention of those who gave this power, to say that in using it the constitution should not be looked into? That a case arising under the constitution should be decided without examining the instrument under which it aries?

This is too extravagant to be maintained.

In some cases, then, the constitution must be looked into by the judges. And if they can open it at all, what part of it are they forbidden to read or to obey?

There are many other parts of the constitution which serve to illustrate this subject.

It is declared that "no tax or duty shall be laid on articles exported from any state." Suppose a duty on the export of cotton, of tobacco, or of flour; and a suit instituted to recover it. Ought judgment to be rendered in such a case? ought the judges to close their eyes on the constitution, and only see the law?

The constitution declares "that no bill of attainder or ex post facto law shall be passed."

If, however, such a bill should be passed, and a person should be prosecuted under it; must the court condemn to death those victims whom the constitution endeavors to preserve?

"No person," says the constitution, "shall be convicted of treason unless on the testimony of two witnesses to the same overt act, or on confession in open court."

Here the language of the constitution is addressed especially to the courts. It prescribes directly for them, a rule of evidence not to be departed from. If the legislature should change that rule, and declare one witness, or a confession out of court, sufficient for conviction, must the constitutional principle yield to the legislative act?

From these, and many other selections which might be made, it is apparent, that the framers of the constitution contemplated that instrument as a rule for the government of courts, as well as of the legislature.

Why otherwise does it direct the judges to take an oath to support it? This oath certainly applies in an especial manner, to their conduct in their official character. How immoral to impose it on them, if they were to be used as the instruments, and the knowing instruments, for violating what they swear to support!

The oath of office, too, imposed by the legislature, is completely demonstrative of the legislative opinion on this subject. It is in these words: "I do solemnly swear that I will administer justice without respect to persons, and do equal right to the poor and the rich; and that I will faithfully and impartially discharge all the duties incumbent on me as, according to the best of my abilities and understanding agreeably to the constitution and laws of the United States."

Why does a judge swear to discharge his duties agreeably to the constitution of the United States, if that constitution forms no rule for his government? if it is closed upon him, and cannot be inspected by him?

If such be the real state of things, this is worse than solemn mockery. To prescribe, or to take this oath, becomes equally a crime.

It is also not entirely unworthy of observation, that in declaring what shall be the supreme law of the land, the constitution itself is first mentioned; and not the laws of the United States generally, but those only which shall be made in pursuance of the constitution, have that rank.

Thus, the particular phraseology of the constitution of the United States confirms and strengths the principle, supposed to be essential to all written constitutions, that a law repugnant to the constitution is void; and that courts, as well as other departments, are bound by that instrument.

3.3 The Louisiana Purchase Bypasses the Amending Process*

Few events were more dramatic in early American history than the purchase of Louisiana in 1803, an event which

---

* Material taken from Thomas Jefferson, *The Works of Thomas Jefferson*, ed. Paul Leicester Ford (New York: Putnam, The Knickerbocker Press, 1905), vol. 10, p. 3-13.

relieved a foreign military threat on America's frontier and practically doubled the size of the country. Then President Thomas Jefferson faced a constitutional dilemma in making this purchase for he had been one who had previously opposed the establishment of the national bank (whose constitutionality was later accepted in *McCulloch v. Maryland*) on the basis that the power to create such a bank was not explicitly granted in the Constitution and could not therefore be exercised.

Consistent with his principles Jefferson therefore proposed an amendment to ratify his action in purchasing Louisiana. When leaders of his own party resisted and fears arose that delay might jeopardize treaty ratification, Jefferson retreated, refusing to allow the lack of explicit constitutional authorization to stand in the path of national progress. Later during the embargo with Great Britain that preceded the War of 1812, Jefferson would show himself capable of exercising similar powers. Jefferson reaped both praise for his actions on behalf of national interests and criticism for failure to practice his own theory of strict constitutional interpretation. Below is a copy of Jefferson's proposed amendment justifying the Louisiana Purchase and his subsequent comments in a letter to a friend.

Proposed Amendment

The province of Louisiana is incorporated with the U.S. and made part thereof. The rights of occupancy in the soil, and of self government, are confirmed to the Indian inhabitants, as they now exist. Pre-emption only of the portions rightfully occupied by them, & a succession to the occupancy of such as they may abandon, with the full rights of possession as well as of property & sovereignty in whatever is not or shall cease to be so rightfully occupied by them shall belong to the U.S.

The legislature of the Union shall have authority to exchange the right of occupancy in portions where the U.S. have full right for lands possessed by Indians within the U.S. on the East side of the Missisipi; to exchange lands on the East side of the river for those of the white inhabitants on the West side thereof and above the latitude of 31 degrees; to maintain in any part of the province such military posts as may be requisite for peace or safety; to exercise police over all persons therein, not being Indiana inhabitants; to work salt springs, or mines of coal, metals and other minerals within the possession of the U.S. or in any others with the consent of the possessors; to regulate trade & intercourse between the Indian inhabitants and all other persons; to explore and ascertain the geography of the province, its productions and other interesting circumstances; to open roads and navigation therein where necessary for beneficial communication; & to establish agencies and factories therein for the cultivation of commerce, peace & good understanding with the Indians residing there.

The legislature shall have no authority to dispose of the lands of the province otherwise than is hereinbefore permitted, until a new Amendment of the constitution shall give that authority. Except as to that portion thereof which lies south of the latitude of 31 degrees; which whenever they deem expedient, they may erect into a territorial Government, either separate or as making part with one of the eastern side of the river, vesting the inhabitants thereof with all the rights possessed by other territorial citizens of the U.S.

Excerpt From Letter to John Breckenridge, August 12, 1803

This treaty must of course be laid before both Houses, because both have important functions to exercise respecting it. They, I presume, will see their duty to their country in ratifying & paying for it, so as to secure a good which would otherwise probably be never again in their power. But I suppose they must then appeal to *the nation* for an additional article to the Constitution, approving & confirming an act which the nation had not previously authorized. The constitution has made no provision for our holding foreign territory, still less for incorporating foreign nations into our Union. The Executive in seizing the fugitive occurrence which so much advances the good of their country, have done an act beyond the Constitution. The Legislature in casting behind them metaphysical subtleties, and risking themselves like faithful servants, must ratify & pay for it, and throw themselves on their country for doing for them unauthorized what we know they would have done for themselves had they been in a situation to do it. It is the case of a guardian, investing the money of his ward in purchasing an important adjacent territory; & saying to him when of age, I did this for your good; I pretend to no right to bind you: you may disavow me, and I must get out of the scrape as I can: I thought it my duty to risk myself for you. But we shall not be disavowed by the nation, and their act of indemnity will confirm & not weaken the Constitution, by more strongly marking out its lines.

Excerpt from Letter to Wilson Cary Nicholas, Sept. 7, 1803.
I am aware of the force of the observations you make on the power given by the Constn to Congress, to admit new States into the Union, without restraining the subject to the territory then constituting the US. But when I consider that the limits of the U S are precisely fixed by the treaty of 1783, that the Constitution expressly declares itself to be made for the U S, I cannot help believing the intention was to permit Congress to admit into the Union new States, which should be formed out of the territory for which, & under whose authority alone, they were then acting. I do not believe it was meant that they might receive England, Ireland, Holland, &c. into it, which would be the case on your construction. When an instrument admits two constructions, the one safe, the other dangerous, the one precise, the other indefinite, I prefer that which is safe & precise. I had rather ask an enlargement of power from the nation, where it is found necessary, than to assume it by a construction which would make our powers boundless. Our peculiar security is in possession of a written Constitution. Let us not make it a blank paper by construction. . . . I confess, then, I think it important, in the present case, to set an example against broad construction, by appealing for new power to the people. If, however, our friends shall think differently, certainly I shall acquiesce with satisfaction; confiding, that the good sense of our country will correct the evil of construction when it shall produce ill effects.

3.4. St. George Tucker Praises the Amending Process*

St. George Tucker, often known as "the American Blackstone," was both a Virginia judge and a Professor of Law at the College of William and Mary where he had succeeded his renowned teacher, George Wythe. In the passages below, Tucker praises the Article V amending process and briefly explores the question as to whether one generation can bind another.

The Virtues of the Amending Process And the Rights of the Living

It [the U.S. Constitution] can not be controlled, or altered without the express consent of the body politic of three fourths of the states in the union, or, of the people, of an equal number of the states. To prevent the necessity of an immediate appeal to the latter, a method is pointed out, by which amendments may be proposed and ratified by the concurrent act of two thirds of both houses of congress, and three fourths of the state legislatures: but if congress should neglect to propose amendments in this way, when they may be deemed necessary, the concurrent sense of two thirds of the state legislatures may enforce congress to call a convention, the amendments proposed by which, when ratified by the conventions of three fourths of the states, become valid, as a part of the constitution. In either mode, the assent of the body politic of the states, is necessary, either to complete, or to originate the measure.

Here let us pause a moment, and reflect on the peculiar happiness of the people of the United States, thus to possess the power of correcting whatever errors may have crept into the constitution, or may hereafter be discovered therein, without the danger of those tremendous scenes which have convulsed every nation of the earth, in their attempts to amelio-

---

* St. George Tucker, *Blackstone's Commentaries with Notes of Reference, to The Constitution and Laws, of the Federal Government of the United States; and of the Commonwealth of Virginia* (Philadelphia: William Young Birch, and Abraham Small, 1803; reprinted South Hackensack, N.J.: Rothman Reprints, Inc., 1969), appendices, pp. 171-3; 371-2.

rate their condition; a power which they have already more than once successfully exercised. "Americans," says a writer whom I have before quoted, "ought to look upon themselves, at present, as almost the sole guardians and trustees of republican freedom: for other nations are not, as we are, at leisure to shew it in its true and most enticing form. Whilst we contemplate with a laudable delight, the rapid growth of our prosperity, let us ascribe it to its true cause, the wholesome operation of our new political philosophy. What blessings we enjoy, over and above what are to be found under the British government, whatever evils we avoid, to which the people of that government are exposed; for all these advantages are we indebted to the separation that has taken place, and the new order of things that has obtained among us. Let us be thankful to the parent of the universe, that he has given us, the first enjoyment of that freedom, which is intended in due time for the whole race of man. Let us diligently study the nature of our situation, that we may better know how to preserve and improve its advantages. But above all, let us study the genuine principles of DEMOCRACY, and steadily practice them, that we may refute the calumnies of those who would bring them into disgrace.

Let us publish to the world, and let our conduct verify our assertions, that by democracy we mean not a state of licentiousness, nor a subversion of order, nor a defiance of legal authority. Let us convince mankind, that we understand by it, a well ordered government, endued with energy to fulfil all its intentions, to act with effect upon all delinquents, and to bring to punishment all offenders against the laws: but, at the same time, not a government of usurpation; not a government of prescription; but a government of compact, upon the ground of equal right, and equal obligation; in which the rights of each individual spring out of the engagement he has entered into, to perform the duties required of him by the community, whereby the same rights in others, are to be maintained inviolate."

That mankind have a right to bind themselves by their own voluntary acts, can scarcely be questioned: but how far have they a right to enter into engagements to bind their posterity likewise? Are the acts of the dead binding upon their living posterity, to all generations; or has posterity the same natural rights which their ancestors have enjoyed before them? And if they have, what right have any generation of men to establish any particular form of government for succeeding generations?

The answer is not difficult: "Government," said the congress of the American States, in behalf of their constituents, "derives its just authority from the consent of the governed." This fundamental principle then may serve as a guide to direct our judgment with respect to the question. To which we may add, in the words of the author of Common Sense, a law is not binding upon posterity, merely, because it was made by their ancestors; but, because posterity have not repealed it. It is the acquiescence of posterity under the law, which continues its obligation upon them, and not any right which their ancestors had to bind them.

Until, therefore, the people of the United States, whether the present, or any future generation, shall think it necessary to alter, or revoke the present constitution of the United States, it must be received, respected, and obeyed among us, as the great and unequivocal declaration of the will of the people, and the supreme law of the land.

Description of and Praise for Article V

Lastly; the fifth article provides the mode by which future amendments to the constitution may be proposed, discussed, and carried into effect, without hazarding a dissolution of the confederacy, or suspending the operations of the existing government. And this may be effected in two different modes: the first on recommendation from congress, whenever two thirds of both houses shall concur in the expediency of any amendment. The second, which secures to the states an influence in case congress should neglect to recommend such amendments, provides, that congress shall, on application from the legislatures of two thirds of the states, call a convention for proposing amendments; which in either case shall be valid to all intents and purposes as part of the constitution, when ratified by the legislatures of three fourths of the several states, or by conventions in three fourths thereof, as the one or the other mode, of the ratification may be proposed by the congress. Both of these provisions appear excellent. Of the utility and practicability of the former, we have already had most satisfactory experience. The latter will probably never be resorted to, unless the federal government should betray symptoms of corruption, which may render it expedient for the states to exert themselves in order to the application of some radical and effectual remedy. Nor can we too much applaud a constitution, which thus provides a safe, and peaceable remedy for its own defects, as they may from time to time be discovered. A change of government in other countries is almost always attended with convulsions which threaten its entire dissolution; and with scenes of horror, which deter mankind from any attempt to correct abuses, or remove oppressions until they have become altogether intolerable. In America we may reasonably hope, that neither of these evils need be apprehended; nor is there any reason to fear that this provision in the constitution will produce any degree of instability in the government; the mode both of originating and of ratifying amendments, in either mode which the constitution directs, must necessarily be attended with such obstacles, and delays, as must prove a sufficient bar against light, or frequent innovations. And as a further security against them, the same article further provides, that no amendment which may be made, prior to the year one thousand eight hundred and eight, shall, in any manner, affect those clauses of the ninth section of the first article, which related to the migration or importation of such persons as the states may think proper to allow; and to the manner in which direct taxes shall be laid: and that no state, without its consent shall be deprived of its equal suffrage in the senate.

3.5 The Hartford Convention Proposes New Amendments*

While the Supreme Court asserted in *Marbury v. Madison* that it was the final interpreter of the Constitution, through much

---

* Found in *The Federalist*, ed. with documents by Paul L. Ford (New York: Henry Holt and Company, 1898), pp. 688-89.

of the early part of the nineteenth century this claim with in tension with claims made by some of the states. In 1798, the Virginia and Kentucky Resolutions (respectively authored by James Madison and Thomas Jefferson and passed by the legislatures in opposition to the Alien and Sedition Acts, the first of which was in apparent contradiction to the guarantees of freedom of speech in the First Amendment) had indicated that states could "interpose" against a law that they thought to be unconstitutional. These resolutions received little support from the other states.

An indication that support for states' rights was not limited to the South, however, came from the Hartford Convention which was called by the New England states during the War of 1812 which they believed to be against their own interests. Below are the resolutions for amendments, and a possible convention, which the Hartford Convention adopted. Few resolutions have been more poorly timed. Delegates arrived in Washington D.C. as the victory in the Battle of New Orleans was being celebrated along with news that a peace treaty had been signed with Great Britain. The Federalist Party, associated in the popular mind with the Hartford Convention, never recovered, but the theme of states' rights which was tied to the Hartford Convention would reappear in the writings of John C. Calhoun and other Southerners.

Proposed Amendments

First.—Representatives and direct taxes shall be apportioned among the several States which may be included within this union, according to their respective numbers of free persons, including those bound to serve for a term of years, and excluding Indians not taxed, and all other persons.

Second.—No new State shall be admitted into the union by Congress in virtue of the power granted by the Constitution, without the concurrence of two-thirds of both Houses.

Third.—Congress shall not have power to lay any embargo on the ships or vessels of the citizens of the United States, in the ports of harbors thereof, for more than sixty days.

Fourth.—Congress shall not have power, without the concurrence to two-thirds of both Houses, to interdict the commercial intercourse between the United States and any foreign nation or the dependencies thereof.

Fifth.—Congress shall not make or declare war, or authorize acts of hostility against any foreign nation, without the concurrence of two-thirds of both Houses, except such acts of hostility be in defense of the territories of the United States when actually invaded.

Sixth.—No person who shall hereafter be naturalized, shall be eligible as a member of the Senate or House of Representatives of the United States, nor capable of holding any civil office under the authority of the United States.

Seventh.—The same person shall not be elected President of the United States a second time; nor shall the President be elected from the same State two terms in succession.

Resolved.—That if the application of these States to the government of the United States, recommended in a foregoing Resolution, should be unsuccessful, and peace should not be concluded, and the defense of these States should be neglected, as it has been since the commencement of the war, it will in the opinion of this Convention be expedient for the Legislatures of the several States to appoint Delegates to another Convention, to meet at Boston, in the State of Massachusetts, on the third Thursday of June next, with such powers and instructions as the exigency of a crisis so momentous may require.

3.6 John C. Calhoun Praises the Amending Process and Ties it to His Doctrine of State Sovereignty*

There was no greater spokesman for the doctrine of state sovereignty than the one-time Vice-President and later Senator from South Carolina, John C. Calhoun. Calhoun became a particularly ardent defender of slavery and the South's interest in this peculiar institution. Calhoun recommended a system of "concurrent majorities" which would in effect have

* Calhoun, *A Discourse on the Constitution and Government of the United States, The Works of John C. Calhoun*, ed. Richard K. Cralle (New York; Russell & Russell, 1968. Reprint of 1851-56 ed)., vol. 1, pp. 279-301.

granted to the South and other regions (albeit not to the slaves and other minorities within these regions) a veto over national legislation. Calhoun argued that states objecting to a constitutional construction by the national government had the right to "nullify," or interpose, against such a law and require that the national government affirm its power to accomplish its object by adoption of a constitutional amendment. While this extraconstitutional mechanism would have wrecked havoc with the federal system, it required that Calhoun be supportive of the amending process, showing that it was effective in counteracting any evil tendencies that might occur from the exercise of the nullifying power and allowing the national government to get authority it needed. In an interesting twist, however, Calhoun still conceded the right of states to secede if they thought the amending process were used for objects not intended by the original compact and unsatisfactory to it. Thus, did the amending process come to play a key part in Calhoun's most controversial doctrines, nullification and secession.

Calhoun on the Amending Process

But the right, with all these consequences, is not more certain than that possessed by the several States, as parties to the compact, of interposing for the purpose of arresting, within their respective limits, an act of the federal government in violation of the constitution; and thereby of preventing the delegated from encroaching on the reserved powers. Without such right, all the others would be barren and useless abstractions, —and just as puerile as the right of judging, without the right of pronouncing an act to be unconstitutional, and, as such, null and void. Nor is this right more certain, than that of the States, in the same character and capacity, to decide on the mode and measure to be adopted to arrest the act, and prevent the encroachment on the reserved powers. It is a right indispensable to all the others, and, without which, they would be valueless. . . .

But, suppose it should prove otherwise; and that the negative power should become so strong as to cause dangerous derangements and disorders in the system;—the constitution makes ample provisions for their correction,—whether produced by the interposition of a State, or the mutual negative, or conflict of power between the two co-ordinate governments. I refer to the amending power. Why it was necessary to provide for such a power;—what is its nature and character;—why it was modified as it is,—and whether it be safe, and sufficient to effect the objects intended,—are the questions, which I propose next to consider.

It is, as has already been explained, a fundamental principle, in forming such a federal community of States, and establishing such a federal constitution and government as ours, that no State could be bound by its separate ratification and adoption. The principle is essentially connected with the independence and sovereignty of the several States. As the several States, in such a community, with such a constitution and government, still retained their separate independence and sovereignty, it followed, that the compact into which they entered, could not be altered or changed, in any way, but by the unanimous assent of all the parties, without some express provision authorizing it. But there were strong objections to requiring the consent of all to make alterations or changes in the constitution. Those who formed it were not so vain as to suppose that they had made a perfect instrument; nor so ignorant as not to see, however perfect it might be, that derangements and disorders, resulting from time, circumstances, and the conflicting elements of the system itself, would make amendments necessary. But to leave it, without making some special provision for the purpose, would have been, in effect, to leave it to any one of the States to prevent amendments; which, in practice, would have been almost tantamount to leaving it without any power to amend;—notwithstanding its necessity. And, hence, the subject of making some special provision for amending the constitution, was forced on the attention of the convention.

There was diversity of opinion as to what the nature and character of the amending power should be. All agreed that it should be a modification of the original creative power, which ordained and established the separate constitutions and governments of the several States; and, by which alone, the proposed constitution and government could be ordained and established: or, to express it differently and more explicitly,—that amendments should be the acts of the several States, voting as States,—each counting one,—and not the act of the government. But there was great diversity of opinion as to what *number* of States should be required to concur, or agree, in order to make an amendment. It was first moved to require the consent of all the States. This was followed by a motion to amend requiring *two thirds*; which was overruled by a considerable majority. It was then moved to require the concurrence of *three fourths*, which was agreed to, and finally adopted without dissent.

To understand fully the reasons for so modifying the original creative power, as to require the concurrence of three fourths to make an amendment, it will be necessary to advert to another portion of the proceedings of the convention, intimately connected with the present question. I refer to that which contains a history of its action in regard to the number of States required to ratify the constitution, before it should become binding between those so ratifying it. It is material to state, that although the article in respect to ratifications, which grew out of these proceedings, stands last in the constitution, it was finally agreed on and adopted before the article in regard to amendments;—and had, doubtless, no inconsiderable influence in determining the number of States required for that purpose.

There was, in reference to both, great diversity of opinion as to the requisite number of States. With the exception of one State, all agreed that entire unanimity should not be required; but the majority divided as to the number which should be required. One of the most prominent leaders of the party, originally in favor of a national government, was in favor of requiring only a bare majority of the States. Another, not less distinguished, was in favor of the same proposition; but so modified as to require such majority to contain, also, a majority of the entire population of all the States; and, in default of this, as many additional States as would be necessary to supply the deficiency. On the other hand, the more prominent members of the party in favor of a federal government, inclined to a large number. One of the most influential of these, moved to require ten States; on which motion the convention was nearly equally divided. Finally, the number nine was agree on;—constituting *three fourths* of all the States represented in all the convention,—and, as nearly as might be, of all the States at that time in the Union. . . .

It remains now to be explained why the particular number, between these two extremes, was finally agreed on. Among other reasons, one, doubtless, is to be found in the fact, that the articles of the then existing confederation, required the consent of nine States to give validity to many of the acts of their Congress;—among which, were the acts declaring war,—granting letters of marque and reprisal in time of peace, and emitting bills, or borrowing money on the credit of the United States. The object of requiring so great a number was, to guard against the abuses of these and the other great and delicate powers contained in the provision. A mere majority of the States, was too few to be intrusted with such powers; and, to make the trust more safe, the consent of nine States was required; which was within a small fraction of *three fourths* of the whole number at that time. The precedent,—and the same consideration which induced the legislatures of all the States to assent to it, in adopting the articles of confederation, must have had, undoubtedly, much weight in determining what number of States should ratify the constitution, before it should become binding between them. If the legislatures of all the States should have unanimously deemed it not unreasonable, that the highest and most delicate acts of the old Congress, when agreed to by nine or more States, should be acquiesced in by the others, it was very natural that the members of the convention should think it not unreasonable to require an equal number to give validity to the constitution, as between them;—leaving it to the others to say whether they would ratify or not. Nine, or *three fourths* of the whole, were unquestionably, regarded as a safe and sufficient guaranty against oppression and abuse, both in the highest acts of the confederacy, and in establishing the constitution between the States ratifying it. And it is equally certain that a smaller number was not regarded either as safe, or sufficient.

The force of these precedents, combined with the reasons for adopting them, must have had great weight in determining the proportional number which should be required to amend the constitution. Indeed, after determining the proportion in the provision for the ratification of the constitution, it would seem to follow, as a matter of course, that the same proportion should be required in the provision for amending it. It would be difficult to assign a reason, why the proportion should be different in the two cases; and why, if *three fourths* should be required in the one, it should not also be required in the other. If it would have been unreasonable and improper in the one, that a few States in proportion should, by their obstinacy, prevent the others from forming a constitution,—it would have been equally so, and for the same reason, that the like proportion should have the power to prevent amendments, however necessary they might be to the well working and safety of the system. So, again, if it would have been dangerous and improper, to permit a bare majority of the States, or any proportion less than that required to make the constitution binding as between the States ratifying,—it would have been no less so to permit such number or proportion to amend it. The two are, indeed, nearly allied, and involve, throughout, the same principle;—and hence, the same diversity of opinion between the two parties in the convention, in reference to both, and the adoption of the same proportion of States in each. I say the same proportion,—for although nine States were rather less than *three fourths* of the whole number when the constitution was ratified,—this proportion of the States was required in order to amend it, (without regard to an inconsiderable fraction,) because of the facility of its application.

But independently of these considerations, there were strong reasons for adopting that proportion in providing a power to amend. It was, at least, as necessary to guard against too much facility as too much difficulty, in amending it. If, to require the consent of all the States for that purpose would be, in effect, to prevent amendments which time should disclose to be,—or change of circumstances make necessary;—so, on the other hand, to require a bare majority only, or but a small number in proportion to the whole, would expose the constitution to hasty, inconsiderate, and even sinister amendments, on the part of the party dominant for the time. If the one would give it too much fixedness, the other would deprive it of all stability. Of the two, the latter would be more dangerous than the former. It would defeat the very ends of a constitution, regarded as a fundamental law. Indeed, it would involve a glaring absurdity to require the separate ratification of nine States to make the constitution binding as between them,—and to provide that a mere majority of States, or even a small one, when compared with the whole number, should have the power, as soon as it went into operation, to amend it as they pleased. It would be difficult to find any other proportion better calculated to avoid this absurdity, and, at the same time, the difficulties attending the other extreme, than that adopted by the convention. While it affords sufficient facility, it guards against too much, in amending the constituion,—and thereby unites stability with the capacity of adjusting itself to all such changes as may become necessary; and thus combines all the requisites that are necessary in the amending power. It hardly admits of a doubt, that these combined reasons,—the conviction that it possessed all the requisites for such a power, in a higher degree than any other proportion,—with the force of the two precedents above explained, induced the convention to adopt it.

Possessing these, it possesses all the requisites, of course, to render the power at once safe in itself, and sufficient to effect the objects for which it was intended. It is safe; because the proportion is sufficiently large to prevent a dominant portion of the Union, or combination of the States, from using the amending power as an instrument to make changes in the constitution, adverse to the interests and rights of the weaker portion of the Union, or a minority of the States. It may not, in this respect, be as perfectly safe as it would be in the unmodified state in which it ordained and established the constitution; but, for all practical purposes, it is believed to be safe as an *amending* power. It is difficult to conceive a case, where so large a portion as *three fourths* of the States would undertake to insert a power, by way of amendment, which, instead of improving and perfecting the constitution, would deprive the remaining *fourth* of any right, essentially belonging to them as members of the Union, or clearly intended to oppress them. There are many powers, which a dominant combination of States would assume by *construction*, and use for the purpose of aggrandizement, which they would not dare to propose to insert as amendments. But should an attempt be successfully made to engraft an amendment for such a purpose, the case would not be without remedy, as will be shown in the proper place.

I say, as large a proportion as *three fourths*;—for the larger the proportion required to do an act, the less is the danger of the power being used for the purpose of oppression and aggrandizement. The reason is plain. With the increase of the proportion, the difficulty of so using it, is increased;—while the inducement is diminished in the same proportion. The former is increased;—because the difficulty of forming combinations for such purpose is increased with the increase of the number required to combine; and the latter decreased, because the greater the number to be aggrandized, and the less the number, by whose oppression this can be effected, the less the inducement to oppression. And hence, by increasing the proportion, the number to be aggrandized may be made so large, and the number to be oppressed so small, as to make the effort bootless;—when the motive to oppress, as well as to abuse power will, of course, cease.

But, while *three fourths* furnish a safe proportion against making changes in the constitution, under the color of amendments, by the dominant portion of the Union, with a view to oppress the weaker for its aggrandizement, the proportion is equally safe, in view of the opposite danger;—as it furnishes a sufficient protection against the combination of a few States to prevent the rest from making such amendments as may become necessary to preserve or perfect it. It thus guards against the dangers, to which a less, or greater proportion might expose the system.

It is not less sufficient than safe to effect the object intended. As a modification of the power which ordained and established the system, its authority is above all others, except itself in its simple and absolute form. Within its appropriate sphere,—that of amending the constitution,—all others are subject to its control, and may be modified, changed and altered at its pleasure. Within that sphere it truly represents the intention of the power, of which it is a modification, when it ordained and established the constitution,—as to the limits to which the system might be safely and properly extended, and beyond which it could not. The same wisdom, which saw the necessity of having as much harmony as possible, in ratifying the constitution, saw, also, the necessity of preserving it, after it went into operation; and therefore required the same proportion of States to make an amendment, as to ratify the instrument, before it could become binding between the States ratifying. It saw, that, if there was danger from *too little*, there was also danger from *too much* union (if I may be allowed so to express myself);—and that, while one led to weakness, the other led to discord and alienation. To guard against each, it so modified the amending power as to avoid both extremes,— and thus to preserve the equilibrium of the powers of the system as originally established, so far as human contrivance could.

Thus the power which, in its simple and absolute form, was the creator, becomes, in its modified form, the preserver of the system. By no other device, nor in any other form, could the high functions appertaining to this character, be safely and efficiently discharged;—and by none other could the system be preserved. It is, when properly understood, the *vis medicatrix* of the system;—its great repairing, healing, and conservative power;—intended to remedy its disorders, in whatever cause or causes originating; whether in the original errors or defects of the constitution itself,—or the operation of time and change of circumstances, or in conflicts between its parts,—including those between the co-ordinate governments. By it alone, can the equilibrium of the various powers and divisions of the system be preserved; as by it alone, can the stronger be prevented from encroaching on, and finally absorbing the weaker. For this purpose, it is, as has been shown, entirely safe and all-sufficient. In performing its high functions, it acts, not as a judicial power, but in the far more elevated and authoritative character of an *amending* power;—the only one in which it can be called into action at all. In this character, it can amend the constitution, by modifying its existing provisions;—or, in case of a disputed power, whether it be between the federal government and one of its co-ordinates,—or between the former and an interposing State,—by declaring, authoritatively, what is the constitution.

Having now explained the nature and object of the amending power, and shown its safety and sufficiency, in respect to the object for which it was provided;—I shall next proceed to show, that it is the duty of the federal government to invoke its aid, should any dangerous derangement or disorder result from the mutual negative of the two co-ordinate governments, or from the interposition of a State, in its sovereign character, to arrest one of its acts,—in case all other remedies should fail to adjust the difficulty.

In order to form a clear conception of the true ground and reason of this duty, it is necessary to premise, that it is difficult to conceive of a case, where a conflict of power could take place between the government of a State, or the State itself in its sovereign character, and the federal government, in which the former would not be in a minority of the States and of their population, estimate in federal numbers; and, of course, the latter is a majority of both. The reason is obvious. If it were otherwise, the remedy would at once be applied through the federal government,—by a repeal of the act asserting the power,—and the question settled by yielding it to the State. Such being the case, the conflict, whenever it takes place, must be between the reserved and delegated powers; the latter, supported by a majority both of the States and of their population, claiming the right to exercise the power,—and the former, by a State constituting one of the minority,—(at least as far as it relates to the power in controversy,)—denying the claim.

Now it is a clear and well established principle, that the party who claims the right to exercise a power, is bound to make it good, against the party denying the right; and that, if there should be an authority higher than either provided, by which the question between them can be adjusted, he, in such case, has no right to assert his claim on his own authority,—

but is bound to appeal to the tribunal appointed, according to the forms prescribed, and to establish and assert his right through its authority.

If a principle, so clear and well established, should, in a case like the one supposed, require confirmation,—it may be found in the fact, that the powers of the federal government are all enumerated and specified in the constitution;—while those belonging to the States embrace the whole residuary mass of powers, not enumerated and specified. Hence, in a conflict of power between the two, the presumption is in favor of the latter, and against the former; and, therefore, it is doubly bound to establish the power in controversy, through the appointed authority, before it can rightfully undertake to exercise is.

But as conclusive as these reasons are, there are others not less so. Among these, it may be stated, that the federal government, being of the party of the majority in such conflicts, may, at pleasure, make the appeal to the amending power; while the State, being of the party of the minority, cannot possibly do so. The reason is plain. To make it, requires, on the part of the State, more than a bare majority. It would then be absurd, to transfer the duty from the party of the majority, which has the power, to that of the minority, which has it not:—and this, too, when, with such a majority, the question of power could be settled in its favor, more easily and promptly, through the federal government itself.

There is also another reason,—if not more conclusive, yet of deeper import. The federal government never will make an appeal to the amending power, in a case of conflict, unless compelled;—nor, indeed, willingly in any case, except with a view to enlarge the powers it has usurped by construction. The only means, by which it can be compelled to make an appeal, are the negative powers of the constitution;—and especially, so far as the reserved powers are concerned,—by that of its co-ordinates,—and State interposition. But to transfer the duty from itself to the States, would, necessarily, have the effect, so far as they are concerned, of leaving it in the full and quiet exercise of the contested power, until the appeal was made and finally acted on;—instead of suspending the exercise of the power, until the decision was pronounced;—as would be the case, if the duty were not transferred. In the latter case, it would have every motive to exert itself to make the appeal, and to obtain a speedy and final action in its favor, if possible; but in the former, it would be the reverse. The motive would be to use every effort to prevent a successful appeal and to defeat action on it; as, in the mean time, it would be left in full possession of the power in question. Nor would it have any difficulty in effecting what it desired; as it would be impossible for the State, even without opposition, to succeed in making an appeal, for the reason already assigned.

Its effect would be a revolution in the character of the system. It would virtually destroy the relation of co-ordinates between the federal government and those of the several States, by rendering the negative of the latter, in case of conflict with it, of no effect. It would supersede and render substantially obsolete, not only the amending power, but the original sovereign power of the several States, as parties to the constitutional compact,—by making them, also, of no effect; and, thereby, elevate the federal government to the absolute and supreme authority of the system, with liberty to assume, by construction, whatever power the cupidity or ambition of a dominant party or section might crave.

It would, in a word, practically transform the federal, into a consolidated national government, against the avowed intention of its framers,—the plain meaning of the constitution itself,—and the understanding of the people of the States, when they ratified and adopted it. Such a result is, itself, the strongest, the most conclusive argument against the position. If there were none other, this, of itself, would be ample to prove, that it is the duty of the federal government to invoke the action of the amending power, by proposing a declaratory amendment affirming the power it claims, according to the forms prescribed in the constitution; and, if it fail, to abandon the power.

On the other hand, should it succeed in obtaining the amendment, the act of the government of the separate State which caused the conflict, and operated as a negative on the act of the federal government, would, in all cases, be overruled; and the latter become operative within its limits. But the result is, in some respects, different,—where a State acting in her sovereign character, and as a party to constitutional compact, has interposed, and declared an act of the federal government to be unauthorized by the constitution,—and, therefore, null and void. In this case, if the act of the latter be predicated on a power consistent with the character of the constitution, the ends for which it was established, and the nature of our system of government;—or, more briefly, if it come fairly within the scope of the amending power, the State is bound to acquiesce, by the solemn obligation which it contracted, in ratifying the constitution. But if it transcends the limits of the amending power,—be inconsistent with the character of the constitution and the ends for which it was established,—or with the nature of the sytem,—the result is different. In such case, the State is not bound to acquiesce. It may choose whether it will, or whether it will not secede from the Union. One or the other course it must take. To refuse acquiescence, would be tantamount to secession; and place it as entirely in the relation of a foreign State to the other States, as would a positive act of secession. That a State, as a party to the constitutional compact, has the right to secede,—acting in the same capacity in which it ratified the constitution,— cannot, with any show of reason, be denied by any one who regards the constitution as a compact,—if a power should be inserted by the amending power, which would radically change the character of the constitution, or the nature of the system; or if the former should fail to fulfil the ends for which it was established. This results, necessarily, from the nature of a compact,—where the parties to it are sovereign; and, of course, have no higher authority to which to appeal. That the effect of secession would be to place her in the relation of a foreign State to the others, is equally clear. Nor is it less so, that it would make here, (not her citizens *individually*,) responsible to them, in that character. All this results, necessarily, from the nature of a compact between sovereign parties.

3.7 Thomas Jefferson Renews His Plea for Periodical Amendment*

The readings in the previous chapter have already demonstrated that Thomas Jefferson's views on constitutional change were more liberal than those of James Madison. Although Madison had responded to Jefferson's idea that "the earth belongs in usufruct to the living" with what many would consider to be forceful refutation, Jefferson continued to advocate constitutional change, especially at the state level. Jefferson treated this subject in the following letter, written over twenty-five years after his correspondence with Madison, in which he proposed that Virginia be divided into a number of wards by which the opinion of the people could be collected and in which he indicated that constitutions were not sacred objects to be revered but instruments to protect the public good..

Desirable Amendments

The sum of these amendments is, 1. General Suffrage. 2. Equal representation in the legislature. 3. An executive chosen by the people. 4. Judges elective or amovable. 5. Justices, jurors, and sheriffs elective. 6. Ward divisions. And 7. Periodical amendments of the constitution.

I have thrown out these as loose heads of amendment, for consideration and correction; and their object is to secure self-government by the republicanism of our constitution, as well as by the spirit of the people; and to nourish and perpetuate that spirit. I am not among those who fear the people. They, and not the rich, are our dependence for continued freedom. And to preserve their independence, we must not let our rulers load us with perpetual debt. We must make our election between *economy and liberty*, or *profusion and servitude*. If we run into such debts, as that we must be taxed in our meat and in our drink, in our necessaries and our comforts, in our labors and our amusements, for our callings and our creeds, as the people of England are, our people, like them, must come

---

* Letter to Samuel Kercheval, July 12, 1816. *The Works of Thomas Jefferson*, ed. Paul L. Ford (C.P. Putnam's Sons: New York: The Knickerbocker Press, 1905), vol. 12, pp. 9-14.

to labor sixteen hours in the twenty-four, give the earnings of fifteen of these to the government for their debts and daily expenses; and the sixteenth being insufficient to afford us bread, we must live, as they now do, on oatmeal and potatoes; have no time to think, no means of calling the mismanagers to account; but be glad to obtain subsistence by hiring ourselves to rivet their chains on the necks of our fellow-suffers. . . .

Some men look at constitutions with sanctimonious reverence, and deem them like the arc [sic] of the covenant, too sacred to be touched. They ascribe to the men of the preceding age a wisdom more than human, and suppose what they did to be beyond amendment. I knew that age well; I belonged to it, and labored with it. It deserved well of its country. It was very like the present, but without the experience of the present; and forty years of experience in government is worth a century of book-reading; and this they would say themselves, were they to rise from the dead. I am certainly not an advocate for frequent and untried changes in laws and constitutions. I think moderate imperfections had better be borne with; because, when once known, we accommodate ourselves to them, and find practical means of correcting their ill effects. But I know also, that laws and institutions must go hand in hand with the progress of the human mind. As that becomes more developed, more enlightened, as new discoveries are made, new truths disclosed, and manners and opinions change with the change of circumstances, institutions must advance also, and keep pace with the times. We might as well require a man to wear still the coat which fitted him when a boy, as civilized society to remain ever under the regimen of their barbarous ancestors. It is this preposterous idea which has lately deluged Europe in blood. Their monarchs, instead of wisely yielding to the gradual change of circumstances, of favoring progressive accommodation to progressive improvement, have clung to old abuses, entrenched themselves behind steady habits, and obliged their subjects to seek through blood and violence rash and ruinous innovations, which, had they been referred to the peaceful deliberations and collected wisdom of the nation, would have been put into acceptable and salutary forms. Let us follow no such examples, nor weakly believe that one generation is not as capable as another of taking care of itself, and of ordering its own affairs. Let us, as our sister States have done, avail ourselves of our reason and experience, to correct the crude essays of our first and unexperienced, although wise, virtuous, and well-meaning councils. And lastly, let us provide in our constitution for its revision at stated periods. What these periods should be, nature herself indicates. By the European tables of mortality, of the adults living at any one moment of time, a majority will be dead in about nineteen years. At the end of that period, then, a new majority is come into place; or, in other words, a new generation. Each generation is as independent as the one preceding, as that was of all which had gone before. It has then, like them, a right to choose for itself the form of government it believes most promotive of its own happiness; consequently, to accommodate to the circumstances in which it finds itself, that received from its predecessors; and it is for the peace and good of mankind that a solemn opportunity of doing this every nineteen or twenty years, should be provided by the constitution; so that it may be handed on, with periodical repairs, from generation to generation, to the end of time, if anything human can so long endure. It is now forty years since the constitution of Virginia was formed. The same tables inform us, that, within that period, two-thirds of the adults then living are now dead. Have then the remaining third, even if they had the wish, the right to hold in obedience to their will, and to laws heretofore made by them, the other two-thirds, who, with themselves, compose the present mass of adults? If they have not, who has? The dead? But the dead have no rights. They are nothing; and nothing cannot own something. Where there is no substance, there can be no accident. This corporeal globe, and everything upon it, belong to its present corporeal inhabitants, during their generation. They alone have a right to direct what is the concern of themselves alone, and to declare the law of that direction; and this declaration can only be made by their majority. That majority, then, has a right to depute representatives to a convention, and to make the constitution what they think will be the best for themselves. But how collect their voice? This is the real difficulty. If invited by private authority, or county or district meetings, these divisions are so large that few will attend; and their voice will be imperfectly, or falsely pronounced. Here, then, would be one of the advantages of the ward divisions I have proposed. The mayor of every ward, on a question like the present, would call his ward together, take the simple yea or nay of its members, convey these to the county court, who would hand on those of all its wards to the proper general authority; and the voice of the whole people would be thus fairly, fully, and peaceably expressed, discussed, and decided by the common reason of the society. If this avenue be shut to the call of sufferance, it will make itself heard through that of force, and we shall go on, as other nations are doing, in the endless circle of oppression, rebellion, reformation; and oppression, rebellion, reformation, again; and so on forever.

3.8 John Marshall Articulates the Need for an Enduring Constitution*

One of the most important cases of the nineteenth century was John Marshall's decision in *McCulloch v. Maryland*. This case arose when the state of Maryland attempted to tax a branch of the national bank which had been established in Baltimore. At issue were two questions: Did the national government have the authority to establish a national bank? and, Did Maryland have the right to tax it? Marshall answered the first question in the affirmative and the second in the negative.

The following selection is from Marshall's answer to the first question. Marshall drew conclusions from the ratification of the Constitution consistent with his own nationalism. Moreover, by giving Congress broad authority to enact legislation under the necessary and proper clause, he made it less necessary to resort to frequent amendments and indicated that the Constitution should be interpreted differently from a legal code. This interpretation, much different from the "strict construction" generally advocated, although arguably not always

* *McCulloch v. Maryland*, 17 U.S. 316 (1819), 402-21.

practiced by Thomas Jefferson and fellow Democratic Republicans, has undoubtedly made the adoption of amendments less necessary than would otherwise be required.

The Constitution and the Bank

The Convention which framed the constitution was indeed elected by the State legislatures. But the instrument, when it came from their hands, was a mere proposal, without obligation, or pretensions to it. It was reported to the then existing Congress of the United States, with a request that it might "be submitted to a Convention of Delegates, chosen in each State by the people thereof, under the recommendation of its Legislature, for their assent and ratification." This mode of proceeding was adopted; and by the Convention, by Congress, and by the State Legislatures, the instrument was submitted to the people. They acted upon it in the only manner in which they can act safely, effectively, and wisely, on such a subject, by assembling in Convention. It is true, they assembled in their several States—and where else should they have assembled? No political dreamer was ever wild enough to think of breaking down the lines which separate the States, and of compounding the American people into one common mass. Of consequence, when they act, they act in their States. But the measures they adopt do not, on that account, cease to be the measures of the people themselves, or become the measures of the State governments.

From these Conventions the constitution derives its whole authority. The government proceeds directly from the people; is "ordained and established" in the name of the people; and is declared to be ordained, "in order to form a more perfect union, establish justice, ensure domestic tranquillity, and secure the blessings of liberty to themselves and to their posterity." The assent of the States, in their sovereign capacity, is implied in calling a Convention, and thus submitting that instrument to the people. But the people were at perfect liberty to accept or reject it; and their act was final. It required not the affirmance, and could not be negatived, by the State governments. The constitution, when thus adopted, was of complete obligation, and bound the State sovereignties. . . .

The government of the Union, then, (whatever may be the influence of this fact on the case,) is, emphatically, and truly, a government of the people. In form and in substance it emanates from them. Its powers are granted by them, and are to be exercised directly on them, and for their benefit.

This government is acknowledged by all to be one of enumerated powers. The principle, that it can exercise only the powers granted to it, would seem too apparent to have required to be enforced by all those arguments which its enlightened friends, while it was depending before the people, found it necessary to urge. That principle is now universally admitted. But the question respecting the extent of the powers actually granted, is perpetually arising, and will probably continue to arise, as long as our system shall exist.

In discussing these questions, the conflicting powers of the general and State governments must be brought into view, and the supremacy of their respective laws, when they are in opposition, must be settled.

If any one proposition could command the universal assent of mankind, we might expect it would be this—that the government of the Union, though limited in its powers, is supreme within its sphere of action. This would seem to result necessarily from its nature. It is the government of all; its powers are delegated by all; it represents all, and acts for all. Though any one State may be willing to control its operations, no State is willing to allow others to control them. The nation, on those subjects on which it can act, must necessarily bind its component parts. But this question is not left to mere reason: the people have, in express terms, decided it, by saying, "this constitution, and the laws of the United States, which shall be made in pursuance thereof," "shall be the supreme law of the land," and by requiring that the members of the State legislatures, and the officers of the executive and judicial departments of the States, shall take the oath of fidelity to it.

The government of the United States, then, though limited in its powers, is supreme; and its laws, when made in pursuance of the constitution, form the supreme law of the land, "any thing in the constitution or laws of any State to the contrary notwithstanding."

Among the enumerated powers, we do not find that of establishing a bank or creating a corporation. But there is no phrase in the instrument which, like the articles of confederation, excludes incidental or implied powers; and which requires that every thing granted shall be expressly and minutely described. Even the 10th amendment, which was framed for the purpose of quieting the excessive jealousies which had been excited, omits the words "expressly," and declares only that the powers "not delegated to the United States, nor prohibited to the States, are reserved to the States or to the people;" thus leaving the question, whether the particular power which may become the subject of contest has been delegated to the one government, or prohibited to the other, to depend on a fair construction of the whole instrument. The men who drew and adopted this amendment had experienced the embarrassments resulting from the insertion of this word in the articles of confederation, and probably omitted it to avoid those embarrassments. A constitution, to contain an accurate detail of all the subdivisions of which its great powers will admit, and of all the means by which they may be carried into execution, would partake of the prolixity of a legal code, and could scarcely be embraced by the human mind. It would probably never be understood by the public. Its nature, therefore, requires, that only its great outlines should be marked, its important objects designated, and the minor ingredients which compose those objects be deduced from the nature of the objects themselves. That this idea was entertained by the framers of the American constitution, is not only to be inferred from the nature of the instrument, but from the language. Why else were some of the limitations, found in the ninth section of the 1st article, introduced? It is also, in some degree, warranted by their having omitted to use any restrictive term which might prevent its receiving a fair and just interpretation. In considering this question, then, we must never forget, that it is *a constitution* we are expounding.

Although, among the enumerated powers of government, we do not find the word "bank" or "incorporation," we find the great powers to lay and collect taxes; to borrow money; to regulate commerce; to declare and conduct a war; and to raise and support armies and navies. The sword and the purse, all the external relations, and no inconsiderable portion of the industry of the nation, are entrusted to its government. It can never be pretended that these vast powers draw after them others of inferior importance, merely because they are inferior. Such an idea can never be advanced. But it may with great reason be contended, that a government, entrusted with such ample powers, on the due execution of which the happiness and prosperity of the nation so vitally depends, must also be entrusted with ample means for their execution. The power being given, it is the interest of the nation to facilitate its execution. It can never be their interest, and cannot be presumed to have been their intention, to clog and embarrass its execution by withholding the most appropriate means. Throughout this vast republic, from the St. Croix to the Gulph [sic] of Mexico, from the Atlantic to the Pacific, revenue is to be collected and expended, armies are to be marched and supported. The exigencies of the nation may require that the treasure raised in the north should be transported to the south, *that* raised in the east conveyed to the west, or that this order should be reversed. Is that construction of the constitution to be preferred which would render these operations difficult, hazardous, and expensive? Can we adopt that construction, (unless the words imperiously require it,) which would impute to the framers of that instrument, when granting these powers for the public good, the intention of impeding their exercise by withholding a choice of means? If, indeed, such be the mandate of the constitution, we have only to obey; but that instrument does not profess to enumerate the means by which the powers it confers may be executed; nor does it prohibit the creation of a corporation, if the existence of such a being be essential to the beneficial exercise of those powers. It is, then, the subject of fair inquiry, how far such means may be employed.

It is not denied, that powers given to the government imply the ordinary means of execution. That, for example, of raising revenue, and applying it to national purposes, is admitted to imply the power of conveying money from place to place, as the exigencies of the nation may require, and of employing the usual means of conveyance. But it is denied that the government has its choice of means; or, that it may employ the most convenient means, if, to employ them, it be necessary to erect a corporation.

On what foundation does this argument rest? On this alone: The power of creating a corporation, is one appertaining to sovereignty, and is not expressly conferred on Congress. This is true. But all legislative powers appertain to sovereignty. The original power of giving the law on any subject whatever, is a sovereign power; and if the government of the Union is restrained from creating a corporation, as a means for performing its functions, on the single reason that the creation of a corporation is an act of sovereignty; if the sufficiency of this reason be acknowledged, there would be some difficulty in sustaining the authority of Congress to pass other laws for the accomplishment of the same objects.

The government which has a right to do an act, and has imposed on it the duty of performing that act, must, according to the dictates of reason, be allowed to select the means; and those who contend that it may not select any appropriate means, that one particular mode of effecting the object is excepted, take upon themselves the burden of establishing that exception.

The creation of a corporation, it is said, appertains to sovereignty. This is admitted. But to what portion of sovereignty does it appertain? Does it belong to one more than to another? In America, the powers of sovereignty are divided between the government of the Union, and those of the States. They are each sovereign, with respect to the objects committed to it, and neither sovereign with respect to the objects committed to the other. We cannot comprehend that train of reasoning which would maintain, that the extent of power granted by the people is to be ascertained, not by the nature and terms of the grant, but by its date. Some State constitutions were formed *before*, some *since* that of the United States. We cannot believe that their relation to each other is in any degree dependent upon this circumstance. Their respective powers must, we think, be precisely the same as if they had been formed at the same time. Had they been formed at the same time, and had the people conferred on the general government the power contained in the constitution, and on the States the whole residuum of power, would it have been asserted that the government of the Union was not sovereign with respect to those objects which were entrusted to it, in relation to which its laws were declared to be supreme? If this could not have been asserted, we cannot well comprehend the process of reasoning which maintains, that a power appertaining to sovereignty cannot be connected with that vast portion of it which is granted to the general government, so far as it is calculated to subserve the legitimate objects of that government. The power of creating a corporation, though appertaining to sovereignty, is not, like the power of making war, or levying taxes, or of regulating commerce, a great substantive and independent power, which cannot be implied as incidental to other powers, or used as a means of executing them. It is never the end for which other powers are exercised, but a means by which other objects are accomplished. No contributions are made to charity for the sake of an incorporation, but a corporation is created to administer the charity; no seminary of learning is instituted in order to be incorporated, but the corporate character is conferred to subserve the purposes of education. No city was every built with the sole object of being incorporated, but is incorporated as affording the best means of being well governed. The power of creating a corporation is never used for its own sake, but for the purpose of effecting something else. No sufficient reason is, therefore, perceived, why it may not pass as incidental to those powers which are expressly given, if it be a direct mode of executing them.

But the constitution of the United States has not left the right of Congress to employ the necessary means, for the execution of the powers conferred on the government, to general reasoning. To its enumeration of powers is added that of making "all laws which shall be necessary and proper, for carrying into execution the foregoing powers, and all other powers vested by this constitution, in the government of the United States, or in any department thereof."

The counsel for the State of Maryland have urged various arguments, to prove that this clause, though in terms a grant of power, is not so in effect; but is really restrictive of the general right, which might otherwise be implied, of selecting means for executing the enumerated powers.

In support of this proposition, they have found it necessary to contend, that this clause was inserted for the purpose of conferring on Congress the power of making laws. That, without it, doubts might be entertained, whether Congress could exercise its powers in the form of legislation.

But could this be the object for which it was inserted? A government is created by the people, having legislative, executive, and judicial powers. Its legislative powers are vested in a Congress, which is to consist of a Senate and House of Representatives. Each house may determine the rule of its proceedings; and it is declared that every bill which shall have passed both houses, shall, before it becomes a law, be presented to the President of the United States. The 7th section describes the course of proceedings, by which a bill shall become a law; and, then, the 8th section enumerates the powers of Congress. Could it be necessary to say, that a legislature should exercise legislative powers, in the shape of legislation? After allowing each house to prescribe its own course of proceeding, after describing the manner in which a bill should become a law, would it have entered into the mind of a single member of the Convention, that an express power to make laws was necessary to enable the legislature to make them? That a legislature, endowed with legislative powers, can legislate, is a proposition too self-evident to have been questioned.

But the argument on which most reliance is placed, is drawn from the peculiar language of this clause. Congress is not empowered by it to make all laws, which may have relations to the powers conferred on the government, but such only as may be "*necessary and proper*" for carrying them into execution. The word "*necessary*," is considered as controlling the whole sentence, and as limiting the right to pass laws for the execution of the granted powers, to such as are indispensable, and without which the power would be nugatory. That it excludes the choice of means, and leaves to Congress, in each case, that only which is most direct and simple.

Is it true, that this is the sense in which the word "necessary" is always used? Does it always import an absolute physical necessity, so strong, that one thing, to which another may be termed necessary, cannot exist without that other? We think it does not. If reference be had to its use, in the common affairs of the world, or in approved authors, we find that it frequently imports no more than that one thing is convenient, or useful, or essential to another. To employ the means necessary to an end, is generally understood as employing any means calculated to produce the end, and not as being confined to those single means, without which the end would be entirely unattainable. Such is the character of human language, that no word conveys to the mind, in all situations, one single definite idea; and nothing is more common than to use words in a figurative sense. Almost all compositions contain words, which, taken in their rigorous sense, would convey a meaning different from that which is obviously intended. It is essential to just construction, that many words which import something excessive, should be understood in a more mitigated sense—in that sense which common usage justifies. The word "necessary" is of this description. It has not a fixed character peculiar to itself. It admits of all degrees of comparison; and is often connected with other words, which increase or diminish the impression the mind receives of the urgency it imports. A thing may be necessary, very necessary, absolutely or indispensably necessary. To no mind would the same idea be conveyed, by these several phrases. This comment on the word is well illustrated, by the passage cited at the bar, from the 10th section of the 1st article of the constitution. It is, we think, impossible to compare the sentence which prohibits a State from laying "imposts, or duties on imports or exports, except what may be *absolutely* necessary for executing its inspection laws," with that which authorizes Congress "to make all laws which shall be necessary and proper for carrying into execution" the powers of the general government, without feeling conviction that the convention understood itself to change materially the meaning of the word "necessary," by prefixing the word "absolutely." This word, then, like others, is used in various senses; and, in its construction, the subject, the context, the intention of the person using them, are all to be taken into view.

Let this be done in the case under consideration. The subject is the execution of those great powers on which the welfare of a nation essentially depends. It must have been the intention of those who gave these powers, to insure, as far as human prudence could insure, their beneficial execution. This could not be done by confiding the choice of means to such narrow limits as not to leave it in the power of Congress to adopt any which might be appropriate, and which were conducive to the end. This provision is made in a constitution intended to endure for ages to come, and, consequently, to be adapted to the various *crises* of human affairs. To have prescribed the means by which government should, in all future times, execute its powers, would have been to change, entirely, the character of the instrument, and give it the properties of a legal code. It would have been an unwise attempt to provide, by immutable rules, for exigencies which, if foreseen at all, must have been seen dimly, and which can be best provided for as they occur. To have declared that the best means shall not be used, but those alone without which the power given would be negatory, would have been to deprive the legislature of the capacity to avail itself of experience, to exercise its reason, and to accommodate its legislation to circumstances. If we apply this principle of construction to any of the powers of the government, we shall find it so pernicious in its operation that we shall be compelled to disgard it. . . .

In ascertaining the sense in which the word "necessary" is used in this clause of the constitution, we may derive some aid from that with which it is associated. Congress shall have power "to make all laws which shall be necessary and *proper* to carry into execution" the power of the government. If the word "necessary" was used in that strict and rigorous sense for which the counsel for the State of Maryland contend, it would be an extraordinary departure from the usual course of the human mind, as exhibited in composition, to add a word, the only possible effect of which is to qualify that strict and rigorous meaning; to present to the mind the idea of some choice of means of legislation not straitened and compressed within the narrow limits for which gentlemen content.

But the argument which most conclusively demonstrates the error of the construction contended for by the counsel for the state of Maryland, is founded on the intention of the Convention, as manifested in the whole clause. To waste time and argument in proving that, without it, Congress might carry its powers into execution, would be not much less idle than to hold a lighted taper to the sun. As little can it be required to prove, that in the absence of this clause, Congress would have some choice of means. That it might employ those which, in its judgment, would most advantageously effect the object to be accomplished. That any means adapted to the end, any means which tended directly to the execution of the constitutional powers of the government, were in themselves constitutional. This clause, as construed by the State of Maryland, would abridge, and almost annihilate this useful and necessary right of the legislature to select its means. That this could not be intended, is, we should think, had it not been already controverted, too apparent for controversy. We think so for the following reasons:

1st. The clause is placed among the powers of Congress, not among the limitations on those powers.

2nd. Its terms purport to enlarge, not to diminish the powers vested in the government. It purports to be an additional power, not a restriction on those already granted. No reason has been, or can be assigned for thus concealing an intention to narrow the discretion of the national legislature under words which purport to enlarge it. The framers of the constitution wished its adoption, and well knew that it would be endangered by its strength, not by its weakness. Had they been capable of using language which would convey to the eye one idea, and, after deep reflection, impress on the mind another, they would rather have disguised the grant of power, than its limitation. If, then, their intention had been, by this clause, to restrain the free use of means which might otherwise have been implied, that intention would have been inserted in another place, and would have been expressed in terms resembling these. "In carrying into execution the foregoing powers, and all others," & c. "no laws shall be passed but such as are necessary and proper." Had the intention been to make this clause restrictive, it would unquestionably have been so in form as well as in effect.

The result of the most careful and attentive consideration bestowed upon this clause is, that if it does not enlarge, it cannot be construed to restrain the powers of Congress, or to impair the right of the legislature to exercise its best judgment in the selection of measures to carry into execution the constitutional powers of the government. If no other motive for its insertion can be suggested, a sufficient one is found in the desire to remove all doubts respecting the right to legislate on that vast mass of incidental powers which must be involved in the constitution, if that instrument be not a splendid bauble.

We admit, as all must admit, that the powers of the government are limited, and that its limits are not to be transcended. But we think the sound construction of the constitution must allow to the national legislature that discretion, with respect to the means by which the powers it confers are to be carried into execution, which will enable that body to perform the high duties assigned to it, in the manner most beneficial to the people. Let the end be legitimate, let it be within the scope of the constitution, and all means which are appropriate, which are plainly adapted to that end, which are not prohibited, but consist with the letter and spirit of the constitution, are constitutional.

3.9 Joseph Story Praises the Amending Process as a Safety Valve*

One of the Constitution's most astute commentators was Joseph Story (1799-1845), Associate Justice of the Supreme Court from 1812-1845 and Professor of Law at Harvard Uni-

---

* Joseph Story, *Commentaries on the Constitution of the United States*, intro by Ronald D. Rotunda and John E. Nowak (Durham: Carolina Academic Press, 1987), pp. 678-82.

versity from 1819 until his death. The following description of the amending process indicates that, long after the Constitution was ratified, its supporters continued to point to Article V as an appropriate mechanism for bringing about necessary constitutional changes without providing for hasty or precipitate alterations. This reading presents an interesting contrast to readings by Sidney George Fisher (Reading 4.4) and John W. Burgess (Reading 5.3) later in this book.

Description and Defense of Article V

The fifth article of the constitution respects the mode of making amendments to it. [Story quotes Article V.]

Upon this subject little need be said to persuade us, at once, of its utility and importance. It is obvious, that no human government can ever be perfect; and that it is impossible to foresee, or guard against all the exigencies, which may, in different ages, require different adaptations and modifications of powers to suit the various necessities of the people. A government, forever changing and changeable, is, indeed, in a state bordering upon anarchy and confusion. A government, which, in its own organization, provides no means of change, but assumes to be fixed and unalterable, must, after a while, become wholly unsuited to the circumstances of the nation; and it will either degenerate into a despotism, or by the pressure of its inequalities bring on a revolution. It is wise, therefore, in every government, and especially in a republic, to provide means for altering, and improving the fabric of government, as time and experience, or the new phases of human affairs, may render proper, in order to promote the happiness and safety of the people. The great principle to be sought is to make the changes practicable, but not too easy; to secure due deliberation, and caution; and to follow experience, rather than to open a way for experiments, suggested by mere speculation or theory.

In regard to the constitution of the United States, it is confessedly a new experiment in the history of nations. Its framers were not bold or rash enough to believe, or to pronounce it to be perfect. They made use of the best lights, which they possessed, to form and adjust its parts, and mould its materials. But they knew, that time might develope many defects in its arrangements, and many deficiencies in its powers. They desired, that it might be open to improvement; and under the guidance of the sober judgment and enlightened skill of the country, to be perpetually approaching nearer and nearer to perfection. It was obvious, too, that the means of amendment might avert, or at least have a tendency to avert, the most serious perils, to which confederated republics are liable, and by which all of them have hitherto been shipwrecked. They knew, that the besetting sin of republics is a restlessness of temperament, and a spirit of discontent at slight evils. They knew the pride and jealousy of state power in confederacies; and they wished to disarm them of their potency, by providing a safe means to break the force, if not wholly to ward off the blows, which would, from time to time, under the garb of patriotism, or a love of the people, be aimed at the constitution. They believed, that the power of amendment was, if one may so say, the safety valve to let off all temporary effervescences and excitements; and the real effective instrument to control and adjust the movements of the machinery, when out of order, or in danger of self-destruction.

Upon the propriety of the power, in some form, there will probably be little controversy. The only question is, whether it is so arranged, as to accomplish its objects in the safest mode; safest for the stability of the government; and safest for the rights and liberties of the people.

Two modes are pointed out, the one at the instance of the government itself, through the instrumentality of congress; the other, at the instance of the states, through the instrumentality of a convention. Congress, whenever two thirds of each house shall concur in the expediency of an amendment, may propose it for adoption. The legislatures of two thirds of the states may require a convention to be called, for the purpose of proposing amendments. In each case, three fourths of the states, either through their legislatures, or conventions, called for the purpose, must concur in every amendment, before it becomes a part of the constitution. That this mode of obtaining amendments is practicable, is abundantly demonstrated by our past experience in the only mode hitherto found necessary, that of amendments proposed by congress. In this mode twelve amendments have already been incorporated into the constitution. The guards, too, against the too hasty exercise of the power, under temporary discontents or excitements, are apparently sufficient. Two thirds of congress, or of the legislatures of the states, must concur in proposing, or requiring amendments to be proposed; and three fourths of the states must ratify them. Time is thus allowed, and ample time, for deliberation, both in proposing and ratifying amendments. They cannot be carried by surprise, or intrigue, or artifice. Indeed, years may elapse before a deliberate judgment may be passed upon them, unless some pressing emergency calls for instant action. An amendment, which has the deliberate judgment of two-thirds of congress, and of three fourths of the states, can scarcely be deemed unsuited to the prosperity, or security of the republic. It must combine as much wisdom and experience in its favour, as ordinarily can belong to the management of any human concerns. In England the supreme power of the nation resides in parliament; and, in a legal sense, it is so omnipotent, that it has authority to change the whole structure of the constitution, without resort to any confirmation of the people. There is, indeed, little danger, that it will so do, as long as the people are fairly represented in it. But still it does, theoretically speaking, possess the power; and it has actually exercised it so far, as to change the succession to the crown, and mould to its will some portions of the internal structure of the constitution.

Upon the subject of the national constitution, we may adopt without hesitation the language of a learned commentator. "Nor," says he, "can we too much applaud a constitution, which thus provides a safe and peaceable remedy for its own defects, as they may, from time to time, be discovered. A change of government in other countries is almost always attended with convulsions, which threaten its entire dissolution; and with scenes of horror, which deter mankind from every attempt to correct abuses, or remove oppressions, until they have become altogether intolerable. In America we may reasonably hope, that neither of these evils need be apprehended. Nor is there any reason to fear, that this provision in the constitution will produce any instability in the government. The mode, both of originating and ratifying amendments, (in either mode, which the constitution directs,) must necessarily be attended with such obstacles and delays, as must prove a sufficient bar against light or frequent innovations. And, as a further security against them, the same article further provides, that no amendment, which may be made prior to the year 1808, shall, in any manner affect those clauses of the ninth section of the first article, which relate to the migration or importation of such persons, as the states may think proper to allow; and to the manner, in which direct taxes shall be laid; and that no state shall, without its consent, be deprived of its equal suffrage in the senate."

3.10 Alexis de Tocqueville Articulates the Relationship Between the Amending Process and Judicial Review*

One of the most perceptive foreign commentators ever to visit America was the French-born Alexis de Tocqueville (1805-59). The following description, one of the most succinct of its day for articulating the relationship that had developed between judicial review and constitutional amendment, comes amidst Tocqueville's well known discussion of the judicial power and its role in preserving American democracy. Tocqueville begins by comparing the U.S. Constitution to those in England and France.

Three Constitutions Compared

In France the Constitution is, (or at least it is supposed to be) immutable; and the received theory is that no power has the right of changing any part of it. In England the Parliament has an acknowledged right to modify the constitution; as, therefore, the constitution may undergo perpetual changes, it does not in reality exist; the Parliament is at once a legislative and a constituent assembly. The political theories of America

---

* Alexis de Tocqueville, *Democracy in America*, trans. by Henry Reeve, rev. ed. (New York: P. F. Collier & Son, 1900), I, pp. 98-101.

are more simple and more rational. An American constitution is not supposed to be immutable as in France, nor is it susceptible of modification by the ordinary powers of society as in England. It constitutes a detached whole, which, as it represents the determination of the whole people, is no less binding on the legislator than on the private citizen, but which may be altered by the will of the people in predetermined cases, according to established rules. In America the constitution may therefore vary, but as long as it exists it is the origin of all authority, and the sole vehicle of the predominating force.

It is easy to perceive in what manner these differences must act upon the position and the rights of the judicial bodies in the three countries I have cited. If in France the tribunals were authorized to disobey the laws on the ground of their being opposed to the constitution, the supreme power would in fact be placed in their hands, since they alone would have the right of interpreting a constitution, the clauses of which can be modified by no authority. They would therefore take the place of the nation, and exercise as absolute a sway over society as the inherent weakness of judicial power would allow them to do. Undoubtedly, as the French judges are incompetent to declare a law to be unconstitutional, the power of changing the constitution is indirectly given to the legislative body, since no legal barrier would oppose the alterations which it might prescribe. But it is better to grant the power of changing the constitution of the people to men who represent (however imperfectly) the will of the people, than to men who represent no one but themselves.

It would be still more unreasonable to invest the English judges with the right of resisting the decisions of the legislative body, since the Parliament which makes the laws also makes the constitution; and consequently a law emanating from the three powers of the State can in no case be unconstitutional. But neither of these remarks is applicable to America.

In the United States the constitution governs the legislator as much as the private citizen; as it is the first of laws it cannot be modified by a law, and it is therefore just that the tribunals should obey the constitution in preference to any law. This condition is essential to the power of the judicature, for to select that legal obligation by which he is most strictly bound is the natural right of every magistrate.

In France the constitution is also the first of laws, and the judges have the same right to take it as the ground of their decisions, but were they to exercise this right they must perforce encroach on rights more sacred than their own, namely, on those of society, in whose name they are acting. In this case the State-motive clearly prevails over the motives of an individual. In America, where the nation can always reduce its magistrates to obedience by changing its constitution, no danger of this kind is to be feared. Upon this point, therefore, the political and the logical reasons agree, and the people as well as the judges preserve their privileges.

Whenever a law which the judge holds to be unconstitutional is argued in a tribunal of the United States he may refuse to admit it as a rule; this power is the only one which is peculiar to the American magistrate, but it gives rise to immense political influence. Few laws can escape the searching analysis of the judicial power for any length of time, for there are few which are not prejudicial to some private interest or other, and none which may not be brought before a court of justice by the choice of parties, or by the necessity of the case. But from the time that a judge has refused to apply any given law in a case, that law loses a portion of its moral cogency. The persons to whose interests it is prejudicial learn that means exist of evading its authority, and similar suits are multiplied, until it becomes powerless. One of two alternatives must then be resorted to: the people must alter the constitution, or the legislature must repeal the law. The political power which the Americans have intrusted to their courts of justice is therefore immense, but the evils of this power are considerably diminished by the obligation which has been imposed of attacking the laws through the courts of justice alone. If the judge had been empowered to contest the laws on the ground of theoretical generalities, if he had been enabled to open an attack or to pass a censure on the legislator, he would have played a prominent part in the political sphere; and as the champion or the antagonist of a party, he would have arrayed the hostile passions of the nation in the conflict. But when a judge contests a law applied to some particular case in an obscure proceeding, the importance of his attack is concealed from the public gaze, his decision bears upon the interest of an individual, and if the law is slighted it is only collaterally. Moreover, although it is censured, it is not abolished; its moral force may be diminished, but its cogency is by no means suspended, and its final destruction can only be accomplished by the reiterated attacks of judicial functionaries. It will readily be understood that by connecting the censorship of the laws with the private interests of members of the community, and by intimately uniting the prosecution of the law with the prosecution of an individual, legislation is protected from wanton assailants, and from the daily aggressions of party spirit. The errors of the legislator are exposed whenever their evil consequences are most felt, and it is always a positive and appreciable fact which serves as the basis of a prosecution.

I am inclined to believe this practice of the American courts to be at once the most favorable to liberty as well as to public order.

3.11 Rhode Island Litigants Debate Changes in the Absence of Constitutional Mechanisms*

While most states adopted constitutions during the American Revolution that provided for a regularized amending process, Rhode Island simply reaffirmed its colonial charter which made no such provision. Moreover, while other states began rewriting their constitutions in the 1820s and 1830s, Rhode Island did not. The result was that the Charter Government did not take many democratizing steps that were being taken elsewhere. Eventually, a rival government headed by Thomas Dorr, vied for the allegiance of Rhode Island citizens and even claimed to have received approval in an election by a majority of Rhode Island's citizens. The Charter Government, how-

* *Luther v. Borden*, 48 U.S. 1 (1849). Plaintiff's arguments from pp. 19-20, 24. Defendant's arguments from pp. 28-9, pp. 30-3.

ever, failed to recognize the legitimacy of this new government.

During the altercations that ensued, Luther Borden, a representatives of the Charter Government, entered the home of Martin Luther, a Dorr Government supporter to arrest him. Martin Luther subsequently sued in federal court, alleging that Luther Borden's actions were simply the illegal acts of a private citizen since the orders under which he had proceeded were not made by a legitimate republican government. In *Luther v. Borden* (1849), Chief Justice Roger Taney declared for the Supreme Court that the matter of whether a government was republican or not was a "political question" for the two elective branches to decide; since the existing government had sided with the Charter Government, these actions were legitimated. Clearly though, this case raised substantial questions about the right to make governmental changes in cases where the written constitution made no provisions for them and in cases where state legislatures resist such change. The case shows that there is sometimes a fine line indeed between the right of revolution and the right of legitimate constitutional change. The case must also have impressed many observers with the wisdom of the federal Constitution in providing for change in a peaceful and regularized fashion.

Arguments for the Plaintiff

And upon these facts the plaintiff in error will maintain, that, by the fundamental principles of government and of the sovereignty of the people acknowledged and acted upon in the United States, and the several States thereof, at least ever since the Declaration of Independence in 1776, the constitution and frame of government prepared, established as above set forth was, and became thereby, the supreme fundamental law of the State of Rhode Island, and was in full force and effect, as such, when the trespass alleged in the plaintiff's writ was committed by the defendants.

That this conclusion also follows from one of the foregoing fundamental principles of the American system of government, which is, that government is instituted by the people, and for the benefit, protection, and security of the people, nation, or community. And that when any government shall be found inadequate or contrary to these purposes, a majority of the community hath an indubitable, inalienable, and indefeasible right to reform, alter, or abolish the same, in such manner as shall be judged most conducive to the public weal.

But that, in the case at bar, the argument is sufficient, even should it limit the right (which the plaintiff disclaims) to a majority of the voting people, such majority having, in fact, adopted and affirmed the said constitution of Rhode Island.

To sustain this general view, the following proposition is submitted as the theory of American government, upon which the decision of this cause must depend.

The institution of American liberty is based upon the principles, that the people are capable of self-government, and have an inalienable right at all times, and in any manner they please, to establish and alter or change the constitution or particular form under which that government shall be effected. This is especially true of the several States composing the Union, subject only to a limitation provided by the United States Constitution, that the State governments shall be republican.

In order to support this proposition, we have to establish the following points:—

1st. That the sovereignty of the people is supreme, and may act in forming government without the assent of the existing government.

2d. That the people are the sole judges of the form of government best calculated to promote their safety and happiness.

3d. That, as the sovereign power, they have a right to adopt such form of government.

4th. That the right to adopt necessarily includes the right to abolish, to reform, and to alter any existing form of government, and to substitute in its stead any other than they may judge better adapted to the purposes intended.

5th. That if such right exists at all, it exists in the States under the Union, not as a right of force, but a right of sovereignty; and that those who oppose its peaceful exercise, and not those who support it, are culpable.

6th. That the exercise of this right, which is a right original, sovereign, and supreme, and not derived from any other human authority, may be, and must be, effected in such way and manner as the people may for themselves determine.

7th. And more especially is this true in the case of the then subsisting government of Rhode Island, which derived no power from the charter or from the people to alter or amend the frame of government, or to change the basis of representation, or even to propose initiatory measures to that end. . . .

So far as the foregoing authorities are proof of any thing, they establish the following position, viz.:—

1. That in the United States no definite, uniform mode has ever been established for either instituting or changing a form of State government.

2. That State legislatures have no power or authority over the subject, and can interfere only by usurpation, any further than, like other individuals, to recommend.

3. That the great body of the people may change their form of government at any time, in a peaceful way, and by any mode of operations that they for themselves determine to be expedient.

4. That even where a subsisting constitution points out a particular mode of change, the people are not bound to follow the mode so pointed out; but may at their pleasure adopt another.

5. That where no constitution exists, and no fundamental law prescribes any mode of amendment, there they must adopt a mode for themselves; and the mode they do adopt, when adopted, ratified, or acquiesced in by a majority of the people, is binding upon all.

Arguments for the Defense

It has been contended by the opposite counsel, that they had a right, in the court below, to prove, by parol, the adoption of their constitution; that every male inhabitant over twenty-one years of age has a natural right to vote; that their votes are binding upon the government; that their government had a right to take the military arsenal by force; and that this court has a right to decide that our government, now and always represented in Congress, was not a legitimate government.

There is no such thing as a natural right to vote. There are three classes of rights: natural, such as those recognized in the Declaration of Independence; civil, such as the rights of property; and political rights. Society has nothing to do with natural rights except to protect them. Civil rights belong equally to all. Every one has the right to acquire property, and even in infants the laws of all governments preserve this. But political rights are matters of practical utility. A right to vote comes under this class. If it was a natural right, it would appertain to every human being, females and minors. Even the Dorr men excluded all under twenty-one, and those who had not resided within the State during a year. But if the State has the power to affix any limit at all to the enjoyment of this right, then the State must be the sole judge of the extent of such restriction. It can confine the right of voting to freeholders, as well as adults or residents for a year. The boasted power of majorities can only show itself under the law, and not against the law, in any government of laws. It can only act upon days and in places appointed by law.

But it is urged by the opposite counsel, that the great doctrine of the sovereignty of the people, and their consequent power to alter the constitution whenever they choose, is the American doctrine, in opposition to that of the Holy Alliance of Europe, which proclaims that all reforms must emanate from the throne. Let us examine this so-called American doctrine. I say that a proposition to amend always comes from the legislative body. (*Mr. Whipple* [the attorney] here examined, seriatim, the Constitution of the United States, and the constitutions of each State, to show that this principle ran through the whole of them.)

Look at the subject in another aspect. In Congress each House must agree, and even then the President may veto a bill. Sixteen millions of people in the large States may be in favor of amending the Constitution, but their will may be thwarted by four millions in the small States. What then becomes of this vaunted American doctrine of popular sovereignty, acting by majorities? There is no such thing in the United States as a forcible revolution. The Constitution forbids it. The framers of it gave to the federal government power to put down a rebellion, because they saw that remedies for all grievances were provided by law.

Mr Daniel Webster, also for the defense:
Our ancestors brought with them all which they thought valuable in England, and left behind them all which they thought were not. Whilst colonies, they sympathized with Englishmen in the Revolution of 1688. There was a general rejoicing. But in 1776 the American people adopted principles more especially adapted to their condition. They can be traced through the Confederation and the present Constitution, and our principles of liberty have now become exclusively American. They are distinctly marked. We changed the government where it required change; where we found a good one, we left it. Conservatism is visible throughout. Let me state what I understand these principles to be.

The first is, that the people are the source of all political power. Every one believes this. Where else is there any power? There is no hereditary legislature, no large property, no throne, no primogeniture. Every body may buy and sell. There is an equality of rights. Any one who should look to any other source of power than the people would be as much out of his mind as Don Quixote, who imagined that he saw things which did not exist. Let us all admit that the people are sovereign. Jay said that in this country there were many sovereigns and no subject. A portion of this sovereign power has been delegated to government, which represents and speaks the will of the people as far as they chose to delegate their power. Congress have not all. The State governments have not all. The Constitution of the United States does not speak of the government. It says the United States. Nor does it speak of State governments. It says the States; but it recognizes government as existing. The people must have representatives. In England, the representative system originated, not as a matter of right, but because it was called by the king. The people complained sometimes that they had to send up burgesses. At last there grew up a constitutional representation of the people. In our system, it grew up differently. It was because the people could not act in mass, and the right to choose a representative is every man's portion of sovereign power. Suffrage is a delegation of political power to some individual. Hence the right must be guarded and protected against force or fraud. That is one principle. Another is, that the qualification which entitles a man to vote must be prescribed by previous laws, directing how it is to be exercised, and also that the results shall be certified to some central power so that the vote may tell. We know no other principle. If you go beyond these, you go wide of the American track. One principle is, that the people often limit their government; another, that they often limit themselves. They secure themselves against sudden changes by mere majorities. The fifth article of the Constitution of the United States is a clear proof of this. The necessity of having a concurrence of two thirds of both houses of Congress to propose amendments, and of their subsequent ratification by three fourths of the States, gives no countenance to the principles of the Dorr men, because the people have chosen so to limit themselves. All qualifications which persons are required to possess before they can be elected are, in fact, limitations upon the power of the electors; and so are rules requiring them to vote only at particular times and places. Our American mode of government does not draw any power from tumultuous assemblages. If any thing is established in that way, it is deceptive. It is true that at the Revolution governments were forcibly destroyed. But what did the people then do? They got together and took the necessary steps to frame new governments, as they did in England when James the Second abdicated. William asked Parliament to assemble and provide for the case. It was a revolution, not because there was a change in the person of the sovereign, but because there was a hiatus which must be filled. It has been said by the opposing counsel, that the people can get together, call themselves so many thousands, and establish whatever government they please. But others must have the same right. We have then a stormy South American liberty, supported by arms to-day and crushed by arms tomorrow. Our theory places a beautiful face on liberty, and makes it powerful for good, producing no tumults. When it is necessary to ascertain the will of the people, the legislature must provide the means of ascertaining it. The Constitution of the United States was established in this way. It was recommended to the States to send delegates to a convention. They did so. Then it was recommended that the States should ascertain the will of the people. Nobody suggested any other mode.

The opposite counsel have cited the examples of the different States in which constitutions have been altered. Only two provided for conventions, and yet conventions have been held in many of them. But how? Always these conventions were called together by the legislature, and no single constitution has ever been altered by means of a convention gotten up by mass meetings. There must be an authentic mode of ascertaining the public will somehow and somewhere. If not, it is a government of the strongest and most numerous. It is said, that, if the legislature refused to call a convention, the case then resembles the Holy Alliance of Europe, whose doctrine it was that all changes must originate with the sovereign. But there is no resemblance whatever. I say that the will of the people must prevail, but that there must be some mode of finding out that will. The people here are as sovereign as the crowned heads at Laybach, but their will is not so easily discovered. They cannot issue a ukase or edict. In 1845, New York passed a law recommending to the people to vote for delegates to a convention; but the same penalties against fraud were provided as in other elections. False oaths were punished in the same way. The will of the people was collected just as in ordinary occasions.

What do the Constitution and laws of the United States say upon this point. The Constitution recognizes the existence of States, and guarantees to each a republican form of government, and to protect them against domestic violence. The thing which is to be protected is the existing State government. This is clear by referring to the act of Congress of 1795. In case of an insurrection against a State, or the government thereof, the President is to interfere. The Constitution proceeds upon the idea, that each State will take care to establish its own government upon proper principles, and does not contemplate these extraneous and irregular alterations of existing governments. . . .

The question which the court was called upon to decide was one of sovereignty. Two legislatures were in existence at the same time. Both could not be legitimate. If legal power had not passed away from the charter government, it could not have got into Dorr's. The position taken on the other side is that it had so passed away, and it is attempted to be proved by votes and proceedings of meetings, &c., out of doors. This court must look elsewhere,—to the Constitution and laws, and acts of the government, of the United States. How did the President of the United States treat this question? Acting under the Constitution and law of 1795, he decided that the existing government was the one which he was bound to protect. He took his stand accordingly, and we say that this is obligatory upon this court, which always follows an executive recognition of a foreign government. The proof offered below, and rejected by the court, would have led to a different result. Its object was to show that the Dorr constitution was adopted by a majority of the people. But how could a court judge of this? Can it know how many persons were present, how many of them qualified voters, and all this to be proved by testimony? Can it order to be brought before it the minutes and registers of unauthorized officers, and have them proved by parol? The decisions of the legislature and courts of Rhode Island conclude the case. . . .

Chapter 4

The Period of Rising Doubts, 1850-1900

The period from 1850-1900 marked some of the first serious criticisms of the actual operation of the Article V amending process. Such criticisms were stimulated both by the nation's apparent inability to use this mechanism to avoid civil war and by the use of a convention—however illegal—to establish the rebel government of the Confederate States of America. After the Civil War, scholars raised questions about the scope and meaning of the three amendments that had been adopted, at least one in highly questionable procedures, in its wake. Commentators further sought to define the operation of the convention mechanism with greater precision so that it would be a tool for needed change rather than a threat to legitimate government. During this same time, scholars were increasingly likely to argue that there was a fine line between judicial interpretation of the Constitution and the incorporation of actual changes in that document.

4.1 Taney Insists that the Words of the Constitution and Their Meaning Remain Unchanged*

Undoubtedly, one of the Supreme Court's most controversial decisions was *Dred Scott v. Sandford* (1857) which many unrealistically hoped might forestall the Civil War by settling the slavery controversy. At issue was the status of Dred Scott, a slave who had been taken by his master, to free territory and

* 60 *Dred Scott v. Sandford,* U.S. 393 (1857); 15 L. Ed. 691, pp. 700-2; 709-10; 712, and 720.

back to a slave state. Had Scott thereby become free? In rendering its negative answer, the Supreme Court majority, led by Chief Justice Roger Taney, asserted that because blacks had not been included in the original designation of "We the People" in 1787, they could not be so included in 1857. Taney's decision indicated that the only way that blacks could become part of the national polity, at least while he and his brethren sat, was by constitutional amendment. Taney further limited congressional powers so that they applied only to limitation of slavery in the territories owned by the federal government in 1787 rather than to those subsequently purchased—thus invalidating the Missouri Compromise of 1820 which had prohibited slavery in the northern parts of the Louisiana Purchase. Taney's method of constitutional interpretation makes for an interesting comparison to that advanced by Chief Justice Marshall in *McCulloch v. Maryland* (Reading 3.8). While accepting the immediate decision as regards the parties in the Dred Scott Case, Abraham Lincoln did not recognize Taney's decision on this issue as being final. The decision was eventually overturned by the Fourteenth Amendment.

Chief Justice Taney:
The words "people of the United States" and "citizens" are synonymous terms, and mean the same thing. They both describe the political body who, according to our republican institutions, form the sovereignty, and who hold the power and conduct the government through their representatives. They are what we familiarly call the "sovereign people," and every citizen is one of this people, and a constituent member of this sovereignty. The question before us is, whether the class of persons described in the plea in abatement compose a portion of this people, and are constituent members of this sovereignty. We think they are not, and that they are not included, and were not intended to be included, under the word "citizens" in the Constitution, and can therefore, claim none of the rights and privileges which that instrument provides for and secures to citizens of the United States. On the contrary, they were at that time considered as a subordinate and inferior class of beings, who had been subjugated by the

dominant race, and whether emancipated or not, yet remained subject to their authority, and had no rights or privileges but such as those who held the power and the government might choose to grant them.

It is not the province of the court to decide upon the justice or injustice, the policy or impolicy of these laws. The decision of that question belonged to the political or law-making power; to those who formed the sovereignty and framed the Constitution. The duty of the court is to interpret the instrument they have framed, with the best lights we can obtain on the subject, and to administer it as we find it, according to its true intent and meaning when it was adopted.

In discussing this question, we must not confound the rights of citizenship which a state may confer within its own limits, and the rights of citizenship as a member of the Union. It does not by any means follow, because he has all the rights and privileges of a citizen of a State, that he must be a citizen of the United States. . . .

It is difficult at this day to realize the state of public opinion in relation to that unfortunate race, which prevailed in the civilized and enlightened portions of the world at the time of the Declaration of Independence, and when the Constitution of the United States was framed and adopted. But the public history of every European nation displays it, in a manner too plain to be mistaken.

They had for more than a century before been regarded as beings of an inferior order; and altogether unfit to associate with the white race, either in social or political relations; and so far inferior, that they had no rights which the white man was bound to respect; and that the negro might justly and lawfully be reduced to slavery for his benefit. He was bought and sold, and treated as an ordinary article of merchandise and traffic, whenever a profit could be made by it. This opinion was at that time fixed and universal in the civilized portion of the white race. It was regarded as an axiom in morals as well as in politics, which no one thought of disputing, or supposed to be open to dispute; and men in every grade and position in society daily and habitually acted upon it in their private pursuits, as well as in matters of public concern, without doubting for a moment the correctness of this opinion.

No one, we presume, supposes that any change in public opinion or feeling, in relation to this unfortunate race, in the civilized nations of Europe or in this country, should induce the court to give to the words of the Constitution a more liberal construction in their favor than they were intended to bear when the instrument was framed and adopted. Such an argument would be altogether inadmissible in any tribunal called on to interpret it. If any of its provisions are deemed unjust, there is a mode prescribed in the instrument itself by which it may be amended; but while it remains unaltered, it must be construed now as it was understood at the time of its adoption. It is not only the same in words, but the same in meaning, and delegates the same powers to the government, and reserves and secures the same rights and privileges to the citizen; and as long as it continues to exist in its present form, it speaks not only in the same words, but with the same meaning and intent with which it spoke when it came from the hands of its framers, and was voted on and adopted by the people of the United States. Any other rule of construction would abrogate the judicial character of this court, and make it the mere reflex of the popular opinion or passion of the day. The court was not created by the Constitution for such purposes. Higher and graver trusts have been confided to it, and it must not falter in the path of duty. . . .

And upon a full and careful consideration of the subject, the court is of opinion that, upon the facts stated in the plea in abatement, Dred Scott was not a citizen of Missouri within the meaning of the Constitution of the United States, and not entitled as such to sue in its courts; and, consequently, that the Circuit Court had no jurisdiction of the case. . . .

The counsel for the plaintiff has laid much stress upon that article in the Constitution which confers on Congress the power "to dispose of and make all needful rules and regulations respecting the territory of other property belonging to the United States;" but, in the judgment of the court, that provision has no bearing on the present controversy, and the power there given, whatever it may be, is confined, and was intended to be confined, to the territory which at that time belonged to, or was claimed by, the United States, and was within their boundaries as settled by the Treaty with Great Britain, and can have no influence upon a territory afterwards acquired from a foreign government. It was a special provision for a known and particular Territory, and to meet a present emergency, and nothing more. . . .

Upon these considerations, it is the opinion of the court that the Act of Congress which prohibited a citizen from holding and owning property of this kind in the territory of the United States north of the line therein mentioned, is not warranted by the Constitution, and is therefore void; and that neither Dred Scott himself, nor any of his family, were made free by being carried into this territory; even if they had been carried there by the owner, with the intention of becoming a permanent resident. . . .

4.2 Amendments Proposed to Avert Civil War*

The doctrines of nullification and secession found increasingly receptive audiences in the South as controversy between the North and South waxed over the slavery issue which was further stimulated by the Supreme Court's controversial decision in the Dred Scott Decision. Despite his conciliatory efforts and reassurances, the election of Abraham Lincoln in 1860, stimulated a number of proposals for amendments which would reassure the Southern states that their institutions were not in jeopardy. Below are amendments proposed by a Peace Conference in 1861, the so-called Corwin Amendment which was actually approved by Congress and ratified by three states, and Lincoln's statement in his First Inaugural Address of his own

---

* Peace convention proposals from *The Federalist*, ed. with illustrative documents by Paul L. Ford (New York: Henry Holt and Company, 1898), pp. 718-20. Corwin amendment found in Herman Ames, *The Proposed Amendments to the Constitution of the United States During the First Century of its History* (New York: Burt Franklin, 1970 reprint of 1896 edition), p. 196. Lincoln's First Inaugural Address from *A Compilation of the Messages and Papers of the Presidents, 1789-1908*, ed. James D. Richardson (Bureau of National Literature and Art, 1908), 6, pp.10-11.

willingness to consider constitutional changes (and even a constitutional convention) which might preserve the Union. Needless to say, none of these proposals was adopted, and bitter war resolved the issue that regularized amending procedures seemed unable to accomplish.

Proposals of the Peace Conference of 1861

SECTION 1. In all the present territory of the United States, north of the parallel of 36° 30′ of north latitude, involuntary servitude, except in punishment of crime, is prohibited. In all the present Territory south of that line, the status of persons held to involuntary service or labor, as it now exists, shall not be changed; nor shall any law be passed by Congress or the Territorial Legislature to hinder or prevent the taking of such persons from any of the States of this Union to said Territory, nor to impair the rights arising from said relation; but the same shall be subject to judicial cognizance in the Federal courts, according to the course of the common law. When any Territory north or south of said line, within such boundary as Congress may prescribe, shall contain a population equal to that required for a member of Congress, it shall, if its form of government be republican, be admitted into the Union on an equal footing with the original States, with or without involuntary servitude, as the constitution of such State may provide.

SEC. 2. No Territory shall be acquired by the United States, except by discovery and for naval and commercial stations, depots, and transit routes, without the concurrence of a majority of all the Senators from States which allow involuntary servitude, and a majority of all the Senators from States which prohibit that relation; nor shall Territory be acquired by treaty, unless the votes of a majority of the Senators from each class of States hereinbefore mentioned be cast as a part of the two-thirds majority necessary to the ratification of such treaty.

SEC. 3. Neither the Constitution nor any amendment thereof shall be construed to give Congress power to regulate, abolish, or control, within any State the relation established or recognized by the laws thereof touching persons held to labor or involuntary service therein, nor to interfere with or abolish involuntary service in the District of Columbia without the consent of Maryland and without the consent of the owners, or making the owners who do not consent just compensation; nor the power to interfere with or prohibit Representatives and others from bringing with them to the District of Colombia, retaining, and taking away, persons so held to labor or service; nor the power to interfere with or abolish involuntary service in places under the exclusive jurisdiction of the United States within those States and Territories where the same is established or recognized; nor the power to prohibit the removal or transportation of persons held to labor or involuntary service in any State or Territory of the United States to any other State or Territory thereof where it is established or recognized by law or usage, and the right during transportation, by sea or river, of touching at ports, shores and landings, and of landing in case of distress, shall exist; but not the right of transit in or though any State or Territory, or of sale or traffic, against the laws thereof. Nor shall Congress have power to authorize any higher rate of taxation on persons held to labor or service than on land. The bringing into the District of Columbia of persons held to labor or service, for sale, or placing them in depots to be afterwards transferred to other places for sale as merchandise, is prohibited.

SEC. 4. The third paragraph of the second section of the fourth article of the Constitution shall not be construed to prevent any of the States, by appropriate legislation, and through the action of their judicial and ministerial officers, from enforcing the delivery of fugitives from labor to the person to whom such service or labor is due.

SEC. 5. The foreign slave-trade is hereby forever prohibited; and it shall be the duty of Congress to pass laws to prevent the importation of slaves, coolies, or persons held to service or labor, into the United States and the Territories from places beyond the limits thereof.

SEC. 6. The first, third and fifth sections, together with this section of these amendments, and the third paragraph of the second section of the first article of the Constitution, and the third paragraph of the second section of the fourth article thereof, shall not be amended or abolished without the consent of all the States.

SEC. 7. Congress shall provide by law that the United States shall pay to the owner the full value of his fugitive from labor, in all cases where the marshal or other officer, whose duty it was to arrest such fugitive, was prevented from so doing by violence and intimidation from mobs or riotous assemblages, or when after arrest such fugitive was rescued by like violence or intimidation, and the owner thereby deprived of the same; and the acceptance of such payment shall preclude the owner from further claim to such fugitive. Congress shall provide by law for securing to the citizens of each State the privileges and immunities of citizens in the several States.

The Corwin Amendment

No amendment shall be made to the Constitution which will authorize or give to Congress the power to abolish or to interfere, within any State, with the domestic institutions thereof, including that of persons held to labor or service by the laws of said State.

Excerpt From Lincoln's First Inaugural Address

This country, with its institutions, belongs to the people who inhabit it. Whenever they shall grow weary of the existing Government, they can exercise their *constitutional* right of amending it or their *revolutionary* right to dismember or overthrow it. I can not be ignorant of the fact that many worthy and patriotic citizens are desirous of having the National Constitution amended. While I make no recommendation of amendments, I fully recognize the rightful authority of the people over the whole subject, to be exercised in either of the modes prescribed in the instrument itself; and I should, under existing circumstances, favor rather than oppose a fair opportunity being afforded the people to act upon it. I will venture to add that to me the convention mode seems preferable, in that it allows amendments to originate with the people themselves, instead of only permitting them to take or reject propositions originated by others, not especially chosen for this purpose, and which might not be precisely such as they would wish to either accept or refuse. I understand a proposed amendment to the Constitution—which amendment, however, I have not seen—has passed Congress, to the effect that the Federal Government shall never interfere with the domestic institutions of the States, including that of persons held to service. To avoid misconstruction of what I have said, I depart from my purpose not to speak of particular amendments so far as to say that, holding such a provision to now be implied constitutional law, I have no objection to its being made express and irrevocable.

4.3 The Confederate Constitution Provides for a New Method of Constitutional Change*

Amendments proved unable to avert Civil War. Subsequently, the Southern states held a convention and drafted a new Constitution. Like the old Articles of Confederation and the doctrines of John C. Calhoun, this Constitution stressed state sovereignty. Below are selections from this Constitution which show its recognition of state sovereignty, its constitutional protection for the institution of slavery, and its amending mechanism which focused more than that of the Constitution of the United States on the convention mechanism. The amending power was never utilized during the short tenure of the Confederacy.

The Preamble

We, the people of the Confederate States, each State acting in its sovereign and independent character, in order to form a permanent federal government, establish justice, insure domestic tranquillity, and secure the blessings of liberty to ourselves and our posterity—invoking the favor and guidance of Almighty God—do ordain and establish this Constitution of the Confederate States of America.

---

* *The Federalist*, ed. Paul L. Ford (New York: Henry Holt and Company, 1898), p. 720, 731.

Article IV, Section 3, para. 3
The Confederate States may acquire new territory; and Congress shall have power to legislate and provide governments for the inhabitants of all territory belonging to the Confederate States, lying without the limits of the several States; and may permit them, at such times, and in such manner as it may by law provide, to form States to be admitted into the Confederacy. In all such territory, the institution of negro slavery as it now exists in the Confederate States, shall be recognized and protected by Congress, by the territorial government; and the inhabitants of the several Confederate States and Territories, shall have the right to take to such territory any slaves, lawfully held by them in any of the States or territories of the Confederate States.

Article V
Upon the demand of any three States, legally assembled in their several Conventions, the Congress shall summon a convention of all the States, to take into consideration such amendments to the Constitution as the said States shall concur in suggesting at the time when the said demand is made; and should any of the proposed amendments to the Constitution be agreed on by the said Convention—voting by States—and the same be ratified by the Legislatures of two-thirds of the several States, or by Conventions in two-thirds thereof—as the one or the other mode of ratification may be proposed by the general Convention—they shall thenceforward form a part of this Constitution. But no State shall, without its consent, be deprived of its equal representation in the Senate.

4.4 Sidney George Fisher Advocates Congressional Sovereignty*

One of the most fascinating American perspectives on the constitutional amending process was that of Sidney George Fisher,

* Fisher, *The Trial of the Constitution*, intro by Harold M. Hyman (Da Capo Press; New York, 1972; Reprint of Philadelphia: J.B. Lippincott & Co., 1862), pp. 25-37, pp. 40-3, pp. 94-7.

a Philadelphia author, lawyer and aristocrat. As Americans were going to war, Fisher advanced the fascinating argument that Congress should amend the Constitution on its own, as in the English system of parliamentary sovereignty. While his argument hardly squared with the American constitutional system, it is noteworthy both in spelling out an alternative to American practice and because Fisher's view of the efficacy of Article V processes were far more jaundiced than that of most previous commentators. Fisher's arguments made an interesting comparison to those of Noah Webster (Reading 2.10).

The Inefficacy of Article V

Among the powers thus reserved to the people is that of altering the Constitution in the manner prescribed by itself. In England the Constitution may be altered by Parliament. Here, organic changes in the Government, according to received opinions, can be made only by a convention elected for the purpose, and in an appointed manner, by the people; there, they can be made by an assembly also elected by the people, and for the same purpose, since it has the same power. In both cases the resort is to the people—that is to say, to popular opinion requiring a change. The difference is that in England the whole power of the people is delegated to Parliament, and the power, therefore, is always ready for action, whilst with us it can only be made available by a difficult and uncertain process, slow, though prompt measures may be important, and uncertain in its results, because the consent of three-fourths of the States or of the people, is necessary before an alteration can be made. The English organic law is the custom of the Government. It is in no danger of sudden and great innovations, for it is the nature of custom or habit to change slowly. It is also its nature to be constantly changing, according to the age, circumstances, and mental condition of an individual or a nation. Safe and gradual change may therefore be predicated of the English Constitution, and such in fact has always been its characteristic.

But how can our Constitution be altered when alteration is necessary? It is a code, partly of old and therefore customary law, but partly and largely of new contrivances. The new portions, where doubtful in their meaning, must be construed, and therefore may be moulded by the practice of the Government and by the Courts, and thus to that extent the Constitution may be altered by the usage of the Government, as it has been. The Government is one of limited, but also of implied powers, and this affords a certain latitude for needed change. But the exigencies of the future may require great and organic changes; the best opinion of the country may demand them, a majority of the people may demand them, and the necessity for them may be obvious to all men able to think upon the subject, which nevertheless may not be three-fourths of the people or of the States. Where, then, is the remedy? If amendments to the Constitution are really necessary they will be made. But the conditions imposed by the Constitution require, first, that two-thirds of both houses of Congress, or the Legislatures of two-thirds of the States shall propose amendments, which must be ratified by the Legislatures of three-fourths of the States, or by conventions in three-fourths of them.

It will be difficult to satisfy these conditions, yet necessary changes in the organic law must be made. On the other hand rash, ignorant, even fatal alterations, in times of popular excitement, may be proposed and hurried through the constitutional forms, by demagogues controlling the masses for a time, and would thus become a part of the Constitution unalterable, even when found mischievous, except by another doubtful and dangerous appeal to three-fourths of the States. The provision in the Constitution for amending it has been called a safety-valve to prevent the explosion of the passions of the people in revolutionary violence. But the efficacy of a safety-valve depends on the promptness with which it can be opened and the width of its throttle. If defective in either of these, when the pressure of steam is too high the boiler will burst.

The English Constitution has been going through a constant process of change for eight hundred years, dating from the Norman conquest. All the changes have been beneficial, and though some have been accompanied by violence, they have all been made by Parliament. No convention for this purpose has ever been elected by the people to exercise their reserved power. Yet feudalism and Romanism have been abolished, Plantagenets, Tudors, and Stuarts controlled, the prerogative of the King diminished, the succession to the Crown altered, the powers of the Legislature enlarged, the tenure of the Judiciary changed, and the whole machinery of the Government modified to secure the rights and liberties of the people and to suit their growth and progress. Through all these stormy centuries this machinery has worked well, because the alterations have been skilfully made, as Lord Coke says, "by an infinite number of *grave and learned men* and by long experience." The process is still going on. "Grave and learned men"—the best minds of the nation—are now pondering the necessity for further change, what that change shall be and how it can be safely and beneficially made. They anxiously consult the indications of popular sentiment, though they summon no conventions of the people. There is no necessity for these, as Parliament is intrusted already with the whole power of the people, and is responsible to them. The action of Parliament is therefore free; members are not delegates to register a foregone conclusion, but meet to deliberate, to compare opinions, to gain light and knowledge. It is almost impossible, therefore, that under the operation of the principle of representation and of a free press, any changes can be made not required both by the wants and the opinions of the people, or that when made they will be resisted.

The Amendment Article in our Constitution has not preserved us from civil war, though the war turned on construction as to the power of Congress over the Territories. The safety-valve did not work, and the boiler has burst. The valve could not be opened, and had it been, would not have let off the steam. The rebellion has tested and illustrated its merits as a means of peacefully altering the Constitution.

The Convention were anxious to protect the Government they had made from the rash spirit of innovation inherent in a democracy. They therefore interposed barriers to restrain it. But it is a spirit that cannot be restrained by any democratic means. A Government powerful enough to resist the people is not a democracy. Instead of a dam to back up the rushing flood of passion, until it should acquire force enough to sweep away all obstructions, it would have been wiser to make channels and conduits to give it easy and safe vent. This part of the Constitution was new, and had, therefore, never been tried by experience. There is nothing like it in the English model, or in any other model known to history. Reserved powers of the people, dormant till roused by a great crisis, then suddenly evoked to deliberate in the midst of a great crisis, on profound and difficult questions of constitutional law and political science, surely this was a new thing under the sun. It looks well enough on paper. This Constitution of ours, thought the Convention, is a wise and good one; it should therefore be guarded and preserved with vigilant care. But time may reveal defects in it that ought to be remedied; may create wants under it that must be supplied. The Constitution, therefore, should be open to alterations, but they should be made only after mature reflection. To secure the requisite caution, the people must not be permitted to vote directly upon proposed changed, but must act through their representatives in Congress, or in the State Legislatures, and through conventions chosen for the purpose. Moreover, as the Constitution is the birthright of the whole people, it should not be altered by a mere majority which may be factitious, or gained by undue influence or the result of transient public excitement. The interest, the opinions and the feelings of a large minority might thus be unjustly disregarded, which minority might be composed of a portion of the people best entitled to respect. As the proposed alterations may affect the rights of the States and their relations to the General Government, they, as such, would in such a case, be entitled to an influential voice, though the vote of a small State would weigh as much as that of a large one. All these points are carefully met and provided for in Article V of the Constitution. [Fisher quotes Article V.]

The whole value of this plan depends on its practical utility. It sets in motion enormous forces. Can it restrain and guide them? Will they allow such a bit to be put into their mouths at all; or if they do, where is the arm strong enough to hold them to the track when lashed to their speed? Questions that involve State rights and popular rights, the power of the people and the power of the Government, affect large interests and excite strong passions. An impetuous and influential minority may think itself endangered or aggrieved, a large majority may demand a change, yet despair of obtaining the requisite two-thirds of Congress or of the State Legislatures, or a party controlling these, may refuse to take the initiatory steps, doubtful of the result, and preferring to carry its measures by a vote of Congress. Yet that vote may be either a criminal usurpation of power, or a modification of the Constitution imperatively demanded by circumstances, and in either case it is sure to be made a party question. It would be so difficult to subject such a question to the process required by the Constitution, that the process cannot be relied on. It would fail when most needed, because then neither party would appeal to it. If they refused, the question must be decided by Congress, or not at all, and a decision by Congress, when its authority is denied, settles nothing; may, in a flagrant case, justify resistance, and in any case affords incitements and arguments to meditated and planned rebellion, which, without such show or reality of right might never have been thought of. For clear, unquestionable authority is obeyed even when severely exercised, whilst doubtful, disputed, or manifestly illegal power is resisted on slight grounds, or even only because it is illegal.

The obstacles therefore to be overcome, before the tribunal contemplated by the Constitution for deciding upon amendments to it, can be created, are so formidable, that they tend rather to excite than to repress the spirit of revolution, whilst they are not strong enough to resist it. In England, Parliament is a "convention to amend the Constitution," duly appointed, always in existence, and always competent to entertain proposals for needed alterations, with full authority to decide them. Possessed of undoubted power, Parliament is likely to act with moderation and caution on a subject so momentous, so surrounded by watchful intelligence, by great interests and opposing forces, because any action at all implies great responsibility. But in the conduct of governments as of individuals, it is often only the first step that counts. A government that is guilty of usurpation, has already thrown off responsibility, and relied for success on other supports than the law affords. This is revolution; and when a government cannot be altered to satisfy the people, revolution is a necessity. It is a remarkable fact that in conservative England, so steadfast in adhering to ancient usage, the power to make changes is always ready to act, without question or form or delay, and the organic law is thus pliable and responsive to the wishes of the people; whilst in democratic America, innovation is guarded against with such jealous care, that it is doubtful whether the means provided by law for making needed change can ever be employed.

It is also doubtful whether they can ever be used with success, so trammelled are they with conditions and so dangerous are they likely to be in action. The Constitution has indeed been once amended in a legal manner [Fisher seems unaware of the Eleventh and Twelfth Amendments]. But this was proposed by the first Congress that sat under it, composed in part of the men who made it, and to satisfy the known wishes of some of the States by which it was ratified. No popular excitement was connected with the amendments, no partisan or sectional interests or passions. They were, indeed, so nearly contemporaneous with the Constitution as to be substantially part of the original structure. The ratification of the amendments was made under the same influences and in the same mood of the popular mind which had induced the acceptance of the Constitution, and the whole was thus virtually one act. There was, moreover, nothing in the amendments themselves to divide opinion; for, as all parties agreed, they were really implied in the first plan. For these reasons, the fact that they were peaceably adopted in the appointed mode is no test of it, and gives no assurance of its future success.

The condition of the country has greatly changed since the war of Independence. From three millions we have grown to be thirty-four millions of people, and from thirteen to be thirty-four States. Trade and manufactures have been created and have flourished, and with them wealth has increased. These have been gathered, for the most part, in the large towns, and with them, also, masses of ignorant population; so that the cities, whilst they are the centres of activity, intelligence, and capital, with all their influences increased by concentration, are also centres of that power which is most dangerous in a democracy. From the varied pursuits of the people, indicated by natural causes, have arisen conflicting interests, and contrasted manners and social forms, in different parts of the country. Slavery and the plantation have created, in the South, ideas, habits and desires that distinguish it from the North; whilst the agricultural Northwest is scarcely less divided from the commercial and manufacturing East. These characteristics show, also, different stages of civilization. New England is the country of schools, colleges, towns, manufactures, and concentrated population, where thought is active and intense, because of universal education, general comfort, diversified industry, and the collision of mind caused by easy and constant intercourse. In the Northwest the people are scattered on isolated farms over a vast expanse. They are intelligent and energetic, but rude and uncultivated— enthralled by a single interest and occupation. The electric currents of thought and knowledge do not freely reach them, and therefore opinion forms itself slowly, and lags behind the quick and eager spirit of the East. In the South education is confined to a small class, governed by a supreme influence and made captive by a social system which directs all thought and endeavor to one idea and one policy.

The Government may press unequally on these powerful sections, and may, justly or unjustly, resist their respective demands. A change may be necessary, to allay discontent, by yielding to reasonable wishes and thus prevent insurrection and civil war. Some contrivance is needed, by which the mature and enlightened opinion of the people may not only act on the measures of Government, but also alter the Constitution; for unless this can be done according to changing circumstances and opinions, physical force is the only resort. But what alterations to make and what will be their effect, are difficult questions, of which not the many but the few are competent to judge. They never have originated with the many, but have always been the work of individuals, or of a very small and select class. This is true of every change in the British Constitution, and every part of its machinery, from Magna

Charta down to the Reform Bill. They were all introduced, not by the people, but to meet their wishes and supply their wants. They were never submitted to them for discussion or decision, but were contrived and provided for them by heads wiser than their own, and then adopted by them, because found to answer their purpose.

The average intelligence of the American people is very high—far higher than that of any other in the world. They can appreciate the benefits of good government, and can perceive defects in it; but it is quite a different thing to be able to furnish a remedy. This requires mental power and cultivation of a higher order. The principles of government are a science; so also is jurisprudence, and so is constitutional law, depending on both, and to be interpreted by the lights of both. No small knowledge of each is required safely to alter the Constitution. The multitude, rich or poor, do not possess the knowledge. Few of them have ever read the Constitution or know anything of the various questions that have arisen under it, or the reasoning by which they have been settled. Information of this sort is not the attribute of the many. No property qualification, however high, would secure a class that possess it. Neither are the masses capable of abstract thought, or able to anticipate the tendencies and remote consequences of changes in organic law. They are not very well acquainted with history, nor can they read or understand Montesquieu, De Lohne, Burke, Vattell, Kent, and Story. They can perceive effects, but only when they happen; they can judge of the results of a law, but can rarely refer them to the true causes. They know what they need, and can feel injustice and oppression. They know the difference between anarchy and order, between poverty and prosperity, between corruption and honesty, between wise men and fools, between virtuous men and villains; but of these things, how to secure the good and how to avoid the evil, they do not know.

They require liberty and security, but the machinery by which these are attained, they cannot contrive, and even when it is constructed for them, they can judge of it only by the effects it produces. For example: an intelligent people demands political power, or the privilege of influencing the measures of government. But the difficulty is how to give them this power, and to contrive some means by which they can exercise it. This end has never yet been fully accomplished, only some approximation to it, by clumsy and inefficient means. The American people think they have got it, because they have universal suffrage and the ballot-box. Perhaps they have only got a sham instead of a reality, and the result of universal suffrage and the ballot-box has been, to place their power beyond their control, in a few unworthy and irresponsible hands. An intelligent people demand of right, power, not only over the action of Government, but its form, that it may be moulded to suit their wants and wishes. They think they have got this power in the fifth article of the Constitution. Perhaps it may turn out that the article, instead of an instrument, as was intended, is an iron fetter that must be broke, before free action can be attained.

Unless connected with real grievances, abstract questions of government do not interest the people. They are beyond the habitual range of their thought, and they cannot be induced to entertain them or act upon them at all. Therefore, in quiet times, appropriate to the consideration of the principles of government, such topics cannot be discussed with any prospect of securing such action as the Constitution requires. To put its cumbrous machinery in motion, the people must be roused, and as the most important organic changes are generally connected with the interests of sections or of classes, the people are very likely to be roused by them, to be divided into parties, to be influenced by passion. They thus become a very unfit tribunal to decide such questions, which are not likely to be tried on their merits. The contest would be for victory, not for truth, a wide field and ample opportunity would be given to the arts of demagogues, and how far the struggle would go, and what would be its result, no one, at the beginning of it, could predict.

Yet to such a tribunal does the Constitution submit organic changes, and such a struggle does it invoke. First in Congress or in the State Legislatures the question must be debated, by which the alarm is sounded. Then it must be discussed before the people, that a convention be elected. Then debated again in that convention. Then again before the people or in the State Legislatures. And all these operations are to be performed by the same people and by the same leaders; for leading party men would be the managers of the process throughout. Why might not the subject be safely committed to Congress, a body as much elected by the people as a convention, and therefore, as likely to represent their wishes? What is the difference between the power of the people delegated to Congress and the power of the same people reserved to themselves, except that the former is always ready to act when an emergency makes it necessary, and the latter cannot act without hindrances and delay.

Congress is more amenable to the control of the people than the convention proposed by the Constitution is likely to be, because the former is a permanent branch of the Government, elected at short intervals, so that at every election it is subjected to the popular control. The convention is, indeed, to be chosen by the people, and its work to be submitted to them for ratification. That done, however, the control of the people, over the convention and over the subject, ceases. The amendment once made, however injurious it may prove, is irrevocable, except by another convention elected by the same difficult forms; for the reserved power of the people having acted, returns to its prison and cannot again act, till summoned in the appointed manner. Is not this power too much hampered to be of use when most needed?

In England Parliament wields the whole power of the nation. But in England, as everywhere else, when the privileges of the people are violated, and their wishes disregarded by the Government, there exists the right of resistance,—a right often exercised in English history, and therefore a custom and part of the unwritten law, undefined, unprovided with legal means for its exercise, but denied by no one. This is the reserved power of the English people, and it is always ready for use, without being trammelled by forms, votes, conventions, or ratifications. By its employment, at long intervals, the English Constitution has grown up to its present symmetry and strength. Coupled with the right of suffrage, this implied and dormant power is a constant check on Parliament, whilst the unquestioned legal authority of Parliament is a check on the people. They influence every measure of Government through the press, the elections, and other organs of opinion, whilst every law affects the interests of members of Parliament. These do not owe their influence in the community to their seats in the Legislature, but are in the Legislature because of their influence in the community, derived from rank, birth, wealth, and character. Land, trade, manufactures, and labor, are all represented in Parliament. Identified thus with the great interests of every class of the people,—informed of their sentiments, and controlled by their votes,—no measure is likely to be adopted by Parliament in opposition to their wishes, or in violation of their rights. Even should this happen, they easily acquiesce, because they know that errors or injustice can be remedied by another Parliament. The interests affected by organic changes in Government are so powerful in England, that changes cannot be made unless really needed and demanded by the people, and then they can be made by a safe and easy process. With us, the process is so difficult that it can rarely be resorted to at all, and so dangerous, that to use it would be only something better than civil war, for it would be likely to provoke one. It implies more intelligence, and more dispassionate calmness of deliberation, than is or can be possessed by any people. . . .

But we cannot throw aside the natural laws that govern society, which declare that a government is made for a people, not a people for the government, and that an intelligent people will have a government to satisfy their intelligence. Either an acorn or the Saxon race, planted in a vessel, made of either clay or paper, too narrow for its expanding force, will break the vessel and become severally an oak, and a free, progressive nation. The reserved power of the people cannot be chained up by fifth articles or by any forms that impede its action, when action is needed, It may well be doubted whether there is or can be such a thing in a political community, as the reserved power of the people, or whether it will be possible, in the nature of things, to contrive a government which can be limited or restrained, except by the wishes, convictions, and interests of the nation, expressed by custom, by votes, by the press, by silent acquiescence, or as Carlyle expresses it, by "not revolting," and if need be, by forcible resistance.

A government must be checked either by these influences or not at all. The received theory of our Constitution is, that it is alterable, not by the Government, but by the people. That is to say, it cannot be altered by representatives of the people assembled in Congress, but it may be altered by representatives of the people assembled in a convention. But suppose Congress made an alteration, which was approved and sustained by the people; that a sudden emergency should arise, when the Government must either exert unconstitutional power or be destroyed. Should the people acquiesce, what power has the Constitution to protect itself? The work of Congress can only be undone by a subsequent Congress, and will be, if the alteration should not satisfy the people, otherwise not. If the change be a wise one and prove beneficial, it will be adopted by the people and become, in time, custom and organic law. So that we get at last to the English doctrine, that Parliament is omnipotent, that it to say, it cannot be legally restrained. Any change in the Constitution may be made by act of Parliament, which may be repealed by another act, if the change is not agreeable to the people. The difference between Congress and Parliament is, that the latter has legal power over the subject, and the former, by the law as generally understood, none at all. But a law that cannot be enforced is a nullity, and so is power that cannot be exerted. The reserved power of the people cannot be exercised, and therefore does not exist. The alleged legal restraint on the power of Congress cannot be enforced, and therefore there is no restraint on it. The whole power of the people, within the sphere of the General Government, does and must, in the nature of things, reside in Congress, and the security of the people consists in their control over Congress by the ballot-box. . . .

But it is not to be supposed, we may be told, that all branches of the Government will conspire to violate the Constitution, neither is it fair to assume that the people would submit, if they did. They would punish and frustrate such at attempt by the ballot-box. True enough, unless the thing done happened to suit their wishes, their passions, their mental and moral condition, which may be high or low. If low, and sinking lower, they will soon lose all power over the Government and will neither care whether, nor know when, the Constitution is disregarded. But if their spirit and intelligence be high and progressive, and be represented by the persons who administer the Government, it is a supposable case that defects in the Constitution, revealed by experience, should be corrected, or changes demanded by necessity should be made, by the combined action of all branches of the Government, with the assent of the people, when prescribed forms cannot be observed, either because, by reason of their intricacy, they cannot be applied at all or not in time to meet a dangerous emergency. Thus changes have been made in the English Constitution, which, because it is custom, is far more certain, definite, and positive than ours. Why have those changes been so made? Is it because of any peculiarity of that law, or is it because of a principle inherent in all free and representative governments? If the latter, then we may hope that alterations of our Constitution will be made in the same way, notwithstanding its fifth article. . . .

"In pursuing the present inquiry, we must bear in mind that we are not to confine our view to the present period, but to look forward to remote futurity. Constitutions of civil government are not to be framed upon a calculation of existing exigencies, but upon a imagination of these with the *probable exigencies of ages* according to the natural and tried course of human affairs. Nothing, therefore, can be more fallacious than to infer the extent of any power proper to be lodged in the National Government, from an estimate of its immediate necessities. There ought to be a capacity to provide for future contingencies as they may happen; and as these are illimitable in their nature, it is impossible safely to limit that capacity." [Quoting Hamilton in Federalist No. 34.] Evidently this great statesman, who helped to make the Constitution, did not consider it a finality, to be altered only according to the forms of the Fifth Article. Clearly, in his opinion, the clause under discussion, granted to Congress, where those forms cannot be observed, sovereign powers to do whatever circumstances may render necessary, subject only to the subsequent assent of the people. . . .

A great mass of incidental and resulting authority has been exercised by the Government, which has been sanctioned by the Courts and by the people. A national bank, a protective tariff, the right to make internal improvements, to acquire foreign territory, to govern it when acquired, to lay an embargo on commerce, to pass alien and sedition laws, and other acts of government, were all denounced as the exercise of authority not expressly granted, and have all passed into the domain of implied power, so far as anything can pass out of doubt into certainty, under our Constitution, a thing impossible, according to the construction given to it by some, who have no small influence over its fate.

The result of these examples and authorities is, that the Government may exercise not only power expressly granted, but all powers not expressly prohibited by the Constitution. But the arguments by which implied power is attributed to Government, sustain also the position that it must have sovereign and absolute power even over the Constitution. This arises, to quote the language of Mr. Madison, in the Federalist (No. 43), from "the absolute necessity of the case; from the great principle of self-preservation; the transcendent law of nature and of nature's God, which declares that the safety and happiness of society are the objects at which all political institutions aim, and to which all such institutions *must be sacrificed*."

Whenever these great objects are in danger, the Government may, and unless false to its trust, always will overstep the limits of the Constitution to preserve them. What a Government can do, and ought to do, is the law of that Government; the supreme law, to which its Constitution must be made to conform. Moreover, whatever the Government thus does, it afterwards ratified by the sentiments and votes of the people, is, for that reason also, the law, whether the thing done was absolutely essential to the purpose or not, for the question of necessity is one not of law, but of fact.

The people of this country have prospered under the Constitution. They have enjoyed the blessings of security, order, and liberty. They have advanced rapidly in wealth and in all the arts and culture of civilization. They, therefore, justly regard the Constitution with reverence and affection. It is impossible to over-estimate its value, or to encourage too earnestly those sentiments which may preserve it from the rude touch of experiment or rash innovation. But, that it may endure, it must be capable of alteration, when an alteration is needed, otherwise it will be destroyed; for a Constitution that cannot be changed for the people, and by the people, must, the moment it is felt as an obstruction, be swept away by the force of opinion, and the march of events. Should it yield to these, its original plan and proportions may be preserved, though it may be gradually modified in parts and subordinate details. It may be thus modified, if our reasoning be correct, without violating its spirit, its essential character, or the intention of its founders.

In a war like the present, when all the elements of discord are let loose, when no man can foresee from what source dangers may arise, or what now dormant forces of passion may be roused, the power of Government must be maintained, or every interest of society may perish in a raging sea of violence and anarchy. An excited people in the midst of civil war, without a Government,—who can describe the manifold horrors and miseries of such a condition? Those who are now assailing the Administration for violating the Constitution, and endeavoring to weaken its authority, would do well to think of this. If they can succeed in their schemes, the Constitution for which they profess so much respect, will soon cease to exist, and the war they deprecate, will speedily be brought with added terrors to their own homes.

The Constitution belongs to the people,—to the people of 1862, not to those of 1787. It must and will be modified to suit the wishes of the former, by their representatives in Congress, must as the English Constitution has been modified by Parliament, or it will be destroyed. The great danger to our Constitution arises not from its pliability, but from its rigid resistance to change. It may be thought, by some, that it would run greater risks if committed to the caprice of the multitude, or to such a Legislature as the multitude elects. But these perils must be encountered in a republic. If the people cannot preserve the Constitution, it must perish, for it cannot be preserved by the Judiciary. The only reliance in a popular Government is on the intelligence of the people, which in our country is so great as to inspire just confidence in the future.

4.5 The Thirteenth Through Fifteenth Amendments

No amendments have altered the Constitution more than the three which were adopted at the end of the Civil War. The Thirteenth Amendment abolished involuntary servitude, or slavery, except in cases of punishment, thus broadening the scope of Lincoln's Emancipation Proclamation (which had applied only behind enemy lines) and giving it a firm foundation in law. The Fourteenth Amendment overturned the *Dred Scott* Decision (1857) that declared that blacks were not and could not be American citizens and went on to designate rights which all citizens would now be guaranteed; it also attempted to take care of other matters like representation, eligibility to run for office, and debt payment arising from the Civil War. The Fifteenth Amendment, for a long time a dead letter of the Constitution evaded by literacy tests, grandfather clauses, all-white primaries, poll taxes, and even physical intimidation, further prohibited discrimination in voting on the basis of race.

Amendment XIII [1865]

SECTION 1. Neither slavery nor involuntary servitude, except as a punishment for crime whereof the party shall have been duly convicted, shall exist within the United States, or any place subject to their jurisdiction.

SECTION 2. Congress shall have power to enforce this article by appropriate legislation.

Amendment XIV [1868]

SECTION 1. All persons born or naturalized in the United States, and subject to the jurisdiction thereof, are citizens of the United States and of the State wherein they reside. No State shall make or enforce any law which shall abridge the privileges or immunities of citizens of the United States; nor shall any State deprive any person of life, liberty, or property, without due process of law; nor deny to any person within its jurisdiction the equal protection of the laws.

SECTION 2. Representatives shall be apportioned among the several States according to their respective numbers, counting the whole number of persons in each State, excluding Indians not taxed. But when the right to vote at any election for the choice of electors for President and Vice-President of the United States, Representatives in Congress, the Executive and Judicial officers of a State, or the members of the Legislature thereof, is denied to any of the male inhabitants of such State, being twenty-one years of age, and citizens of the United States, or in any way abridged, except for participation in rebellion, or other crime, the basis of representation therein shall be reduced in the proportion which the number of such male citizens shall bear to the whole number of male citizens twenty-one years of age in such State.

SECTION 3. No person shall be a Senator or Representative in Congress, or elector of President and Vice-President, or hold any office, civil or military, under the United States, or under any State, who, having previously taken an oath, as a member of Congress, or as an officer of the United States, or as a member of any State legislature, or as an executive or judicial officer of any State, to support the Constitution of the United States, shall have engaged in insurrection or rebellion against the same, or given aid or comfort to the enemies thereof. But Congress may by a vote of two-thirds of each House, remove such disability.

SECTION 4. The validity of the public debt of the United States, authorized by law, including debts incurred for payment of pensions and bounties for services in suppressing insurrection or rebellion, shall not be questioned. But neither the United States nor any State shall assume or pay any debt or obligation incurred in aid of insurrection or rebellion against the United States, or any claim for the loss of emancipation of any slave; but all such debts, obligations and claims shall be held illegal and void.

SECTION 5. The Congress shall have power to enforce, by appropriate legislation, the provisions of this article.

Amendment XV [1870]

SECTION 1. The right of citizens of the United States to vote shall not be denied or abridged by the United States or by any State on account of race, color, or previous condition of servitude.

SECTION 2. The Congress shall have power to enforce this article by appropriate legislation.

4.6 Judge John Jameson Warns Against Sovereign Constitutional Conventions*

In addition to the illegal convention which led to the formation of the Confederate States of America, a number of states went through the process of altering their constitutions by conventions. Delegates to a number of these conventions took the position that they were sovereigns with complete power to do what they chose to do. These events led Judge John Jameson to make the most exhaustive study of constitutional conventions ever published in the United States. Jameson argued that conventions were not sovereign but were subordinate to the state constitutions. Below are excerpts from the Preface to Jameson's book in which he casts light on his motives for writing and from the passage from his first chapter where he attempted to distinguish different types of conventions.

The Motive For Jameson's Treatise

In 1862, certain influential members of the Illinois Constitutional Convention, then in session, set up for that body, in debate, a claim of inherent powers amounting almost to absolute sovereignty,—maintaining, for instance, that though the Act of the General Assembly under which the Convention had met required it to submit the fruit of its labors to the people,

---

* John Jameson, *A Treatise on Constitutional Conventions; Their History, Powers, and Modes of Proceeding*, 4th ed. (Chicago: Callaghan and Company, 1887), iii-iv, pp. 1-16.

for ratification or rejection, it might lawfully refuse to do so and put the Constitution it should frame in operation without any reference whatever to the people. At the same time rumors were current throughout the State that there were in that body, seeking to control it, many members of a secret organization supposed to be disloyal to the Union, called the "Knights of the Golden Circle." Alarmed by this claim of power, which he deemed excessive, as well as by these sinister rumors, the author commenced a study of the Convention as an American institution from its foundation and in all its aspects and relations, with a view to ascertain whether the claim of power referred to was warranted either by history or by constitutional principles. The result was the text of the first edition of this work. Because, in the course of his examination of the Convention system, the author found reason to believe, as he thought, that the origin, functions, and powers of the institution had been widely misapprehended, and that, as conceived by the "natural man," without knowledge or experience, jumping to conclusions respecting it hastily, it had been and was a source of extreme danger to the republic, the work was published by him in the autumn of 1866. The same considerations, strengthened by subsequent reflection and research, and by the change of sentiment in regard to the subject, which he could not but observe after the first edition of his work was published, a change as apparent as it was gratifying, not only in the press and in the debates of our Conventions and legislatures, but in the courts, have impelled the author to issue subsequent editions of the work until this, the fourth edition, now appears. His object in writing it having been simply to throw light upon a part of our constitutional apparatus which had not previously attracted the attention of lawyers and publicists, should the work have effected this, whatever the result otherwise may have been, the author will regard the many years of labor devoted by him to its preparation as not spent in vain.

The Various Kinds of Conventions

It is my purpose, in the following pages, to inquire into the history, powers, and modes of proceeding of the CONSTITU-

TIONAL CONVENTION, one of the most important and most characteristic of the political institutions of the United States.

Of the American system of government, the two leading principles are, first, that laws and Constitutions can be rightfully formed and established only by the people over whom they are to be put in force; and, secondly, that the people being a corporate unit, comprising all the citizens of the state, and, therefore, too unwieldy to do this important work directly, agents or representatives must be employed to do it, and that, in such numbers, so selected, and charged respectively with such functions, as to make it reasonably certain that the will of the people will be not only adequately but speedily executed.

The function of framing and enacting the statute law is commonly, by the practice of all representative governments, intrusted to a numerous body, called a legislature. Constitutions, on the other hand, considered as written instruments, are the work of various agencies, according to the genius of special circumstances of the states concerned, some being formed by the executive branch of the government, some by the legislature, and some by a body for that purpose specially chosen and commissioned. Thus, in England, this duty is exclusively committed to King, Lords, and Commons in Parliament assembled. Under the imperial *regimes* of the first and the third Napoleons, in France, the *plebiscites*, determining the form and powers of the government, though nominally the work of the Senate, were and are really dictated by those monarchs. With us, in America, there is set apart a special agency, to which is confided wholly, or mainly, the business of fundamental legislation,—the Constitutional Convention. It is this agency which frames our Constitution, and which, generally, as changes in them become necessary, is charged with maturing the needed amendments. In some cases, under authority for that purpose expressly given, it both forms and establishes our fundamental codes, but commonly it acts in conjunction with some other department of the existing government; the one presenting, after mature deliberation, in the form of proposals, a connected scheme, and the other by its sanction imparting to that scheme the force and vigor of law.

To any society, far enough advanced in civilization to demand as well the ascertainment as the protection of its civil and political rights, no institution could be of more interest than one charged thus with the *role* of both founder and restorer of its social machinery. Is this institution, it might be asked, subject to any law, to any restriction? What claims does it itself put forth, and what do the precedents teach, in relation to its nature and powers? When called into existence, is it the servant, or the master, of the people, by whom it was spoken into being? Whatever be its relations to the general source of political power, whether those of subordination or of independence, what is the place in our system, what are the relations to other governmental agencies, the normal functions and powers, of an institution, that, however hedged about by legal restraints, obviously exhibits more features that are menacing to republican liberty than any other in our whole political structure.

To the interest attaching to the Convention, thus, from abstract considerations, has been added a greater, resulting from the connection of that institution with recent political events. The desolating war of secession, which closed, in 1865, could hardly have been inaugurated but for the use made by the revolting faction of that institution. For reasons, which will be more fully explained hereafter, it had come to be a maxim in the practical jurisprudence of the United States, at least in some of the States, that whatever had been done by a Constitutional Convention, had been done by the people, "in their primary and sovereign capacity," and was therefore absolutely unquestionable, on legal or constitutional grounds; and there were not wanting those who arrogated to that ill-defined assembly, as by an extension to it of the absurd maxim, that "the voice of the people is the voice of God," an omnipotence transcending that higher law, to which ordinary legislative assemblies acknowledge themselves at all times subject. When to this, which is deemed one of the most impudent heresies of our times, was added its fellow, the dogma of State sovereignty, with its corollary, the duty of State allegiance, the transformation of a loyal community into a band of parricides seeking to pull down the edifice of our liberties, need be but the work of a day. To effect it, there was needed but a vote of a few conspirators, sitting as a Constitutional Convention, pretending to utter the voice of the people, and refusing to submit their ordinances to the test of a popular vote, under the false plea that neither the theory of the Convention system nor the practice of the fathers made such a submission necessary.

This picture of treachery and cunning, playing upon popular ignorance for their country's ruin, describes with precision the historical drama that culminated in the secession of the States of the South, in 1860-1. For, surely, it is not too much to say that without the moral effect of those disorganizing maxims, which impressed upon Southern consciences the duty of "going with one's State," there could have been no victories won by the armies of treason, even had an outbreak of hostilities been possible.

Of an institution to which are conceded a position so important and influence so decisive, but of which the true character and relations are so ill understood as to give rise to widespread misapprehensions, no apology is needed for an attempt to develop their history and illustrate the nature and principles.

Before entering upon the task indicated, it is important to clear the way by carefully discriminating the institution in question from others known under the same general designation of *Conventions*, but differing from it in their essential principles and function. To do this, will be the principal object of this chapter.

There are known to the social life of our times, in America four species of *Conventions*, namely:—

I. THE SPONTANEOUS CONVENTION, or PUBLIC MEETING.

II. THE ORDINARY LEGISLATIVE CONVENTION, or GENERAL ASSEMBLY.

III. THE REVOLUTIONARY CONVENTION.

IV. THE CONSTITUTIONAL CONVENTION.

These will now be considered in their order.

I. BY SPONTANEOUS CONVENTIONS, I mean those voluntary assemblages of citizens, which characterize free communities in advanced stages of civilization, having for their purpose agitation or conference in respect of their industrial, religious, political, or other social interests. These gatherings are at once the effects and the causes of social life and activity, doing for the state what the waves do for the sea: they prevent stagnation, the precursor of decay and death. They are among the most efficient manufactories of public opinion; or, rather, they are public opinion in the making,—public opinion fit to be the basis of political action, because sound and wise, and not a mere echo of party cries and platforms. Spontaneous assemblages, for such purposes, of the masses of a people, betoken a very high state of civilization, or instincts that are sure to develop into it. To be possible, in perfection, as we see them amongst us, freedom must be ripe and well-nigh universal. But when rulers and social institutions do not favor them, to their occurrence at all would be necessary a native passion for liberty strong enough to break all chains, and which could be daunted by no perils. We are prepared, therefore, to believe that it is only our own race, here and in England, that has thus far successfully vindicated the right of freely assembling. This right was asserted in England as early as the twelfth century, history telling us of the "*conventus publicos propria authoritate*," or voluntary meetings of the people, under the protection of the common law. With some fluctuations, as the work of social development proceeded, this right became more firmly rooted in the parent soil, and from it a vigorous scion was planted in America, which has exhibited a still stronger vitality, and now overspreads the land. A common and most invaluable provision of our constitutions, State and Federal, guarantees to the people the right "peaceably to assemble and petition the government for a redress of grievances." The right, thus expressed, involves those of discussing all measures of the government; of embodying in resolutions or remonstrance the general sentiment in regard to the policy and the acts of the public authorities; and, in general, of exercising the privilege, without which freedom is impossible, of saying and hearing whatsoever one pleases, being at the same time responsible for abuses of that privilege. Such is the Spontaneous Convention: a body which meets upon the call of any individual; adjourns when it pleases; is wholly unofficial; whose determinations have no efficacy whatever, except as expressions of matured or maturing opinion; which is subject to no laws but the *lex parliamentaria*,—common sense applied to the action of numerous assemblies,—and the law which enjoins upon all men to keep the peace; and yet a body which is quite as important to the continued healthy life of a commonwealth as either of the four species of Conventions mentioned.

II. The second species of Conventions, consisting of our GENERAL ASSEMBLIES, is so well known, that I need not dwell upon it. A General Assembly is, in our American system, a collection of representatives of the people, freely elected in pursuance of the Constitution, and empowered to enact the ordinary statute law. Deriving its existence and powers from the people, through the Constitution, it can do nothing except by the authority contained in that instrument, and is, therefore, official, or vicarious, but at the same time subaltern,—the people being the principal and paramount source of power. Yet, as we shall have occasion to note hereafter, though subordinate in relation to the people, considered as the creator of the government and Constitution, the legislature is nevertheless *prima inter pares*, when compared with other departments of the government; or, as it has been expressed by speculative writers, is more nearly sovereign than any of the departments which are ordinarily regarded as coordinate with it.

III. The third species of Conventions, as its name implies, is a part of the apparatus of revolution. It consists of those bodies of men who, in times of political crisis, assume, or have cast upon them, provisionally, *the function of government*. They either supplant or supplement the existing governmental organization. The principal characteristics of this species are, that they are *dehors* the law; that they derive their powers, if justifiable, from necessity,—the necessity, in default of the regular authorities, or protection and guidance to the Commonwealth,—or, if not justifiable, from revolutionary force and violence; that they are possessed, accordingly, to an indeterminate extent, depending on the circumstances of each case, *of governmental powers*; finally, *that they are not subaltern or ancillary to any other institution whatever, but lords paramount of the entire political domain*. To this may be added, that they are of no definite numbers or organization, comprising sometimes one and sometimes several chambers, and composed indifferently of ex-officers of the government that was, of persons possessing neither office nor the qualifications requisite for it, nor even for the elective franchise, or of a mixture of all of these together, as chance may have tossed them to the surface. The general purpose of the Revolutionary Convention, moreover, is to bridge over a chasm between two orders of things: an order that has expired or been extinguished; and an order emerging, under the operation of existing social forces, to replace it. In short, a Revolutionary Convention is simply a PROVISIONAL GOVERNMENT.

Examples of the Revolutionary Convention have been numerous in the political history of the world, and they are becoming daily more so. Among the most famous and, for our purpose, the most important, are those held in England in 1660 and 1689.

In those cases the ruling dynasty having abdicated the throne, or been expelled from it, there was in the kingdom not only no organized government, but no central authority legally competent to institute one. There was, it is true, the people of England, but they could not so assemble as to act as a unit. The parliament had ceased, in law, to exist with the reign of the monarch by whose writ it had been summoned, and no new parliament could be legally called, because for that the royal writ was absolutely necessary. In these alarming crises, and as the last and only resource for temporary government, as well as for providing the initial points of new organizations, Conventions were summoned. That called in 1660 consisted of persons elected by the several constituencies of the realm, as for a lawful parliament, but elected illegally, on the recommendation of a rump of the old Parliament, which had been dispersed by the army under Richard Cromwell, and, for that reason, as Macaulay observes, more accurately described as a *Convention*, as having been called without the royal writ. The Convention of 1689, summoned by the Prince of Orange, afterwards William III., on his accession by force to the throne left vacant by James II., consisted of persons elected in a similar manner, on the call of the usurping prince, issued at the recommendation of the lords spiritual and temporal at the time in London, forming a *quasi* House of Lords, and of old members of the House of Commons, together with the magistrates of the city of London, acting as a House of Commons. This Convention, also, though made up of members chosen by the electors for members of Parliament, in their several districts, was not styled or considered a Parliament, because called by a person not constitutionally authorized, acting on the advice of an assembly, which, though regarded by the nation with a large measure of the respect due to a Parliament, on account of the eminence and former official station of its members, was yet without a shadow of legal authority. The proceeding was revolutionary, and so universally admitted to be. Such were the two great English Conventions, the models after which most subsequent bodies of the same class have been formed or organized, both in this country and in Europe, and of which, as we shall see, our Constitutional Conventions are special adaptations or modifications. They were Provisional Governments,—the only governments England had during the periods of their existence. And for our purpose it will be interesting to note further, that the English Convention of 1689, having taken steps, as a revolutionary body, to settle the succession to the throne, passed a bill declaring itself to be a parliament, and from that time acted as such in conjunction with the king it had itself called to the throne.

Interesting examples of the Revolutionary Convention are found in our own history. The first occurred in New England simultaneously with the English Convention of 1689, its assembling being the result, in part, of the same causes which led to that, but, in part, of causes local to New England. Both, however, were called and composed in a similar manner, and organized after the same model, that of 1660, convened at the time of the Restoration.

The leading facts in the history of that held in New England are as follows: —

Whilst the tyrannical acts of James II. were, in England, exciting the discontents which finally led to his abdication, those of Sir Admond Andros, the Governor of Massachusetts, were arousing the fiercest opposition in New England, against both the colonial and the imperial administrations. It is believed that as early as January, 1689, before the news of the landing of the Prince of Orange in England had reached the colony, arrangements had been made in the latter to rise against the unpopular governor. So soon as that news arrived an outbreak occurred. On the 18th of April, a "Declaration of the Gentlemen, Merchants, and Inhabitants of Boston and the country adjacent," was published, recounting their oppressions, and announcing their purpose to "seize upon the persons of those few ill men which have been (next to our sins) the grand authors of our miseries." The governor and the magistrates and crown officers adhering to him, were accordingly thrown into prison; the castle was occupied by colonial militia, and an English frigate, lying in the harbor, was forced to surrender. On the day following this revolutionary outbreak, the leaders in the movement with twenty-two others, whom they now associated, formed themselves into a Provisional Government, under the name of a "Council for the Safety of the People and Conservation of the Peace." Feeling the weakness of their position, since they "held their place neither by deputation from the sovereign nor by election of the people," and hesitating to set up again the charter, "formally condemned by the Kings' courts," "they decided to call a *Convention*, to consist of two delegates from each town in the jurisdiction, except Boston, which was to send four. This Convention met on the 9th of May, and attempted to put the charter in force, but meeting with opposition from the magistrates, steps were taken to call a second Convention with "express instructions from their towns," Fifty-four towns sent delegates to this latter Convention, the large majority of them with instructions to insist on the resumption of the charter.

After two days' debate, the governor and magistrates, chosen at the last election under the charter, were prevailed upon "to assume the trusts committed to them, and, in concert with the delegates recently elected, to form a General Court," or Legislature, "and administer the colony, for the present, according to the ancient forms."

Two days after this revolutionary government was established, a ship arrived from England with the news that the revolution there had succeeded, and bring orders to the authorities to proclaim King William and Queen Mary.

The Convention, organized as above stated, by which this revolution was effected, was evidently of the species I have denominated Revolutionary Conventions. It rested for its warrant upon necessity, and sought its ends through force. It was a *government*, intended to supplant another government, and not merely a political institution designed to be subservient to a government conceived of as existing in full activity.

Thus the *Revolutionary Convention* became domesticated in America. Since this first appearance, there have been numerous others, a few during the colonial condition, but most of them in the course of our two great civil revolutions, those of 1776 and 1861. As we shall see in a subsequent chapter, most of the organizations, by which, under the names of "provincial Conventions," or "Provincial Congresses," the first of those revolutions was consummated, and all of those by which the late secession movement was carried through, were strictly Revolutionary Conventions.

One of the best known examples of the Revolutionary Convention is the National Convention, by which was effected the bloody overthrow of the old feudal monarchy of France at the close of the last century. Enough has been said, however, to show the characteristic feature of an institution, too often, as we shall see, confounded with the Constitutional Convention, to which I now pass.

IV. The last species of the Convention is the CONSTITUTIONAL CONVENTION. It differs from the last preceding, in being, as its name implies, *constitutional*; not simply as having for its object the framing or amending of Constitutions, but as being within, rather than without, the pale of the fundamental law; as ancillary and subservient and not hostile and paramount to it. This species of Convention sustains an official relation to the state, considered as a political organization. It is charged with a definite, and not a discretionary and indeterminate, function. It always acts under a commission, for a purpose ascertained and limited by law or by custom. Its principal feature, as contradistinguished from the Revolutionary Convention, is, that at every step and moment of its existence, it is subaltern,—it is evoked by the side and at the call of a government preexisting and intended to survive it, for the purpose of administering to its special needs. It never supplants the existing organization. It never governs. Though called to look into and recommend improvements in the fundamental laws, it *enacts* neither them nor the statute law; and it performs no act of administration. As John Randolph said in the Virginia Convention of 1829, it is called as counsel to the people, "as a state physician, to propose remedies for the state's diseases." But it is a physician whose ministrations are confined to the extraordinary maladies requiring a fundamental change in the Constitution, not to those constantly recurring but petty disorders which demand the interposition of the ordinary legislature.

It is apparent that institutions, whose definitions thus mutually exclude each other, cannot be the same, however similar the names by which they are popularly known.

But it may happen, (instances will be hereafter mentioned in which it has happened,) that the Constitutional Convention may, by usurpation, assume one or more of the powers of the Revolutionary Convention; or that the latter may exercise those of the former. How, in such a case, is the usurping body to be classed? This question is one of great importance, but is susceptible of a ready answer.

A Revolutionary Convention, because it is, *ex vi termini*, unlimited, in respect of both the kind and the degree of its powers, may take upon itself the functions of either of the three lower species of conventions, under the same warrant by which it justifies the assumption of revolutionary powers. A body which can, violently and without law, uproot all existing institutions, can clearly do the lesser act of digesting, or even of enacting, amendments to the Constitution. But, in doing so, it does not change its original character; it is still a Revolutionary Convention, and all its acts must stand on the footing of those which involve the widest stretch of power.

But the converse of this proposition does not hold true. If a Constitutional Convention step outside the circle of the law, it does not continue to be a Constitutional Convention, but, so far, becomes that whose powers or methods it assumes,—a Revolutionary Convention. It leaves the domain of law, which is one of specified and restricted powers, and enters upon that of arbitrary discretion, within which law is silent, and where he is master who wields the greater force.

Whenever, therefore, a Constitutional Convention, appointed, as we shall see it usually is, for a specific duty under the Constitution, presumes to overpass the limits imposed by its commission, by custom, or by the maxims of political prudence, and to do acts requiring the exercise of a *revolutionary discretion*, it ceases to be a Constitutional, and becomes, in the eye of the law, *ab initio*, a Revolutionary Convention.

If I mistake not, in the confounding of the distinctions noted in the preceding sections between the Constitutional and the Revolutionary Convention, will be found the origin of the most fatal misconceptions attaching to any part of our political system. To show how those misconceptions arise, as well as to obviate their effects by bringing into as clear a light as possible the distinctions indicated, it is necessary to inquire into the genesis and historical development of the Constitutional Convention.

The history of that institution may be summed up in a few words; it is an adaptation to the exigencies of constitutional life and government, in the United States, of the Revolutionary Convention, as derived from our English ancestors of 1660 and 1689. How the transformation occurred, by which the wild scion from the woods was domesticated in the garden of the Constitution and made to subserve the purposes of regulated life, will now be shown.

When the American colonies assumed the position in *independent States*, the revolt, by which the change in their political relations was accomplished, was conducted by revolutionary conventions in the several States, patterned after those described in the previous sections of this chapter. In other words, our fathers borrowed the revolutionary machinery which history showed to have been so efficacious in the time of Charles II. and James II., as they also, in general, inherited the political principles and the forms of administration of the mother-country. Thus, the institution was planted upon American soil.

The next step, if less obvious, was not less important. The Revolution accomplished, when our fathers came to embody the rights achieved by it in institutions independent of the crown, two circumstances led them to establish governments limited to the exercise of granted powers. The first of these was affection for their charters, so long, in many of the colonies, the most effective barriers against parliamentary oppression; the second, apprehension of an American monarchy,—a mere phantom, as we now know, but a phantom which, at that time, to many imaginations, threatened immediate and serious evils. However this may be, the tendency indicated was universal, and has given character to our political institutions to this day.

But it was not forgotten that the colonial charters were mere royal grants, and that the tenures by which they were held had sometimes been very insecure. Here, it is true, there was no sovereign authority but the people, represented chiefly by the General Assemblies, a circumstance which might be thought to render the wrongful abrogation of their characters improbable, if not impossible. But as the worst oppressions, experienced by them as colonies, had been at the hands of Parliament,—a popular assembly, in theory, if not in fact, representing the Commons of the whole empire,—might not their own assemblies in time become the oppressors, especially if allowed to retain not only the power of ordinary legislation, but that transcendent one exercised by the English Parliament, of framing the organic law?

This apprehension, nearly universal at the time of our separation, led the statesmen of the Revolution to seek some other depositary of the latter power. This they found in Conventions, called by the governments in force in the several colonies, modelled, in point of structure and organization, after the Revolutionary Conventions, with which they were so familiar, but charged with the single function of maturing the charters, or Constitution, rendered necessary by the altered condition of their affairs. As thus used, the Convention ceased to be the revolutionary body which had alone been known by that name in former times. But it was the same institution, for our fathers knew no other, but the same with important differences. Brought into operation as a regular constitutional agency, in aid of a system established, it was shorn of the extraordinary powers possessed by it when it was itself the government; the government, too, of a state in a time of social upheaval and transition, in which the laws were silent, and those intrusted with the public administration were restrained by no law but that of the strongest.

It is not my purpose here to trace at any great length the limits of this new development. It is enough to observe, that the change began with the Revolution, of the fruits of which it constituted so valuable and characteristic a part. It was not accomplished, however, in a moment, nor can it be said to be even yet completely consummated, since there are doubts and misconceptions widely prevalent regarding it, which are inconsistent with the idea of a perfect development of the new institution. An important step in that development has only lately been taking, in the case of the Lecompton Convention, so-called, of the Territory of Kansas. In the discussion of that case, in 1857-9, the question, whether or not a Constitutional Convention has power either to refuse to submit the fruit of its deliberations to those who are to be governed by it, or to submit it to them in such a way as to deprive them substantially of a voice in determining its form and character, was for the first time definitely settled. The same process will doubtless continue in the future.

When the first Constitutions were framed for the colonies, in 1776, the limits and distinctions, above explained, were far less understood than they have since become. In a subsequent chapter, it will be seen that the most important principle in the convention system—that which requires the Constitutional Convention to be kept totally disconnected, as well in theory as in practice, from the Revolutionary Convention—was sometimes, in those early days, disregarded. The statesmen of the Revolutionary period, though familiar with the principles and, to some extent, with the administration of the English government, were necessarily less so with those that were springing up about them; and of the features indispensable to be impressed upon an old institution coming now to be employed for a new constitutional purpose, so as to render its working easy and safe, they were wholly ignorant. Accordingly, in their first essays at constitution making, partly from this ignorance and partly from the urgent needs of the time, they allowed the functions of the Constitutional Convention, in some cases, to be exercised by its revolutionary prototype,—the Revolutionary Conventions assuming the duty, with others, of framing their first constitutions.

But, if the necessity of keeping the two institutions distinct was not at first generally apparent, it required but little experience of actual administration to convince men as intelligent and jealous of their liberties as our fathers, that if, to the function of suggesting, the Constitutional Conventions, become so common amongst them, should join that of establishing, their Constitutions of government, and not only so, but of framing and administering the ordinary laws of their respective States, as being but the less involved in the greater power, there would be practically no security at all for their liberties. Accordingly, we find that the cases in which the incompatible functions indicated were actually accumulated in the same hands were confined to the first years of the war, when the idea had not been dissipated that a satisfactory peace with England would soon make unnecessary the continuance of the State organizations, thus far regarded as temporary establishments for the government of the colonies, whilst the contest with England should continue.

We are to conceive of the Constitutional Convention, then, as an adaptation to constitutional uses of an institution originally revolutionary; that is, whose methods and principles of action, as well as whose purposes, were alien and hostile to established laws and Constitutions. And this is the real occasion of most of the misconceptions prevalent as to its true character. Thus, the notion has been common among even the well-informed, that the Constitutional Convention is above the law, the Constitution, and the government, all of which it may, therefore, it is conceived, respect and obey or not at its discretion; that it is possessed, in short, of the powers of its revolutionary namesake.

The origin of this misconception is ignorance of the simple facts of our constitutional history above detailed, and of the principles of our political system. To determine the rightful powers of the institution as adapted to our constitutional uses, men point to the English Conventions of 1660 and 1689, to that of the latter year in Massachusetts, to those by which our first Revolution was, in the various American colonies, begun and consummated. Those bodies, which, unquestionably, in many cases, framed Constitutions, were known to be possessed of other and extraordinary powers. They were called by high-sounding titles: "The Estates of the Realm;" "the People in their Primary and Sovereign Capacity;"—phrases, in whose indefiniteness could be discovered, or concealed, all possible attributions of power. The error has received additional currency from the extraordinary proceedings of the Conventions held in France, particularly that which piloted here upon the breakers in the closing years of the last century. Was not the Convention of our first ally, it is asked, which uprooted the monarchy and laid the foundations of the French Republic, an institution borrowed from us,—an institution, therefore, which has not here developed the extraordinary powers, exhibited by it in France, only because our occasions have never called them forth. The upshot of this reasoning is, the establishment of the axiom, that a Constitutional Convention wields all the powers, which, by the law of nature or of nations, are conceded to exist in the sovereign for which it acts—a degree of omnipotence to which, in a government of law, there can be found no parallel, and which is inconsistent with the fundamental principles of American liberty.

The Constitutional Convention, then, I consider as an exotic, domesticated in our political system, but in the process so transformed as to have become an essentially different institution from what it was as a Revolutionary Convention. . . .

4.7 The Slaughterhouse Cases Interpret the Fourteenth Amendment*

As indicated in an earlier reading, the Amendments adopted after the Civil War are among the most important in the entire document. The Fourteenth Amendment, which reversed the notorious *Dred Scott* decision is especially important, serving as a lynchpin for the rights of those who were once held in bondage. But just exactly how far did this Amendment intend to go in transferring rights which had traditionally rested for protection at the state level to the national government? This was the critical issue raised by the *Slaughterhouse Cases* of 1873, the Supreme Court's first attempt at interpreting the amendment.

At issue was an act by the Louisiana legislature, apparently motivated by a combination of greed and health concerns, which required all New Orleans butchers to do their work in specified abattoirs. Those whose livelihood was jeopardized by these new regulations came to Court alleging that their privileges and immunities as United States citizens had been abridged. The radically different answers the members of the majority and dissenting opinions gave to this plea indicates that even amendments may not put an end to constitutional questions, and that questions of language and intention are often as complicated in assessing amendments as in assessing the text of the Constitution itself.

Selection From Justice Miller's Opinion for the Court

Twelve articles of amendment were added to the Federal Constitution soon after the original organization of the govern-

---

* *The Butchers' Benevolent Association of New Orleans* v. *The Crescent City Live-Stock Landing and Slaughterhouse Company*, 83 U.S. 36 (1873); 21 L. Ed. 394, pp. 405-10 and 414-5.

ment under it in 1789. Of these all but the last were adopted so soon afterwards as to justify the statement that they were practically contemporaneous with the adoption of the original; and the twelfth, adopted in eighteen hundred and three, was so nearly so as to have become, like all the others, historical and of another age. But within the last eight years three other articles of amendment of vast importance have been added, by the voice of the people, to that now venerable instrument.

The most cursory glance at these articles discloses a unity of purpose, when taken in connection with the history of the times, which cannot fail to have an important bearing on any question of doubt concerning their true meaning. Nor can such doubts, when any reasonably exist, be safely and rationally solved without a reference to that history; for in it is found the occasion and the necessity for recurring again to the great source of power in this country, the people of the States, for additional guaranties of human rights; additional powers to the Federal Government; additional restraints upon those of the States. Fortunately that history is fresh within the memory of us all, and its leading features, as they bear upon the matter before us, free from doubt.

The institution of African slavery, as it existed in about half the States of the Union, and the contests pervading the public mind for many years, between those who desired its curtailment and ultimate extinction and those who desired additional safeguards for its security and perpetuation, culminated in the effort, on the part of most of the States in which slavery existed, to separate from the Federal Government, and to resist its authority. This constituted the war of the rebellion, and whatever auxiliary causes may have contributed to bring about this war, undoubtedly, the overshadowing and efficient cause was African slavery.

In that struggle slavery, as a legalized social relation, perished. It perished as a necessity of the bitterness and force of the conflict. When the armies of freedom found themselves upon the soil of slavery they could do nothing less than free the poor victims whose enforced servitude was the foundation of the quarrel. And when hard pressed in the contest these men (for they proved themselves men in that terrible crisis) offered their services and were accepted by thousands to aid in suppressing the unlawful rebellion, slavery was at an end wherever the Federal Government succeeded in that purpose. The Proclamation of President Lincoln expressed an accomplished fact as to a large portion of the insurrectionary districts, when he declared slavery abolished in them all. But the war being over, those who had succeeded in re-establishing the authority of the Federal Government were not content to permit this great act of emancipation to rest on the actual results of the contest or the Proclamation of the Executive, both of which might have been questioned in after times, and they determined to place this main and most valuable result in the Constitution of the restored Union as one of its fundamental articles. Hence the 13th article of amendment of that instrument . . .

Among the first Acts of legislation adopted by several of the States in the legislative bodies which claimed to be in their normal relations with the Federal Government, were laws which imposed upon the colored race onerous disabilities and burdens, and curtailed their rights in the pursuit of life, liberty and property, to such an extent that their freedom was of little value, while they had lost the protection which they had received from their former owners from motives both of interest and humanity. . . .

We repeat, then, in the light of this recapitulation of events, almost too recent to be called history, but which are familiar to us all; and on the most casual examination of the language of these amendments, no one can fail to be impressed with the one pervading purpose found in them all, lying at the foundation of each, and without which none of them would have been even suggested; we mean the freedom of the slave race, the security and firm establishment of that freedom, and the protection of the newly made freeman and citizen from the oppressions of those who had formerly exercised unlimited dominion over him. It is true that only the 15th Amendment, in terms, mentions the negro by speaking of his color and his slavery. But it is just as true that each of the other articles was addressed to the grievances of that race, and designed to remedy them as the fifteenth.

We do not say that no one else but the negro can share in this protection. Both the language and spirit of these articles are to have their fair and just weight in any question of construction. Undoubtedly, while negro slavery alone was in the mind of the Congress which proposed the 13th article, it forbids any other kind of slavery, now or hereafter. If Mexican peonage or the Chinese coolie labor system shall develop slavery of the Mexican or Chinese race within our territory, this Amendment may safely be trusted to make to void. And so, if other rights are assailed by the States which properly and necessarily fall within the protection of these articles, that protection will apply though the party interested may not be of African descent. But what we do say, and what we wish to be understood, is, that in any fair and just construction of any section or phrase of these amendments, it is necessary to look to the purpose which we have said was the pervading spirit of them all, the evil which they were designed to remedy, and process of continued addition to the Constitution until that purpose was supposed to be accomplished, as far as constitutional law can accomplish it. . . .

[Looking at the Fourteenth Amendment] the distinction between citizenship of the United States and citizenship of a State is clearly recognized and established. Not only may a man be a citizen of the United States without being a citizen of a State, but an important element is necessary to convert the former into the latter. He must reside within the State to make him a citizen of it, but it is only necessary that he should be born or naturalized in the United States to be a citizen of the Union.

It is quite clear, then, that there is a citizenship of the United States and a citizenship of a State, which are distinct from each other and which depend upon different characteristics or circumstances in the individual. . . .

Of the privileges and immunities of the citizens of the United States, and of the privileges and immunities of the citizen of the State, and what they respectively are, we will presently consider; but we wish to state here that it is only the former which are placed by this clause under the protection of the Federal Constitution, and that the latter, whatever they may be are not intended to have any additional protection by this paragraph of the Amendment.

If, then, there is a difference between the privileges and immunities belonging to a citizen of the United States as such, and those belonging to the citizen of the State as such, the latter must rest for their security and protection where they have heretofore rested; for they are not embraced by this paragraph of the Amendment. . . .

The constitutional provision . . . did not create those rights, which it called privileges and immunities of citizens of the States. It threw around them in that clause no security for the citizen of the State in which they were claimed or exercised. Nor did it profess to control the power of the state governments over the rights of its own citizens.

Its sole purpose was to declare to the several States, that whatever those rights, as you grant or establish them to your own citizens, or as you limit or qualify, or impose restrictions on their exercise, the same, neither more nor less, shall be the measure of the rights of citizens of other States within your jurisdiction.

It would be the vainest show of learning to attempt to prove by citations of authority, that up to the adoption of the recent Amendments, no claim or pretense was set up that those rights depended on the Federal Government for their existence or protection, beyond the very few express limitations which the Federal Constitution imposed upon the States—such, for instance, as the prohibition against *ex post facto* laws, bills of attainder, and laws impairing the obligation of contracts. But with the exception of these and a few other restrictions, the entire domain of the privileges and immunities of citizens of the States, as above defined, lay within the constitutional and legislative power of the States, and without that of the Federal Government. Was it the purpose of the 14th Amendment, by the simple declaration that no State should make or enforce any law which shall abridge the privileges and immunities of citizens of the United States, to transfer the security and protection of all the civil rights which we have mentioned, from the States to the Federal Government? And where it is declared that Congress shall have the power to enforce that article, was it intended to bring within the power of Congress the whole domain of civil rights heretofore belonging exclusively to the States?

All this and more must follow, if the proposition of the plaintiffs in error be sound. For not only are these rights subject to the control of Congress whenever in its discretion any of them are supposed to be abridged by state legislation, but that body may also pass laws in advance, limiting and restricting the exercise of legislative power by the States, in their most ordinary and usual functions, as in its judgment it may think proper on all such subjects. And still further, such a construction followed by the reversal of the judgments of the Supreme Court of Louisiana in these cases, would constitute this court a perpetual censor upon all legislation of the States, on the civil rights of their own citizens, with authority to nullify such as it did not approve as consistent with those rights, as they existed at the time of the adoption of this Amendment. The argument, we admit, is not always the most conclusive which is drawn from the consequences urged against the adoption of a particular construction of an instrument. But when, as in the case before us, these consequences are so serious, so far reaching and pervading, so great a departure from the structure and spirit of our institutions; when the effect is to fetter and degrade the state governments by subjecting them to the control of Congress, in the exercise of powers heretofore universally conceded to them of the most ordinary and fundamental character; when in fact it radically changes the whole theory of the relations of the state and Federal Governments to each other and of both these governments to the people; the argument has a force that is irresistible, in the absence of language which expresses such a purpose too clearly to admit of doubt.

We are convinced that no such results were intended by the Congress which proposed these Amendments, nor the Legislatures of the States, which ratified them.

Having shown that the privileges and immunities relied on in the argument are those which belong to citizens of the States as such, and that they are left to the state governments for security and protection, and not by this article placed under the special care of the Federal Government, we may hold ourselves excused from defining the privileges and immunities of citizens of the United States which no State can abridge, until some case involving those privileges may make it necessary to do so.

But lest it should be said that no such privileges and immunities are to be found if those we have been considering are excluded, we venture to suggest some which owe their existence to the Federal Government, its national character, its Constitution, or its laws.

One of these is well described in the case of *Crandall v. Nevada*, 6 Wall., 36 (73 U.S. XVIII., 745). It is said to be the right of the citizens of this great country, protected by implied guaranties of its Constitution, "to come to the seat of government to assert any claim he may have upon that government, to transact any business he may have with it, to seek its protection, to share its offices, to engage in administering its functions. He has the right of free access to its seaports, through which all operations of foreign commerce are conducted, to the sub-treasuries, land-offices, and courts of justices in the Several States." And quoting from the language of *Chief Justice* Taney in another case, it is said "that, for all the great purposes for which the Federal Government was established, we are one people with one common country; we are all citizens of the United States;" and it is as such citizens that their rights are supported in this court in *Crandall v. Nevada*.

Another privilege of a citizen of the United States is to demand the care and protection of the Federal Government over his life, liberty and property when on the high seas or within the jurisdiction of a foreign government. Of this there can be no doubt, nor that the right depends upon his character as a citizen of the United States. The right to peaceably assemble and petition for redress of grievances, the privilege of the writ of *habeas corpus*, are rights of the citizen guarantied [sic] by the Federal Constitution. The right to use the navigable waters of the United States, however they may penetrate the territory of the several States, and all rights secured to our citizens by treaties with foreign nations, are dependent upon citizenship of the United States, and not citizenship of a State.

One of these privileges is conferred by the very article under consideration. It is that a citizen of the United States can, of his own volition, become a citizen of any State of the Union by a *bona fide* residence therein, with the same rights as other citizens of that State. To these may be added the rights secured by the 13th and 15th articles of amendment, and by the other clause of the fourteenth, next to be considered.

But it is useless to pursue this branch of the inquiry, since we are of opinion that the rights claimed by these plaintiffs in error, if they have any existence, are not privileges and immunities of citizens of the United States within the meaning of the clause of the 14th Amendment under consideration. . . .

The adoption of the first eleven amendments to the Constitution so soon after the original instrument was accepted, shows a prevailing sense of danger at that time from the federal power. And it cannot be denied that such a jealousy continued to exist with many patriotic men until the breaking out of the late civil war. It was then discovered that the true danger to the perpetuity of the Union was in the capacity of the state organizations to combine and concentrate all the powers of the State, and of contiguous States, for a determined resistance to the General Government.

Unquestionably this has given great force to the argument, and added largely to the number of those who believe in the necessity of a strong national government.

But, however pervading this sentiment, and however it may have contributed to the adoption of the Amendments we have been considering, we do not see in those Amendments any purpose to destroy the main features of the general system. Under the pressure of all the excited feeling growing out of the war, our statesmen have still believed that the existence of the States with powers for domestic and local government, including the regulation of civil rights, the rights of persons and of property, was essential to the perfect working of our complex form of government, though they have thought proper to impose additional limitations on the States, and to confer additional power on that of the Nation.

But whatever fluctuations may be seen in the history of public opinion on this subject during the period of our national existence, we think it will be found that this court, so far as its functions required, has always held with a steady and an even hand, the balance between state and federal power, and we trust that such may continue to be the history of its relation to that subject so long as it shall have duties to perform which demand of it a construction of the Constitution, or of any of its parts.

The judgments of the Supreme Court of Louisiana in these cases are affirmed.

Selections from Justice Field's dissenting opinion

The first clause of the fourteenth Amendment changes this whole subject, and removes it from the region of discussion and doubt. It recognizes in express terms, if it does not create, citizens of the United States, and it makes their citizenship dependent upon the place of their birth, or the fact of their adoption, and not upon the Constitution or laws of any State or the condition of their ancestry. A citizen of a State is now only a citizen of the United States residing in that State. The fundamental rights, privileges and immunities which belong to him as a free man and a free citizen, now belong to him as a citizen of the United States, and are not dependent upon his citizenship of any State. The exercise of these rights and privileges, and the degree of enjoyment received from such exercise, are always more or less affected by the condition and the local institutions of the State, or city, or town where he resides. They are thus affected in a State by the wisdom of its laws, the ability of its officers, the efficiency of its magistrates, the education and morals of its people, and by many other considerations. This is a result which follows from the constitution of society, and can never be avoided, but in no other way can they be affected by the action of the State, or by the residence of the citizen therein. They do not derive their existence from its legislation, and cannot be destroyed by its power.

The Amendment does not attempt to confer any new privileges or immunities upon citizens, or to enumerate or define those already existing. It assumes that there are such privileges and immunities which belong of right to citizens as such, and ordains that they shall not be abridged by state legislation. If this inhibition has no reference to privileges and immunities of this character, but only refers, as held by the majority of the court in their opinion, to such privileges and immunities as were before its adoption specially designated in the Constitution or necessarily implied as belonging to citizens of the United States, it was a vain and idle enactment, which accomplished nothing, and most unnecessarily excited Congress and the people on its passage. With privileges and immunities thus designated no State could ever have interfered by its laws, and no new constitutional provision was required to inhibit such interference. The supremacy of the Constitution and the laws of the United States always controlled any state legislation of that character. But if the Amendment refers to the natural and inalienable rights which belong to all citizens, the inhibition has a profound significance and consequence.

What, then, are the privileges and immunities which are secured against abridgement by state legislation?

In the 1st section of the Civil Rights Act Congress has given its interpretation to these terms, or at least has stated some of the rights which, in its judgment, these terms include; it has there declared that they include the right "to make and enforce contracts, to sue, be parties and give evidence; to inherit, purchase, lease, sell, hold, and convey real and personal property, and to full and equal benefit of all laws and proceedings for the security of person and property." That Act, it is true, was passed before the 14th Amendment, but the Amendment was adopted, as I have already said, to obviate objections to the Act, or, speaking more accurately, I should say, to obviate objections to legislation of a similar character, extending the protection of the National Government over the common rights of all citizens of the United States. Accordingly, after its ratification Congress re-enacted the Act under the belief that whatever doubts may have previously existed of its validity, they were removed by the Amendment. May 31, 1870, 16 Stat. at L., 144.

The terms "privileges and immunities" are not new in the Amendment; they were in the Constitution before the Amendment was adopted. They are found in the 2d section of the 4th article, which declares that "the citizens of each State shall be entitled to all privileges and immunities of citizens in the several States," and they have been the subject of frequent consideration in judicial decisions. In *Corfield v. Coryell*, 6 Wash. (C. C.), 380, *Mr. Justice* Washington said he had "no hesitation in confining these expressions to those privileges and immunities which were, in their nature, fundamental; which belong of right to citizens of all free governments, and which have at all times been enjoyed by the citizens of the several States which compose the Union, from the time of their becoming free, independent and sovereign;" and, in considering what those fundamental privileges were, he said that perhaps it would be more tedious than difficult to enumerate them, but that they might be "all comprehended under the following general heads: protection by the government; the enjoyment of life and liberty, with the right to acquire and possess property of every kind, and to pursue and obtain happiness and safety; subject, nevertheless, to such restraints as the government may justly prescribe for the general good of the whole." This appears to me to be a sound construction of the clause in question. The privileges and immunities designated are those which of right belong to the citizens of all free governments. Clearly among these must be placed the right to pursue a lawful employment in a lawful manner, without other restraint than such as equally affects all persons. . . .

4.8 Christopher Tiedeman Expounds His View of Constitutional Interpretation*

Among the most influential legal commentators of the late nineteenth and early twentieth century, few ranked higher than Christopher Tiedeman, law professor and author of a number of influential law treatises. Like many others of his day, Tiedeman was especially concerned that the Constitution serve the interests of property rights as it had increasingly

* Tiedeman, *The Unwritten Constitution of the United States: A Philosophical Inquiry into the Fundamentals of American Constitutional Law*, (New York: G. P. Putnam's Cons, 1890), pp. 155-65.

come to do (however largely via the due process clause of the Fourteenth Amendment rather than the privileges and immunities clause which had been rejected in the Slaughterhouse Cases) through Supreme Court decisions from this era. In 1890, Tiedeman published a book entitled, *The Unwritten Constitution*, in which he indicated that, not unlike the British Constitution, the U.S. Constitution was often changed by interpretation rather than by formal amendment. Indeed, the Court might even, as it had done in the Slaughterhouse Cases, severely restrict the meanings of amendments if not, in fact, repeal them.

If this were the case, however, one might call into question the whole value of a written constitution. It is this objection, which Tiedeman dealt with in his final chapter and which is reproduced below. His answer suggests the way that defenders of property rights in his day looked to unelected judges and justices to protect that which they otherwise feared might be taken from them by the people.

The Real Value of Written Constitutions.

If it be true, as the foregoing pages indicate, that all political constitutions undergo a constant and gradual evolution, keeping pace with the development of civilization, whether there be a written constitution or not; that these changes generally take place without formal amendments to the written constitution, the question would naturally arise: Of what value then is a written constitution which demonstrates its superiority over an unwritten constitution? The student who has been in the habit—which is still very common, if not universal, with practical lawyers and judges—of beginning his inquiry into constitutional law with the fundamental postulate that all constitutional rules have their root in the written declarations of the sovereign power, and that these declarations must be observed and obeyed in the spirit and meaning with which they were first promulgated,—such a student is apt, if he concedes the truth of the present thesis, to conclude that the superiority of written over purely unwritten constitutions has been dissipated altogether.

Not so. There is still room for the claim that the written constitution has in it elements which fundamentally change the character of the government, and which the unwritten constitution cannot possibly claim. Not only this, but the further claim may be substantiated that, with a full understanding of the real value of written constitutions, and a differentiation of that real value from its supposed but fictitious value, the superiority of written over purely unwritten constitutions is enhanced rather than diminished.

In the pursuit of this inquiry, it is necessary, as elsewhere, to take cognizance of the existence and effect of the two opposing social forces, which are present everywhere in bodies-politic, and which were prominently distinguishable at the time when the present Federal Constitution was adopted, viz.: the force of consolidation or centralization, and the force of disintegration. In every body-politic, in the effort to reconcile the claims of legal order and personal freedom from restraint, there are those who, on the one hand, are willing to sacrifice personal liberty to the cause of law and order, only as far as this sacrifice is absolutely necessary to the public safety; while, on the other hand, there are those who place so high a value upon law and order, that they are willing and are clamorous for the sacrifice of personal liberty, whenever that sacrifice promotes the public welfare. The first class of political units translate the Latin maxim, *salus populi suprema lex*, the *safety* of the people is the highest law; while the second class understand by that maxim that the *welfare* of the people is the highest law. The first class are therefore always afraid of the tyranny of officials; while the second class dread the power of the *demos*. The first class are anxious to impose restraints upon the power of the officials; while the second class are anxious to diminish as far as possible the influence of the people on legislation. The first class are thoroughly democratic in spirit; the second class, thoroughly aristocratic.

It is needless to state that both of these political classes were present in full force during the first years of our national existence. In the sense in which the terms have here been explained, George Washington, Alexander Hamilton, James Madison, John Randolph, and others, who took the same view of politics, were Aristocrats; while Samuel Adams, George Clinton, Thomas Jefferson, Patrick Henry, etc., were Democrats. The Aristocrats, dreading the absolutism of a democratic majority, sought to establish a government, which, although representative and popular in character, could be conducted and controlled by the better elements of society, and whose actual administration would be as free as possible from the influence of the masses. Hence, in the constitutional convention, they proposed the establishment of a strong national government, with such checks and safeguards thrown around the exercise of the power of amendment, as to give permanency to the form and character of the government, and to prevent radical changes in response to every popular clamor. The Democrats were, on the other hand, in constant fear of the establishment in this country of another George III., under the guise of a popular executive. They fought for their liberties step by step, the result of the contest being that the Federal Constitution became a collection of compromises. But, in order that the opposing element may not easily or inadvertently secure any increase of power for the Federal Government, the Democrats were likewise anxious to impose restraints upon the power of amendment. Both parties then concurred in the same conclusion, proceeding from opposite standpoints, and resting the conclusions upon different reasons.

But in their desire to impose restraints upon the exercise of official and popular power, respectively, they did not stop with making it difficult to amend the Constitution. Legislation was also made difficult by dividing the legislative power between three different independent bodies or departments of the government, the President, the Senate, and the House of Representatives, and requiring the concurrence of all, in order to make new laws, or to change existing ones,—except that the two houses of Congress were permitted, by a two-thirds vote in each house, to pass a law over the veto of the President.

The further provision is made, in the procurement of the same ends, that the President, the members of the Senate, and the House of Representatives, shall not all be elected at the same time. Taken as a whole, it was the most ingenious device for the prevention of legislation that the world has ever known; and after the adoption of the Constitution, both parties, from their respective standpoints, extolled these features of the Constitution, perhaps beyond their true value, losing sight of the great loss which ensures from unwise legislation, because of the supreme difficulty to secure its repeal or modification.

But all these checks and balances, set down in a written constitution, would be unavailing, if the means of securing their observance were not likewise provided in the exalted and extraordinary power of the courts to declare when a law, passed by Congress, or an act, committed by an official, is in contradiction of some provision of the Constitution. There is no express grant to the courts of such a power; it is simply deduced from the necessity of determining when there is a conflict which law they must apply to the cause of action, the law of Congress or the rule of the Constitution. Hence the courts have no authority to pass upon the constitutionality of legislation, except when the settlement of this question is necessary in deciding a *bona-fide* cause or action, brought before the court by *bona-fide* litigants. But whenever it becomes in this way necessary to pass upon the constitutionality of national and State legislation, the decision of the court is binding upon all the parties to the suit, and upon all others whose rights are in any way affected by the judgment of the court.

The same dread of the possession of absolute power by any department of the government is to be observed in the limitations of this extraordinary judicial power. The Supreme Court of the United States is not placed by the Constitution above the other departments of the government, with the power to prohibit any unconstitutional exercise of power by them. Not at all. This power to pass upon the constitutionality of a law or official act is only acquired by the court as an incident of its duty to enforce the law between parties litigant. The judgment of the United States Supreme Court on a constitutional question is not binding upon the President or upon Congress. Each department is required to obey the Constitution, according to the light in which the question under discussion is viewed by it. Andrew Jackson vetoed the bill providing for the maintenance of a system of banks by the Federal Government, on the ground that the bill was unconstitutional, although the Supreme Court had pronounced a similar bill to be within the constitutional power of Congress. Furthermore, Mr. Jefferson refused to obey the order of the court in Marbury v. Madison (1 Cranch, 137), while Mr. Lincoln ignored the opinion of Chief-Justice Taney, that the presidential proclamation of the suspension of the writ of *habeas corpus* was an unconstitutional exercise of authority. This is not all. The Supreme Court is still further shorn of its power by giving the Congress the power to increase the number of the Supreme Court judges, and thus, with the aid of the President, to change the composition and tendencies of the court. If at any time the Supreme Court should too persistently withstand any popular demand in a case in which the people will not submit to the judicial negative, by an increase in the number of the judges and the appointment to the newly created judgeships of men who will do the people's bidding, the popular will may be realized.

I do not think there can be much doubt that the danger of official tyranny has been successfully dissipated in the American constitutional system,—except so far as such tyranny may be demanded by a popular majority,—by the frequency of the elections and the short terms of service. Officials of all classes are too anxious to secure popular approval to make the administration of their offices a popular menace. They have their fingers constantly upon the public pulse, and every expression of popular approval and disapproval is noted. Indeed, the direct and constant responsibility of almost all classes of officials to public opinion, through frequent popular elections, goes very far towards nullifying any superior merit which the written constitution possesses over an unwritten constitution. For those officials, instead of attempting to throttle the popular will, are too ready to obey every popular caprice, it matters not how grievously the written Constitution may be thereby violated. And were the judges of the federal bench elected for short terms of service, and by popular election, as is the case in many of the States with respect to the

State judiciary, the written Constitution would serve very little purpose. It is not needed for the protection of the people against the tyranny of the officials; its only value is to serve as a check upon the popular will in the interest of the minority. By making the federal judiciary hold office during good behavior, and by providing in the Constitution for one Supreme Court, which cannot be abolished by congressional action, the means have been provided, in ordinary times of peace, of protecting the minority against the absolutism of a democratic majority. It enables a small body of distinguished men, whose life-long career is calculated to produce in them an exalted love of justice and an intelligent appreciation of the conflicting rights of individuals, and the life-tenure of whose offices serves to withdraw them from all fear of popular disapproval; it enables these independent, right-minded men, in accordance with the highest law, to plant themselves upon the provisions of the written Constitution, and deny to popular legislation the binding force of law, whenever such legislation infringes a constitutional provision. This is the real value of the written Constitution. It legalized, and therefore makes possible and successful, the opposition to the popular will.

But this opposition, when most successful, does not serve as a complete barrier to the popular will. Not only do the judges themselves fall under the influence of the prevalent sense of right, and ordinarily give in their decisions an accurate expression of it, but the various checks upon this veto power of the courts also serve to make their action only a dilatory proceeding; or, to adopt the happy expression of James Russell Lowell, this overruling power of the Supreme Court is an obstacle "in the way of the people's whim, not of their will." But with this limitation, extensive as it is, the written Constitution serves a most beneficent purpose. If one professes any faith at all in popular government, he must confess to a desire that the popular will shall prevail, and that the danger to the commonwealth lies not in the people's will but in their whims and ill-considered wishes. And even if the student does not have any faith in popular government, he must admit that, with an enlightened and spirited people, who know their strength, and who know that the living power in all municipal law proceeds from them, it is an absolute impossibility to suppress the popular will. Happy is that country whose constitutional system enables it to enjoy the blessings of popular government, while at the same time it is protected from the evils of hasty and passionate legislation. And while, perhaps, the constitutional system of this country has not developed exactly in accordance with the wishes and expectations of Washington, Hamilton, Madison, and their co-workers, yet if it were possible for them to know the results actually achieved, they would be satisfied with the knowledge that they had in a measure succeeded is establishing, what exists nowhere else, a popular government without democratic absolutism.

4.9 The Supreme Court Reverses Course Amid Calls for a New Constitutional Amendment*

The history of constitutional interpretation and amendment contains many ironies. In few cases are such ironies more evident than in the cases below. In the first case, *Munn v. Illinois* (1877) the Supreme Court rejected, as it had done in the Slaughterhouse Cases, attempts to interpret the due process clause of the Fourteenth Amendment in a substantive fashion so as to limit state regulation of industries, in this case, grain elevators. In the same year that a legal scholar was advocating an amendment to reverse this decision, the Court in *Chicago, Milwaukee, and St. Paul Railway Company v. Minnesota* (1890) effectively reversed course on its own, making interpretations standard which Munn had seemed to rule out as impossible. The Supreme Court's romance with the notion of "substantive due process" continued intermittently until its reversal of course in 1937, once again without the adoption of a constitutional amendment. (See Reading 6-9)

---

* *Munn v. Illinois*, 94 U.S. 94 U.S. 113 (1877), 24 L. Ed. pp. 83-4, and 87. Chas. C. Marshall, "A New Constitutional Amendment," 24 *American Law Review* (1890), pp. 909; 912-13; 929-31; *The Chicago, Milwaukee, and St. Paul Railway Company v. Minnesota*, 134 U.S. 418 (1890), 33 L. Ed. 970, p. 981.

***Munn v. Illinois*, Chief Justice Waite**

The question to be determined in this case is whether the General Assembly of Illinois can, under the limitations upon the legislative power of the States imposed by the Constitution of the United States, fix by law the maximum of charges for the storage of grain in warehouses at Chicago and other places in the State . . .

The Constitution contains no definition of the word "deprive," as used in the 14th Amendment. To determine its signification, therefore, it is necessary to ascertain the effect which usage has given it, when employed in the same or a like connection. . . .

From this it is apparent that, down to the time of the adoption of the 14th Amendment, it was not supposed that statutes regulating the use, or even the price of the use, of private property necessarily deprived an owner of his property without due process of law. Under some circumstances they may, but not under all. The Amendment does not change the law in this particular; it simply prevents the States from doing that which will operate as such a deprivation.

This brings us to inquire as to the principles upon which this power of regulation rests, in order that we may determine what is within and what without its operative effect. Looking, then, to the common law, from whence came the right which the Constitution protects, we find that when private property is "affected with a public interest it ceases to be *juris privati* only." . . . Property does become clothed with a public interest when used in a manner to make it of public consequence, and affect the community at large. When, therefore, one devotes his property to a use in which the public has an interest, he, in effect, grants to the public an interest in that use, and must submit to be controlled by the public for the common good, to the extent of the interest he has thus created. He may withdraw his grant by discontinuing the use; but, so long as he maintains the use, he must submit to the control. . . .

We know that this is a power which may be abused; but that is no argument against its existence. For protection against abuses by Legislatures the people must resort to the polls, not to the courts. . . .

Response in the Law Journals

[The article begins with quotations from *Munn v. Illinois* and other cases indicating the position that the Court had taken.] The Court of Appeals of the State of New York has within the last year or two approved the doctrine of the case referred to by the learned writers quoted above. This throws the weight of judicial authority very heavily in favor of the validity of that doctrine as a fundamental principle of jurisprudence. The possibility of retracing steps, of reversing or distinguishing, or of otherwise nullifying it through the courts is put quite beyond possibility. Our inquiry is whether these cases have truly discovered in our legislatures an inherent power on which our constitutions impose no check—a power hitherto unsuspected by the citizen and before which rights and property which he has always regarded as in his absolute possession and control may forever disappear. Our further inquiry is, if such a power exists, how may it be properly controlled. . . .

The prodigious consequences which may flow from these cases cannot be overlooked. Our boasted security in property rights falls away for the lack of a constitutional guaranty against this sovereign power thus discovered in our legislatures. It is apparent that against the whim of a temporary majority, inflamed with class-prejudice, envy or revenge, the property of no man is safe. And the danger is even greater in an age teeming with shifting theories of social reform and economic science, which seem to have but one common principle—the subjection of private property to governmental control for the good—or alleged good—of the public.

The State and Federal Constitutions contain, of course, two clauses which might appear at the first glance to have been framed to protect business or property where the legislature by its enactments so fixed prices or charges as to interfere with such business or property. One clause provides that a citizen shall not be deprived of his property except by "due process of law." The other clause forbids the acquisition by the State of private property for public use without compensation. The former clause as contained in the fourteenth amendment of the Federal Constitution has been sometimes regarded in the discussion of these very matters, as an express constitutional limitation on the delegation of power by the people to the State legislatures contained in the State constitutions. But it is clear that if, according to law, all property affected by a public use or interest, is in its very nature subject to legislative control, then for the legislature to control its use is in no sense to deprive a citizen of such property contrary to the law of the land. What the citizens owns is not absolute property but a *qualified and contingent interest in property*. Control by the legislature is its necessary incident, and such control, when exercised through a statute, is in its very self "due process of law." It is equally clear, for the same reasons, that such legislative control is not the appropriation of private property to public use. When the legislature exercises such control it does not appropriate property, for up to the extent of such control there is no property. Furthermore, these two clauses of the constitution have long been determined not to protect rights or property indirectly impaired by the exercise on the part of the state of any of its divers sovereign powers. The exercise of the taxing power, the police power, and the power of eminent domain have often indirectly resulted not only in impairing rights and property, but in stripping the citizen of them; but to such cases of indirect loss the courts have almost universally refused to apply the constitutional provisions now under discussion. The cases arising under the liquor legislation of the country clearly illustrate the point. Admitting that the ancient power of Parliament in social and economic legislation exists as an element of sovereignty to-day, and conceding that in our country the true sovereign—the people—has delegated this power, together with all legislative power to the legislature, imposing thereon no restraints excepting those expressly mentioned in the constitution, it is clear that this power of social or economic legislation must at once take its place beside the other analogous power of taxation, eminent domain and police regulation and that our constitutional guaranties can be applied to the first to no greater extent than to the three powers last mentioned. Hence it becomes apparent that the species of property under consideration is without constitutional guaranty against legislative control, for no clauses other than those considered exist in the constitutions, which could be invoked. . . .

If, as has been claimed, the Munn case and the Budd case are arrant absurdities, time might quite obliterate them or modifying decisions bury them out of sight, but if there is a living principle of Anglo-Saxon law underlying them, the evidence of which we have tried to set forth, something more may be necessary to secure property rights against legislative encroachments. . . .

Mr. Justice Field and Judge Peckham [dissenters in the cases Marshall opposes] are jurists of such eminence that their opinions have been as carefully read and will perhaps be regarded with as much attention in the future as the opinions of their respective courts; but the view is submitted with all deference that before their opinion can be carried out an amendment to the Federal and State constitutions is now necessary. [Here Marshall notes in a footnote that some believe the Chicago Railroad Case has overturned Munn, but he argues that the cases clearly differ.]. . . .

It is perhaps the natural course of things that the first great question in American political history should have been the question of personal liberty and that the second great question is that now before the American people, the question of private property. In the latter there are elements which "could furnish forth," a history surpassing in importance that of the slavery question. The latter was a struggle between sections. The property question must be a struggle between classes. In the one, America as the civilized nation last to abolish her slaves closed an epoch in history. In the latter there is much to show that she will open an epoch. That is the contrast. But there is a significant parallel. Years ago the Supreme Court of the United States introduced the slavery struggle with the Dred Scott decision. To-day it may be that it has introduced the property struggle with the decision of Munn v. Illinois. Each decision leaves a wide section of human rights unprotected by constitutional guarantees. Each is met with a storm of criticism from the advocates of the "higher law." Each is the opinion of a divided court. Each is accompanied with dissenting opinions of jurists of the highest rank and lastly each reveals a defect where all was supposed to be perfection and that defect is properly remedial only by constitutional amendment.

To devise and apply the remedy is the future work of legislatures and courts. Both the evil and the necessity of a remedy suggest the words of Henry Sumner Maine: "The Americans settled in a country of boundless unexhausted wealth have never been tempted to engage in socialistic legislation; but as far as they have gone a large measure of success cannot be denied to them,—success which has all but dispelled the old ill-fame of democracies. The short history of the United States has at the same time established one momentous negative conclusion: *When a democracy governs, it is not safe to leave unsettled any important question concerning the exercise of public powers.*"

Chicago, Milwaukee, and St. Paul Railway v. Minnesota, Justice Blatchford

By the second section of the Statute in question, it is provided that all charges made by a common carrier for the transportation of passengers or property shall be equal and reasonable. Under this provision, the carrier has a right to make equal and reasonable charges for such transportation. In the present case, the return alleged that the rate of charge fixed by the Commission was not equal or reasonable, and the supreme court held that the Statute deprived the Company of the right to show that judicially. The question of the reasonableness of a rate of charge for transportation by a railroad company, involving as it does the element of reasonableness both as regards the company and as regards the public, is eminently a question for judicial investigation, requiring due process of law for its determination. If the company is deprived of the power of charging reasonable rates for the use of its property, and such deprivation takes place in the absence of an investigation by judicial machinery, it is deprived of the lawful use of its property, and thus, in substance and effect, of the property itself, without due process of law and in violation of the Constitution of the United States; and in so far as it is thus deprived, while other persons are permitted to receive reasonable profits upon their invested capital, the company is deprived of the equal protection of the laws.

4.10 Justice Harlan Urges His Brethren to Respect *Stare Decisis**

In one of its most dramatic decision of the second half of the nineteenth century, the Supreme Court declared in *Pollock v. Farmers' Loan & Trust Co.* that the national income tax was unconstitutional. This decision was at odds with previous practice and with the Court's own earlier decisions. In the selection below, Justice Harlan indicates his reservations about the Court's position and raises some interesting questions about the proper role of *stare decisis*, or precedent, in judicial decision-making. Harlan even indicates at one point that he favors an amendment to overturn this decision; the Sixteenth Amendment did, of course, eventually bring Harlan's wish into realization.

Mr. Justice Harlan, Dissenting

The practice of a century, in harmony with the decisions of the court, under which uncounted millions have been collected by taxation, ought to be sufficient to close the door against further inquiry, based upon the speculations of theorists, and the varying opinions of statesmen who participated in the discussions, sometimes very bitter, relating to the form of government to be established in place of the Articles of Confederation under which, it has been well said, Congress could declare everything and do nothing.

But this view has not been accepted in the present cases, and the questions involved in them have been examined just as if they had not been settled by the long practice of the government, as well as by judicial decisions covering the entire period since 1796 and giving sanction to that practice. It seems to me that the court has not given to the maxim of *stare*

---

* *Pollock v. Farmers' Loan & Trust Co.*, 158 U.S. (1895), pp. 662-3, 671-2, 674, and 685.

decisis the full effect to which it is entitled. While obedience to that maxim is not expressly enjoined by the Constitution, the principle that decisions, resting upon a particular interpretation of that instrument, should not be lightly disregarded where such interpretation has been long accepted and acted upon by other branches of the government and by the public, underlies our American jurisprudence. There are many constitutional questions which were earnestly debated by statesman [sic] and lawyers in the early days of the Republic. But having been determined by the judgments of this court, they have ceased to be the subjects of discussion. While, in a large sense, constitutional questions may not be considered as finally settled, unless settled rightly, it is certain that a departure by this court from a settled course of decisions on grave constitutional questions, under which vast transactions have occurred, and under which the government has been administered during great crises, will shake public confidence in the stability of the law. . . .

Why do I say that the decision just rendered impairs or menaces the national authority? The reason is so apparent that it need only be stated. In its practical operation this decision withdraws from national taxation not only all incomes derived from real estate, but tangible personal property, "*invested* personal property, bonds, stocks, investments of all kinds," and the income that may be derived from such property. This results from the fact that by the decision of the court, all such personal property and all incomes from real estate and personal property, are placed beyond national taxation otherwise than by *apportionment* among the states *on the basis* simply *of population*. No such apportionment can possibly be made without doing gross injustice to the many for the benefit of the favored few in particular states. Any attempt upon the part of Congress to apportion among the states, upon the basis simply of their population, taxation of personal property or of incomes, would tend to arouse such indignation among the freemen of America that is would never be repeated. When, therefore, this court adjudges, as it does now adjudge, that Congress cannot impose a duty or tax upon personal property, or upon income arising either from rents of real estate or from personal property, including invested personal property, bonds, stocks, and investments of all kinds, except by apportioning the sum to be so raised among the states according to population, it *practically* decides that, *without an amendment of the Constitution*—two thirds of both Houses of Congress and three fourths of the states concurring—such property and incomes can never be made to contribute to the support of the national government. . . .

If this new theory of the Constitution, as I believe it to be, if this new departure from the same way marked out by the fathers and so long followed by this court, is justified by the fundamental law, the American people cannot too soon amend their Constitution. . . .

If the decision of the majority had stricken down all the income tax sections, either because of unauthorized exemptions, or because of defects that could have been remedied by subsequent legislation, the result would not have been one to cause anxiety or regret; for, in such a case, Congress could have enacted a new statute that would not have been liable to constitutional objections. But the serious aspect of the present decision is that by a new interpretation of the Constitution, it so ties the hands of the legislative branch of the government, that without an amendment of that instrument, or unless this court, at some future, should return to the old theory of the Constitution, Congress cannot subject to taxation—however great the needs or pressing the necessities of the government—either the invested personal property of the country, bonds, stocks, and investments of all kinds, or the income arising from the renting of real estate, or from the yield of personal property, except by the grossly unequal and unjust rule of apportionment among the states. Thus, undue and disproportioned burdens are placed upon the many, while the few, safely entrenched behind the rule of apportionment among the states on the basis of numbers, are permitted to evade their share of responsibility for the support of the government ordained for the protection of the rights of all.

I cannot assent to an interpretation of the Constitution that impairs and cripples the just powers of the national government in the essential matter of taxation, and at the same time discriminates against the greater part of the people of our country. . . .

Chapter 5

Tides of Progressivism and Reform

The criticisms of the amending process which had begun near the Civil War period did not subside with the adoption of the three post-war amendments. Progressives reasoned that a Constitution which could change only after a revolution might not be changeable enough. Influenced by developments in the natural sciences, scholars urged readers to take a more organic and less rigid view of the Constitution, and a number of them proposed ways that Article V might itself be liberalized. Amid all the criticisms of Article V, it proved itself capable of inaugurating four changes in the space of seven years, changes that would provide for a national income tax, democratize elections to the U.S. Senate, establish national alcoholic prohibition and grant women the right to vote.

5.1 Woodrow Wilson Contrasts the Darwinian to the Newtonian View of the Constitution*

Woodrow Wilson was a political scientist and academician long before he become President of the United States. Like other progressives, Wilson believed that the amending process made constitutional change excessively difficult. In the first passage below, Wilson explains this difficulty; in the second, he appears to commend a method of constitutional interpretation which should partially get around this difficulty. Wilson's reference to Charles Darwin indicate how changes in other areas of thought might have influenced theories of constitutional

---

* Wilson, *Congressional Government: A Study in American Politics* (Boston: Houghton Mifflin Company, 1885 and 1913), pp. 242-3 and Wilson, *Constitutional Government in the United States* (New York: Columbia University Press, 1908), pp. 54-7.

amendment and interpretation. It may also be significant that Wilson was a lifelong admirer of British institutions and may have preferred the British method of change to that instituted in America.

The Difficulty of the Amending Process

It is at once curious and instructive to note how we have been forced into practically amending the Constitution without constitutionally amending it. The legal processes of constitutional change are so slow and cumbersome that we have been constrained to adopt a serviceable framework of fictions which enables us easily to preserve the forms without laboriously obeying the spirit of the Constitution, which will stretch as the nation grows. It would seem that no impulse short of the impulse of self-preservation, no force less than the force of revolution, can nowadays be expected to move the cumbrous machinery of formal amendment erected in Article Five. That must be a tremendous movement of opinion which can sway two thirds of each House of Congress and the people of three fourths of the States. Mr. Bagehot has pointed out that one consequence of the existence of this next to immovable machinery "is that the most obvious evils cannot be quickly remedied," and "that a clumsy working and a curious technicality mark the politics of a rough-and-ready people. The practical arguments and legal disquisitions in America," continues he, "are often like those of trustees carrying out a misdrawn will,—the sense of what they mean is good, but it can never be worked out fully or defended simply, so hampered is it by the old words of an old testament." But much the greater consequence is that we have resorted, almost unconscious of the political significance of what we did, to extra-constitutional means of modifying the federal system where it has proved to be too refined by balances of divided authority to suit practical uses,—to be out of square with the main principle of its foundation, namely, government by the people through their representatives in Congress.

The Newtonian and the Darwinian Views

It is difficult to describe any single part of a great governmental system without describing the whole of it. Governments are living things and operate as organic wholes. Moreover, governments have their natural evolution and are one thing in one age, another in another. The makers of the Constitution constructed the federal government upon a theory of checks and balances which was meant to limit the operation of each part and allow to no single part or organ of it a dominating force; but no government can be successfully conducted upon so mechanical a theory. Leadership and control must be lodged somewhere; the whole art of statesmanship is the art of bringing the several parts of government into effective cooperation for the accomplishment of particular common objects, —and party objects at that. Our study of each part of our federal system, if we are to discover our real government as it lives, must be made to disclose to us its operative coordination as a whole: its places of leadership, its method of action, how it operates, what checks it, what gives it energy and effect. Governments are what politicians make them, and it is easier to write of the President than of the presidency.

The government of the United States was constructed upon the Whig theory of political dynamics, which was a sort of unconscious copy of the Newtonian theory of the universe. In our own day, whenever we discuss the structure of development of anything, whether in nature or in society, we consciously or unconsciously follow Mr. Darwin; but before Mr. Darwin, they followed Newton. Some single law, like the law of gravitation, swung each system of thought and gave it its principle of unity. Every sun, every planet, every free body in the spaces of the heavens, the world itself, is kept in its place and reined to its course by the attraction of bodies that swing with equal order and precision about it, themselves governed by the nice poise and balance of forces which give the whole system of the universe its symmetry and perfect adjustment. The Whigs had tried to give England a similar constitution. They had had no wish to destroy the throne, no conscious desire to reduce the king to a mere figurehead, but had intended only to surround and offset him with a system of constitutional checks and balances which should regulate his otherwise arbitrary course and make it at least always calculable.

They had made no clear analysis of the matter in their own thoughts; it has not been the habit of English politicians, or indeed of English-speaking politicians on either side of the water, to be clear theorists. It was left to a Frenchman to point out to the Whigs what they had done. They had striven to make Parliament so influential in the making of laws and so authoritative in the criticism of the king's policy that the king could in no matter have his own way without their cooperation and assent, though they left him free, the while, if he chose, to interpose an absolute veto upon the acts of Parliament. They had striven to secure for the courts of law as great an independence as possible, so that they might be neither overawed by parliament nor coerced by the king. In brief, as Montesquieu pointed out to them in his lucid way, they had sought to balance executive, legislature, and judiciary off against one another by a series of checks and counterpoises, which Newton might readily have recognized as suggestive of the mechanism of the heavens.

The makers of our federal Constitution followed the scheme as they found it expounded in Montesquieu, followed it with genuine scientific enthusiasm. The admirable expositions of the *Federalist* read like thoughtful applications of Montesquieu to the political needs and circumstances of America. They are full of the theory of checks and balances. The President is balanced off against Congress, Congress against the President, and each against the courts. Our statesmen of the earlier generations quoted no one so often as Montesquieu, and they quoted him always as a scientific standard in the field of politics. Politics is turned into mechanics under his touch. The theory of gravitation is supreme.

The trouble with the theory is that government is not a machine, but a living thing. It falls, not under the theory of the universe, but under the theory of organic life. It is accountable to Darwin, not to Newton. It is modified by its environment, necessitated by its tasks, shaped to its functions by the sheer pressure of life. No living thing can have its organs offset against each other as checks, and live. On the contrary, its life is dependent upon their quick cooperation, their ready response to the commands of instinct or intelligence, their amicable community of purpose. Government is not a body of blind forces; it is a body of men, with highly differentiated functions, no doubt, in our modern day of specialization, but with a common task and purpose. Their cooperation is indispensable, their warfare fatal. There can be no successful government without leadership or without the intimate, almost instinctive, coordination of the organs of life and action. This is not theory, but fact, and displays its force as fact, whatever theories may be thrown across its track. Living political constitutions must be Darwinian in structure and in practice.

Fortunately, the definitions and prescriptions of our constitutional law, though conceived in the Newtonian spirit and upon the Newtonian principle, are sufficiently broad and elastic to allow for the play of life and circumstance. Though they were Whig theorists, the men who framed the federal Constitution were also practical statesmen with an experienced eye for affairs and a quick practical sagacity in respect of the actual structure of government, and they have given us a thoroughly workable model. If it had in fact been a machine governed by mechanically automatic balances, it would have had no history; but it was not, and its history has been rich with the influences and personalities of the men who have conducted it and made it a living reality. The government of the United States has had a vital and normal organic growth and has proved itself eminently adapted to express the changing temper and purposes of the American people from age to age.

5.2 Lord Bryce Notes the Desirability of a Flexible Constitution*

One of the most astute foreign observers of American institutions was Lord James Bryce. As an Englishman, Bryce was respectful of American institutions but tended to believe that British institutions were generally better. In latter works, Bryce would elaborate a distinction between "rigid" constitu-

---

* Bryce, *The American Commonwealth*, 3rd ed. (New York: The Macmillan Company, 1906), 1, pp. 364, 367-71.

tions like that of the United States, and "flexible" constitutions like that of Great Britain, terminology which seemed in and of itself to suggest the superiority of the latter to the former. In the passage below, Bryce describes the amending system of the United States, choosing, however, to let defenders of America's "rigid" Constitution have their say.

The Amending Process in America

The men who sat in the Convention of 1787 were not sanguine enough, like some of the legislating sages of antiquity, or like such imperial codifiers as the Emperor Justinian, to suppose that their work would stand unaltered for all time to come. [Bryce proceeds to outline the procedures established in Article V and provides a brief history of their use.]

Many amendments to the Constitution have been at various times suggested to Congress by Presidents, or brought forward in Congress by members, but very few of these have ever obtained the requisite two-thirds vote of both Houses. In 1789, however, and again in 1807, amendments were passed by Congress and submitted to the States for which the requisite majority of three-fourths of the States was not obtained; and in February and March 1861 an amendment forbidding the Constitution to be ever so amended as to authorize Congress to interfere with the "domestic institutions," including slavery, of any State, was passed in both Houses, but never submitted to the States, because war broke out immediately afterwards. It would doubtless, had peace been preserved, have failed to obtain the acceptance of three-fourths of the States, and its effect could only have been to require those who might thereafter propose to amend the Constitution so as to deal with slavery, to propose also the repeal of this particular amendment itself.

The moral of these facts is not far to seek. Although it has long been the habit of the Americans to talk of their Constitution with almost superstitious reverence, there have often been times when leading statesmen, perhaps even political parties, would have materially altered if it they could have done so. There have, moreover, been some alterations suggested in it, which the impartial good sense of the wise would have approved, but which have never been submitted to the States, because it was known they could not be carried by the requisite majority. If, therefore, comparatively little use has been made of the provisions for amendment, this has been due, not solely to the excellence of the original instrument, but also to the difficulties which surround the process of change. Alterations, though perhaps not large alterations, have been needed, to cure admitted faults or to supply dangerous omissions, but the process has been so difficult that it has never been successfully applied, except either to matters of minor consequence involving no party interests (Amendments xi. and xii.), or in the course of a revolutionary movement which had dislocated the Union itself (Amendments xiii. xiv. xv.).

Why then has the regular procedure for amendment proved in practice so hard to apply?

Partly, of course, owing to the inherent disputatiousness and perversity (what the Americans call "cussedness") of bodies of men. It is difficult to get two-thirds of two assemblies (the Houses of Congress) and three-fourths of forty-four commonwealths, each of which acts by two assemblies, for the State legislatures are all double-chambered, to agree to the same practical proposition. Except under the pressure of urgent troubles, such as were those which procured the acceptance of the Constitution itself in 1788, few persons or bodies will consent to forego objections of detail, perhaps in themselves reasonable, for the mere sake of agreeing to what others have accepted. They want to have what seems to themselves the very best, instead of a second best suggested by some one else. Now, bodies enjoying so much legal independence as do the legislatures of the States, far from being disposed to defer to Congress or to one another, are more jealous, more suspicious, more vain and opinionated, than so many individuals. Nothing but a violent party spirit, seeking either a common party object or individual gain to flow from party success, makes them work together.

If an amendment comes to the legislatures recommended by the general voice of their party, they will be quick to adopt it. But in that case it will encounter the hostility of the opposite party, and parties are in most of the Northern States pretty evenly balanced. It is seldom that a two-thirds majority in either House of Congress can be secured on a party issue; and of course such majorities in both Houses, and a three-fourths majority of State legislatures on a party issue, are still less probable. Now, in a country pervaded by the spirit of party, most questions either are at starting, or soon become, controversial. A change in the Constitution, however useful its ultimate consequences, is likely to be for the moment deemed more advantageous to one party than to the other, and this is enough to make the other party oppose it. The mere fact that a proposal comes from one side, rouses the suspicion of the other. There is always that dilemma of which England has so often felt the evil consequences. If a measure of reform is pressing, it becomes matter of party contention, and excites passion. If it is not pressing, neither party, having other and nearer aims, cares to take it up and push it through. In America, a party amendment to the Constitution can very seldom be carried. A non-party amendment falls into the category of those things which, because they are everybody's business, are the business of nobody.

It is evident when one considers the nature of a Rigid or Supreme constitution, that some method of altering it so as to make it conform to altered facts and ideas is indispensable. A European critic may remark that the American method has failed to answer the expectations formed of it. The belief, he will say, of its authors was that while nothing less than a general agreement would justify alteration, that agreement would exist when omissions impeding its working were discovered. But this has not come to pass. There have been long and fierce controversies over the construction of several points in the Constitution, over the right of Congress to spend money on internal improvements, to charter a national bank, to impose a protective tariff, above all, over the treatment of slavery in the Territories. But the method of amendment was not applied to any of these questions, because no general agreement could be reached upon them, or indeed upon any but secondary matters. So the struggle over the interpretation of a document which it was found impossible to amend, passed from the law courts to the battle-field. Americans reply to such criticisms by observing that the power of amending the Constitution is one which cannot prudently be employed to conclude current political controversies, that if it were so used no constitution could be either rigid or reasonably permanent, that some latitude of construction is desirable, and that in the above-mentioned cases amendments excluding absolutely one or other of the constructions contended for would either have tied down the legislature too tightly or have hastened a probably inevitable conflict.

Ought the process of change to be made easier? say by requiring only a bare majority in Congress, and a two-thirds majority of States? American statesmen think not. A swift and easy method would not only weaken the sense of security which the rigid Constitution now gives, but would increase the troubles of current politics by stimulating a majority in Congress to frequently submit amendments to the States. The habit of mending would turn into the habit of tinkering. There would be too little distinction between changes in the ordinary statute law, which require the agreement of majorities in the two Houses and the President, and changes in the more solemnly enacted fundamental law. And the rights of the States, upon which congressional legislation cannot now directly encroach, would be endangered. The French scheme, under which an absolute majority of the two Chambers, sitting together, can amend the Constitution; or even the Swiss scheme, under which a bare majority of the voting citizens, coupled with a majority of the Cantons, can ratify constitutional changes drafted by the Chambers, in pursuance of a previous popular vote for the revision of the Constitution, is considered by the Americans dangerously lax. The idea reigns that solidity and security are the most vital attributes of a fundamental law.

From this there has followed another interesting result. Since modifications or developments are often needed, and since they can rarely be made by amendment, some other way of making them must be found. The ingenuity of lawyers has discovered one method of interpretation, while the dexterity of politicians has invented a variety of devices whereby legislation may extend, or usage may modify, the express provisions of the apparently immovable and inflexible instrument.

5.3 John W. Burgess Suggests an Amending Alternative*

Often regarded as the founder of modern American political Science, John W. Burgess of Columbia University agreed with many of his contemporaries that the amending process was too difficult. In the following selection, Burgess both explains and critiques the operation of the amending process in America and recommends an alternative. Burgess's surprisingly modern concerns with procedural matters surrounding the amending process, while undoubtedly reflecting his own scholarly concerns, may have been furthered by questions surrounding the adoption of the Fourteenth Amendment.

The Organization of the State in the U.S. Constitution

As I have already indicated, the proper standpoint from which to examine the organization of the state within the constitution is its relation, on the one side, to the revolutionary organization of the state back of the constitution or, if the political society back of the constitution has outgrown that original organization, to the existing social conditions back of the constitution and, on the other side, to the government created in the constitution. In an earlier chapter of this work, I have endeavored to show that the real organization of the United States as the sovereign, the state, in our present system, was in the constituent convention. This, like the Continental Congress, was a single body, representing the whole people of the United States and passing its resolves by simple majority. The people of the United States, as a whole, were behind this body, and gave it the power to ignore practically the Confederate Congress and the legislatures of the commonwealths, and, while formally submitting its work to ratification by the immediate representatives of the people in the common-

---

* Burgess, Selections from *Political Science and Comparative Constitution Law*, intro by Richard M. Pious (Farmingdale, New York: Dabor Social Science Publications, 1978 reprint of 1890), pp. 12-24.

wealths, chosen by the people for that especial purpose, to really ordain the constitution. As I have shown, this theory of the character and position of the convention is the only one which will give scientific explanation to its acts, and the only one which fits in with the natural status and relations of what we may term American political society. The organization of the state *within* the constitution, however, is of a double, and perhaps of a triple or quadruple, character. Article V provides, in the first place, for an organization apparently very nearly correspondent with the original organization back of the constitution, *viz*; a convention for proposing amendments, and conventions of the people resident within the several commonwealths for ratifying the same. According to the letter of the law, however, the general convention is only an initiating body, and a three-fourths majority of the separate conventions is the real constituent. This was the apparent relation between the original convention of 1787 and the separate conventions within the commonwealths; but, as I have shown, that body really exercised constituent powers when it framed an entirely new constitution, designated the bodies who should ratify it, and fixed the majority necessary for ratification. It is probable that another convention, representing in a single body the whole people of the United States, upon a truthful basis of representation, would have such a moral power as to carry its resolves through the separate conventions unchanged, unless some absorbing sectional interest should control the conventions in more than one-fourth of the commonwealths. In such a case the national convention might be able to propose and cause to be applied a different method of ratification from that provided in the existing constitution, as did the convention of 1787; but this would be revolution again, as that was, and not existing law.

It will be seen that the constitution does not elaborate the details of this form of organization of the state. It therefore impliedly leaves that to the Congress. The Congress has never touched the subject, and the constitution has never been changed by the sovereign under this form of organization. From a theoretical standpoint, this is much to be regretted. We have here upon paper an organization of the sovereignty separate from the organs of government. It is a great advance in constitutional law, and if it could be actually applied to practice, it would give us the vantage-ground for the solution of the many difficulties which arise out of confounding the state with the government.

The second form of organization of the state within the constitution vests the sovereign power in the Congress and the legislatures of the commonwealths, the former originating, and the latter ratifying, the changes in constitutional law. The confederate constitution of 1781 vested the amending power in these same bodies; but that constitution required unanimity in the ratifying bodies, with the simple majority of the commonwealths represented in the proposing body, while the present constitution requires only a three-fourths majority of the ratifying bodies, with a two-thirds majority of both houses of the proposing body. This difference is fundamental. It stamps the present system as consolidated over against the confederalism of the other. When any one commonwealth can be bound against its will, confederation is overcome.

The difficulty with this form of organization is that it identifies the organization of the state with the organs of government, and promotes that confusion of thought in dealing with the subjects of public law which arises from the lack of a sufficiently clear distinction of state from government. This is felt in a different way in our system from what it is in the English. We do not lose thereby the juristic test of constitutional law, as the English do. Only that which passes both Congress and the legislatures of the commonwealths is constitutional law, while ordinary statute law is made by these bodies separately. But we become confused upon the still more important point as to whether the sovereignty is in the United States or in the commonwealths; and we are led to misconceive the real character of the commonwealths, and to think of them really as states instead of merely as governments. This is also true, in some degree, when the ratifying bodies are conventions of the people resident within the commonwealths; but it is much easier to comprehend that these bodies, created directly by the constitution of the United States and solely for United States purposes, are institutions of the United States, than that the legislatures of the commonwealths are such, even when acting in this capacity alone.

The advantage, on the other hand, of this form of organization of the sovereignty lies in its convenience. The bodies called upon to act are always in existence. It is not necessary, therefore, to exhaust time and energy and incur special expense to call them out of potential into actual being. It is to be presumed, moreover, that those accustomed to the work of legislation know best when and where the organic law should be changed or supplemented. The former consideration especially has, no doubt, determined the practice in our system. All the changes in our constitutional law have been made by the sovereignty under this form of organization.

In the third place, it will be seen from an examination of this article of the constitution relating to this subject that the Congress may direct which method of ratification shall be followed. The Congress may, therefore, combine itself with conventions of the people within the commonwealths or may combine the general convention with the legislatures of the commonwealths. Either would be a more convenient form of organization than the first form treated. The combination of the general convention with the commonwealth legislatures, however, would be confusing upon the most vital topic of our system. The combination of the Congress with the conventions within the commonwealths would, on the other hand, furnish us a form of organization much less liable to misconception and, at the same time, fairly convenient.

Congress, as I have indicated, has never ordained any such combinations; and in the method actually followed, Congress has not elaborated any complete system of procedure. Anything approaching an exhaustive regulation of this subject would require an express determination of the following questions, *viz*; whether the proposed amendment is subject to the President's veto power; how the submission of the same to the legislatures of the commonwealths is to be effected; whether the two houses of the commonwealth legislatures are to sit in joint session; whether the resolutions of these bodies upon the proposition or propositions of Congress are subject to the usual veto power of the executives of the respective commonwealths; what period is to be set for and to the deliberations of these bodies upon the proposition or propositions of the Congress; how the acts of these bodies shall be communicated to the Congress; whether a commonwealth legislature can reconsider its resolution either before or after notification of the same to Congress, and from what date an approved proposition shall be deemed in force as a part of the constitution. All we have upon this subject from the Congress is contained in the formula of the resolution submitting a proposition for ratification which reads: "Resolved by the Senate and House of Representatives of the United States of America in Congress assembled, two-thirds of both Houses concurring, "That the following article be proposed to the legislatures of the several states, as an amendment to the constitution of the United States; which when ratified by three-fourths of the said legislatures shall be valid as part of the said constitution; and in the direction as to promulgation, which reads: "Whenever official notice is received at the Department of State that any amendment proposed to the Constitution of the United States has been adopted, according to the provisions of the Constitution, the Secretary of State shall forthwith cause the amendment to be published in the newspapers authorized to promulgate the laws, with his certificate, specifying the States" (commonwealths) "by which the same may have been adopted, and that the same has become valid, to all intents and purposes, as a part of the Constitution of the United States."

It will be seen from an examination of the first of these provisions, that Congress treats the origination of the propositions of amendment as exempt from the veto power of the President. The resolutions of this nature are not printed in the statutes as approved by the President, but as signed by the speaker of the House of Representatives and the president of the Senate, and attested by the clerk of the House of Representatives and by the secretary of the Senate. The constitution of the United States declares, however, that "every order, resolution, or vote to which the concurrence of the Senate and House of Representatives may be necessary (except on a question of adjournment)" is subject to the President's veto. There certainly seems to be here a repugnance between the law and the practice. It is sometimes said that this question is one of no practical consequence, since the two-thirds majority necessary to pass the proposition in the first place could override the President's veto. I think this a superficial view. The President may veto the resolutions of Congress, no matter by how great majority originally passed. If he does, the resolutions are thereby subjected to a second consideration and vote, and it is not at all improbable that the President's objections may produce a change in the vote sufficient to defeat the original proposition, or to cause a modification of the same.

Moreover, it will be seen that the practice of Congress is to connect the determination of the question as to whether the proposition or propositions of amendment shall be submitted to conventions of the people within the several commonwealths or to the legislatures thereof with the passage of the proposition or propositions, thus avoiding the veto of the President upon that point. The question of determining the bodies to whom submission shall be made is certainly a distinct one from the internal question of the proposition itself. It is a question determined *finally* by the Congress and not dependent for validity upon ratification, as is the content of the proposition. It might well be claimed that though the content of the proposition should be fixed by Congress alone, yet the act of submission should be in the form of a law; *i.e.* should be subject to the President's veto. If this be not so, then I do not see that it would ever be necessary, in the determination of this question, to unite more than a simple majority in the houses of Congress, since the constitution simply prescribes that Congress shall determine which of the two methods of ratification shall be followed, without designating the majority necessary to do so. It must be confessed that the language of the constitution upon this most important subject is not clear, and that the practice of Congress has some appearance of repugnance to it; but happily we have a decision of the Court which declares that the procedure followed by the Congress is in conformity with the constitution.

After the submission, the Congress leaves everything to the legislatures of the commonwealths until their ratifications, in sufficient number to make the proposition a valid part of the constitution, are in the hands of the Secretary of State of the United States. One question may be said to have been touched and a settlement indicated, in the practice, during this stage of the procedure, *viz*; that a commonwealth may always reconsider its refusal to ratify, but that ratification once voted cannot be withdrawn, neither after the sufficient number shall have ratified to make the proposition a part of the constitution, but before promulgation, nor before the sufficient number shall have been reached. I say this settlement of the question is only indicated, not fully fixed. It is certainly the only sound view of the subject. When the official report of ratification from any commonwealth is in the hands of the Secretary of State of the United States, all further power over the subject has passed from that commonwealth. It may with some reason be held that another point is implied in the precedents, *viz*; that no commonwealth may insert any change in the proposition of the Congress nor ratify conditionally. Certainly the insertion of any change would be an exceeding of the powers conferred by the constitution of the United States upon the legislatures of the commonwealths in regard to this subject. The constitution confers upon them only ratifying powers; *i.e.* it confers upon them no powers of initiation. It is not so certain, however, that the legislatures of the commonwealths can attach no conditions to their ratifications. For example, if a legislature should ratify, and fix a certain date past which its ratification would not hold unless the legislatures of three-fourths of the commonwealths should have ratified before or upon that date, it is not certain that this would not be valid as within the powers of the legislature. The constitution of the United States does not fix the date within which ratifications must be made. Congress has not done so, and certainly there are scientific objections to having a proposition so long undecided as to become obsolete. Nevertheless, I think the sound view of the subject, from the standpoint of political science, is that the legislatures should not be allowed to affix any conditions whatever to their ratifications. I think also that the sound interpretation of the constitution of the United States must arrive at the same result. The only power which the legislatures have upon this subject is derived from an express grant in the constitution of the United States; and since that grant speaks only of ratification, it is the reasonable conclusion that if ratification, in any other than its primary and simplest form, is allowed at all, it must be by permission of the Congress, antecedently given; because the attachment of any conditions to the ratification would be an exercise of the power of initiation, and the constitution vests the whole power of initiation upon this subject in the Congress.

I cannot sympathize with that unreserved commendation of the fifth article of the constitution of the United States indulged in by Mr. Justice Story and other commentators. When I reflect that, while our natural conditions and relations have been requiring a gradual strengthening and extension of the powers of the central government, not a single step has been taken in this direction through the process of amendment prescribed in that article, except as the result of civil war, I am bound to conclude that the organization of the sovereign power within the constitution has failed to accomplish the purpose for which it was constructed. I am not of those who believe that we have done with war in the world yet. I believe that much of the civilization of the world is still to be wrought out through its apparently destructive agency. But I do say this: that when a state must have recourse to war to solve the internal questions of its own politics, this is indisputable evidence that the law of its organization within the constitution is imperfect; and when a state cannot so modify and amend its constitution from time to time as to express itself truthfully therein, but must writhe under the bonds of its constitution until it perishes or breaks them asunder, this is again indisputable evidence that the law of its organization within the constitution is imperfect and false. To my mind the error lies in the artificially excessive majorities required in the production of constitutional changes. According to the census of 1880, it was possible for less than 3,000,000 of people to successfully resist more than 45,000,000 in any attempt to amend the constitution under the present process. The argument in favor of these artificial majorities is that innovation is too strong an impulse in democratic states, and must be regulated; that the organic law should be changed only after patience, experience and deliberation shall have demonstrated the necessity of the change; and that too great fixedness of the law is better than too great fluctuation. This is all true enough; but, on the other hand, it is equally true that development is as much a law of state life as existence. Prohibit the former, and the latter is the existence of the body after the spirit has departed. When, in a democratic political society, the well-matured, long and deliberately formed will of the undoubted majority can be persistently and successfully thwarted, in the amendment of its organic law, by the will of the minority, there is just as much danger to the state from revolution and violence as there is from the caprice of the majority, where the sovereignty of the bare majority is acknowledged. The safeguards against too radical change must not be exaggerated to the point of dethroning the real sovereign.

There is another way, a better way and a natural way of securing deliberation, maturity and clear consciousness of purpose without antagonizing the actual source of power in the democratic state, *viz*; by repetition of vote. If, for example, the Congress should, in joint session and by simple majority, resolve upon a proposition of amendment, and give notice of the same to the people in time for the voters to take the matter into consideration in the election of the members of the House of Representatives for the next succeeding Congress; and if the succeeding Congress should then repass the proposition in joint session and by like majority; and if then it should be sent to the legislatures of the commonwealths for ratification by the houses thereof, acting in joint assembly and resolving by simple majority vote; and if then the vote of each legislature should have the same weight in the count as that of the respective commonwealth in the election of the President of the United States, and an absolute majority of all the votes to which all of the commonwealths were entitled should be made necessary and sufficient for ratification,—why would not this be an organization of the sovereign, of the state within the constitution, which would be truthful to the conditions of our national democratic society and our federal system of government; which would secure all needful deliberation in procedure and maturity in resolution; which would permit changes when the natural conditions and relations of our state and society demanded them; and which would give us an organization of the state convenient in practice and, at the same time, sufficiently distinct from the organization of the government to prevent confusion of thought in reference to the spheres and powers of the two organizations?

To reach such an organization of the state within the constitutional legally would, of course, require the amendment of the provision of the constitution for amendment. This may be done legally in the manner prescribed for making any amendment, since no part of the constitution is withdrawn by the constitution from the process, except the quality of the commonwealths in the senatorial representation. The only question would be as to whether this exception must be connected with the new law of amendment. It seems to me that the letter of the constitution and the intentions of the framers would require this, unless the new law should be ratified by the legislature of every commonwealth. If this be not true, then a commonwealth might be deprived indirectly of its equal representation in the Senate without its own consent, while by the existing law it cannot in any manner be so deprived. From the standpoint of political science, on the other hand, I regard this legal power of the legislature of a single commonwealth to resist successfully the will of the sovereign as unnatural and erroneous. It furnishes the temptation for the powers back of the constitution to reappear in revolutionary organization and solve the question by power, which bids defiance to a solution according to law. There is a growing feeling among our jurists and publicists that, in the interpretation of the constitution, we are not to be strictly held by the intentions of the framers, especially since the whole fabric of our state has been so changed by the results of rebellion and civil war. They are beginning to feel, and rightly too, that present conditions, relations and requirements should be the chief consideration, and that when the language of the constitution will bear it, these should determine the interpretation. From this point of view all the great reasons of political science and of jurisprudence would justify the adoption of a new law of amendment by the general course of amendment now existing, without the attachment of the exception; and in dealing with the questions of public law, we must not, as Mirabeau finely expressed it, lose the *grande morale* in the *petite morale*.

5.4 Herman Ames Assesses the Difficulty of the Amending Process*

In the first study ever to be made of the proposals for constitutional amendment which had been introduced into Congress, Professor Herman Ames counted over 1,700 proposals, many of course redundant, which had been offered in the nation's first one hundred years. Considering that only fifteen of these amendments were proposed and ratified by the necessary majorities, Ames, like others of the period concluded that the existing amending process was too rigid.

The Difficulties of Amendment

In summarizing the results of the attempts to amend the Constitution during the first century of its history, we find that besides the fifteen amendments now a part of the organic law, only four have been proposed by Congress to the States for ratification. Two of these, one on the apportionment of Representatives, the other on titles of nobility, failed of adoption by only one ratification. In addition, nine have passed the Senate and nine the House of Representatives.

The failure to secure amendments in the past does not seem to prevent the frequent introduction of new proposals to change the Constitution. In the Forty-ninth Congress there were no less than fifty-four resolutions, and in the Fiftieth Congress forth-eight, to amend the Constitution.

---

* Herman Ames, *The Proposed Amendments to the Constitution of the United States During the First Century of its History* (New York: Burt Franklin, 1970 reprint of 1896 edition), pp. 300-04, footnotes omitted.

In the light of the history of the different movements to secure amendments, we cannot believe that the expectation of the framers of the Constitution has been fulfilled. Nothing of strength has been added to the Constitution by amendment except in the case of the "reconstruction amendments," and these were carried only after a civil war.

Why, it may be asked, have so few of the more than eighteen hundred propositions looking to the amendment of our fundamental law been successful? In part because some were suggested as cures for temporary evils, others were trivial or impracticable, still others found a place in that unwritten constitution which has grown up side by side with the written document, and whose provisions are often as effective as those contained in the organic law; but the real reason for the failure of those other amendments which have been called for repeatedly by the general public has been due to the insurmountable constitutional obstacles in their way. "It would seem," as a well-known American writer has truly said, "that no impulse short of the impulse of self-preservation, no force less than the force of revolution, can nowadays be expected to move the cumberous machinery in Article V."

When we contrast the paucity of amendments with the frequency of constitutional revision and change in the States, it is the more striking. Only one of the original States lives under its first constitution, namely, Massachusetts, and that instrument has been amended far more than the Federal document. It is doubtless true that this tendency to change has been in some instances carried too far, and that the constitutions of some of our States enter so much into detail that their provisions partake more of the nature of the statutory than the fundamental law. Still many salutary changes have been effected, and these constitutions are, in consequence, much better adapted to meet the needs of the present age. The fact that the modern State constitutions have entered so largely into technique and detail render them less likely to be permanent and increases the necessity of amendment. This being true, one of the demands of the time is for greater facility in procuring amendments.

Fortunately, the Federal Constitution, owing to the fact that it deals only with the most general elements of government, has proved so elastic as to adapt itself to new contingencies and circumstances, and thus the necessity of amendment has been reduced to a minimum. There still remains, however, certain desirable reforms, rendered apparent by more than a century's experience and the changed conditions of our people and age. Although constructive statesmanship did not end with the adoption of the Constitution, as some would have us believe, and although there exists to-day more wisdom and capacity in matters pertaining to the science of government than at the time the Constitution was formed, still it has proved to be impossible to secure these reforms because they can be effected only by a formal amendment.

Nearly all Americans will agree that a rigid constitution has its excellencies, but is there not a limit to the degree of rigidity desirable? Did not the framers of our Federal Constitution, while seeking "to avoid the dangers attending a too frequent change of their fundamental code," advert "to an opposite danger to be equally shunned—that of making amendments too difficult?" Has not the mode provided proved to be of such a character that in some instances "discovered faults" have been perpetuated? While continuing to follow the wise injunction of the "Father of the Country" "to resist with care the spirit of innovation upon the principles of the Constitution," may we not do well to make such constitutional modifications as "experience"—"the surest standard by which to test the real tendency of existing constitutions"—has shown desirable? Certainly the facts plainly show that the cause of the difficulty is, to use the words of Chief Justice Marshall, that the machinery of procuring an amendment is "unwieldly and cumbrous." The majorities required are too large. Under the present system, according to the population given in the census of 1890, it was possible for eleven States with a population of less than 2,350,000 to defeat any constitutional amendment although it was desired by the more than 60,000,000 inhabitants of the other States.

"When in a democratic political society," says Professor Burgess, "the well matured, long and deliberately formed will of the undoubted majority can be persistently and successfully thwarted, in the amendment of its organic law, by the will of the minority, there is just as much danger to the State from revolution and violence as there is from the caprice of the majority, where the sovereignty of the bare majority is acknowledged."

5.5 J. Allen Smith Accuses the Founders of Creating an Aristocracy*

Many progressive spokesmen, frustrated in their initial reform efforts, began to blame the American Founders for what they considered to be the excessive rigidity of the document. Few critics were harsher or took a more conspiratorial tone than did Professor J. Allen Smith who argued that the difficulty of the amending process was in fact the Founder's way of insuring that the aristocratic elements of society would prevail over democratic ones. Smith's critique seems to foreshadow those of Charles Beard, *An Economic Interpretation of the Constitution*, and others that would follow although Smith was more critical of judicial review than were some of these scholars. It is interesting that Smith took some hope from the Article V convention mechanism; it is significant that calls for such a convention were one major factor that apparently led Congress to propose on its own the Seventeenth Amendment for direct election of Senators.

The Significance of the Amending Process

All democratic constitutions are flexible and easy to amend. This follows from the fact that in a government which the people really control, a constitution is merely the means of securing the supremacy of public opinion and not an instrument for thwarting it. Such a constitution can not be regarded as a check upon the people themselves. It is a device for securing to them that necessary control over their agents and

---

* Smith, *The Spirit of American Government* (Cambridge, MA: Belknap Press, 1965 reprint of 1907), pp. 40-64, pp. 346-8. Footnotes in text are omitted.

representatives, without which popular government exists only in name. A government is democratic just in proportion as it responds to the will of the people; and since one way of defeating the will of the people is to make it difficult to alter the form of government, it necessarily follows that any constitution which is democratic in spirit must yield readily to changes in public opinion.

Monarchical and aristocratic constitutions on the other hand are always extremely conservative. Inasmuch as they express the opinion and guarantee the privileges of a dominant class, they are bulwarks erected against popular change. The privileged classes of any society regard stability as the chief political desideratum. They resist, and if possible prevent, those legal and political readjustments which the general progress of society makes necessary. Their interests are furthered in proportion as the system is one which renders change difficult.

With this distinction in mind let us examine the Constitution of the United States. Was it the intention of the framers of this instrument that it should be merely a check upon the governmental machinery with the view of establishing popular control over it, or was it expected to constitute a check upon the people themselves? That is was not intended that the people should be given direct and complete control over the general policy of the government is clear from the fact that the Constitution was made so difficult to amend; for the right to control the political machinery, implies of necessity the right to make such changes in it from time to time, as are needed to make this control effective. It is evident from the views expressed in the Convention that one object of the Constitution was to secure stability by placing the government beyond the direct influence of public opinion.

Madison, who has been called the "father of the Constitution," thought it "ought to secure the permanent interests of the country against innovation." Hamilton said "all communities divide themselves into the few and the many. The first are the rich and well born, the other the mass of the people . . . [the latter] are turbulent and changing; they seldom judge or determine right." Therefore he advocated a permanent senate which would be able to "check the imprudence of democracy."

Gouverneur Morris observed that "the first branch [of the proposed Federal Congress], originating from the people, will ever be subject to *precipitancy*, *changeability*, and *excess*. . . . This can only be checked by *ability* and *virtue* in the second branch . . . [which] ought to be composed of men of great and established property—*aristocracy*; men who, from pride, will support consistency and permanency; and to make them completely independent, they must be chosen *for life*, or they will be a useless body. Such an aristocratic body will keep down the turbulence of democracy."

This dread of the consequences of popular government was shared to a greater or less extent by nearly all members of that Convention. Their aim was to find a cure for what they conceived to be the evils of an excess of democracy.

"Complaints," says Madison in *The Federalist*, "are everywhere heard from our most considerate and virtuous citizens, equally the friends of public and private faith, and public and personal liberty, that our governments are too unstable, that the public good is disregarded in the conflicts of rival parties, and that measures are too often decided, not according to the rules of justice and the rights of the minor party, but by the superior force of an interested and overbearing majority."

This criticism of the American government of the Revolutionary period gives us the point of view of the framers of the Constitution. We should remember, however, that the so-called majority rule to which Madison attributed the evils of that time had nothing in common with majority rule as that term is now understood. Under the laws then in force the suffrage was greatly restricted, while the high property qualifications required for office-holding had the effect in many cases of placing the control of legislation in the hands of the wealthier part of the community. But undemocratic as the system was, it was not sufficiently undemocratic to suit the framers of the Constitution. It was no part of their plan to establish a government which the people could control. In fact, popular control was what they were seeking to avoid. One means of accomplishing this was to make amendment difficult, and this accordingly was done. We need not be surprised that no provision was made for its original adoption, or subsequent amendment by direct popular vote.

The fact that the people can not directly propose, or even ratify changes in the fundamental law, is a substantial check upon democracy. But in addition to this, another check was provided in the extraordinary majority necessary to amend the Constitution. That it requires a two-thirds majority of both houses of Congress, or an application from the legislature in two-thirds of the states to merely set the machinery for constitutional amendment in motion, and that it requires for ratification of amendments proposed, the assent of legislatures or conventions in three-fourths of the states, ought to give one some idea of the extreme difficulty of changing our Constitution.

Patrick Henry clearly saw that this lack of adequate provision for amendment was destructive of democracy. [Smith quotes Henry's argument at the Virginia ratifying convention]

That such a small minority of the people should have the power under our constitutional arrangements to prevent reform, can hardly be reconciled with the general belief that in this country the majority rules. Yet small as was this minority when the Constitution was adopted, it is much smaller now than it was then. In 1900 one forth-fourths of the population distributed so as to constitute a majority in the twelve smallest states could defeat any proposed amendment. As a matter of fact it is impossible to secure amendments to the Constitution, unless the sentiment in favor of change amounts almost to a revolution. Only at critical times in our history have constitutional amendments been adopted. During sixty-one years from 1804 to 1865, and since 1870, no amendments have been made. The fifteen amendments were all adopted, either during the turbulent period of American politics during which immediately followed the ratification of the Constitution, or during the reconstruction period after the Civil War. That it is not possible in ordinary times to change the Constitution is evident from the fact that of some twenty-two hundred propositions for amendment only fifteen have been adopted, and these during the periods above mentioned.

"The argument in favor of these artificial majorities," says Professor Burgess, "is that innovation is too strong an impulse in democratic states, and must be regulated; that the organic law should be changed only after patience, experience and deliberation shall have demonstrated the necessity of the change; and that too great fixedness of the law is better than too great fluctuation. This is all true enough; but, on the other hand, it is equally true that development is as much a law of state life as existence. Prohibit the former, and the latter is the existence of the body after the spirit has departed. When, in a democratic political society, the well-matured, long and deliberately formed will of the undoubted majority can be persistently and successfully thwarted, in the amendment of its organic law, by the will of the minority, there is just as much danger to the state from revolution and violence as there is from the caprice of the majority, where the sovereignty of the bare majority is acknowledged. The safeguards against too radical change must not be exaggerated to the point of dethroning the real sovereign."

What Professor Burgess seems to overlook is the fact that the framers of the Constitution deliberately intended to dethrone the numerical majority. The restrictions which they placed upon the exercise of the amending power were not only not inconsistent with the form of government which they established, but as a matter of fact absolutely necessary to ensure its preservation, since without such a limitation of the power to amend, the majority could easily overcome all other checks upon its authority.

This feature of the Constitution, which nominally provides for amendment, but really makes it an impossibility, is perhaps the best proof we could have that the Constitution as framed and adopted represented the views of a minority who intended by this means to perpetuate their influence. But, we are told, this can not be the case since the states were free to accept or reject it. Let us not forget, however, that at no stage of the proceedings was the matter referred directly to the people. Bryce says: "Had the decision been left to what is now called 'the voice of the people,' that is, to the mass of the citizens all over the country, voting at the polls, the voice of the people would probably have pronounced against the Constitution." Moreover, "the Convention met," as he observes, "at the most fortunate moment in American History [for securing the adoption of such a constitution]. . . . Had it been attempted four years earlier or four years later at both of which times the waves of democracy were running high, it must have failed." But even under these favoring conditions it was no easy task to get the states to adopt it. The advocates of the Constitution employed every argument and influence that could contribute to the desired result. They appealed with telling effect to the dread of European aggression. This induced many who had little sympathy with the proposed plan of government, to acquiesce in its adoption, believing that some sort of a strong government was necessary for purposes of defence. It was also boldly charged that money was employed to overcome opposition where other means of persuasion failed.

Our natural inclination is to disbelieve anything that reflects on the political methods employed by the founders of our government. Nevertheless, the widespread belief that the politicians and public men of that time were less corrupt than those of to-day is, as Professor McMaster says, a pure delusion. "A very little study of long-forgotten politics will suffice to show that in filibustering and gerrymandering, in stealing governorships and legislatures, in using force at the polls, in colonizing and in distributing patronage to whom patronage is due, in all the frauds and tricks that go to make up the worst form of practical politics, the men who founded our state and national governments were always our equals, and often our masters." Of one thing we may be reasonably certain—the Constitution as adopted did not represent the political views of a majority of the American people—probably not even a majority of those entitled to vote. . . .

The Constitution would certainly have been rejected, notwithstanding the influences that were arrayed in favor of its adoption, but for the belief that it would shortly be amended so as to remove some of its more objectionable features. In the large and influential states of Massachusetts, New York, and Virginia it was ratified by very small majorities, though each of these states accompanied its acceptance of the Constitution with various recommendations for amendment. As a result of these suggestions from the states ratifying it, the first Congress in 1789 framed and submitted the first ten amendments. The eleventh amendment was the outgrowth of the Supreme Court decision in the case of Chisholm v. The State of Georgia. In this case the court held, contrary to the interpretation given to the Constitution by Hamilton when defending it in *The Federalist*, that a private plaintiff could sue a state in the Federal Court. This decision aroused a storm of indignation, and Congress in 1794 proposed the Eleventh Amendment, which counteracted the effect of this decision. The Twelfth Amendment, proposed by Congress in 1803, merely changed the method of electing the President to meet the requirements of the party system which had then come into existence.

These first twelve amendments were all adopted during the infancy of the Constitution, and while it was still regarded as an experiment. But though they had the effect of quieting public opinion and allaying the fears of the people concerning the new form of government, they made no important changes in the Constitution, leaving all its main features as originally adopted. The same may be said of the last three amendments, which were the result of the Civil War. They were proposed and ratified, as Bryce says, "under conditions altogether abnormal, some of the lately conquered states ratifying while actually controlled by the Northern armies, others as the price which they were obliged to pay for the readmission to Congress of their senators and representatives." These amendments were really carried through, not by the free choice of three-fourths of the states, as the Constitution requires, "but under the pressure of a majority which had triumphed in a great war," and used military and political coercion to accomplish what otherwise could not have been brought about. Nothing could have been farther from the intention of the victorious Northern states at that time than any important change in the form of character of the government which they had waged a gigantic civil war to defend and enforce. Slavery, it is true, was abolished to remove forever the bone of contention between the North and the South. But the Constitution survived the Civil War, unchanged in all its essential features, and more firmly established than ever.

That the plan of government originally established has undergone no important modification by constitutional amendment can not be ascribed to the fact that important changes have not been suggested. With the growth of more liberal views concerning government many attempts have been made to remove the constitutional barriers erected by our forefathers to stay the progress of democracy. Among the political reforms contemplated by this numerous class of proposed amendments may be mentioned a shorter term for United States senators and election by popular vote; direct election of the President and the abolition of his veto power; a shorter term for Federal judges and their removal by the President on the joint address of both houses of Congress. The aim of all these proposed amendments has been the same, viz., to make the Constitution accord better with the democratic spirit of the time. It is interesting to observe, however, that with the single exception of the proposed election of United States senators by popular vote, not one of these had the support of either house of Congress, much less the two-thirds majority in both, or a majority in the legislatures of two-thirds of the states, as required to authorize their submission for ratification or rejection. Even this measure, which has passed the House of Representatives several times by an overwhelming vote, has been entirely ignored by the Senate.

No proposal, then, to make any important change in the Constitution has ever obtained the preliminary two-thirds majority, to say nothing of the majority in three-fourths of the states, necessary for its adoption.

That the majority required to propose an amendment is almost prohibitive of change, is shown by the record of popular elections and the journals of representatives bodies. From the presidential election year of 1828, the first for which we have a record of the popular vote, down to 1900, the largest majority ever received by any candidate for the Presidency was that of Andrew Jackson in 1828, when he had less than 56 per cent. of the popular vote. Nine elections since Jackson's time resulted in the choice of a President by less than a popular majority. No candidate in any presidential election from 1876 to 1900 inclusive has carried two-thirds of the states.

It is still more difficult for any important reform measure to secure a two-thirds majority in a representative assembly, as the proceedings of Congress and our state legislatures abundantly prove. This is true for the reason that a wealthy minority can exert an influence over such bodies out of all proportion to its numerical strength at the polls. Hence even a bare majority can seldom be obtained for any measure which interferes with or restricts the privileges of organized wealth. A two-thirds majority under such circumstances is practically impossible. And when we remember that any proposed amendment to the Constitution must twice run the gauntlet of representative assemblies, receiving first a two-thirds majority in both houses of Congress and later a majority in both houses of the legislature or in conventions in three-fourths of the states, we readily see that this provision effectually precludes the possibility of any important amendment.

One of the principal objections to the Articles of Confederation—that they lacked a practical amending power—applies, then, with no less force to the Constitution itself. In one respect the Constitution is even more rigid than were the Articles of Confederation, since the Congress of the Confederation was the court of last resort for passing on the constitutionality of its own legislation. This gave to Congress under the Confederation at least a limited power of virtually amending the Articles of Confederation by the ordinary process of law-making—a power possessed by the legislature in all countries where the system of checks and balances is not recognized. Under the Constitution, however, this power to amend the fundamental law can be exercised only to a very limited extent by Congress, since the interpretation of the Constitution by that body for the purposes of law-making is subject to revision at the hands of the Federal Judiciary. The Constitution, then, more effectually prevents changes desired by the majority than did the Articles of Confederation, since the former guards against the possibility of amendment under the guise of ordinary legislation while the latter did not.

Another distinction must be borne in mind. The Articles of Confederation made amendment difficult in order to prevent the general government from encroaching on the rights of the several states. It was not so much a disposition to make change impossible, or even difficult, as, by keeping the general government within established bounds, to leave the several states free to regulate their own affairs and change their institutions from time to time to suit themselves.

This view finds support in the character of the early state constitutions. These were shaped by the same revolutionary movement which produced the Declaration of Independence, and were largely influenced in their practical working by the "self-evident" truths proclaimed in the latter. One of the axioms of political science embodied in the Declaration of Independence was the right of the people to alter or abolish the existing form of government. This principles, however, was expressly recognized in but few of the earlier state constitutions, which, as a rule, contained no provision for future amendment. But such provision was not really necessary, inasmuch as the power of the legislature was limited only by its responsibility to the electorate. A mere majority of the qualified voters might demand and secure the enactment of laws which would virtually amend the constitution. From this time on, however, we see a strong tendency to specify in the constitution itself the manner in which it could be changed; and by the time that the framers of the Federal Constitution met in Philadelphia in 1787 a majority of the state constitutions contained provisions of this kind. [Smith proceeds to cite various state amending provisions.]

We see, then, that several of the early state constitutions expressly gave, either directly to a majority of the qualified voters, or to their representatives, the right to amend; and even in Massachusetts, New Hampshire, and Delaware, whose constitutions expressly limited the power of the majority, the limitation was not effective, since the majority could push through under the guise of ordinary legislation, measures which virtually amounted to an exercise of the amending power. Such limitations on the power of the majority did not become effective until a judiciary not directly responsible to the people, acquired the right to declare acts of the legislature null and void.

An examination of these features of the various state constitutions in force in 1787 shows clearly the reactionary character of the Federal Constitution. It repudiated entirely the doctrine then expressly recognized in some of the states and virtually in all, that a majority of the qualified voters could amend the fundamental law. And not only did it go farther than any state constitution in expressly limiting the power of the majority, but it provided what no state constitution had done—the means by which its limitations on the power of the majority could be enforced.

A comparison of this feature of our Constitution with the method of amendment in other countries is interesting and instructive. In England no distinction is made between constitutional amendments and other legislation. And since the Crown has lost the veto power and the House of Commons established its right to override the opposition of the House of Lords, the most radical changes may be made without even the checks which impede ordinary legislation in the United States.

In France amendment of the Constitution is almost as easy as in England, though a distinction is made between this and ordinary legislation. When both the Senate and Chamber of Deputies decide by an absolute majority in each that amendment is necessary, they meet in joint session as a National Assembly for that purpose. An absolute majority of the members composing the National Assembly is required to change the Constitution.

Amendments to the Federal Constitution of Australia may be proposed by an absolute majority of both Houses of Parliament. Not less than two nor more than six months after the proposed amendment has been passed by both houses, it must be submitted to the qualified voters in each state. But if either house by an absolute majority passes a proposed amendment which is rejected by the other house, and passes it again by an absolute majority after an interval of three months, the Governor-General may submit the proposed amendment to the qualified voters. A proposed amendment is adopted if it is approved by a majority of all those voting and also by a majority in a majority of the states.

In Switzerland the question whether the Federal Constitution ought to be amended must be submitted to a popular vote whenever demanded by either house of the Federal Assembly or by fifty thousand voters (about one-fifteenth of the voting population). A proposed amendment is adopted if it receives a majority of all the votes cast and at the same time a majority in a majority of the Cantons, a provision copied, as we have seen, in the Federal Constitution of Australia.

These constitutions show the general tendency at the present time to make the majority supreme. In the countries which have been most influenced by democratic ideas constitutional barriers against change have largely or wholly disappeared. A constitution is in no proper sense the embodiment of the will of the people unless it recognizes the right of the majority to amend. Checks which prevent legal and political readjustment are a survival from monarchy and aristocracy and are not found in any full-fledged democracy. Constitutions which are really democratic contain only such checks upon the people, if indeed they can be called checks, as are calculated to insure the deliberate expression of the popular will. Constitutional provisions designed to obstruct amendment are not only an anomaly in popular government, but they are in the very nature of the case inoperative. This follows from the fact that the law-making body, whether it be the people themselves or a representative assembly, is the final interpreter of the constitution and may enact laws which virtually amend it. To make such provisions really effective the constitution must vest the power to prevent legislation in some branch of the government not directly responsible to the people. Usually this is a King or hereditary class. Our Constitution, however, provides a substitute for these in its general system of checks and especially in the independence of our national judiciary, which in addition to the exercise of ordinary judicial functions is also practically a branch of the legislature. . . .

The Convention Mechanism

The most important feature of the Constitution from the standpoint of democracy is the provision contained in Article V, requiring Congress "on the application of the legislatures of two-thirds of the several states" to "call a convention for proposing amendments." The progress of democracy in the various state governments is likely to compel resort to this method of changing the Federal Constitution if the Senate much longer persists in disregarding the will of the people. In fact, this is, in the opinion of the conservative class, the one fatal defect in the scheme of constitutional checks established by our forefathers. It in reality opens the door to the most revolutionary changes in our political arrangements. Congress can not refuse to call a general constitutional convention when two-thirds of the states demand it, and this convention might propose an entirely new constitution framed in accord with the most advanced ideas of democracy. It might also follow the precedent set by the framers of our present Constitution and prescribe an entirely new method of ratification, as our more conservative forefathers did when they disregarded the then existing provision governing the amendment of the Articles of Confederation. It is true that they ignored the established method of amending as well as the instructions from the states by which they were appointed, in order to bring about the adoption of a political system more acceptable to the conservative classes. But what has been done in the interest of the minority may also be done in the interest of the majority. A new Federal constitution might be framed which could eliminate the whole system of checks on the people and provide for direct ratification by a majority of the voters, as has already been done in the case of most of our state constitutions. If the Constitution does not yield sufficiently to satisfy the popular demand for reform, it is possible that the reactionary forces will, in their anxiety to defeat moderate democratic measures, arouse sufficient opposition on the part of the people to compel sweeping constitutional changes.

The fact that two-thirds of the states can require Congress to call a convention of all the states to propose changes in the

Constitution is a matter of no small importance. True, even this method of initiating changes in the system would be very difficult, since the smaller states would naturally fear an attempt to establish a more equitable plan of representation, and the special and privileged interests of all sorts which have found the present system satisfactory would use every means at their command to prevent the states from resorting to this power. It is possible, if not indeed probable, that a serious and concerted attempt by the people to force changes in the Constitution by this method would sufficiently alarm the opponents of democracy to convince them of the wisdom and expediency of such amendments as would appease the popular clamor for reform without going too far in the direction of majority rule. To prevent the complete overthrow of the system, which might be the outcome if the states were compelled to assume the initiative in amending the Constitution, the minority may accept the inevitable, and, choosing what appears to them to be the lesser of two evils, allow Congress to propose such amendments as the people are determined to bring about.

5.6 Walter Dodd Reconsiders Judge Jameson's View of Constitutional Conventions*

The Progressive Era marked a time of reform of many state constitutions as well as of the national document. In the selection below, a scholar questions Judge Jameson's view that such state conventions were completely subordinate to the state legislatures. Although Dodd's immediate subject was state constitutional revision, it is easy to see how his thesis might also be applied to a national constitutional convention.

The Legal Position of the Constitutional Convention

A constitutional convention is a body called together for a limited purpose—that of framing and submitting to the people or of framing and adopting a new constitution, or of revising

---

* Walter F. Dodd, *The Revision and Amendment of State Constitutions* (Baltimore: The Johns Hopkins Press, 1910), pp. 72-80.

and amending an old constitution. The convention has become in our constitutional system a regular organ for the expression of state will with reference to the state's fundamental law. It is in no sense a revolutionary or extra-constitutional body and does not supersede in any way the organs of the existing state government. The existing state government continues in full operation until superseded by a new government organized under the constitution framed or adopted by the convention.

Bearing in mind the limited functions of a constitutional convention, we must inquire here as to what are the relations of the convention to the organs of the regular state government, and especially as to the relations between the convention and the regular legislative body of the state. We have already referred to the fact that in all of the states except New York and Michigan legislative acts are necessary for the calling of constitutional conventions. Can the legislature, in the exercise of this power, place limitations upon a convention, requiring it not to consider certain subjects, or that it insert certain provisions in the new constitution, or that it submit its work for the approval of the people, when such submission is not required by the existing constitution?

Judge J.A. Jameson in his work on *Constitutional Conventions* took the position that a convention is absolutely bound by restrictions placed upon it in the legislative act by which it is called. Judge Jameson took this view because he thought it necessary that a convention be completely subordinate to the existing government, but even he hesitated to push this doctrine to its extreme limits; for example, he thought that a convention might disregard a legislative requirement that its work be not submitted to the people, and also took the position that the legislative limitations upon a convention "must be in harmony with the principles of the convention system, or, rather, not inconsistent with the exercise by the convention, to some extent, of its essential and characteristic functions." This amounts to a statement that the convention is not absolutely subordinate to the regular state legislature, and is in direct contradiction to Jameson's fundamental thesis.

Under a number of the present state constitutions it may be definitely said that a legislature may not bind a convention in any way. In New York and Michigan conventions assemble without any legislative action, when authorized by a vote of the people; in these states, constitutional provisions were adopted for the express purpose of making conventions entirely independent of legislative control and any effort by the legislature to control the convention's action would clearly be a violation of the constitution. The same statement holds with reference to the Missouri constitution, by the terms of which the only step to be taken by the legislature is that submitting to the people the question as to whether a convention shall be held. And the same is probably true with reference to constitutions which impose upon the legislature the one specific duty of providing for the election of delegates after the people have decided that a convention shall be held. Inasmuch as both bodies are legislative in character, a specific power conferred upon the regular legislature may perhaps be said by implication to exclude any other control over the convention by the regular legislative body. The Alabama constitution of 1901 expressly confers full power upon a convention to act in the drafting of a new constitution.

But in many cases there are no constitutional provisions expressly or impliedly restraining legislative interference with conventions. What principles should control in states whose constitutions simply empower the assembling of conventions under a legislative act, or where the constitutions contain no provision with reference to conventions? In some cases the view has been taken that the people, by voting for delegates under a legislative act or by acting thereunder, themselves adopt the restrictions placed upon the convention by such an act, and that the restrictions sought to be placed upon the convention by the legislature thus become restrictions imposed by the people, but in most cases this would clearly not be true. The popular action in connection with a convention may be had in several ways. The question of calling a convention may, in certain states, be determined by the legislature without consulting the people, and an election may be called for the purpose of electing delegates to such convention; it is clear, of course, that the people in voting for delegates to a convention have no way of expressing either approval or disapproval of the terms of the act under which the convention is called; here clearly there is no popular adoption of restrictions sought to be imposed upon a convention by legislative act. In Oregon and Oklahoma there must be submitted to the people the act under which it is proposed to call a convention, but here, while the people have a greater control, it may be necessary for them to pass upon two questions in one, to determine not only whether they want a convention but also whether they want one under the terms proposed by the legislature; even here the act calling a convention cannot be said to be an act of the people. Popular participation to a still greater extent may be obtained by the separate submission of the two question, (a) whether a convention is desired, and (b) then, if a convention is desired, whether the people approve the act under which the legislature proposes to call the convention; and here there may be said to be a popular approval of the legislative act.

But the more usual practice is for the question of calling a convention to be submitted to the people, and if they approve, for the legislature to enact a law under which the convention is elected and assembled. Now it cannot be said that the people, by their preliminary vote determining whether or not a convention shall be called, delegate to the legislature power to impose restrictions upon such convention; they simply vote for or against a convention, and there would be a strong presumption that in voting for a convention, they meant to vote for one with full power to propose or adopt a revision of the state constitution. This was the case in the Pennsylvania decision cited above: the question of holding a convention was submitted to the people and decided in the affirmative; the subsequent legislative act calling the convention sought to impose certain restrictions upon the convention, and the court then said that these restrictions were imposed by the people; the facts found by the court did not conform to the real facts of the case.

The presumption in favor of a convention's having full power to act in the framing of a new constitution would, of course, not apply where no constitutional revision had been in contemplation either by the legislature or by the people, but where a convention had been called by legislative act to determine a particular question of public policy, or to interpret a clause of the existing constitution, as in New York in 1801, in South Carolina in 1832-33, and in Mississippi in 1850-51.

Under Judge Jameson's theory a constitutional convention called by a vote of the people may be restricted by simple legislative act so that it may not revise or propose the revision of any part of the existing constitution which the legislature may forbid it to touch. The convention is made subordinate to an organ of the existing government. Judge Jameson proceeded on the assumption that a constitutional convention must possess sovereign power—that is, all of the power of the state—or that it must be strictly subordinate to the regular legislature. He could conceive of no middle ground between these extremes. In attempting to demolish the theory that the convention is sovereign, he went to the other extreme and really made the legislature the supreme body with respect to the alteration of state constitutions, for under his view a convention may be restrained by a legislature as to what shall be placed in the constitution, and no alteration can be made without legislative consent. Judge Jameson pushed his theory to its logical conclusion and held that a convention, even after elected and assembled, might be dissolved by legislative act, or that the legislature might prevent the submission of this work to the people.

The process of piece-meal amendment of state constitutions is absolutely under the control of the state legislatures, except in the states which have adopted the popular initiative. By the ordinary amending procedure no action may be taken except upon the initiative of the legislature: this method of altering constitutions is absolutely subject to legislative control. The calling of constitutional conventions is also to a large extent subject to legislative control, but the convention method of altering constitutions is the one more independent of the regular legislature, unless Judge Jameson's theory be adopted. The convention loses a large part of its usefulness as an organ of the state if it be treated as strictly subject to control by the regular legislative body. This view was well expressed by the judiciary committee of the New York convention of 1894: "It is of the greatest importance that a body chosen by the people of this state to revise the organic law of the State, should be as free from interference from the several departments of government as the legislative, executive and judiciary are, from interference by each other. Unless this were so, the will of the people might easily be nullified by the existing judiciary or legislature. Should the latter attempt to enact a law prohibiting the constitutional convention from restricting the existing power of the legislature, the act would be at once recognized as an unwarranted invasion of the rights of the people."

The better view would seem to be that the convention is a regular organ of the state (although as a rule called only at long intervals)—neither sovereign nor subordinate to the legislature, but independent within its proper sphere. Under this view the legislature cannot bind the convention as to what shall be placed in the constitution, or as to the exercise of its proper duties. If then we say that the convention is independent of the regular legislature in the exercise of its proper duties, it will be necessary to discuss for a moment what are its proper functions. These are simply to propose a new constitution or to propose constitutional amendments to the people for approval; or, in states where the submission of constitutions is not required, to frame and adopt a constitution if they think proper. In this sphere, and in the exercise of powers incidental to its proper functions, it would seem that constitutional conventions should not be subject to control by legislative acts.

5.7 Herbert Croly Critiques the Amending Process as an Obstacle to Democracy*

One of the best known progressive spokesmen was Herbert Croly, author of the influential book, *The Promise of American Life*. Like Smith, Croly believed that a major obstacle to

---

* Croly, *Progressive Democracy* (New York: The Macmillan Company, 1914), pp. 130-31; pp. 230-37.

democratic reform was the rigidity of the constitutional amending process.

The Amending Process in the Early Republic

The modern democrat should also recognize that the least democratic article in the Constitution contributed effectively to the desirable stability of the early American political system. The machinery of amendment provided by the Constitution did more than anything else to emancipate that instrument from popular control. Its revision required such an emphatic preponderance of approving public opinion that no proposed amendment could be carried by any one political group. All parties understood the futility of inserting amendments in their partisan programs. Proposed changes in the fundamental Law rarely became a matter of practical political discussion. American political controversy was condemned, consequently, to an unedifying superficiality; but there was one great compensation. When Solon imposed a new constitution on Athens, he wanted the original instrument to have a fair trial. He decreed that it should remain unchanged for ten years. The early American law-givers had a plausible excuse for desiring an analogous period of political conformity during the early years of the new Republic. A feeling of security was peculiarly desirable during the first two generations—more desirable, perhaps, than was a greater sincerity and intensity of political experience. The Constitution was really king. Once the kingdom of the Word had been ordained, it was almost as seditious to question the Word as it was to plot against the kingdom. A monarch exists to be obeyed. In the United States, as in other monarchies, unquestioning obedience was erected into the highest of political virtues.

The Amending Process as an Obstacle to Democracy

The way to continue the work of nationalization is not to continue to worship the forms, but to find, wherever necessary, new methods and forms better adapted to contemporary needs and a genuine formative ideal. Although the ideal of social justice with which constitutional government was associated has increased in authority, the program whereby that ideal was to be realized has been profoundly modified. If the new forms and methods are not supplied, the tendency towards disintegration, which is natural in a democratic state, will not be overcome by a really effective unity of purpose and spirit.

The traditional system possessed one specific form which, just as a matter of political mechanics, did more than anything else to convert a constitutional democracy into semi-democratic constitutionalism. This form consisted in the amending clause of the Constitution, which made the process of amendment almost insuperably difficult. That its excessive difficulty of amendment had some immediately desirable results during the early years of the Republic has already been asserted; but at the present time it is unquestionably the most formidable legal obstacle in the path of progressive democratic fulfilment. Professor Munroe Smith is justified in declaring "that the first article of any sincerely intended progressive program must be the amendment of the amending clause of the Constitution." In practice the monarchy of the Law hangs suspended to the nail of this particular bit of writing, and as long as it remains intact the political destinies of the American people will have to rest to an unnecessary and unwholesome extent upon the dicta of a board of judicial trustees.

The new machinery of amendment ought to be very much more easily worked than the old. It must make the Constitution alterable at the demand and according to the dictates of a preponderant prevailing public opinion. Instead of requiring the assent of two-thirds of Congress and the legislatures of three-fourths of the states, the power of revision should be possessed by a majority of the electorate. The only limitations placed on this power should be a method of procedure which allowed sufficient time for deliberation and a certain territorial distribution of the prevailing majority. The form proposed by Senator La Follette is probably the best which has been drafted. It provides for the submission of amendments either by a majority of both houses of Congress or by one-fourth of the states, and their acceptance by a majority of all the voters voting, provided that this majority is distributed throughout a majority of the states.

The necessity of any such revision of the amending clause has been contested because two amendments to the Constitution have recently been proposed and ratified. The successful adoption of these two amendments will have the effect of making the revision of Article V seem less necessary. It may well serve to delay the serious discussion of the matter and to diminish for some time its practical political importance. But in the long run progressive democracy cannot possibly submit to the abridgement of popular political responsibility which is implied by the present amending clause. It cannot wait until two-thirds of a Congress and the legislatures of three-fourths of the states are convinced of the desirability of any proposed modification. The existing method calls for amendment practically by unanimous consent. It removes proposals to revise the Constitution from the realm of partisan political controversy, and it necessitates the retention of means, similar to those which have been used in the past, to give the needed flexibility to the development of the Constitutional system—means which, as we have already seen, placed the political destinies of the American people under the immediate direction of a group of benevolent guardians.

A close connection has assuredly existed between the amount of discretionary authority actually exercised by the Supreme Court and the difficulty of amending the Constitution. No doubt a Federal system with an ambiguous dividing line between the central and state government required the aggrandizement of the courts for another purpose. No doubt, also, the logic of the whole system, based as it was on the supremacy of the Word rather than on that of a gradually educated and enlightened will, tended in the same direction. Nevertheless the supremacy of the Law and consequently the guardianship of the robe was based in practice upon the extreme difficulty of amending the Constitution. The nominal authority of King Demos was always admitted; and this nominal authority did not become effective, in part because it could not become effective by the use of the regular legal machinery. As long as such intractable machinery is preserved intact, a nation blessed with political common-sense will be driven to adopt other and less essentially democratic means of keeping its Law adapted to its needs.

The other method which has been used most frequently in the past was the assumption by the Supreme Court of a constructive political responsibility. At present the Court seeks to evade such a responsibility whenever it can with any show of reason; but time was when it cordially greeted the opportunity to pass essentially political judgments. In order to find clear instances of this tendency, it is not necessary to go as far back as the Dred Scott decision. The period in which the Supreme Court exercised its powers with the largest latitude and with the most complete conviction of the essentially political nature of its duties occurred after the War. Again and again doubtful interpretations were imposed upon the Constitution by the preference of one judge—interpretations which, if not modified by the Court itself, required for their alteration the express voluntary action of two-thirds of Congress and three-quarters of the states. In the Slaughter-House cases it did not hesitate by a vote of five to four to bestow a meaning on the Fourteenth Amendment which, in the opinion of many commentators on the Constitution, was both arbitrary and unwise. By a similar majority it altered the prevailing reading of one provision of the Constitution and declared invalid the income tax. In these and many similar cases it welcomed the chance of writing the preference of a bare majority of the Court into the Supreme Law. That any such preference exhibited by five good lawyers embodied the majesty of reason, while an opposing opinion maintained by four equally good lawyers embodied palpable unreason could, one would think, hardly be maintained with a serious contenance. Yet it has been maintained, and the practice flourished for many years, in spite of the fact that it ignored the official theory supposed to determine the use of the judicial veto—the theory that laws should not be invalidated unless the violation of the Constitution was beyond reasonable doubt.

Of late years the Supreme Court has more and more avoided rather than welcomed political responsibility. The strong tendency towards social legislation, which set in at the very end of the nineteenth century, met with some resistance in the beginning from the Supreme Court; but as the movement grew in volume, the resistance diminished. The absurdity of the attempt by a small body of lawyers in a democracy to convert their political preferences into law under the cover of constitutional construction is being recognized. The judicial veto is being exercised by the Supreme Court only in the cases of manifest excesses and flagrant abuses of legislative authority. The tendency is, consequently, to throw the burden of political decisions on legislative bodies, which are supposed to be responsible immediately to public opinion. Instead of amplifying the scope of the individual rights guaranteed to American citizens by the Constitution and correspondingly restricting the exercise of the police power, they are allowing the police power to shelter an increasing array of interferences with individual liberties. The authority which the courts have exercised under the due process of law and equal rights clauses will gradually be pared down just as it was gradually built up, until finally the restraints put on the legislative power, both local and Federal, by the courts will become comparatively innocuous. A similar tendency was exhibited in recent decisions respecting the regulation by the states of railroad rates. The Court affirmed national control under certain conditions over intra-state rates, but left that control to be exercised by Congress. If this disposition continues and becomes even more emphatic, as it almost certainly will, the development of the American legal system will depend far more than it has in the past upon the will of the legislatures.

Any such shifting of the centre of gravity of the American political system would, however, count in favor of a revision of Article V rather than against it. Assuredly the exercise of a discretionary political power by a body of men directly representative of some phase of public opinion is preferable to its exercise by a body of men who technically are not at all responsible to public opinion. But the substitution of Congressional for judicial authority should not be pushed too far. Any tendency to Congressional omnipotence will have to face the opposition of deep and wholesome American political tradition—the tradition which distrusted the concentration of too much responsibility and power in any one department of the organized government. The courts were allowed to become the final regulators of the American political system, only because they were supposed to act, not from preference, interest or will, but in the light of a purely rational interpretation of a body of permanent political truth. But public opinion has never exhibited any intention of allowing essentially wilful political instruments, like Congress or the state legislatures, to become all-powerful within their respective jurisdictions. The relaxation of judicial control over legislative action will and should be accompanied by an increasing purpose to substitute some other kind of control.

The suspicion with which American public opinion has regarded the work of American legislatures has most assuredly been justified. Representative bodies which have exhibited such meagre powers of self-control can hardly be intrusted with complete legal authority over the lives and property of citizens and the policy of the state. The most important legislature in the United States has not in either of its branches succeeded in adopting a set of rules which combines the efficient transaction of public business with any sufficient freedom of discussion. Moreover, all American legislative bodies, Congress included, have proved wholly incapable of saving themselves from the enervating and disintegrating effect of excessive indulgence in special legislation. The causes of this ill-success of American legislatures are so numerous and raise so many doubtful matters of discussion that they cannot be considered in this connection; but whatever the cause, any early or complete bestowal of confidence by public opinion on Congress is neither to be expected nor desired. The more power Congress obtains at the expense of the judiciary, the greater will be the pressure to redress the balance by means of an increase of popular control—which can be accomplished only by the release of direct popular power over the Constitution.

Such is the one effective way in which the American people can obtain the legal direction of their own political destiny—the one effective way in which the Constitution can be made at once the instrument of democracy and a vitally educational influence on American national development. Then the social treasure of the American democracy will no longer be locked up in an inaccessible safe which cannot be opened except by conforming to a most complicated and difficult ritualistic combination. It will be placed directly in the custody of the people themselves, which will help the people to realize their own responsibility. It is a singular fact that in the past the American system was supposed to derive its democracy from what was in reality its least democratic aspect. It was democratic, not by virtue of the powers which the electorate were permitted to exercise through the agency of the government, but through the powers which the Law reserved to the people. But the powers which the Constitution reserved to the people were, as a consequence of the difficulty of amendment, even more effectually preserved from them. In so far as the Constitution was democratic, the amending clause converted its democracy into a golden hoard, to which access could be obtained only at rare intervals and after an heroic effort.

5.8 Justice Holmes Calls for An Organic Constitution*

Implicit in many critiques of the amending process and in many of the commendations of the British system was the notion that the Constitution should be interpreted flexibly rather than rigidly. While this plea was hardly new—consider Marshall's language in *McCulloch v. Maryland* (1819)—it can be argued that constitutional interpretation began to be even less wedded to constitution text than in earlier eras. One of the most striking pleas for an organic Constitution came from a Justice better known for his philosophic skepticism than for his belief in progressive advancement. Justice Oliver Wendell Holmes, Jr. penned his defense of an organic Constitution in a case dealing with the constitutionality of a migratory bird treaty between the United States and Great Britain (acting on behalf of Canada). Previously, courts had ruled that national regulations over game violated the powers reserved to the states under the Tenth Amendment. Now the Court had to decide if it was possible for the Court to do by treaty that

* *Missouri v. Holland*, 252 U.S. 416 (1920), pp. 433-4.

which it could not do by legislation alone. Holmes responded that it could, taking care to emphasize, however, that state powers under the treaty-making power would also be subject to some constitutional limitations.

The Organic Constitution

Acts of Congress are the supreme law of the land only when made in pursuance of the Constitution, while treaties are declared to be so when made under the authority of the United States. It is open to question whether the authority of the United States means more than the formal acts prescribed to make the convention. We do not mean to imply that there are no qualifications to the treaty-making power; but they must be ascertained in a different way. It is obvious that there may be matters of the sharpest exigency for the national well being that an act of Congress could not deal with but that a treaty followed by such an act could, and it is not lightly to be assumed that, in matters requiring national action, "a power which must belong to and somewhere reside in every civilized government" is not to be found. *Andrews v. Andrews*, 188 U.S. 14, 33. What was said in that case with regard to the powers of the States applies with equal force to the powers of the nation in cases where the States individually are incompetent to act. We are not yet discussing the case before us but only are considering the validity of the test proposed. With regard to that we may add that when we are dealing with words that also are a constituent act, like the Constitution of the United States, we must realize that they have called into life a being the development of which could not have been foreseen completely by the most gifted of its begetters. It was enough for them to realize or to hope that they had created an organism; it has taken a century and has cost their successors much sweat and blood to prove that they created a nation. The case before us must be considered in the light of our whole experience and not merely in that of what was said a hundred years ago. The treaty in question does not contravene any prohibitory words to be found in the Constitution. The only question is whether it is forbidden by some invisible radiation from the general terms of the Tenth Amendment. We must consider what this country has become in deciding what that Amendment has reserved.

5.9 The Progressive Era Amendments

The great irony about all the Progressive critiques of the amending process was that, in the end, major progressive reforms were effected through this much maligned mechanism and in relatively short order. Federal judges were not, as some had suggested, given elected terms of office, but the national income tax (which had been ruled unconstitutional in *Pollock v. Farmers' Loan & Trust Company*, 1895) was legalized, provision was made for direct election of Senators, national alcoholic prohibition was imposed, and American women were finally accorded the right to vote. The texts of these four amendments are provided below. It is interesting to note that the Eighteenth Amendment is the first to include a ratification deadline of seven years within its text, thereby resolving an issue that would become prominent in other amending controversies.

Amendment XVI [1913]
The Congress shall have power to lay and collect taxes on incomes, from whatever source derived, without apportionment among the several States, and without regard to any census or enumeration.

Amendment XVII [1913]
The Senate of the United States shall be composed of two Senators from each State, elected by the people thereof, for six years; and each Senator shall have one vote. The electors in each State shall have the qualifications requisite for electors of the most numerous branch of the State legislatures.

When vacancies happen in the representation of any State in the Senate, the executive authority of such State shall issue writs of election to fill such vacancies: *Provided*, That the legislature of any State may empower the executive thereof to make temporary appointments until the people fill the vacancies by election as the legislature may direct.

This amendment shall not be so construed as to affect the election or term of any Senator chosen before it becomes valid as part of the Constitution.

Amendment XVIII [1919]

SECTION 1. After one year from the ratification of this article the manufacture, sale, or transportation of intoxicating liquors within, the importation thereof into, or the exportation thereof from the United States and all territory subject to the jurisdiction thereof for beverage purposes is hereby prohibited.

SECTION 2. The Congress and the several States shall have concurrent power to enforce this article by appropriate legislation.

SECTION 3. This article shall be inoperative unless it shall have been ratified as an amendment to the Constitution by the legislatures of the several States, as provided in the Constitution, within seven years from the date of the submission hereof to the States by the Congress.

Amendment XIX [1920]

The right of citizens of the United States to vote shall not be denied or abridged by the United States or by any State on account of sex.

Congress shall have the power to enforce this article by appropriate legislation.

Chapter 6

Conservative Reaction and Court Challenges

Even before the Progressive Era amendments were ratified, some conservative legal theorists had begun to warn that certain provisions in the Constitution were subject to implicit limitations. Although these widespread arguments ultimately proved unavailing, they set the groundwork for a number of legal challenges which led to some important judicial decisions in the area of amendments. By 1937, conservatives found that their most prized constitutional doctrines protecting laissez-faire economics were in jeopardy. In the famous "switch in time that saved nine," the Supreme Court, once the bastion of property rights, beat a retreat from earlier doctrines that left conservatives complaining, much like liberals before them, that the Constitution had been amended without consulting the people.

6.1 Thomas Cooley Speculates About Limits on the Amending Process*

Probably the most influential legal theorist of his day, Professor Thomas Cooley was a strong advocate of judicial protection of property rights. Long before adoption of the Progressive Era amendments, Cooley began to question whether reformers might not go too far. In the essay below, which undoubtedly influenced a generation of legal scholars, Cooley raised the possibility that there might be implicit

---

* Cooley, "The Power to Amend the Federal Constitution," *Michigan Law Journal* 1 (April, 1893), pp. 113, 117-20.

constitutional limits on the substance of amendments that could be proposed. The fascinating aspect of this essay is that it does not appear to be directed to the reversal of any existing amendments, Cooley clearly accepting the legitimacy of the fifteen amendments already ratified.

Limits on the Amending Process

But as the future could not be fully foreseen, there was embodied in the constitution itself a provision for further amendments; amendments which might originate either in the congress or in the states, and when regularly proposed and acted upon by the states, three-fourths of the states concurring in them, should become a part of the constitution itself, [sic] And it was supposed that if any very serious evil in government should at any time in the future threaten or actually arise, it would as a matter of course be guarded against or cured in this way. It was supposed that by this method ample means were provided so that it should be beyond the power of the government, (which for the time being was nothing but an agency of the sovereign people, and not in itself possessing the sovereignty), to oppress the people to that point where they would feel called upon to resort to an attempt at revolution for the purpose of a redress of grievances. In this way therefore it was supposed that provision was made whereby this assumption in the constitution that it was to endure forever would be made reasonably certain of realization, since the constitution itself was capable of easy and peaceful modification to provide for all sorts of contingencies and to remove all conceivable evils. . . .

Let us now turn to the question whether this one expressed limitation to the amendment of the constitution is now the sole limitation upon the power of congress and of the states to amend. It certainly is the sole limitation except these temporary ones to which I have referred that it has heretofore been deemed important should be declared,—should be made a part of the constitution itself. But in my view there are limitations that are far more important than this, that stand unquestionably as restrictions upon the power to amend; and although they may not occur to the mind at once, yet, when they are mentioned, it seems to me it must be as clear as anything concerning this instrument can be, that they do exist; that they must in the nature of things exist; and if there should ever be an attempt to amend the constitution in the particulars to which I shall now refer, it would be held by the proper constituted authorities that the offer was altogether futile. Let me suggest, for example, that three-fourths of the states possessing the power to amend in the manner pointed out by the constitution should, by reason of some prejudice against the section of the union comprising the remaining fourth, proceed to so amend the constitution as to set off that other fourth from the union,—to detach it,—to exclude,—put out the states within it from the union altogether. There is nothing in this constitution that in terms forbids it. Will any one say it may be done? Let me suppose that three-fourths of the states should proceed in respect to the other fourth to establish a rule of taxation that they did not see fit at the same time to apply to themselves. Will any one say that that rule could be adopted by an amendment to the constitution, accepted according to the terms of the instrument, basing his opinion on the fact that it is not forbidden? Let me suppose that an amendment should be proposed creating a special order within the states; a privileged class,—a nobility if you please;—that influence sufficient should be found in three-fourths of the states to secure the acceptance of an amendment to the constitution that should set over us a privileged order. We see at once the amendment is not forbidden in the constitution. Can the privileged order therefore be created? Let me suppose that by amendments proposed and adopted, not perhaps all at once, but by a gradual process, we should at length reach the point when we should have over us a king; a hereditary monarch,—an absolute ruler;—"We the people," have unquestionably the sovereignty and thereby supposed to be empowered to do anything we please, may we not, if we see fit, in this form and by the process which we have chosen to adopt, if we reach the conclusion by and by that we will be better governed by a king than by the rulers we elect,—can we not amend amend the constitution to provide for it? And so I might go on illustrating the question I am raising at this point by reference to the different governments that exist on the face of the globe, and inquire whether we may not, when three-fourths of our people see fit to adopt the method whereby some other people are governed; whether we may not under this provision which we have so carefully framed and by which we have expressly made a single exception only, proceed to set up for ourselves such a government as we take a fancy to, and which we find in existence somewhere else?

Now replying to this question, I first call your attention the amendments that have been made to the constitution heretofore. Every one of them, as you will see when you come to consider them carefully, has been in one direction. They each and all have been in the direction of further extending the democratic principles which underlie our constitution. They have increased instead of limiting popular rights; they have enlarged instead of restricting equality of privilege. Not one of them has been in the direction of restoring what was rejected by the people when they declared their independence of the mother country and set up governments for themselves. All of them were entirely harmonious with the general principles of the instrument into which they were brought, and were intended to perfect instead of disfiguring it. That they were, in their nature, proper amendments if assented to by the people, was questioned by no one.

Now an amendment, as I understand it, in the very nature of the case, must be in harmony with the thing amended, so far at least as concerns its general spirit and purpose. It must not be something so entirely incongruous that, instead of amending or reforming it, it overthrows or revolutionizes it. To convert a democratic republic into a government ruled by a privileged aristocracy or by a king, through an amendment of its constitution, is simply an impossibility. The change would not be an amendment but a revolution. The full privilege of amendment, no matter how completely expressed or declared, would not warrant it, because it could not come within the meaning of the term. And any step in the direction of establishing a government which is entirely out of harmony with that which has been created under the constitution, or which is in the direction of taking the power of the state from the people and of substituting principles of government which were rejected when the constitution was established, though it may be taken in the most formal and deliberate manner, and in precise conformity to the method of amendment established by the constitution, is inoperative in the very nature of things, unless it be taken expressly as a revolutionary proceeding, to be accepted if need be, and upheld, by force. The framers of the constitution must very well have understood that this was the case, and must have acted upon this understanding; and they abstained from forbidding such changes because they would be illegitimate as amendments, and for that reason impossible under the term they were making use of. Their thought was upon changes which in coming into the instrument would find suitable place there because of their harmony with the general purpose: changes that would avoid the necessity or repel the inclination for any resort to revolution; but not such as would favor or accomplish one. In other words, the power of amendment was introduced for preservation not destruction, and the intent is too obvious to admit of any question.

I assert then without hesitation, that we have created a constitution of a democratic republic for the protection and perpetuation of popular rights, and on an assumption that whatever is done under it will be done in conformity with the principles which underlie that constitution. Of nothing is that more especially true than of the provision respecting amendments. If the makers of the constitution, in limiting this provision, stopped short of forbidding such changes as would be inharmonious, they did so because it was not in their thought that any such changes could for a moment be considered by congress or by the states as admissible, since in the completed instrument no place could possibly be found for them, however formal might be the process of adoption; and as foreign matter, they would just as certainly be declared inadmissible and therefore invalid without an express inhibition as with it. The fruit grower does not forbid his servants engrafting the witch-hazel or the poisonous sumac on his apple trees; the process is forbidden by a law higher and more imperative than any he could declare, and to which no additional force could possibly be given by re-enactment under his orders. The principle is as imperative in the political world as in the realm of inanimate nature, and is quite as little in need of express declaration. We may amend indefinitely, but the amendments must be harmonious with the original structure, as it has become by changes made in the spirit which it then expressed.

6.2 George Ticknor Curtis Sees the Ninth and Tenth Amendments As Limitations on Article V*

In a book generally acknowledged for its comprehensive treatment of the U.S. Constitution, historian George Ticknor Curtis argued that the Ninth and Tenth Amendments were intended to serve as limits on Article V. This argument, which never met with success before the U.S. Supreme Court, nonetheless retained currency for more than thirty years and helped fuel arguments, some of which we will see in the following pages, that there were inherent limits on Article V.

Limitations on the Amending Power

ONE of the most important subjects that can engage the attention of the statesmen and people of this country is the extent and scope of the power to amend the Constitution of the United States. Very little aid on this subject can be derived from the mode in which the constitution of a state may be amended; for the Constitution of the United States contains in itself a positive text, which at once prescribes the mode in which it may be amended, and limits the power of amendment.

In considering this text, however—Article V. of the Constitution—it is necessary also to consider the force and operation of the Ninth and Tenth Amendments, because they may have some bearing upon the original article which embraces the amending power.

---

* George Ticknor Curtis, *Constitutional History of the United States: From Their Declaration of Independence to the Close of their Civil War* (New York: Da Capo Press, 1974; reprint of New York: Harper & Brothers, 1896), pp. 152-3 and 159-163.

The public bodies which are to be the agents for amending the Constitution are those which are authorized to propose amendments, and those which are authorized to adopt them and make them a part of the instrument.

The first of these are the two houses of Congress, acting by a two-thirds vote of each, or a convention of all the states, called by the Congress on the application of the legislatures of two thirds of the several states. The ratifying bodies in either case are the legislatures of three fourths of the several states, or conventions in three fourths thereof, as the one or the other mode of ratification may be proposed by the Congress. Thus it appears that two thirds of both houses of Congress may propose amendments, or the legislatures of two thirds of the several states may apply to have a convention of all the states called for the proposing of amendments, in which case the Congress must make the call; and it further appears that the amendments, when proposed by either form of action, may be ratified by the legislatures of three fourths of the states, or by conventions in three fourths thereof, as the one or the other mode of ratification may be directed by the Congress when the amendments are proposed. So that there may be one fourth of the several states that must submit to the will of three fourths thereof, if the three fourths ratify any amendment that has been constitutionally proposed, although the one fourth may not accede to it. This is a great and far-reaching power, but it is carefully defined and regulated; and the question arises, What, if any, are its limitations? What is to secure the constitutional minority of the states from an exercise of power by the constitutional majority that will prostrate their state sovereignties and destroy their autonomy?

It will be observed that the amending power is not a power to be exercised by a majority of the people of the United States, acting as a mass of individuals, or as a collective people. It is to be exercised by three fourths of the states, a constitutional majority of the members of the Union fixed for this special purpose. It may thus happen that a proposed amendment would be ratified by a less number than a majority of the people of all the states, because of the mode of ratification and the fixed constitutional number of the state legislatures or state conventions which would have the power to ratify it.

All this shows, on the one hand, how careful the framers of the Constitution were, in shaping the amending power, to preserve the state sovereignties; and, on the other hand, how far their system removes the amending power from the action of the people of the United States regarded as a nation.

No one can read the ten amendments of the Constitution which were prepared by the First Congress in 1789, and were ratified by the states in 1789-91, without perceiving how necessary they were to supplement the instrument that came from the Convention of 1787, and was adopted in 1787-88. . . .

It is proper to observe here that the first ten amendments, unlike some of those which were adopted at a much later period, were designed as restraints imposed on the Federal Government, and not on the state governments. The whole tenor of these texts, and the contemporaneous history, show that they had their origin in the fear that in the powers granted by the Constitution to the government of the United States the safety of the states and their people had not been sufficiently guarded. Designed as restrictive and explanatory clauses, to apply to the powers granted to that government, their language is susceptible of no other meaning. Accordingly, it has been repeatedly held by the Supreme Court of the United States that none of them affects the conditions of the states, or the powers which the states or their people may rightfully exercise.

The powers which the states may not rightfully exercise, according to the original Constitution, as it first took effect, were those which were subjected to the prohibitions expressly laid upon every state by Article I., Section 10. These are the prohibitions referred to in Amendment X., which reserves to the states respectively, or to the people, all powers which had not been so prohibited, and all which had not been delegated to the United States.

At a subsequent period, when the Thirteenth, Fourteenth, and Fifteenth Amendments were adopted, other prohibitions were added which restrained the states in the exercise of certain powers that they previously had. Whenever, therefore, it is sought, in a judicial or any other proceeding, to show that a state is restrained by the Constitution, as now amended, from exercising any power which the original text of the Constitution did not prohibit, the restraint must be found in one of the amendments adopted in 1789 or subsequently. For all other restraints on the state powers the inquirer must consult Article I., Section 10, of the Constitution as it was originally framed and adopted. The Ninth and Tenth Amendments are in themselves express fundamental provisions, fixing immutably the reserved rights of the states. If three fourths of the states were to undertake to repeal them, or to remove them from their place in the foundations of the Union, it would be equivalent to a revolution. There would remain nothing but the dominant force of three fourths of the states, and this would soon end in a complete consolidation of the physical force of the nation, to be followed by a different system of government of a despotic character.

It seems to me, therefore, that while it is within the amending power to change the framework of the government in some respects, it is not within that power to deprive any state, without its own consent, of any rights of self-government which it did not cede to the United States by the Constitution, or which the Constitution did not prohibit it from exercising. In other words, I think the power of amending the Constitution was intended to apply to amendments which would modify the mode of carrying into effect the original provisions and powers of the Constitution, but not to enable three fourths of the states to grasp new power at the expense of any unwilling state.

Take, as an example, some of the amendments adopted at a later period; for instance, those which took from the states the power to continue slavery, or involuntary servitude—a power which every state unquestionably held before those amendments became a part of the Constitution. Or, take the provisions of Amendment XIV, which prohibited any state from assuming or paying any debt incurred in aid of insurrection or rebellion against the United States—a thing which any state could have done but for this inhibition.

It is not necessary to consider here the mode in which these later amendments were required to be adopted by the people of the Confederate States, who had waged war against the government of the United States. When I come to treat specifically of these later amendments, it will appear that notwithstanding some degree of compulsion was used to bring about their acceptance and ratification by the people of the Southern States—a method of proceeding that was certainly not in accordance with the intent and spirit of the amending power—yet these later amendments, both by the ratifications given to them by the Southern States and by the universal acquiescence of their people, are now properly regarded as parts of the Constitution, although we may regret that any kind of compulsion was used. But suppose these amendments had not been proposed and adopted under peculiar circumstances; that, like the earlier amendments, they had been submitted to the people of all the states, to be acted upon freely, without any conditions affecting their standing in the Union, and that three fourths of all the states had adopted them, and one fourth had refused their assent, would any of the constitutional minority of the states have been rightfully deprived of the power to continue slavery, or to assume and pay the Confederate debt, or any debt contracted in aid of the insurrection against the United States?

The true answer to this question, I think, is to be found in the *Ninth* and *Tenth* of the first amendments; for I cannot interpret those amendments as meaning anything less than reservation to the several states of all powers of government which they had not granted to the United States by the Constitution, or which the Constitution had not prohibited them from exercising.

I conclude, therefore, that there are rights of the several states of which they cannot be deprived by an amendment to the Constitution besides their right to equal suffrage in the Senate. We must consider whether a proposed amendment would relate only to the structure of the government, or whether it would relate to some right of the people of a state which was not touched by the original Constitution, and which the states meant to reserve, and did reserve, by the *Ninth* and

Tenth of the amendments. These amendments have certain clauses as applicable to the amending as to all the other powers embraced in the Constitution. It is quite true that the *amending* power is not a power to be exercised by the government of the United States as that government exercises its power of legislation. It is a specific power, vested as a final authority in three fourths of the states. But when we come to inquire whether three fourths of the states can, by amending the Constitution, deprive any state of a right of which the Constitution did not deprive it, as it was first adopted, we must, I think, reach the conclusions which I have indicated.

The grand effort of the Federal Convention of 1787, which framed the Constitution of the United States, was to make a system of government for the Union which, while having certain specific powers ceded to it by the people of each state, would be consistent with the preservation of the state sovereignties in all other respects. The discovery that was made in the process of forming the Federal Constitution was that sovereignty—which is our American sense means only the political authority of the people—is divisible according to the subjects on which it acts; that some powers of government can be vested in one class of public agents, and all others can be retained by the people in whom they primarily reside; and thus that the individual inhabitants of separate, political communities can be acted on by two distinct government, each of which has its appropriate sphere. But this mode of constituting a mixed political system required that the Federal or Central Government should, by express provision, be made supreme and paramount in the exercise of all the powers ceded to it by the people of the several states. That the people of the several states would retain all the original and inherent powers not parted with by cession to the Federal Government was assumed to be a fundamental implication, resulting from the fact that the powers granted to the Federal Government were specific, described, limited, and enumerated, and did not comprehend all the powers of sovereignty. But when the Constitution, as originally framed and promulgated, came before the people of the several states for adoption and ratification, they were not content to leave this very important matter to implication; they demanded an express reservation of all the powers which were not to be ceded by the people of the several states to the Federal Government, or which they were not to be prohibited from exercising. Accordingly the Tenth Amendment, adopted in 1789-91, was made to declare:

"The powers not delegated to the United States by the Constitution, nor prohibited by it to the States, are reserved to the States respectively, or to the people."

By this reservation every state remains a self-governing political community, in respect to its own inhabitants, in every relation in which those inhabitants are not by the Constitution of the United States placed under the authority of the Federal Government.

It is this mass of rights, privileges, and powers not vested in the Federal Government, but retained by the people of each state, that constitutes the state sovereignty. It follows, as a necessary consequence from this system, that the people of every state in this Union have under their entire control every relation of their inhabitants that is not under the control of the United States by reason of some provision in the Federal Constitution. With the domestic relations of their inhabitants the states can deal as they see fit.

6.3 The Constitutionality of the Eighteenth Amendment*

Arguments like Cooley's began to be applied as conservatives attempted to resist the Progressive Era amendments. In the reading below from a series of seven cases which were consolidated for consideration by the Supreme Court, arguments are first reproduced on the issue of whether the Eighteenth Amendment was unconstitutional. This is followed by the Court's opinion rejecting that argument. While the decision seems to be a prudent one, questions must certainly remain (especially in light of the subsequent repeal of the Eighteenth Amendment) as to the desirability of incorporating certain

---

* National Prohibition Cases, 253 U.S. 350 (1920), pp. 354-56; 361-67; 385-88; 381-3; 388; 393; 401; 410-11.

kinds of changes into the text of the fundamental law of the land.

Arguments for Mr. Rice for State of Rhode Island:
Mr. [Herbert A.] Rice, for the State of Rhode Island, in No. 29, Original, confined his argument to the validity of the Amendment. Various objections were stated, the one chiefly elaborated being that the Amendment is an invasion of the sovereignty of the complaining State and her people, not contemplated by the amending clause of the Constitution. The amending power, it was contended, is not a substantive power but a precautionary safeguard inserted incidentally to insure the ends set forth in that instrument against errors and oversights committed in its formation. Amendments, as the term indeed implies, are to be limited to the correction of such errors.

The doctrine that any and every change may be introduced in guise of amendment is a novelty subversive of fundamental principles. It would bring about a constitutional revolution, converting the sovereignty of the people into a sovereignty of officials. It would permit the boundary between federal and state authority, established by the Constitution, to be shifted at will, as officials might be influenced by political cowardice or expediency, and would ultimately reduce the States to mere dependencies of the Federal Government.

All sovereignty resides in the people. The Constitution therefore was submitted for ratification to conventions chosen directly by the people. The possibility of federal encroachment upon state sovereignty was the subject of principal concern when the Constitution was in process of adoption, and, practically as a part of the process, the first ten amendments were added to prevent such encroachments. And it was generally understood and agreed that the boundaries set between state and federal powers were fundamental and permanent.

It is "This Constitution" that may be amended. "This Constitution" is not a code of transient laws but a framework of government and an embodiment of fundamental principles. By an amendment, the identity or purpose of the instrument is not to be changed; its defects may be cured, but "This

Constitution" must remain. It would be the greatest absurdity to contend that there was a purpose to create a limited government and at the same time to confer upon that government a power to do away with its own limitations. All of the prior amendments have been declaratory and interpretative or have had relation to a power or to a subject-matter dealt with in the instrument itself. The amending function (under Art. V) is purely federal. The State is not a party to an amendment and her people do not participate. A legislature in ratifying does not act for the State and cannot limit her sovereign powers. A State is bound in respect of sovereign powers only by the explicit act of her whole people. To be valid, an amendment must have such relation to the general grant of powers and to the scope and purposes of the Constitution as will carry an implication of assent on the part of the people of the United States, springing from their adoption of the Constitution.

In the case of this so-called amendment, the representatives of the people of the United States have attempted, not to amend the Constitution of the United States, but to amend the constitution of every State in the Union. If the amending function is construed as coextensive with absolute sovereignty, then the basis of our political system is no longer the right of the people of a State to make and alter their constitution, for their political institutions are at the mercy of others and may be changed against their will.

Argument of [Elihu] Root:

I. The substantive and operative part of the so-called Eighteenth Amendment is contained in its first section. This provision does not relate to the powers or organization of government, as does an ordinary constitutional provision. On the contrary, it is itself an exercise of the legislative power of government, and a direct act of legislation regulating the conduct of life of the individual. The first question before the court is, therefore, whether Article V of the Constitution authorizes any amendment which in substance and effect is merely a police regulation or statute.

To uphold such a power of amendment would do violence to what Hamilton (Federalist, No. 22, p. 135, Ford's ed.)

described as "the fundamental maxim of republican government . . . which requires that the sense of the majority should prevail." If the so-called Eighteenth Amendment be a valid part of the Constitution, its repeal can hereafter be perpetually prevented by a minority, for if but one State more than one-fourth of the States refuse to assent thereto, it is irrepealable. The census of 1910 discloses that there are in the Union thirteen States whose aggregate population does not equal five per cent. of the entire population of the United States. Consequently, however vast the majority of the population in the future may be who are persuaded by experience that this direct legislative regulation of their lives and personal habits was or has become unwise and unnecessary, they will be helpless to change the law if there be dissent on the part of a minority representing only five per cent of the population or perhaps less.

There is plainly a distinction in this respect between the so-called amendment as adopted and as it would be if it had conferred *power* upon Congress to prohibit the use of intoxicating liquors. An amendment in the latter form would, it is true, be precisely as irrepealable as the one here in question, but the conduct of individual life thereunder would at all times be within the control of representatives of the majority of the people. Congress would then have the power to prohibit intoxicants or not, completely or qualifiedly, as it from time to time deemed best; and if the majority of the people then desired prohibition, Congress could respond to their wish; and if, on the other hand, the majority thereafter became persuaded that extreme prohibition was no longer necessary, in that respect also Congress could effectuate the will of the people. In every free government the direct regulation of the lives of the people by legislation should at all times be in the hands of the majority, however the powers of government may be distributed and allocated.

This fundamental consideration differentiates sharply the Eighteenth Amendment from the Thirteenth Amendment, to which the Eighteenth bears a superficial resemblance. As is now universally conceded, slavery was the creation of positive law, and it was always unauthorized unless some exercise of government permitted it. A constitutional declaration that slavery was prohibited would, therefore, in substance, be only the withdrawal from every governmental authority of the *power* to license or permit involuntary servitude. That amendment, consequently, only affected the *powers* of government, and did not constitute, as does the so-called Eighteenth Amendment, a direct legislative exercise of those powers.

Article V of the Constitution should not be construed to confer unlimited legislative power upon the amending authorities. To assume that it does is inconsistent with the plain provision of §2 of Article I of the Constitution that "*all* legislative powers herein granted shall be vested in a Congress of the United States," and with the terms of Article V itself, as the proceedings of the Constitutional Convention disclose that the framers themselves understood those terms. The framers undoubtedly regarded the power to amend only as authorizing the inclusion of matter of the same general character as the instrument or thing to be amended; and as all the constitutions of their day were concerned solely with the distribution and limitation of the powers of government, and not with the direct exercise thereof by the constitution makers themselves, no amendment of the latter sort would have been deemed appropriate or germane by them.

It does not advance the discussion to urge that *the people* can adopt any amendment to the Constitution they see fit. No doubt an amendment of any sort could be adopted by the same means as were employed in the adoption of the Constitution itself. In that manner alone do or can *the people* themselves act. But the amending authorities provided for in Article V of the Constitution, as clearly appears from the debates in the Constitutional Convention, are only *agents* of the people and not the people themselves. They must, therefore, act within the authority conferred in Article V, and that authority does not embrace the right under color of amendment to adopt mere sumptuary laws which are not constitutional amendments in truth or essence. The people could by appropriate proceedings amend the Constitution so as to impair such vital rights as freedom of religion, but it is inconceivable that any such unlimited power has been delegated to the amending agents, who may represent but a minority of the people. The census discloses that there are three-fourths of the States of the Union whose total population amounts to less than forty-five per cent. of the people of the United States, and two-thirds of a quorum of both houses of Congress may, therefore, likewise represent only a minority of the population.

Ratification by state legislatures does not as matter of fact provide an opportunity for the people to express their will regarding the proposed Eighteenth Amendment as the calling of conventions might have done. Thus, for example, the Missouri legislature ratified it, notwithstanding an express provision of the Missouri constitution (Art. II, 3) forbidding them so to do, and in Ohio ratification by the legislature was subsequently rejected by the people at the polls, while in other States the people have been denied all right to have the question of ratification referred to them for approval.

If, as contended by the defendants, the power of amendment vested in Congress and three-fourths of the state legislatures be absolute and unrestricted, then there would be no limitation whatever upon their legislative authority. They could then by amendment establish a state religion, or oppress or discriminate against any denomination, or authorize the taking away of life, liberty and property, without due process of law, etc., etc. This would destroy the most essential limitation upon power under the American system of government, which is that the rights of the individual citizen shall be protected by withholding from the legislative function the power to do certain things inconsistent with individual liberty. This was the reason of the irresistible demand for the first ten amendments.

When the Federal Constitution was adopted, the people of practically every State had limited by bills of rights their own governments in their own States, which were composed of men elected by themselves. We are not at liberty to assume that in and by Article V it was contemplated that they were vesting legislative power without limitation in the Congress and the legislatures of three-quarters of the States. For these reasons and others it is submitted that the adoption of the so-called Eighteenth Amendment by the agents of the people was beyond the amending power of such agents and therefore invalid.

II. The Eighteenth Amendment, furthermore, if valid, would tend to undermine a fundamental principle of our federal system. As Chief Justice Chase declared in *Texas v. White*, 7 Wall. 700, 724, "the Constitution, in all its provisions, looks to an indestructible Union, composed of indestructible States." Manifestly, the federal system of government created in the Constitution contemplated indestructible States—not indestructible geographic units merely, but indestructible self-governing, local sovereignties. The establishment of our dual system of government must necessarily imply that neither government shall be permitted to destroy the other, and that the States must be preserved, not as mere electoral and administrative districts of a unified and consolidated national government, but as true local, self-governing sovereignties, inviolate and indestructible members of a dual, and not a consolidated, system of government, and with a permanent and effectual reason for being, namely, the possession of the power and the right to exercise forever the functions of internal and local self-government.

The so-called Eighteenth Amendment *directly* invades the police powers of the States and *directly* encroaches upon their right of local self-government. If this amendment be valid, then any amendment which directly impairs the police powers of the States and absolutely withdraws from them their right to local self-government in any important particular, heretofore, indisputably a matter of internal concern, must likewise be valid. In other words, if the so-called Eighteenth Amendment be lawful, then the States are not in truth indestructible. It must be manifest that the precedent necessarily erected by the holding that the Eighteenth Amendment is constitutional, would authorize the complete subversion of our dual and federal system of government. It is submitted that the authority conferred in Article V to amend the Constitution carries no power to destroy its federal principle in a most fundamental aspect.

The Civil War amendments afford no justification for the Eighteenth Amendment. Their primary purpose was to crystallize into the Constitution some of the essentials of a free republican government, and it was expressly made the constitutional duty of the Federal Government to guarantee to the States such a form of government. This federal duty the Civil War amendments helped to realize; and the fact that, as an incident and indirectly, they interfered to some extent with the States is of not consequence. They are not like the Eighteenth Amendment, which is germane to no original federal duty, and which directly, primarily and deliberately invades the right of the States to govern themselves.

The Solicitor General and Assistant Attorney General Frierson:

The questions as to whether the Eighteenth Amendment is of such a nature as to be within the amending power provided by Article V of the Constitution, and whether the Eighteenth Amendment has, in fact, been ratified, are questions committed by the Constitution to the political branch and not to the judicial branch of the Government. . . .

The Eighteenth Amendment, establishing a fundamental rule of law, is an amendment within the meaning of Article V of the Constitution. The Constitution and the amendments heretofore adopted are full of rules of law by which the activities of the various agencies of government, both state and federal, and the rights and duties of persons are fixed or regulated. The Thirteenth Amendment, particularly, is almost an exact prototype of the Eighteenth Amendment and operates upon individuals in the same way. It has always been understood that there is no limitation upon the character of amendments which may be adopted, except such limitations as are imposed by Article V itself. Washington's Writings, vol. XII, pp. 4-5, 222. With these specific limitations, whatever amendments or changes Congress may deem necessary to propose are incorporated in the Constitution if ratified in the manner provided by Article V. Gales and Seaton, Annals of Congress, vol. 1, p. 712.

The fact that the Eighteenth Amendment confers upon Congress a power which had previously belonged exclusively to the States does not prevent that Amendment from being within the amending power conferred by Article V of the Constitution. A provision to the effect should, without its consent, "be affected in its internal police" by an amendment to the Constitution was twice proposed in the Convention and twice rejected. Elliot's Debates, vol. 1, pp. 316-317; Madison's Papers, pp. 531-532, 551-552. In scope, the amending power is now limited as to but one subject, namely, the equal representation of the States in the Senate. Willoughby on the Constitution, 227. Many of the amendments heretofore adopted have taken away from the States powers previously reserved to them. This is particularly true of the Thirteenth, Fourteenth, and Fifteenth Amendments. *Minor v. Happersett*, 21 Wall. 162, 172.

No State by any provision of its laws or its constitution can make the ratification of an amendment to the Constitution of the United States by its legislature subject to a referendum vote of the people. The only method of ratification mentioned in the Constitution is through representatives assembled either in the legislature or a convention called for that purpose. It is clearly contemplated that the action of the State in ratifying shall not be by direct vote of the people but by their representatives, and the body, or bodies, who shall be recognized as acting for the States are specifically named. A legislature in ratifying an amendment, therefore, derives its power not from the State or the people of the State but from the people of the United States through the Constitution of the United States. This power can not be abrogated, limited, or restricted by any state statute or constitution. . . .

Justice Van Devanter for the Court:

We here are concerned with seven cases involving the validity of that [the 18th] Amendment and of certain general features of the National Prohibition Law, known as the Volstead Act . . . The cases have been elaborately argued at the bar and in printed briefs; and the arguments have been attentively considered, with the result that we reach and announce the following conclusions on the questions involved:

1. The adoption by both houses of Congress, each by a two-thirds vote, of a joint resolution proposing an amendment to the Constitution sufficiently shows that the proposal was deemed necessary by all who voted for it. An express declaration that they regarded it as necessary is not essential. None of the resolutions whereby prior amendments were proposed contained such a declaration.

2. The two-thirds vote in each house which is required in proposing an amendment is a vote of two-thirds of the members present—assuming the presence of a quorum—and not a vote of two-thirds of the entire membership, present and absent. *Missouri Pacific Ry. Co. v. Kansas*, 248 U.S. 276.

3. The referendum provisions of state constitutions and statutes cannot be applied, consistently with the Constitution of the United States, in the ratification or rejection of amendments to it. *Hawke v. Smith, ante*, 221.

4. The prohibition of the manufacture, sale, transportation, importation and exportation of intoxicating liquors for beverage purposes, as embodied in the Eighteenth Amendment, is within the power to amend reserved by Article V of the Constitution.

5. That Amendment, by lawful proposal and ratification, has become a part of the Constitution, and must be respected and given effect the same as other provisions of that instrument.

6. The first section of the Amendment—the one embodying the prohibition—is operative throughout the entire territorial limits of the United States, binds all legislative bodies, courts, public officers and individuals within those limits, and of its own force invalidates every legislative act—whether by Congress, by a state legislature, or

by a territorial assembly—which authorizes or sanctions what the section prohibits.

7. The second section of the Amendment—the one declaring "The Congress and the several States shall have concurrent power to enforce this article by appropriate legislation"—does not enable Congress or the several States to defeat or thwart the prohibition, but only to enforce it by appropriate means.

8. The words "concurrent power" in that section do not mean joint power, or require that legislation thereunder by Congress, to be effective, shall be approved or sanctioned by the several States or any of them; nor do they mean that the power to enforce is divided between Congress and the several States along the lines which separate or distinguish foreign and interstate commerce from interstate affairs.

9. The power confided to Congress by that section, while not exclusive, is territorially coextensive with the prohibition of the first section, embraces manufacture and other intrastate transactions as well as importation, exportation and interstate traffic, and is in no wise dependent on or affected by action or inaction on the part of the several States or any of them.

10. That power may be exerted against the disposal for beverage purposes of liquors manufactured before the Amendment became effective just as it may be against subsequent manufacture for those purposes. In either case it is a constitutional mandate or prohibition that is being enforced.

11. While recognizing that there are limits beyond which Congress cannot go in treating beverages as within its power of enforcement, we think those limits are not transcended by the provision of the Volstead Act (Title II, 1), wherein liquors containing as much as one-half of one

per cent. of alcohol by volume and fit for use for beverage purposes are treated as within that power. . . .

Chief Justice White (concurring) expresses disappointment
I profoundly regret that in a case of this magnitude, affecting as it does an amendment to the Constitution dealing with the powers and duties of the national and state governments, and intimately concerning the welfare of the whole people, the court has deemed it proper to state only ultimate conclusions without an exposition of the reasoning by which they have been reached.

I appreciate the difficulties which a solution of this case involves and the solicitude with which the court has approached them, but it seems to my mind that the greater the perplexities the greater the duty devolving upon me to express the reasons which have led me to the conclusion that the Amendment accomplishes and was intended to accomplish the purposes now attributed to it.

Justice McKenna (dissenting) expresses regret
The court in applying it [the 18th amendment] has dismissed certain of the bills, reversed the decree in one, and affirmed the decrees in four others. I am unable to agree with the judgments reversing No. 794 and affirming Nos. 696, 752, 788 and 837.

I am, however, at a loss how, or to what extent, to express the grounds for this action. The court declares conclusions only, without giving any reasons for them. The instance may be wise—establishing a precedent now, hereafter wisely to be imitated. It will undoubtedly decrease the literature of the court if it does not increase lucidity. However, reasons for the conclusions have been omitted, and my comment upon them may come from a misunderstanding of them, their present import and ultimate purpose and force.

There are, however, clear declarations that the Eighteenth Amendment is part of the Constitution of the United Sates, made so in observance of the prescribed constitutional procedure, and as part of the Constitution of the United States is to be respected and given effect like other provisions of that instrument. With these conclusions I agree. . . .

The Eighteenth Amendment is part of the Constitution of the United States, therefore of as high sanction as Article VI. There seems to be a denial of this, based on Article V. That Article provides that the amendments proposed by either of the ways there expressed "shall be valid to all Intents and Purposes, as Part of this Constitution." Some undefinable power is attributed to this in connection with Article VI, as if Article V limits in some way, or defeats, an amendment to the Constitution inconsistent with a previously existing provision. What other purpose could an amendment have? And it would be nullified by the mythical power attributed to Article V, either alone or in conjunction with Article VI. A contention that ascribes such power to those articles is untenable. The Eighteenth Amendment is part of the Constitution and as potent as any other part of it.

Mr. Justice Clarke concurring in first 7 and 10 paragraphs and dissenting from remaining three.

Doubtless such a construction as I am proposing would not satisfy the views of extreme advocates of prohibition or of its opponents, but in my judgment it is required by the salutary rule of constitutional construction referred to, the importance of which cannot be overstated. It is intended to prevent courts from re-writing the Constitution in a form in which judges think it should have been written instead of giving effect to the language actually used in it; and very certainly departures from it will return to plague the authors of them. It does not require the eye of a seer to see contention at the bar of this court against liberal, paramount, congressional definition of intoxicating liquors as strenuous and determined as that which we have witnessed over the strict definition of the Volstead Act. . . .

In the *Slaughter-House* [16 Wall. 36], and other cases, this court was urged to give a construction to the Fourteenth Amendment which would have radically changed the whole constitutional theory of the relations of our state and federal governments by transferring to the general government that police power, through the exercise of which the people of the various States theretofore regulated their local affairs in conformity with the widely differing standards of life, of conduct and of duty which must necessarily prevail in a country of so great extent as ours, with its varieties of climate, of industry and of habits of the people. But this court, resisting the pressure of the passing hour, maintained the integrity of state control over local affairs to the extent that it had not been deliberately and clearly surrendered to the general government, in a number of decisions which came to command the confidence of the generation active when they were rendered and which have been regarded by our succeeding generation as sound and wise and highly fortunate for our country.

The cases now before us seem to me to again present questions of like character to, and of not less importance than, those which were presented in those great cases, and I regret profoundly that I cannot share in the disposition which the majority of my associates think should be made of them.

6.4 The Illegality of Attempts to Ratify Amendments by State Referenda*

The following two cases, the first challenging the Eighteenth and the second the Nineteenth Amendment, arose out of attempts by a state to specify that constitutional amendments would be ratified by state referenda.

Mr. Justice Day

The question for our consideration is: Whether the provision of the Ohio constitution, adopted at the general election, November, 1918, extending the referendum to the ratification by the General Assembly of proposed amendments in the Federal Constitution is in conflict with Article V of the Constitution of the United States. The Amendment of 1918 provides: "The people also reserve to themselves the legislative power of the referendum on the action of the general assembly ratifying

---

* *Hawke v. Smith*, No. 1, 253 U.S. 221, pp. 225-30 (1920); No. 2, 253 U.S. 231, p. 232.

any proposed amendment to the constitution of the United States." . . .

The framers of the Constitution realized that it might in the progress of time and the development of new conditions require changes, and they intended to provide an orderly manner in which these could be accomplished; to that end they adopted the Fifth Article.

This article makes provision for the proposal of amendments either by two-thirds of both houses of Congress, or on application of the legislatures of two-thirds of the States; thus securing deliberation and consideration before any change can be proposed. The proposed change can only become effective by the ratification of the legislatures of three-fourths of the States, or by conventions in a like number of States. The method of ratification is left to the choice of Congress. Both methods of ratification, by legislatures or conventions, call for action by deliberative assemblages representative of the people, which it was assumed would voice the will of the people.

The Fifth Article is a grant of authority by the people to Congress. The determination of the method of ratification is the exercise of a national power specifically granted by the Constitution; that power is conferred upon Congress, and is limited to two methods, by action of the legislatures of three-fourths of the States, or conventions in a like number of States. *Dodge v. Woolsey*, 18 How. 331, 348. The framers of the Constitution might have adopted a different method. Ratification might have been left to a vote of the people, or to some authority of government other than that selected. The language of the article is plain, and admits of no doubt in its interpretation. It is not the function of courts or legislative bodies, national or state, to alter the method which the Constitution has fixed.

All of the amendments to the Constitution have been submitted with a requirement for legislative ratification; by this method all of them have been adopted.

The only question really for determination is: What did the framers of the Constitution mean in requiring ratification by "*Legislatures*"? That was not a term of uncertain meaning when incorporated into the Constitution. What it meant when adopted it still means for the purpose of interpretation. A Legislature was then the representative body which made the laws of the people. The term is often used in the Constitution with this evident meaning. Article I, §2, prescribes the qualifications of electors of congressmen as those "requisite for electors of the most numerous branch of the state legislature." Article I, §3, provided that senators shall be chosen in each State by the legislature thereof, and this was the method of choosing senators until the adoption of the Seventeenth Amendment which made provision for the election of senators by vote of the people, the electors to have the qualifications requisite for electors of the most numerous branch of the state legislature. That Congress and the States understood that this election by the people was entirely distinct from legislative action is shown by the provision of the amendment giving the legislature of any State the power to authorize the Executive to make temporary appointments until the people shall fill the vacancies by election. It was never suggested, so far as we are aware, that the purpose of making the office of Senator elective by the people could be accomplished by a referendum vote. The necessity of the amendment to accomplish the purpose of popular election is shown in the adoption of the amendment. In Article IV the United States is required to protect every State against domestic violence upon application of the legislature, or of the Executive when the legislature cannot be convened. Article VI requires the members of the several legislatures to be bound by oath, or affirmation, to support the Constitution of the United States. By Article I, §8, Congress is given exclusive jurisdiction over all places purchased by the consent of the legislature of the State in which the same shall be. Article IV, §3, provides that no new States shall be carved out of old States without the consent of the legislatures of the States concerned.

There can be no question that the framers of the Constitution clearly understood and carefully used the terms in which that instrument referred to the action of the legislatures of the States. When they intended that direct action by the people should be had they were no less accurate in the use of apt phraseology to carry out such purpose. The members of the

House of Representatives were required to be chosen by the people of the several States. Article I, §2.

The constitution of Ohio in its present form, although making provision for a referendum, vests the legislative power primarily in a General Assembly consisting of a Senate and House of Representatives. Article II, §1, provides:

"The legislative power of the state shall be vested in a general assembly consisting of a senate and house of representatives, but the people shall reserve to themselves the power to propose to the general assembly laws and amendments to the constitution, and to adopt or reject the same at the polls on a referendum vote as hereinafter provided."

The argument to support the power of the State to require the approval by the people of the State of the ratification of amendments to the Federal Constitution through the medium of a referendum rests upon the proposition that the Federal Constitution requires ratification by the legislative action of the States through the medium provided at the time of the proposed approval of an amendment. This argument is fallacious in this—ratification by a State of a constitutional amendment is not an act of legislation within the proper sense of the word. It is but the expression of the assent of the State to a proposed amendment.

At an early day this court settled that the submission of a constitutional amendment did not require the action of the President. The question arose over the adoption of the Eleventh Amendment. *Hollingsworth v. Virginia*, 3 Dall. 378. In that case it was contended that the amendment had not been proposed in the manner provided in the Constitution as an inspection of the original roll showed that it had never been submitted to the President for approval in accordance with Article I, 7, of the Constitution. The Attorney General answered that the case of amendments is a substantive act, unconnected with the ordinary business of legislation, and not within the policy or terms of the Constitution investing the President with a qualified negative on the acts and resolutions of Congress. In a foot-note to this argument of the Attorney General, Justice Chase said: "There can, surely, be no necessity to answer that argument. The negative of the president applies only to the ordinary cases of legislation: He has nothing to do with the proposition or adoption of amendments to the constitution." The court by a unanimous judgment held that the amendment was constitutionally adopted.

It is true that the power to legislate in the enactment of the laws of a State is derived from the people of the State. But the power to ratify a proposed amendment to the Federal Constitution has its source in the Federal Constitution. The act of ratification by the State derives its authority from the Federal Constitution to which the State and its people have alike assented.

Justice Day, Second Case

This case presents the same question as that already decided in No. 582, *ante*, 221, the only different being that the amendment involved is the proposed Nineteenth Amendment to the Constitution extending the right of suffrage to women. The Supreme Court of Ohio upon the authority of its decision in *Hawke v. Smith* (No. 581) *ante*, 221, held that the constitution of the State requiring such submission by a referendum to the people, did not violate Article V of the Federal Constitution, and for that reason rendered a like judgment as in No. 582.

For the reasons stated in our opinion in NO. 582 the judgment of the Supreme Court of Ohio must be.

Reversed.

6.5 Arthur W. Machen, Jr. Questions the Validity of the Fifteenth Amendment*

In the following article, suggestive of many that would be written in the first three decades of this century, a prominent attorney questions the validity of the Fifteenth Amendment. These arguments were ultimately ignored in the Supreme Court's decision in *Myers v. Anderson*, but similar arguments continued to be repeated in a number of subsequent cases.

---

* Machen, "Is the Fifteenth Amendment Void?" *Harvard Law Review* (January 1910) 23: 170-179; 182-3; 189-91.

Is the Fifteenth Amendment Void?

I.

The power of three fourths of the states to amend the Constitution of the United States would seem to be subject to two classes of limitations,—(1) inherent and (2) express.

I. The inherent limitation is that the so-called amendment must be a real amendment, and not the substitution of a new constitution. It may alter many of the vital provisions of the original instrument; but so much of the old constitution must be left that the new provisions may be regarded as merely engrafted on the old stock. A wholly new constitution can be adopted only by the same authority that adopted the present constitution, namely, "the people of the United States," represented by the concurrent action of conventions in all the several states within which the constitution is to be operative.

To draw the line between a mere amendment of the old constitution and an instrument which makes such radical changes as to be fairly regarded only as a new constitution is difficult, not to say impossible. All that can be done is to give a few illustrations that would seem to fall on one side or the other of the line.

Of mere amendments which cannot be deemed to amount to a new constitution, excellent examples are furnished by the first twelve amendments. The Thirteenth Amendment, profoundly as it altered the social system in the slaveholding states, nevertheless falls on the same side of the line. The most important provision of the Fourteenth Amendment—the provision that no state shall deprive any person of life, liberty or property without due process of law, or deny to any person within its jurisdiction the equal protection of the laws—also falls within the same category. It is a new limitation on the powers of the states, but it does not so radically alter their relations as to amount virtually to a new constitution.

On the other hand, one may imagine so-called amendments which would in substance amount to the total abrogation of the old constitution. For instance, the Constitution contemplates a Federal Union, and a Federal Union of all the states;

and probably a change which should destroy this fundamental character of the government would not be an "Amendment." Thus, a so-called amendment substituting two or more independent confederacies in the place of the union of all the states would seem not to be within the power of constitutional amendment. Even more clearly, a provision abolishing the several state governments and providing that all the powers of the British Parliament should be lodged in a national congress would be more than a mere amendment. . . .

The provision, however, that no state without its consent shall be deprived of its equal suffrage in the Senate, being perpetual, is still in full force, and merits the most careful consideration.

In the first place, this proviso necessarily requires the continuance of the Senate as an integral part of the federal legislature. A state could not be deprived of its equal suffrage in the Senate merely by abolishing the Senate, or reducing it to a body merely advisory, concentrating all legislative power in the House of Representatives.

In the next place, this proviso necessitates the continued existence of the several states. As no state can be deprived, even by constitutional amendment, of its equal suffrage in the Senate, it follows that no state can be deprived of its own existence. In order that a state may enjoy equal suffrage in the Senate, it must continue to exist. Its identify must be preserved.

Moreover, the words "without its consent" necessarily imply that the state shall continue to exist as a body capable of consenting, or in other words as an autonomous political community. That a constitutional amendment may cut down the powers of the state may be conceded; but that it cannot deprive the state of its capacity for self-government within its sphere as thus restricted would seem equally clear. The inherent limitation of the power of amendment would perhaps of itself be sufficient to prevent any such change in the Constitution. For the Constitution in all its features contemplates a federal union of self-governing states; and any abrogation of that feature would seem to be more than a mere amendment. But however this may be, the matter is made quite clear by the proviso that no state shall be deprived of its equal suffrage in the Senate without its own consent.

The proviso was, therefore, aptly described in The Federalist as "a palladium to the residuary sovereignty of the states."

The same clause would seem necessarily to imply that the composition of a state cannot be altered without its own consent; for the guaranty of equal suffrage was in favor of the states as they existed in 1789 and as they might subsequently be changed by their own consent or in pursuance of their own laws. If this were not so, the guaranty of equal suffrage in the Senate might be nullified merely by changing the state itself. For example, it will hardly be claimed that three fourths of the states by a constitutional amendment could force a territorial addition upon a small state and thus by enlarging its electorate deprive the residents of the original territorial limits of the state of their exclusive right to elect members of their state legislature and thus indirectly to choose two United States senators. For example, would it be possible for three fourths of the states by a constitutional amendment to provide that the island of Porto Rico, with a population largely in excess of the present State of Rhode Island, should be annexed to that state without its consent, and that the inhabitants of Porto Rico should have the right to vote in state elections anything in the constitution or laws of Rhode Island to the contrary notwithstanding? Would not such a constitutional amendment deprive Rhode Island of its suffrage in the Senate? It is true that two senators would continue to sit nominally as senators from Rhode Island, but the Rhode Island which they would represent would not be the Rhode Island known to the Constitution. That Rhode Island would be swallowed up and lost. The name might remain: the substance would be gone.

Hence, it appears that the prohibition of any constitutional amendment depriving any state of its equal suffrage in the Senate implies as a necessary corollary that no constitutional amendment shall alter the composition of a state; and, therefore, it becomes pertinent to inquire what a state is, and how and of whom or what it is composed. When the Constitution declares that "No State without its consent shall be deprived of its equal suffrage in the Senate," what is meant by "State"?

What is a state? In favor of whom, or of what, is this guarantee.

A state may be defined as a political community united under an organized government and exercising sovereignty over a certain territory; the purely geographical sense is derivative and figurative. . . .

This principle that the word "state" in the Constitution means primarily the body of citizens invested with political rights has been recognized from the very foundation of the Union. . . .

Now, in the provision that "no state without its consent shall be deprived of its equal suffrage in the Senate," the word "state" is certainly not used in the geographical sense; for the expression "its consent" shows that the word refers to some person or persons, or to some organization or corporation, capable of consenting. A geographical area cannot consent; and if we should read "no geographical area without its consent shall be deprived of its equal suffrage in the Senate," the clause would become nonsense. Therefore the word "state" in this place means either the citizens of the state or the government of the state, or else it indicates a blending of the two ideas of people and government. Hence, the clause we are now considering means either that "the citizens or voters of no state without their consent shall be deprived of their equal suffrage in the Senate," or else that "the government of no state without its consent shall be deprived of its equal suffrage in the Senate." In the one aspect, the prohibition would prevent any constitutional amendment enlarging the class of people who constitute the citizenship or electorate of the state, and in the other aspect it would prevent any change in the government or political institutions of the state. If, as is not unlikely, the word "state" in this article of the Constitution refers both to the people of the state and to its government, the prohibition would extend to any change in the class of people who constitute the state, or in their government or political institutions.

A constitutional amendment which should attempt to alter the class of persons who compose the state, and constitute its electorate and repository of political power, would be objectionable on both grounds, even though no change were made in the territorial jurisdiction of the state. It would deprive the state as originally constituted of its suffrage in the Senate. For instance, imagine a constitutional amendment which, without altering the territorial jurisdiction of Rhode Island, should provide that all residents of the city of New York, or of the territory of Porto Rico, or of the Philippine Islands, should have the right to vote in elections for members of the Rhode Island legislature. Such a constitutional amendment would as completely swamp Rhode Island as if foreign territory had been annexed. It would deprive the original citizens of Rhode Island of their exclusive right to elect two senators.

II.

Now let us investigate exactly what changes in the law were attempted to be made by the Fifteenth Amendment, or by the Thirteenth, Fourteenth, and Fifteenth Amendments operating in conjunction. We shall then be in a position to determine whether or not the Fifteenth Amendment exceeds the express or implied limitations of the power of constitutional amendment.

By the common law of all the states, the negroes were slaves—chattels. They were not part of the body politic. They were in no sense citizens. They were "on the same footing with living property of the brute creation." Upon these propositions there has never been any difference of legal opinion, however justly the law which assigned this status of mere property to human beings may have been assailed as barbarous, and however heartily we may rejoice that such a law has ceased to exist.

As more fully explained below, a bitter dispute arose shortly before the Civil War whether even free negroes were, or could be made, citizens and members of the body politic. But those who would answer that question in the affirmative never asserted that slaves were citizens or constituted part of the "people" of the state in which they were held in bondage, or of the United States. . . .

Now, it is these negro slaves, these strangers to the social compact, whom the Fifteenth Amendment attempts to invest with the highest political right. Let us disregard for the moment the various states of the process; for unless the power of constitutional amendment extents to the conversion *per saltum* of slaves into voting citizens, the same result cannot be accomplished more gradually by a series of constitutional amendments.

It will thus be seen that the change is a most serious one in the composition of the state and in its scheme of government. It amounts to a forcible annexation to the state of a large number of persons who had never before constituted part of its body politic, who were not its citizens, and who under its laws were no more entitled to political rights than the Zulus of Africa or the Bushmen of Australia. The case is the same in principle as if an extensive and populous foreign territory had been annexed to the state without its consent.

Take as an illustration a state like South Carolina within whose borders the negroes outnumbered the whites. Notwithstanding their numerical majority they were mere property, and enjoyed no political or even civil rights. They were not members of the body politic, and were not parties to the social compact. The white people and they alone constituted the State of South Carolina. Now, could a constitutional amendment without the consent of the government of South Carolina, or of those persons who constituted that state, annex to their body politic the large black majority in their midst and give these blacks—whom South Carolina had never recognized as her citizens—the power to outvote the whites in the election of members of the state legislature and thus indirectly in the choice of two United States senators? Would not such a constitutional amendment deprive the people whom alone the original Constitution of the United States and the laws of South Carolina recognized as constituting that state—would it not deprive them of their "equal suffrage," or indeed of any suffrage at all, in the Senate?

The Fifteenth Amendment amounts to a compulsory annexation to each state that refused to ratify it of a black San

Domingo within its borders. It is no less objectionable than the annexation of the San Domingo in the Spanish main.

Before the Amendment, the white people of South Carolina had the right and power to elect two senators of the United States—the same representation in the Senate as the white people of Vermont. After the Amendment, if it is valid, the white people of Vermont, a state which contains virtually no negroes and which therefore is virtually unaffected by the Amendment, continue to be entitled to elect two senators; but the white people of South Carolina have none at all.

III.

But it will be objected that this argument carries too far,—that the negroes were already converted into citizens, or members of the body politic, by the Thirteenth and Fourteenth Amendments, although not clothed with the elective franchise, and that if it were impossible to alter the composition or membership of the state, those amendments, upon which scores of judicial decisions have turned, would be invalid, and human slavery would still be constitutionally possible in the United States.

To this supposed *reductio ad absurdum* of the argument there are at least three answers.

1. The Thirteenth Amendment merely released the slaves from the dominion of their masters and did not invest them with any rights of citizenship against the will of the states in which they might reside. . . .

2. The Fourteenth Amendment did undoubtedly purport to convert the freedmen into "citizens of the United States and of the State wherein they reside"; and to that extent attempts to alter the membership or composition of the states. If it were admitted that the argument above deduced from the provision that no state without its consent shall be deprived of its equal suffrage in the Senate would, if sound, prevent this change in the citizenship or membership of the body politic, even though the elective franchise was not conferred upon the new members, the only result would be to strike out of the Fourteenth Amendment the seven words "and of the State

wherein they reside." There is no conclusive authority that the words quoted are a valid part of the Amendment; and all the important provisions of that Amendment, such as the guaranty of due process of law and of the equal protection of the laws, would remain undisturbed. That an argument leads to the elimination of those seven words can, therefore, hardly be deemed a *reductio ad absurdum*.

3. But it may well be doubted whether the elevation of the negroes to citizenship in the states by the Fourteenth Amendment is more than a matter of sentiment or name, and whether in that light it could be regarded as infringing the guaranty of political autonomy implied in the proviso that no state shall be deprived of its equal suffrage in the Senate without its own consent. The Fourteenth Amendment gives negroes the right to sue and be sued in the federal courts as citizens of the state of their residence; but to confer that privilege is certainly within the scope of a constitutional amendment. It also protects them in other states from discrimination in respect to the fundamental rights of person and property, under the provision that citizens of each state shall be entitled to the privileges and immunities of citizens in the several states; but that too is within the scope of constitutional amendment. It does little, if anything, more of practical importance. It is at most a grant of the civil rights pertaining to citizenship in a state.

Certainly the citizenship attempted to be conferred by the Fourteenth Amendment does not imply the enjoyment of any political rights or share in the government. The case of women is the most familiar example of the truth of this proposition. The state is entitled to withhold the suffrage from such of its citizens as it chooses and (unless the Fifteenth Amendment may restrict the power) on such grounds as it chooses. The objection to the Fifteenth Amendment is not merely that it alters the technical citizenship or membership of the state, but also that it alters its political institutions and destroys its political autonomy.

In view of these facts, it may be doubted whether the argument advanced above necessarily goes to the extent of invalidating the provision in the Fourteenth Amendment that all persons born or naturalized within the United States and subject to the jurisdiction thereof are citizens of the state wherein they reside; but if the argument does necessarily carry to that length, there is no reason to shrink from that conclusion. Certainly, that fact, if it be a fact, is no reason for denying the soundness of the argument. . . .

IX.

A final objection is that it is now too late to question the validity of the Fifteenth Amendment. Many answers may be given to this objection.

In the first place, as was mentioned at the very outset of this article, not only has the question never been expressly raised in the Supreme Court of the United States, but there is no decision of that tribunal in which a different result would have been reached if the Fifteenth Amendment had never been conceived. If that amendment is proved to be invalid, there is not a single decision of the Supreme Court which would have to be on that account acknowledged to have been wrongly decided. Consequently, the doctrine of *stare decisis* furnishes no obstacle to holding that the Fifteenth Amendment is invalid. . . .

Mere lapse of time is no bar against attacking the validity of the amendment. If twenty years must elapse in order to toll a private right of entry, how long a period is necessary to bar the most sacred constitutional rights of sovereign states? . . .

Moreover, the Fifteenth Amendment has never been acquiesced in unreservedly throughout the country. . . .

6.6 The Supreme Court Rules that Ratifications of Amendments Must Reflect a Contemporaneous Consensus*

A number of cases arose from the National Prohibition Amendment. In the one reproduced here, the Court was called upon to decide both when the amendment was intended to go into effect and whether the amendment was inoperative

---

* *Dillon v. Gloss*, 256 U.S. 368 (1921). pp. 371-77.

because of the ratification time limit which Congress had included with it.

Time Limits for Constitutional Amendments (Justice Van Devanter)

. . . this article [V] says nothing about the time within which ratification may be had—neither that it shall be unlimited nor that it shall be fixed by Congress. What, then, is the reasonable inference or implication? Is it that ratification may be had at any time, as within a few years, a century, or even a longer period; or that it must be had within some reasonable period which Congress is left free to define? Neither the debates in the Federal convention which framed the Constitution nor those in the state conventions which ratified it shed any light on the question.

The proposal for the 18th Amendment is the first in which a definite period for ratification was fixed. Theretofore twenty-one amendments had been proposed by Congress and seventeen of these had been ratified by the legislatures of three fourths of the states,—some within a single year after their proposal and all within four years. Each of the remaining four had been ratified in some of the states, but not in a sufficient number. Eight years after the partial ratification of one an effort was made to complete its ratification, and the legislature of Ohio passed a joint resolution to that end, after which the effort was abandoned. Two, after ratification in one less than the required number of states, had lain dormant for a century. The other, proposed March 2, 1861, declared: "No amendment shall be made to the Constitution which will authorize or give to Congress the power to abolish or interfere, within any state, with the domestic institutions thereof, including that of persons held to labor or service by the laws of said state." Its principal purpose was to protect slavery and at the time of its proposal and partial ratification it was a subject of absorbing interest, but after the adoption of the 13th Amendment it was generally forgotten. Whether an amendment proposed without fixing any time for ratification, and which after favorable action in less than the required number of states had lain dormant for many years, could be resurrected and its ratification completed, had been mooted on several occasions, but was still an open question.

These were the circumstances in the light of which Congress, in proposing the 18th Amendment, fixed seven years as the period for ratification. Whether this could be done was questioned at the time and debated at length, but the prevailing view in both Houses was that some limitation was intended and that seven years was a reasonable period.

That the Constitution contains no express provision on the subject is not in itself controlling; for with the Constitution, as with a statute or other written instrument, what is reasonably implied is as much a part of it as what is expressed. An examination of Article 5 discloses that it is intended to invest Congress with a wide range of power in proposing amendments. Passing a provision long since expired, it subjects this power to only two restrictions: one that the proposal shall have the approval of two thirds of both Houses, and the other excluding any amendment which will deprive any state, without its consent, of its equal suffrage in the Senate. A further mode of proposal—as yet never invoked—is provided, which is, that on application of the two thirds of the states Congress shall call a convention for the purpose. When proposed in either mode, amendments, to be effective, must be ratified by the legislatures, or by conventions, in three fourths of the states, "as the one or the other mode of ratification may be proposed by the Congress." Thus the people of the United States, by whom the Constitution was ordained and established, have made it a condition to amending that instrument that the amendment be submitted to representative assemblies in the several states and be ratified in three fourths of them. The plain meaning of this is (a) that all amendments must have the sanction of the people of the United States, the original fountain of power, acting through representative assemblies, and (b) that ratification by these assemblies in three fourths of the states shall be taken as a decisive expression of the people's will and be binding on all.

We do not find anything in the Article which suggests that an amendment, once proposed, is to be open to ratification for all time, or that ratification in some of the states may be separated from that in others by many years and yet be effective. We do find that which strongly suggests the contrary. First, proposal and ratification are not treated as unrelated acts, but as succeeding steps in a single endeavor, the natural inference being that they are not to be widely separated in time. Secondly, it is only when there is deemed to be a necessity therefore that amendments are to be proposed, the reasonable implication being that when proposed they are to be considered and disposed of presently. Thirdly, as ratification is but the expression of the approbation of the people and is to be effective when had in three fourths of the states, there is a fair implication that it must be sufficiently contemporaneous in that number of states to reflect the will of the people in all sections at relatively the same period, which, of course, ratification scattered through a long series of years would not do. These considerations and the general purport and spirit of the Article lead to the conclusion expressed by Judge Jameson "that an alteration of the Constitution proposed to-day has relation to the sentiment and the felt needs of to-day, and that, if not ratified early while that sentiment may fairly be supposed to exist, it ought to be regarded as waived, and not again to be voted upon, unless a second time proposed by Congress." That this is the better conclusion becomes even more manifest when what is comprehended in the other view is considered; for, according to it, four amendments proposed long ago—two in 1789, one in 1810, and one in 1861—are still pending and in a situation where their ratification in some of the states many years since by representatives of generations now largely forgotten may be effectively supplemented in enough more states to make three fourths by representatives of the present or some future generation. To that view few would be able to subscribe, and in our opinion it is quite untenable. We conclude that the fair inference or implication from Article 5 is that the ratification must be within some reasonable time after the proposal.

Of the power of Congress, keeping within reasonable limits, to fix a definite period for the ratification we entertain no doubt. As a rule the Constitution speaks in general terms, leaving Congress to deal with subsidiary matters of detail as the public interests and changing conditions may require; and Article 5 is no exception to the rule. Whether a definite period for ratification shall be fixed, so that all may know what it is and speculation on what is a reasonable time may be avoided, is, in our opinion, a matter of detail which Congress may determine as an incident of its power to designate the mode of ratification. It is not questioned that seven years, the period fixed in this instance, was reasonable, if power existed to fix a definite time; nor could it well be questioned considering the periods within which prior amendments were ratified.

The provisions of the act which the petitioner was charged with violating and under which he was arrested (Title 2, 3, 16) were the terms of the act (Title 3, 21) to be in force from and after the date when the 18th Amendment should go into effect, and the latter by its own terms was to go into effect one year after being ratified. Its ratification, of which we take judicial notice, was consummated January 16, 1919. That the Secretary of State did not proclaim its ratification until January 29, 1991, is not material, for the date of its consummation, and not that on which it is proclaimed, controls. It follows that the provisions of the act with which the petitioner is concerned went into effect January 16, 1920. His alleged offense and his arrest were on the following day; so his claim that these provisions had not gone into effect at the time is not well grounded.

6.7 The Supreme Court Upholds The Validity of the Nineteenth Amendment*

The arguments of conservatives about limits on the power of constitutional amendment were taken seriously enough that they became the basis for challenges to a number of amend-

* *Fairchild v. Hughes*, 258 U.S. 126 (1922), pp. 126-30. *Leser v. Garnett*, 258 U.S. 130, pp. 135-7.

ments. In the first case here, the petitioner is seeking an injunction against the Nineteenth Amendment; Brandeis rejects this plea as not being suitable for judicial action. In the second case, also challenging the validity of the Nineteenth Amendment, the petitioner is rejected on more substantive grounds.

Refusal to Enjoin the Nineteenth Amendment (Justice Brandeis)

On July 7, 1920, Charles S. Fairchild of New York brought this suit in the Supreme Court of the District of Columbia against the Secretary of State and the Attorney General. The prayers of the bill are that "the so-called Suffrage Amendment [the Nineteenth to the Federal Constitution] be declared unconstitutional and void"; that the Secretary of State be restrained from issuing any proclamation declaring that it has been ratified; and that the Attorney General be restrained from enforcing it. There is also a prayer for general relief and for an interlocutory injunction. The plaintiff, and others on whose behalf he sues, are citizens of the United States, taxpayers and members of the American Constitutional League, a voluntary association which describes itself as engaged in diffusing "knowledge as to the fundamental principles of the American Constitution, and especially that which gives to each State the right to determine for itself the question as to who should exercise the elective franchise therein."

The claim to relief was rested upon the following allegations. The legislatures of thirty-four of the States have passed resolutions purporting to ratify the Suffrage Amendment; and from one other State the Secretary of State of the United States has received a certificate to that effect purporting to come from the proper officer. The proposed Amendment cannot, for reasons stated, be made a part of the Constitution through ratification by the legislatures; and there are also specific reasons why the resolutions already adopted in several of the States are inoperative. But the Secretary has declared that he is without power to examine into the validity of alleged acts of ratification, and that, upon receiving from one additional State the customary certificate, he will issue a proclamation declaring that the Suffrage Amendment has been adopted. Furthermore, "a force bill" has been introduced in the Senate which provides fine and imprisonment for any person who refuses to allow women to vote; and if the bill is enacted, the Attorney General will be required to enforce its provisions. The threatened proclamation of the adoption of the Amendment would not be conclusive of its validity, but it would lead election officers to permit women to vote in States whose constitutions limit suffrage to men. This would prevent ascertainment of the wishes of the legally qualified voters, and elections, state and federal, would be void. Free citizens would be deprived of their right to have such elections duly held; the effectiveness of their votes would be diminished; and the election expenses would be nearly doubled. Thus irremediable mischief would result. . . .

Plaintiff's alleged interest in the question submitted is not such as to afford a basis for this proceeding. It is frankly a proceeding to have the Nineteenth Amendment declared void. In form it is a bill in equity; but it is not a case within the meaning of 2 of Article III of the Constitution, which confers judicial power on the federal courts, for no claim of plaintiff is "brought before the court[s] for determination by such regular proceedings as are established by law or custom for the protection or enforcement of rights, or the prevention, redress, or punishment of wrongs." See *In re Pacific Railway Commission*, 32 Fed. 241, 255, quoted in *Muskrat v. United States*, 219 U.S. 346, 356. The alleged wrongful act of the Secretary of State, said to be threatening, is the issuing of a proclamation which plaintiff asserts will be vain but will mislead election officers. The alleged wrongful act of the Attorney General, said to be threatening, is the enforcement, as against election officers, of the penalties to be imposed by a contemplated act of Congress which plaintiff asserts would be unconstitutional. But plaintiff is not an election officer; and the State of New York, of which he is a citizen, had previously amended its own constitution so as to grant the suffrage to women and had ratified this Amendment. Plaintiff has only the right, possessed by every citizen, to require that the Government be administered according to law and that the public moneys be not wasted. Obviously this general right does not entitle a private citizen to institute in the federal courts a suit to secure by indirection a determination whether a statute if passed, or a constitutional amendment about to be adopted, will be valid. . . .

The Validity of the Nineteenth Amendment (Justice Brandeis) On October 12, 1920, Cecilia Streett Waters and Mary D. Randolph, citizens of Maryland, applied for and were granted registration as qualified voters in Baltimore City. To have their names stricken from the list Oscar Leser and others brought this suit in the court of Common Pleas. The only ground of disqualification alleged was that the applicants for registration were women, whereas the constitution of Maryland limits the suffrage to men. Ratification of the proposed Amendment to the Federal Constitution, now known as the Nineteenth, 41 Stat. 362, had been proclaimed on August 26, 1920, 41 Stat. 1823, pursuant to Rev. Stats. 205. The Legislature of Maryland had refused to ratify it. The petitioners contended, on several grounds, that the Amendment had not become part of the Federal Constitution. The trial court overruled the contentions and dismissed the petition. Its judgment was affirmed by the Court of Appeals of the State, 139 Md. 46; and the case comes here on writ of error. That writ must be dismissed; but the petition for a writ of certiorari, also duly filed, is granted. The laws of Maryland authorized such a suit by a qualified voter against the Board of Registry. Whether the Nineteenth Amendment has become part of the Federal Constitution is the question presented for decision.

The first contention is that the power of amendment conferred by the Federal Constitution and sought to be exercised does not extend to this Amendment, because of its character. The argument is that so great an addition to the electorate, if made without the State's consent, destroys its autonomy as a political body. This Amendment is in character and phraseology precisely similar to the Fifteenth. For each the same method of adoption was pursued. One cannot be valid and the Other invalid. That the Fifteenth is valid, although rejected by six States including Maryland, has been recognized and acted on for a century. See *United States v. Reese*, 92 U.S. 214; *Neal v. Delaware*, 103 U.S. 370; *Guinn v. United States*, 238 U.S. 347; *Myers v. Anderson*, 238 U.S. 368. The suggestion that the Fifteenth was incorporated in the Constitution, not in accordance with law, but practically as a war measure which has been validated by acquiescence, cannot be entertained.

The second contention is that in the constitutions of several of the thirty-six States named in the proclamation of the Secretary of State there are provisions which render inoperative the alleged ratifications by their legislatures. The argument is that by reason of these specific provisions the legislatures were without power to ratify. But the function of a state legislature in ratifying a proposed amendment to the Federal Constitution, like the function of Congress in proposing the amendment, is a federal function derived from the Federal Constitution; and it transcends any limitations sought to be imposed by the people of a State. *Hawke v. Smith, No. 1*, 253 U.S. 221; *Hawke v. Smith, No. 2*, 253 U.S. 231; *National Prohibition Cases*, 253 U.S. 350, 386.

The remaining contention is that the ratifying resolutions of Tennessee and of West Virginia are inoperative, because adopted in violation of the rules of legislative procedure prevailing in the respective States. The question raised may have been rendered immaterial by the fact that since the proclamation of the legislatures of two other States—Connecticut and Vermont—have adopted resolutions of ratification. But a broader answer should be given to the contention. The proclamation by the Secretary certified that from official documents on file in the Department of State it appeared that the proposed Amendment was ratified by the legislatures of thirty-six States, and that it "has become valid to all intents and purposes as a part of the Constitution of the United States." As the legislatures of Tennessee and of West Virginia had power to adopt the resolutions of ratification, official notice to the Secretary, duly authenticated, that they had done so was conclusive upon him, and, being certified to by his proclamation, is conclusive upon the courts. . . .

6.8 The Supreme Court Upholds the Validity of the Eighteenth Amendment*

In the case reprinted here, the Supreme Court decided that the Eighteenth Amendment did not require ratification by special state conventions. Ironically, the Twenty-First Amendment repealing Prohibition was ratified by such state conventions.

The role of state ratifying conventions (Justice Roberts)

The appellees contended in the court below, and here, that notwithstanding the plain language of Article V, conferring upon the Congress the choice of method of ratification, as between action by legislatures and by conventions, this Amendment could only be ratified by the latter.

They say that it was the intent of its framers, and the Constitution must, therefore, be taken impliedly to require, that proposed amendments conferring on the United States new direct powers over individuals shall be ratified in conventions; and that the Eighteenth is of this character. They reach this conclusion from the fact that the framers thought that ratification of the Constitution must be by the people in convention assembled and not by legislatures, as the latter were incompetent to surrender the personal liberties of the people to the new national government. From this and other considerations, hereinafter noticed, they ask us to hold that Article V means something different from what it plainly says.

In addition they urge, that if there be any doubt as to the correctness of their construction of Article V, the Tenth Amendment removes it.

The District Court refused to follow this reasoning. It quashed the indictment, not as a result of analysis of Article V and Amendment X, but by resorting to "political science," the "political thought" of the times, and a "scientific approach to the problem of government." These, it thought, compelled it to declare the convention method requisite for ratification of an amendment such as the Eighteenth. The appellees do not

* *United States v. Sprague*, 282 U.S. 716 (1931), pp. 729-34.

attempt to justify the lower court's action by the reasons it states, but by resubmitting to us those urged upon that court and by it rejected.

The United States asserts that Article V is clear in statement and in meaning, contains no ambiguity, and calls for no resort to rules of construction A mere reading demonstrates that this is true. It provides two methods for proposing amendments. Congress may propose them by a vote of two-thirds of both houses; or, on the application of the legislatures of two-thirds of the States, must call a convention to propose them. Amendments proposed in either way become a part of the Constitution, "when ratified by the legislatures of three-fourths of the several States or by conventions in three-fourths thereof, *as the one or the other mode of ratification may be proposed by the Congress. . . .*"

The choice, therefore, of the mode of ratification, lies in the sole discretion of Congress. Appellees, however, point out that amendments may be of different kinds, as, *e.g.*, mere changes in the character of federal means or machinery, on the one hand, and matters affecting the liberty of the citizen on the other. They say that the framers of the Constitution expected the former sort might be ratified by legislatures, since the States as entities would be wholly competent to agree to such alterations, whereas they intended that the latter must be referred to the people because not only of lack of power in the legislatures to ratify, but also because of doubt as to their truly representing the people. Counsel advert to the debates in the convention which had to do with the submission of the draft of the Constitution to the legislatures or to conventions, and show that the latter procedure was overwhelmingly adopted. They refer to many expressions in contemporary political literature and in the opinions of this court to the effect that the Constitution derives its sanctions from the people and from the people alone. In spite of the lack of substantial evidence as to the reasons for the changes in statement of Article V from its proposal until it took final form in the finished draft, they seek to import into the language of the Article dealing with amendments, the views of the convention with respect to the proper method of ratification of the instrument as a whole. They say that if the legislatures were considered incompetent to surrender the people's liberties when the ratification of the Constitution itself was involved, *a fortiori* they are incompetent now to make a further grant. Thus, however clear the phraseology of Article V, they urge we ought to insert into it a limitation on the discretion conferred on the Congress, so that it will read, "as the one or the other mode of ratification may be proposed by the Congress, as may be appropriate in view of the purpose of the proposed amendment." This can not be done.

The Constitution was written to be understood by the voters; its words and phrases were used in their normal and ordinary as distinguished from technical meaning; where the intention is clear there is no room for construction and no excuse for interpolation or addition. [Roberts cites a number of previous cases and legal commentators.]

If the framers of the instrument had any thought that amendments differing in purpose should be ratified in different ways, nothing would have been simpler than so to phrase Article V as to exclude implication or speculation. The fact that an instrument drawn with such meticulous care and by men who so well understood how to make language fit their thought does not contain any such limiting phrase affecting the exercise of discretion by the Congress in choosing one or the other alternative mode of ratification is persuasive evidence that no qualification was intended.

The Court has repeatedly and consistently declared that the choice of mode rests solely in the discretion of Congress. *Dodge v. Woolsey*, 18 How. 331, 348; *Hawke v. Smith* (No. 1), 253 U.S. 221; *Dillon v. Gloss*, 256 U.S. 368; *National Prohibition Cases*, 253 U.S. 350. Appellees urge that what was said on the subject in the first three cases cited is *dictum*. And they argue that although in the last mentioned it was said the "Amendment *by lawful proposal and ratification*, has become part of the Constitution," the proposition they now present was not before the Court. While the language used in the earlier cases was not in the strict sense necessary to a decision, it is evident that Article

V was carefully examined and that the Court's statements with respect to the power of Congress in proposing the mode of ratification were not idly or lightly made. In the *National Prohibition Cases,* as shown by the briefs, the contentions now argued were made—the only difference between the presentation there and here being one of form rather than of substance.

The Tenth Amendment provides:

"The powers not delegated to the United States by the Constitution, nor prohibited by it to the States, are reserved to the States respectively, or to the people."

Appellees assert this language demonstrates that the people reserved to themselves powers over their own personal liberty, and that the legislatures are not competent to enlarge the powers of the federal government in that behalf. They deduce from this that the people never delegated to the Congress the unrestricted power of choosing the mode of ratification of a proposed amendment. But the argument is a complete *non sequitur.* The Fifth Article does not purport to delegate any governmental power to the United States, nor to withhold any from it. On the contrary, as pointed out in *Hawke v. Smith* (No. 1), *supra,* that Article is a grant of authority by the people to Congress, and not to the United States. It was submitted as part of the original draft of the Constitution to the people in conventions assembled. They deliberately made the grant of power to Congress in respect to the choice of the mode of ratification of amendments. Unless and until that Article be changed by amendment, Congress must function as the delegated agent of the people in the choice of the method of ratification.

The Tenth Amendment was intended to confirm the understanding of the people at the time the Constitution was adopted, that powers not granted to the United States were reserved to the States or to the people. It added nothing to the instrument as originally ratified and has no limited and special operation, as is contended, upon the people's delegation by Article V of certain functions to the Congress.

The United States relies upon the fact that every amendment has been adopted by the method pursued in respect of the Eighteenth. Appellees reply that all these save the Eighteenth dealt solely with governmental means and machinery rather than with the rights of the individual citizen. But we think that several amendments touch rights of the citizens, notably the Thirteenth, Fourteenth, Fifteenth, Sixteenth and Nineteenth, and in view of this, weight is to be given to the fact that these were adopted by the method now attacked. *The Pocket Veto Case, supra.*

For these reasons we reiterate what was said in the *National Prohibition Cases, supra,* that the "amendment by lawful proposal and ratification, has become a part of the Constitution."

6.9 Dissent From the Switch in Time That Saved Nine*

Up to 1937, the Supreme Court of the United States strongly resisted many of President Franklin Roosevelt's New Deal initiatives, usually taking the position that this legislation was an invasion of the "liberty of contract" thought to be implicit in the due process clause of the Fourteenth Amendment. Commentators began to explore amendments that might be adopted or ways that the Court might be curbed (see Osmond K. Fraenkel, "What Can be Done About the Constitution and the Supreme Court?" 37 *Columbia Law Review* (1937), pp. 212-26). After his landslide election in 1936, Roosevelt offered a plan to "pack" the Court, adding one new justice, up to fifteen, for every justice over the age of 70. While this plan was never adopted, shortly thereafter, the Supreme Court rejected its earlier line of precedents and began deferring to state and congressional judgments in matters of economic regulation. In the reading reproduced below, Justice Sutherland, one of four judicial conservatives on the Supreme Court, objected to the Court's abandonment of its earlier precedents and accused it of rewriting, or amending, the Constitution (perhaps ignoring the fact that many considered the Court's own earlier reading of liberty of contract into the due process clause as a

* *West Coast Hotel v. Parrish,* 300 U.S. 379, p. 404.

form of unsanctioned judicial amendment of the Constitution). At issue was a Washington law providing for minimum wages; the majority of the Supreme Court, in upholding this law, effectively struck down their own earlier holding in *Adkins v. Children's Hospital*, 261 U.S. 525 (1923).

Justice Sutherland dissents

The judicial function is that of interpretation; it does not include the power of amendment under the guise of interpretation. To miss the point of difference between the two is to miss all that the phrase "supreme law of the land" stands for and to convert what was intended as inescapable and enduring mandates into mere moral reflections.

If the Constitution, intelligently and reasonably construed in the light of these principles, stands in the way of desirable legislation, the blame must rest upon that instrument, and not upon the court for enforcing it according to its terms. The remedy in that situation—and the only true remedy—is to amend the Constitution. Judge Cooley, in the first volume of his Constitutional Limitations (8th ed.), p. 124, very clearly pointed out that much of the benefit expected from written constitutions would be lost if their provisions were to be bent to circumstances or modified by public opinion. He pointed out that the common law, unlike a constitution, was subject to modification by public sentiment and action which the courts might recognize; but that "a court or legislature which should allow a change in public sentiment to influence it in giving to a written constitution a construction not warranted by the intention of its founders, would be justly chargeable with reckless disregard of official oath and public duty; and if its course could become a precedent, these instruments would be of little avail. . . . What a court is to do, therefore, is *to declare the law as written*, leaving it to the people themselves to make such changes as new circumstances may require. The meaning of the constitution is fixed when it is adopted, and it is not different at any subsequent time when a court has occasion to pass upon it.

6.10 The Ratification of the Child Labor Amendment*

In a number of cases prior to 1937, the Supreme Court had struck down congressional efforts to regulate child labor either through use of its taxing power or of its power over interstate commerce. In June 1924, the Congress subsequently proposed the following amendment by the necessary majorities: Section 1—The Congress shall have power to limit, regulate, and prohibit the labor of persons under eighteen years of age. Section 2—The power of the several States is unimpaired by this article except that the operation of State laws shall be suspended to the extent necessary to give effect to legislation enacted by Congress.

A number of questions were raised about the ratification of this eventually unsuccessful amendment by the state of Kansas, including whether the Lieutenant Governor of Kansas could cast a deciding vote when the legislature was tied, whether Kansas could ratify an amendment previously rejected, and how long a state had to ratify an amendment. While the Court accepted jurisdiction of these issues, it held that many such questions were "political questions" left to the resolution of elective branches of the government. In so doing, the Court arguably abandoned an important role it had previously assumed in policing the borders amendment controversies. Ironically, the need for a child labor amendment was negated by subsequent judicial interpretations of the Constitution which recognized congressional power acting in pursuit of its taxing and commerce powers to regulate this subject.

Mr. Chief Justice Hughes

First. The jurisdiction of this Court.—Our authority to issue the writ of certiorari is challenged upon the ground that petitioners have no standing to seek to have the judgment of the state court reviewed, and hence it is urged that the writ of certiorari should be dismissed. We are unable to accept that view. . . .

---

* *Coleman v. Miller*, 307 U.S. 433 (1939), pp. 437-9; 446-54; 457-8, and 473-4.

We find the cases cited in support of the contention, that petitioners lack an adequate interest to invoke our jurisdiction to review, to be inapplicable. Here, the plaintiffs include twenty senators, whose votes against ratification have been overridden and virtually held for naught although if they are right in their contentions their votes would have been sufficient to defeat ratification. We think that these senators have a plain, direct and adequate interest in maintaining the effectiveness of their votes. . . .

The contention to the contrary is answered by our decisions in *Hawke v. Smith, supra*, and *Leser v. Garnett, supra*. . . .

Second. The participation of the Lieutenant Governor.—Petitioners contend that, in the light of the powers and duties of the Lieutenant Governor and his relation to the Senate under the state constitution, as construed by the supreme court of the state, the Lieutenant Governor was not a part of the "legislature" so that under Article V of the Federal Constitution, he could be permitted to have a deciding vote on the ratification of the proposed amendment, when the senate was equally divided.

Whether this contention presents a justiciable controversy, or a question which is political in its nature and hence not justiciable, is a question upon which the Court is equally divided and therefore the Court expressed no opinion upon that point.

Third. The effect of the previous rejection of the amendment and of the lapse of time since its submission.

1. The state court adopted the view expressed by textwriters that a state legislature which has rejected an amendment proposed by the Congress may later ratify. The argument in support of that view is that Article V says nothing of rejection but speaks only of ratification and provides that a proposed amendment shall be valid as part of the Constitution when ratified by three-fourths of the States; that the power to ratify is thus conferred upon the State by the Constitution and, as a ratifying power, persists despite a previous rejection. The opposing view proceeds on an assumption that if ratification by "conventions" were prescribed by the Congress, a convention could not reject and, having adjourned *sine die*, be

reassembled and ratify. It is also premised in accordance with views expressed by text-writers, that ratification if once given cannot afterwards be rescinded and the amendment rejected, and it is urged that the same effect in the exhaustion of the State's power to act should be ascribed to rejection; that a State can act "but once, either by convention or through its legislature."

Historic instances are cited. In 1865, the Thirteenth Amendment was rejected by the legislature of New Jersey which subsequently ratified it, but the question did not become important as ratification by the requisite number of States had already been proclaimed. The question did arise in connection with the adoption of the Fourteenth Amendment. The legislatures of Georgia, North Carolina and South Carolina had rejected the amendment in November and December, 1866. New governments were erected in those States (and in others) under the direction of Congress. The new legislatures ratified the amendment, that of North Carolina on July 4, 1868, that of South Carolina on July 9, 1868, and that of Georgia on July 21, 1868. Ohio and New Jersey first ratified and then passed resolutions withdrawing their consent. As there were then thirty-seven States, twenty-eight were needed to constitute the requisite three-fourths. On July 9, 1868, the Congress adopted a resolution requesting the Secretary of State to communicate "a list of the States of the Union whose legislatures have ratified the fourteenth article of amendment," and in Secretary Seward's report attention was called to the action of Ohio and New Jersey. On July 20th Secretary Seward issued a proclamation reciting the ratification by twenty-eight States, including North Carolina, South Carolina, Ohio and New Jersey, and stating that it appeared that Ohio and New Jersey had since passed resolutions withdrawing their consent and that "it is deemed a matter of doubt and uncertainty whether such resolutions are not irregular, invalid and therefore ineffectual." The Secretary certified that if the ratifying resolutions of Ohio and New Jersey were still in full force and effect, notwithstanding the attempted withdrawal, the amendment had become a part of the Constitution. On the following day the Congress adopted a concurrent resolution which, reciting that three-fourths of the States having ratified (the list including North Carolina, South Carolina, Ohio and New Jersey), declared the Fourteenth Amendment to be a part of the Constitution and that it should be duly promulgated as such by the Secretary of State. Accordingly, Secretary Seward, on July 28th, issued his proclamation embracing the States mentioned in the congressional resolution and adding Georgia.

Thus the political departments of the Government dealt with the effect both of previous rejection and of attempted withdrawal and determined that both were ineffectual in the presence of an actual ratification. While there were special circumstances, because of the action of the Congress in relation to the governments of the rejecting states (North Carolina, South Carolina and Georgia), these circumstances were not recited in proclaiming ratification and the previous action taken in these States was set forth in the proclamation as actual previous rejections by the respective legislatures. This decision by the political departments of the Government as to the validity of the adoption of the Fourteenth Amendment has been accepted.

We think that in accordance with this historic precedent the question of the efficacy of ratifications by state legislatures, in the light of previous rejection or attempted withdrawal, should be regarded as a political question pertaining to the political departments, with the ultimate authority in the Congress in the exercise of its control over the promulgation of the adoption of the amendment.

The precise question as now raised is whether, when the legislature of the State, as we have found, has actually ratified the proposed amendment, the Court should restrain the state officers from certifying the ratification to the Secretary of State, because of an earlier rejection, and thus prevent the question from coming before the political departments. We find no basis in either Constitution or statute for such judicial action. Article V, speaking solely of ratification, contains no provision as to rejection. Nor has the Congress enacted a statute relating to rejections. The statutory provision with respect to constitutional amendment is as follows:

"Whenever official notice is received at the Department of State that any amendment proposed to the Constitution of the United States has been adopted, according to the provisions of the Constitution, the Secretary of State shall forthwith cause the amendment to be published, with his certificate, specifying the States by which the same may have been adopted, and that the same has become valid, to all intents and purposes, as a part of the Constitution of the United States."

The statute presupposes official notice to the Secretary of State when a state legislature had adopted a resolution of ratification. We see no warrant for judicial interference with the performance of that duty. See *Leser v. Garnett, supra*, p. 137.

2. The more serious question is whether the proposal by the Congress of the amendment had lost its vitality through lapse of time and hence it could not be ratified by the Kansas legislature in 1937. The argument of petitioners stresses the fact that nearly thirteen years elapsed between the proposal in 1924 and the ratification in question. It is said that when the amendment was proposed there was a definitely adverse popular sentiment and that at the end of 1925 there had been rejection by both houses of the legislatures of sixteen States and ratification by only four States, and that it was not until about 1933 that an aggressive campaign was started in favor of the amendment. In reply, it is urged that Congress did not fix a limit of time for ratification and that as unreasonably long time had not elapsed since the submission; that the conditions which gave rise to the amendment had not been eliminated; that the prevalence of child labor, the diversity of state laws and the disparity in their administration, with the resulting competitive inequalities, continued to exist. Reference is also made to the fact that a number of the States have treated the amendment as still pending and that in the proceedings of the national government there have been indications of the same view. It is said that there were fourteen ratifications in 1933, four in 1935, one in 1936, and three in 1937.

We have held that the Congress in proposing an amendment may fix a reasonable time for ratification. *Dillon v. Gloss*, 256 U.S.. 368. There we sustained the action of the Congress in providing in the proposed Eighteenth Amendment that it should be inoperative unless ratified within seven years. No limitation of time for ratification is provided in the instant case either in the proposed amendment or in the resolution of submission. But petitioners content that, in the absence of a limitation by the Congress, the Court can and should decide what is a reasonable period within which ratification may be had. We are unable to agree with that contention.

It is true that in *Dillon v. Gloss* the Court said that nothing was found in Article V which suggested that an amendment once proposed was to be open to ratification for all time, or that ratification in some States might be separated from that in others by many years and yet be effective; that there was a strong suggestion to the contrary in that proposal and ratification were but succeeding steps in a single endeavor; that as amendments were deemed to be prompted by necessity, they should be considered and disposed of presently; and that there is a fair implication that ratification must be sufficiently contemporaneous in the required number of States to reflect the will of the people in all sections at relatively the same period; and hence that ratification must be within some reasonable time after the proposal. These considerations were cogent reasons for the decision in *Dillon v. Gloss* that the Congress had the power to fix a reasonable time for ratification. But it does not follow that, whenever Congress has not exercised that power, the Court should take upon itself the responsibility of deciding what constitutes a reasonable time and determine accordingly the validity of ratifications. That question was not involved in *Dillon v. Gloss* and, in accordance with familiar principle, what was there said must be read in the light of the point decided.

Where are to be found the criteria for such a judicial determination? None are to be found in Constitution or statute. In their endeavor to answer this question petitioners' counsel have suggested that at least two years should be allowed; that six years would not seem to be unreasonably long; that seven years had been used by the Congress as a reasonable period; that one year, six months and thirteen days was the average time used in passing upon amendments which have been ratified since the first ten amendments; that three years, six months and twenty-five days has been the longest time used in ratifying. To this list of variables, counsel add that "the nature and extent of publicity and the activity of the public and of the legislatures of the several States in relation to any particular proposal should be taken into consideration." That statement is pertinent, but there are additional matters to be examined and weighed. When a proposed amendment springs from a conception of economic needs, it would be necessary, in determining whether a reasonable time had elapsed since its submission, to consider the economic conditions prevailing the country, whether these had so far changed since the submission as to make the proposal no longer responsible to the conception which inspired it or whether conditions were such as to intensify the feeling of need and the appropriateness of the proposed remedial action. In short, the question of a reasonable time in many cases would involve, as in this case it does involve, an appraisal of a great variety of relevant conditions, political, social and economic, which can hardly be said to be within the appropriate range of evidence receivable in a court of justice and to which it would be an extravagant extension of judicial authority to assert judicial notice as the basis of deciding a controversy with respect to the validity of an amendment actually ratified. On the other hand, these conditions are appropriate for the consideration of the political departments of the Government. The questions they involve are essentially political and not justiciable. They can be decided by the Congress with the full knowledge and appreciation ascribed to the national legislature of the political, social and economic conditions which have prevailed during the period since the submission of the amendment.

Our decision that the Congress has the power under Article V to fix a reasonable limit of time for ratification in proposing an amendment proceeds upon the assumption that the question, what is a reasonable time, lies within the congressional province. If it be deemed that such a question is an open one when the limit has not been fixed in advance, we think that it should also be regarded as an open one for consideration of the Congress when, in the presence of certified ratifications by three-fourths of the States, the time arrives for the promulgation of the adoption of the amendment. The decision by the Congress, in its control of the action of the Secretary of State, of the question whether the amendment had been adopted within a reasonable time would not be subject to review by the courts. . . .

Black's Concurring Opinion—Joined by Roberts, Frankfurter (who also wrote a separate concurrence) and Douglas

The Constitution grants Congress exclusive power to control submission of constitutional amendments. Final determination by Congress that ratification by three-fourths of the States has taken place "is conclusive upon the courts." In the exercise of that power, Congress, of course, is governed by the Constitution. However, whether submission, intervening procedure or Congressional determination of ratification conforms to the commands of the Constitution, calls for decisions by a "political department" of questions of a type which this Court has frequently designated "political." And decision of a "political question" by the "political department" to which the Constitution has committed it "conclusively binds the judges, as well as all other officers, citizens and subjects of . . . government." Proclamation under authority of Congress that an amendment has been ratified will carry with it a solemn assurance by the Congress that ratification has taken place as the Constitutional commands. Upon this assurance a proclaimed amendment must be accepted as a part of the Constitution leaving to the judiciary its traditional authority of interpretation. To the extent that the Court's opinion in the present case even impliedly assumes a power to make judicial interpretation of the exclusive constitutional authority of Congress over submission and ratification of amendments, we are unable to agree.

Butler's Dissent joined by Justice McReynolds

Upon the reasoning of our opinion in that case [*Dillon v. Gloss*], I would hold that more than a reasonable time had elapsed and that the judgment of the Kansas supreme court should be reversed.

The point that the question—whether more than a reasonable time had elapsed—is not justiciable but one for Congress after attempted ratification by the requisite number of States, was not raised by the parties or by the United States appearing as *amicus curiae*; it was not suggested by us when ordering reargument. As the Court, in the *Dillon* case, did directly decide upon the reasonableness of the seven years fixed by the Congress, it ought not now, without hearing argument upon the point, hold itself to lack power to decide whether more than 13 years between proposal by Congress and attempted ratification by Kansas is reasonable.

6.11 The Twentieth and Twenty-First Amendments

Although no constitutional amendments were adopted from 1920 through 1932, two amendments were ratified in the following year. The first, relatively inconsequential, was intended to limit the time that "lame duck" Presidents and members of Congress served; it may thus be considered a continuation of the Progressive democratizing reforms. This amendment also toyed, as would a later amendment, with the problem of the death of an elected President. The second amendment repealed prohibition, one of the campaign promises of the incoming Democratic Administration in 1932. This was the first and only amendment to be ratified by state conventions, chosen as a means of bypassing conservative and "dry" state legislatures.

AMENDMENT XX

SECTION 1. The terms of the President and Vice President shall end at noon on the 20th day of January, and the terms of Senators and Representatives at noon on the 3d day of January, of the years in which such terms would have ended if this article had not been ratified; and the terms of their successors shall then begin.

SECTION 2. The Congress shall assemble at least once in every year, and such meeting shall begin at noon on the 3d day of January, unless they shall by law appoint a different day.

SECTION 3. If, at the time fixed for the beginning of the term of the President, the President elect shall have died, the Vice President elect shall become President. If a President shall not have been chosen before the time fixed for the beginning of his term, or if the President elect shall have failed to qualify, then the Vice President elect shall act as President until a President shall have qualified; and the Congress may by law provide for the case wherein neither a President elect nor a Vice President elect shall have qualified, declaring who shall then act as President, or the manner in which one who is to act shall be selected, and such person shall act accordingly until a President or Vice President shall have qualified.

SECTION 4. The Congress may by law provide for the case of the death of any of the persons from whom the House of Representatives may choose a President whenever the right of choice shall have devolved upon them, and for the case of the death of any of the persons from whom the Senate may choose a Vice President whenever the right of choice shall have devolved upon them.

SECTION 5. Sections 1 and 2 shall take effect on the 15th day of October following the ratification of this article.

SECTION 6. This article shall be inoperative unless it shall have been ratified as an amendment to the Constitution by the legislatures of three-fourths of the several States within seven years from the date of its submission.

AMENDMENT XXI

SECTION 1. The eighteenth article of amendment to the Constitution of the United States is hereby repealed.

SECTION 2. The transportation or importation into any State, Territory, or possession of the United States for delivery or use therein of intoxicating liquors, in violation of the laws thereof, is hereby prohibited.

SECTION 3. This article shall be inoperative unless it shall have been ratified as an amendment to the Constitution by conventions in the several States, as provided in the Constitution, within seven years from the date of the submission hereof to the States by the Congress.

Chapter 7

The Modern Era

Despite over two-hundred years of constitutional history, questions remain about whether substantive changes to the Constitution are desirable, about procedural questions which continue to surround the process (especially the still untried convention mechanism), and about the proper relationship between changes initiated by constitutional amendment and those inaugurated by the judiciary or other governmental branches.

Five amendments were ratified in the period from 1951 to 1971, but more controversial amendments which would have guaranteed equal rights for women or treated the District of Columbia as a state were defeated, and still more radical proposals which would have significantly changed the relation between the nation and the state or among the three branches of the national government were never reported to the states. Similarly, proposals to overturn the Supreme Court's recent decisions permitting flag-burning were not accepted by the necessary majorities in Congress.

A number of proposals—for example, for a balanced budget and for a line-item presidential veto—do, however, continue to be items of national discussion. Moreover, many Americans were surprised when a congressional pay amendment, originally proposed as part of the Bill of Rights, was putatively ratified in 1992. The ratification of this amendment and the more general history of the amending process certainly indicate that the amending process has often been utilized in the past during times when some have despaired of it ever being exercised again. As long as the U.S. Constitution survives, the amending process is likely to continue to be a subject of continuing importance and concern that merits scholarly attention.

7.1 The Amending Provisions and the First Amendment*

After the Supreme Court's "switch in time" in 1937, it increasingly tended to address issues connected with civil rights and liberties not directly connected to property rights. Among the guarantees receiving increased attention were those of the First Amendment. In this case, the Court was faced with the issue as to whether the government could revoke United States citizenship on the basis that it had been obtained by fraud. In deciding that the government had not in this case met its strong burden of proof, the Court explored the relationship between the guarantees in Article V and those in the First Amendment.

Mr. Justice Murphy:
The claim that petitioner was not in fact attached to the Constitution and well disposed to the good order and happiness of the United States at the time of his naturalization and for the previous five year period is twofold: *First*, that he believed in such sweeping changes in the Constitution that he simply could not be attached to it; *Second*, that he believed in and advocated the overthrow by force and violence of the Government, Constitution and laws of the United States.

In support of its position that petitioner was not in fact attached to the principles of the Constitution because of his membership in the League and the Party, the Government has directed our attention first to petitioner's testimony that he subscribed to the principles of those organizations, and then to certain alleged Party principles and statements by Party Leaders which are said to be fundamentally at variance with the principles of the Constitution. At this point it is appropriate to mention what will be more fully developed later—that under our traditions beliefs are personal and not a matter of mere association, and that men in adhering to a political party or

* *Schneiderman v. United States*, 320 U.S. 118 (1942), pp. 135-142.

other organization notoriously do not subscribe unqualifiedly to all of its platforms or asserted principles. Said to be among those Communist principles in 1927 are: the abolition of private property without compensation; the erection of a new proletarian state upon the ruins of the old bourgeois state; the creation of a dictatorship of the proletariat; denial of political rights to others than members of the Party or of the proletariat; and the creation of a world union of soviet republics. Statements that American democracy "is a fraud" and that the purposes of the Party are "utterly antagonistic to the purposes for which the American democracy, so called, was formed," are stressed.

Those principles and views are not generally accepted—in fact they are distasteful to most of us—and they call for considerable change in our present form of government and society. But we do not think the Government has carried its burden of proving by evidence which does not leave the issue in doubt that petitioner was not in fact attached to the principles of the Constitution and well disposed to the good order and happiness of the United States when he was naturalized in 1927.

The constitutional fathers, fresh from a revolution, did not forge a political strait-jacket for the generations to come. Instead they wrote Article V and the First Amendment, guaranteeing freedom of thought, soon followed. Article V contains procedural provisions for constitutional change by amendment without any present limitation whatsoever except that no State may be deprived of equal representation in the Senate without its consent. Cf. *National Prohibition Cases*, 253 U.S. 350. This provision and the many important and far-reaching changes made in the Constitution since 1787 refute the idea that attachment to any particular provision or provisions is essential, or that one who advocates radical changes is necessarily not attached to the Constitution. *United States v. Rovin*, 12 F. 2d 942, 944-45. As Justice Holmes said, "Surely it cannot show lack of attachment to the principles of the Constitution that . . . [one] thinks it can be improved." *United States v. Schwimmer*, *supra* (dissent). Criticism of, and the sincerity of desires to improve, the Constitution should not be judged by conformity to prevailing thought because, "if there is any principle of the Constitution that more imperatively calls for attachment than any other it is the principle of free thought—not free thought for those who agree with us, but freedom for the thought that we hate." *Id.* See also Chief Justice Hughes dissenting in *United States v. Macintosh, supra,* p. 635. Whatever attitude we may individually hold toward persons and organizations that believe in or advocate extensive changes in our existing order, it should be our desire and concern at all times to uphold the right of free discussion and free thinking to which we as a people claim primary attachment. To neglect this duty in a proceeding in which we are called upon to judge whether a particular individual has failed to manifest attachment to the Constitution would be ironical indeed.

Our concern is with what Congress meant to be the extent of the area of allowable thought under the statute. By the very generality of the terms employed it is evident that Congress intended an elastic test, one which should not be circumscribed by attempts at precise definition. In view of our tradition of freedom of thought, it is not to be presumed that Congress in the Act of 1906, or its predecessors of 1795 and 1802, intended to offer naturalization only to those whose political views coincide with those considered best by the founders in 1787 or by the majority in this country today. Especially is this so since the language used, posing the general test of "attachment" is not necessarily susceptible of so repressive a construction. The Government agrees that an alien "may think that the laws and the Constitution should be amended in some or many respects" and still be attached to the principles of the Constitution within the meaning of the statute. Without discussing the nature and extent of those permissible changes, the Government insists that an alien must believe in and sincerely adhere to the "general political philosophy" of the Constitution. Petitioner is said to be opposed to that "political philosophy," the minimum requirements of which are set forth in the margin. [A note quotes from the brief: "The test is . . . whether he substitutes revolution for evolution, destruction for construction, whether he believes in an ordered society, a government of laws, under which the powers of government are granted by the people but under a grant which itself preserves to the individual and to minorities certain rights or freedoms which even the majority may not take away; whether, in sum, the events which began at least no further back than the Declaration of Independence, followed by the Revolutionary War and the adoption of the Constitution, establish principles with respect to government, the individual, the minority and the majority, by which ordered liberty is replaced by disorganized liberty."] It was argued at the bar that since Article V contains no limitations, a person can be attached to the Constitution no matter how extensive the changes are that he desires, so long as he seeks to achieve his ends within the framework of Article V. But we need not consider the validity of this extreme position for if the Government's construction is accepted, it has not carried its burden of proof even under its own test.

The district court did not state in its findings what principles held by petitioner or by the Communist Party were opposed to the Constitution and indicated lack of attachment. . . .

With regard to the Constitutional changes he desired petitioner testified that he believed in the nationalization of the means of production and exchange with compensation, and the preservation and utilization of our "democratic structure . . . as far as possible for the advantage of the working classes." He stated that the "dictatorship of the proletariat" to him meant "not a government, but a state of things" in which "the majority of the people shall really direct their own destinies and use the instrument of the state for these truly democratic ends." None of this is necessarily incompatible with the "general political philosophy" of the Constitution as outlined above by the Government. It is true that the Fifth Amendment protects private property, even against taking for public use without compensation. But throughout our history many sincere people whose attachment to the general constitutional scheme cannot be doubted have, for various and even divergent reasons, urged differing degrees of governmental ownership and control of natural resources, basic means of production, and banks and the media of exchange, either with or without compensation. And something once regarded as a species of private property was abolished without compensating the owners when the institution of slavery was forbidden. Can it be said that the author of the Emancipation Proclamation and the supporters of the Thirteenth Amendment were not attached to the Constitution? We conclude that lack of attachment to the Constitution is not shown on the basis of the changes which petitioner testified he desired in the Constitution.

7.2 Justice Frankfurter Asserts the Primacy of the Amending Process*

One of the most enigmatic and scholarly justices ever to sit on the U.S. Supreme Court, Felix Frankfurter, an F.D.R. appointee with a reputation for liberalism, became one of the Court's strongest advocates for judicial restraint and deference to the judgments of the people's elected representatives. The quotation below is from a case involving the Fifth Amendment immunity against self-incrimination in which the Court decided, with Frankfurter as spokesman, that the Fifth Amendment privilege did not apply in cases where a defendant was granted immunity for his testimony.

The Necessity for Amendments as a Vehicle of Change

Nothing new can be put into the Constitution except through the amendatory process. Nothing old can be taken out without the same process.

No doubt the constitutional privilege may, on occasion save a guilty man from his just desserts. It was aimed at a more far-reaching evil—a recurrence of the Inquisition and the Star Chamber, even if not in their stark brutality. Prevention of the greater evil was deemed of more importance than occurrence of the lesser evil. Having had much experience with a tendency in human nature to abuse power, the Founders

* *Ullman v. United States*, 350 U.S. 422, 428 (1956).

sought to close the doors against like future abuses by law-enforcing agencies.

As no constitutional guarantee enjoys preference, so none should suffer subordination or deletion.

7.3 Proposed Reforms by the Council of State Governments*

Much of the impetus for reform since the "switch in time" has come from the judicial branch. Although the guarantees in the Bill of Rights originally applied only to the national government, the Supreme Court has subsequently applied most of the guarantees in the Bill of Rights to the states via the due process clause of the Fourteenth Amendment (generally known as the process of "selective incorporation"). It has also initiated major reforms in the area of civil rights, privacy rights, and other areas.

In one of its most important decisions, *Baker v. Carr*, 369 U.S. 186 (1962), the Supreme Court declared that the issue of state legislative apportionment would no longer be considered a "political question" but would now be subject to judicial consideration. Two years later, the Supreme Court declared in *Reynolds v. Sims* 377 U.S. 533, that both houses of state legislatures would have to be apportioned according to the "one-person-one-vote" standard. Together with other "activist" rulings, this decision initiated a fire-storm of criticism. It appears that the nation may have been but one vote shy of the necessary number of state petitions to call a constitutional convention to reconsider this issue.

Even before the decision in *Reynolds v. Sims*, many states had begun to see the handwriting on the wall. Below are three amendments which were proposed by the Council of State Governments in 1963 which, had they been adopted, would have drastically altered the current federal system. The second was a response to *Baker v. Carr*.

---

* The texts of these amendments are taken from "Amending the Constitution to Strengthen the States in the Federal System," *State Government* 36 (Winter, 1963), pp. 11-14.

Proposed Change in the Amending Process:

Section 1. Article V of the Constitution of the United States is hereby amended to read as follows: The Congress, whenever two-thirds of both Houses shall deem it necessary, or, on the application of the Legislatures of two-thirds of the several states, shall propose amendments to this Constitution, which shall be valid to all intents and purposes, as part of this Constitution, when ratified by the Legislatures of three-fourths of the several states. Whenever applications from the Legislatures of two-thirds of the total number of states of the United States shall contain identical texts of an amendment to be proposed, the President of the Senate and the Speaker of the House of Representatives shall so certify, and the amendment as contained in the application shall be deemed to have been proposed, without further action by Congress. No State, without its consent, shall be deprived of its equal suffrage in the Senate.

Section 2. This Article shall be inoperative unless it shall have been ratified as an amendment to the Constitution by the Legislatures of three-fourths of the several states within seven years from the date of its submission.

The Proposed Apportionment Amendment

Section 1. No provision of this Constitution, or any amendment thereto, shall restrict or limit any state in the apportionment of representation in its legislature.

Section 2. The judicial power of the United States shall not extend to any suit in law or equity, or to any controversy, relating to apportionment of representation in a state legislature.

Section 3. This article shall be inoperative unless it shall have been ratified as an amendment to the Constitution by the Legislatures of three-fourths of the several States within seven years from the date of its submission.

Proposed Amendment to Create a Court of the Union

Section 1. Upon demand of the legislatures of five states, no two of which shall share any common boundary, made within two years after the rendition of any judgment of the Supreme

Court relating to the rights reserved to the states or to the people by this Constitution, such judgment shall be reviewed by a Court composed of the chief justices of the highest courts of the several states to be known as the Court of the Union. The sole issue before the Court of the Union shall be whether the power or jurisdiction sought to be exercised on the part of the United States is a power granted to it under this Constitution.

Section 2. Three-fourths of the justices of the Court of the Union shall constitute a quorum, but it shall require concurrence of a majority of the entire Court to reverse a decision of the Supreme Court. In event of incapacity of the chief justice of the highest court of any state to sit upon the Court of the Union, his place shall be filled by another justice of such state court selected by affirmative vote of a majority of its membership.

Section 3. On the first Monday of the third calendar month following the ratification of this amendment, the chief justices of the highest courts of the several states shall convene at the national capital, at which time the Court of the Union shall be organized and shall adopt rules governing its procedure.

Section 4. Decisions of the Court of the Union upon matters within its jurisdiction shall be final and shall not thereafter be overruled by any court and may be changed only by an amendment of this Constitution.

Section 5. The Congress shall make provision for the housing of the Court of the Union and the expenses of its operation.

Section 6. This article shall be inoperative unless it shall have been ratified as an amendment to the Constitution by the Legislatures of three-fourths of the several States within seven years from the date of its submission.

7.4 Amendments Twenty-Two Through Twenty-Six

Five amendments were ratified from 1951 to 1971, although none brought about major changes in constitutional structures or principles. The Twenty-Second Amendment reinstated ruling custom from George Washington to Franklin Roosevelt, namely the tradition of a two-term presidential limit. The Twenty-Third Amendment modified the electoral college so as to give votes to the District of Columbia. The Twenty-Fourth Amendment outlawed the poll tax in federal elections. The Twenty-Fifth Amendment provided for cases of Presidential disability and Vice-Presidential vacancies, and the Twenty-Sixth Amendment prohibited denial of the right to vote to those eighteen or older.

Amendment XXII [1951]

Section 1. No person shall be elected to the office of the President more than twice, and no person who has held the office of President, or acted as President, for more than two years of a term to which some other person was elected President shall be elected to the office of the President more than once. But this Article shall not apply to any person holding the office of President when this Article was proposed by the Congress, and shall not prevent any person who may be holding the office of President, or acting as President, during the term within which the Article becomes operative from holding the office of President or acting as President during the remainder of such term.

Section 2. This article shall be inoperative unless it shall have been ratified as an amendment to the Constitution by the legislatures of three-fourths of the several States within seven years from the date of its submission to the States by the Congress.

Amendment XXIII [1961]

Section 1. The District constituting the seat of Government of the United States shall appoint in such manner as the Congress may direct:

A number of electors of President and Vice President equal to the whole number of Senators and Representatives in Congress to which the District would be entitled if it were a State, but in no event more than the least populous State; they shall be in addition to those appointed by the States, but they shall be considered, for the purposes of the election of President and Vice President, to be electors appointed by a State;

and they shall meet in the District and perform such duties as provided by the twelfth article of amendment.

Section 2. The Congress shall have power to enforce this article by appropriate legislation.

Amendment XXIV [1964]

Section 1. The right of citizens of the United States to vote in any primary or other election for President or Vice President, for electors for President or Vice President, or for Senator or Representative in Congress, shall not be denied or abridged by the United States or any State by reason of failure to pay any poll tax or other tax.

Section 2. The Congress shall have power to enforce this article by appropriate legislation.

Amendment XXV [1967]

Section 1. In case of the removal of the President from office or his death or resignation, the Vice President shall become President.

Section 2. Whenever there is a vacancy in the office of the Vice President, the President shall nominate a Vice President who shall take the Office upon confirmation by a majority vote of both houses of Congress.

Section 3. Whenever the President transmits to the President pro tempore of the Senate and the Speaker of the House of Representatives his written declaration that he is unable to discharge the powers and duties of his office, and until he transmits to them a written declaration to the contrary, such powers and duties shall be discharged by the Vice President as Acting President.

Section 4. Whenever the Vice President and a majority of either the principal officers of the executive departments, or of such other body as Congress may by law provide, transmit to the President pro tempore of the Senate and the Speaker of the House of Representatives their written declaration that the President is unable to discharge the powers and duties of his office, the Vice President shall immediately assume the powers and duties of the office as Acting President.

Thereafter, when the President transmits to the President pro tempore of the Senate and the Speaker of the House of Representatives his written declaration that no inability exists, he shall resume the powers and duties of his office unless the Vice President and a majority of either the principal officers of the executive department, or of such other body as Congress may by law provide, transmit within four days to the President pro tempore of the Senate and the Speaker of the House of Representatives their written declaration that the President is unable to discharge the powers and duties of his office. Thereupon Congress shall decide the issue, assembling within 48 hours for that purpose if not in session. If the Congress, within 21 days after receipt of the latter written declaration, or, if Congress is not in session, within 21 days after Congress is required to assemble, determines by two-thirds vote of both houses that the President is unable to discharge the powers and duties of his office, the Vice President shall continue to discharge the same as Acting President; otherwise, the President shall resume the powers and duties of his office.

Amendment XXVI [1971]

Section 1. The right of citizens of the United States, who are eighteen years of age, or older, to vote shall not be denied or abridged by the United States or by any state on account of age.

Section 2. The Congress shall have the power to enforce this article by appropriate legislation.

7.5 The Supreme Court Affirms Extra-constitutional Rights Over Vigorous Dissent*

One of the most controversial decisions in modern jurisprudence was the decision in *Griswold v. Connecticut*. In this case, the Supreme Court majority struck down a Connecticut statute forbidding the prescription or use of birth control devices—a decision which prepared the way for the Court's even more controversial decision in *Roe* v. *Wade*, 410 U.S. 113 (1973)

---

* *Griswold* v. *Connecticut*, 381 U.S. 479 (1965), pp. 481-86, 520-23.

legalizing most abortions. The majority decision in *Griswold*, written by Justice Douglas, relied on a right to privacy not specifically stated in the Constitution but rather based on constitutional penumbras from a number of constitutional provisions including those in the First, Third, Fourth, Fifth, Ninth, and Fourteenth Amendments. In the dissent, Justice Black, who like Douglas, had been appointed by Franklin Roosevelt, questioned this broad interpretation of the Constitution and counterposed it against the use of the amending process.

Justice William Douglas:
Coming to the merits, we are met with a wide range of questions that implicate the Due Process Clause of the Fourteenth Amendment. Overtones of some arguments suggest that *Lochner v. New York*, 198 U.S. 45, should be our guide. But we decline that invitation. . . We do not sit as a super-legislature to determine the wisdom, need, and propriety of laws that touch economic problems, business affairs, or social conditions. This law, however, operates directly on an intimate relation of husband and wife and their physician's role in one aspect of that relation.

The association of people is not mentioned in the Constitution nor in the Bill of Rights. The right to educate a child in a school of the parents' choice—whether public or private or parochial—is also not mentioned. Nor is the right to study any particular subject or any foreign language. Yet the First Amendment has been construed to include certain of those rights.

By *Pierce* v. *Society of Sisters*, *supra*, the right to educate one's children as one chooses is made applicable to the States by the force of the First and Fourteenth Amendments. By *Meyer* v. *Nebraska*, *supra*, the same dignity is given the right to study the German language in a private school. In other words, the State may not, consistently with the spirit of the First Amendment, contract the spectrum of available knowledge. The right of freedom of speech and press includes not only the right to utter or to print, but the right to distribute, the right to receive the right to read (*Martin* v. *Struthers*, 319 U.S. 141,143) and freedom of inquiry, freedom of thought, and freedom to teach (see *Wieman* v. *Updegraff*, 344 U.S. 183, 195)—indeed the freedom of the entire university community. *Sweezy* v. *New Hampshire*, 354 U.S. 234, 249-50; 261-263; *Barenblatt* v. *United States*, 360 U.S. 109, 112; *Baggett* v. *Bullitt*, 377 U.S. 360, 369. Without those peripheral rights the specific rights would be less secure. And so we reaffirm the principle of the *Pierce* and the *Meyer* cases.

In *NAACP* v. *Alabama*, 357 U.S. 449, 462, we protected the "freedom to associate and privacy in one's associations," noting that freedom of association was a peripheral First Amendment right. Disclosure of membership lists of a constitutionally valid association, we held, was invalid "as entailing the likelihood of a substantial restraint upon the exercise by petitioner's members of their right to freedom of association." *Ibid.* In other words, the First Amendment has a penumbra where privacy is protected from governmental intrusion. In like context, we have protected forms of "association" that are not political in the customary sense but pertain to the social, legal, and economic benefit of the members. *NAACP* v. *Button*, 371 U.S. 415, 530-431. In *Schware* v. *Board of Bar Examiners*, 353 U.S. 232, we held it not permissible to bar a lawyer from practice, because he had once been a member of the Communist Party. The man's "association with that Party" was not shown to be "anything more than a political faith in a political party" (*id.*, at 244) and was not action of a kind proving bad moral character. *Id.*, at 245-246.

Those cases involved more than the "right of assembly"—a right that extends to all irrespective of their race or ideology. *De Jonge* v. *Oregon*, 299 U.S. 353. The right of "association," like the right of belief (*Board of Education* v. *Barnette*, 319 U.S. 634), is more than the right to attend a meeting; it includes the right to express one's attitudes or philosophies by membership in a group or by affiliation with it or by other lawful means. Association in that context is a form of expression of opinion; and while it is not expressly included in the First Amendment its existence is necessary in making the express guarantees fully meaningful.

The foregoing cases suggest that specific guarantees in the Bill of Rights have penumbras, formed by emanations from those guarantees that help give them life and substance. See *Poe* v. *Ullman*, 367 U.S. 497, 516-522 (dissenting opinion). Various guarantees create zones of privacy. The right of association contained in the penumbra of the First Amendment is one, as we have seen. The Third Amendment in its prohibition against the quartering of soldiers "in any house" in time of peace without the consent of the owner is another facet of that privacy. The Fourth Amendment explicitly affirms the "right of the people to be secure in their persons, houses, papers, and effects, against unreasonable searches and seizures." The Fifth Amendment in its Self-Incrimination Clause enables the citizen to create a zone of privacy which government may not force him to surrender to his detriment. The Ninth Amendment provides: "The enumeration in the Constitution, of certain rights, shall not be construed to deny or disparage others retained by the people." . . .

The present case, then, concerns a relationship lying within the zone of privacy created by several fundamental constitutional guarantees. And it concerns a law which, in forbidding the use of contraceptives rather than regulating their manufacture or sale, seeks to achieve its goals by means having a maximum destructive impact upon that relationship. Such a law cannot stand. . . .

We deal with a right of privacy older than the Bill of Rights—older than our political parties, older than our school system. Marriage is a coming together for better or for worse, hopefully enduring, and intimate to the degree of being sacred. It is an association that promotes a way of life, not causes; a harmony in living, not political faiths; a bilateral loyalty, not commercial or social projects. Yet it is an association for as nobel a purpose as any involved in our prior decisions.

Justice Hugo Black:
I repeat so as not to be misunderstood that this Court does have power, which it should exercise, to hold laws unconstitutional where they are forbidden by the Federal Constitution. My point is that there is no provision of the Constitution which either expressly or impliedly vests power in this Court to sit as a supervisory agency over acts of duly constituted leg-

islative bodies and set aside their laws because of the Court's belief that the legislative policies adopted are unreasonable, unwise, arbitrary, capricious or irrational. The adoption of such a loose, flexible, uncontrolled standard for holding laws unconstitutional, if ever it is finally achieved, will amount to a great unconstitutional shift of power to the courts which I believe and am constrained to say will be bad for the courts and worse for the country. Subjecting federal and state laws to such an unrestrained and unrestrainable judicial control as to the wisdom of legislative enactments would, I fear, jeopardize the separation of governmental powers that the Framers set up and at the same time threaten to take away much of the power of States to govern themselves which the Constitution plainly intended them to have.

I realize that many good and able men have eloquently spoken and written, sometimes in rhapsodical strains, about the duty of this Court to keep the Constitution in tune with the times. The idea is that the Constitution must be changed from time to time and that this Court is charged with a duty to make those changes. For myself, I must with all deference reject that philosophy. The Constitution makers knew the need for change and provided for it. Amendments suggested by the people's elected representatives can be submitted to the people or their selected agents for ratification. That method of change was good for our Fathers, and being somewhat old-fashioned I must add it is good enough for me. And so, I cannot rely on the Due Process Clause or the Ninth Amendment or any mysterious and uncertain natural law concept as a reason for striking down this state law. The Due Process Clause with an "arbitrary and capricious" or "shocking to the conscience" formula was liberally used by this Court to strike down economic legislation in the early decades of this century, threatening, many people thought, the tranquility and stability of the Nation. See, e.g., *Lochner v. New York*, 198 U.S. 45. That formula, based on subjective considerations of "natural justice," is no less dangerous when used to enforce this Court's views about personal rights than those about economic rights. I had thought that we had laid that formula, as a means for striking down state legislation to rest once and for all in cases like *West Coast Hotel Co. v. Parrish*, 300 U.S. 379; *Olsen v. Nebraska ex rel. Western Reference & Bond Assn.*, 313 U.S. 236, and many other opinions. . . .

7.6 Justice Black Objects to Judicial Amendment of the Constitution*

The Twenty-Fourth Amendment, ratified in 1964, had outlawed the use of poll taxes in federal elections. Despite the restrictive language of this amendment, in *Harper v. Virginia Board of Elections*, the Supreme Court also outlawed the use of such taxes in state and local elections, relying on the Equal Protection Clause of the Fourteenth Amendment. As in *Griswold*, Justice Black objected to what he considered substitution of judicial constitution-writing for use of the amending process.

Justice Hugo Black in Dissent:
Another reason for my dissent from the Court's judgment and opinion is that it seems to be using the old "natural-law-due-process formula" to justify striking down state laws as violations of the Equal Protection Clause. I have heretofore had many occasions to express my strong belief that there is no constitutional support whatever for this Court to use the Due Process Clause as though it provided a blank check to alter the meaning of the Constitution as written so as to add to it substantive constitutional changes which a majority of the Court at any given time believes are needed to meet present-day problems. Nor is there in my opinion any more constitutional support for this Court to use the Equal Protection Clause, as it has today, to write into the Constitution its notions of what it thinks is good governmental policy. If basic changes as to the respective powers of the state and national governments are needed, I prefer to let those changes be made by amendment as Article V of the Constitution provides. For a majority of this Court to undertake that task, whether purporting to do so under the Due Process or the Equal Protection Clause

* *Harper* v. *Virginia Board of Elections*, 383 U.S. 663 (1966), pp. 675-79.

amounts, in my judgment, to an exercise of power the Constitution makers with foresight and wisdom refused to give the Judicial Branch of the Government. I have in no way departed from the view I expressed in *Adamson v. California*, 332 U.S. 46, 90, decided June 23, 1947, that the "natural-law-due-process formula" under which courts make the Constitution mean what they think it should at a given time "has been used in the past, and can be used in the future, to license this Court, in considering regulatory legislation, to roam at large in the broad expanses of policy and morals and to trespass, all too freely, on the legislative domain of the States as well as the Federal Government."

The Court denies that it is using the "natural-law-due-process formula." It says that its invalidation of the Virginia law "is founded not on what we think governmental policy should be, but on what the Equal Protection Clause requires." I find no statement in the Court's opinion, however, which advances even a plausible argument as to why the alleged discriminations which might possibly be effected by Virginia's poll tax law are "irrational," "unreasonable," "arbitrary," or "invidious" or have no relevance to a legitimate policy which the State wishes to adopt. The Court gives no reason at all to discredit the long-standing beliefs that making the payment of a tax a prerequisite to voting is an effective way of collecting revenue and that people who pay their taxes are likely to have a far greater interest in their government. The Court's failure to give any reasons to show that these purposes of the poll tax are "irrational," "unreasonable," "arbitrary," or "invidious" is a pretty clear indication to me that none exist. I can only conclude that the primary, controlling, predominant, if not the exclusive reason for declaring the Virginia law unconstitutional is the Court's deep-seated hostility and antagonism, which I share, to making payment of a tax a prerequisite to voting.

The Court's justification for consulting its own notions rather than following the original meaning of the Constitution, as I would, apparently is based on the belief of the majority of the Court that for this Court to be bound by the original meaning of the Constitution is an intolerable and debilitating evil; that our Constitution should not be "shackled to the political theory of a particular era," and that to save the country from the original Constitution the Court must have constant power to renew it and keep it abreast of this Court's more enlightened theories of what is best for our society. It seems to me that this is an attack not only on the great value of our Constitution itself but also on the concept of a written constitution which is to survive through the years as originally written unless changed through the amendment process which the Framers wisely provided. Moreover, when a "political theory" embodied in our Constitution becomes outdated, it seems to me that a majority of the nine members of this Court are not only without constitutional power but are far less qualified to choose a new constitutional political theory than the people of this country proceeding in the manner provided by Article V.

The people have not found it impossible to amend their Constitution to meet new conditions. The Equal Protection Clause itself is the product of the people's desire to use their constitutional power to amend the Constitution to meet new problems. Moreover, the people, in §5 of the Fourteenth Amendment, designated the governmental tribunal they wanted to provide additional rules to enforce the guarantees of that Amendment. The branch of Government they chose was not the Judicial Branch but the Legislative.

7.7 The Court Takes Note of the Equal Rights Amendment*

In 1972, Congress approved the Equal Rights Amendment and passed it on to the states for approval. In the meantime, the Supreme Court had rendered a number of decisions widening the protection of women under the equal protection clause of the Fourteenth Amendment. By 1973, in *Frontiero v. Richardson*, four of nine justices examining differential rules for dependency enforced in the military in regard to males and females were willing to declare that gender classifications were one of a number of "suspect categories" deserving special judi-

---

* *Frontiero v. Richardson*, 411 U.S. 677 (1973), pp. 691-2.

cial scrutiny and requiring the showing of a "compelling state interest." While concurring in the result in this case, Justice Lewis Powell urged caution, pointing out that, while the Equal Rights Amendment had been voted on by Congress, it had not yet been ratified by the states. His opinion raises continuing questions about the interplay between constitutional amendment and judicial interpretation.

Text of the Proposed Equal Rights Amendment:
Section 1. Equality of rights under the law shall not be denied or abridged by the United States or by any State on account of sex.

Section 2. The Congress shall have the power to enforce, by appropriate legislation, the provisions of this article.

Section 3. This amendment shall take effect two years after the date of ratification.

Powell's concurring opinion:
I agree that the challenged statutes constitute an unconstitutional discrimination against servicewomen in violation of the Due Process Clause of the Fifth Amendment, but I cannot join the opinion of Mr. Justice BRENNAN, which would hold that all classifications based upon sex, "like classifications based upon race, alienage, and national origin," are "inherently suspect and must therefore be subjected to close judicial scrutiny." *Ante*, at 682. It is unnecessary for the Court in this case to characterize sex as a suspect classification, with all of the far-reaching implications of such a holding. *Reed v. Reed*, 404 U.S. 71 (1971), which abundantly supports our decision today, did not add sex to the narrowly limited group of classifications which are inherently suspect. In my view, we can and should decide this case on the authority of *Reed* and reserve for the future any expansion of the rationale.

There is another, and I find compelling, reason for deferring a general categorizing of sex classifications as invoking the strictest test of judicial scrutiny. The Equal Rights Amendment, which if adopted will resolve the substance of this precise question, has been approved by the Congress and submitted for ratification to the States. If this Amendment is duly adopted, it will represent the will of the people accomplished in the manner prescribed by the Constitution. By acting prematurely and unnecessarily, as I view it, the Court has assumed a decisional responsibility at the very time when state legislatures, functioning within the traditional democratic process, are debating the proposed Amendment. It seems to me that this reaching out to pre-empt by judicial action a major political decision which is currently in process of resolution does not reflect appropriate respect for duly prescribed legislative processes.

There are times when this Court, under our system, cannot avoid a constitutional decision on issues which normally should be resolved by the elected representatives of the people. But democratic institutions are weakened, and confidence in the restraint of the Court is impaired, when we appear unnecessarily to decide sensitive issues of broad social and political importance at the very time they are under consideration within the prescribed constitutional processes.

7.8 A Law Professor Argues for Extension of the Equal Rights Amendment*

The proposed Equal Rights Amendment was reported to the states with a seven year deadline in its authorizing resolution. As the end of this deadline approaches and only thirty-five of the necessary thirty-eight states had ratified, Congress considered whether it had authority to extend this deadline and whether it would require a two-thirds voting majority to do so. In the following testimony, a law professor later appointed as a U.S. Circuit Judge in the U.S. Court of Appeals, D.C. Circuit argued that Congress could extend the deadline by a simple majority vote.

---

* Testimony of Ruth Bader Ginsburg, Professor of Law, Columbia Law School. *Equal Rights Amendment Extension*, Hearings Before the Subcommittee on Civil and Constitutional Rights of the Committee on the Judiciary, House of Representatives, Ninety-Fifth Congress, First and Second Sessions on H.J. Res. 638 (November 1, 4, and 8, 1977; and May 17,18, 19, 1978. (U.S. Government Printing Office: Washington, 1978), pp. 121-5.

Testimony of Ruth Bader Ginsberg:
It is my firm opinion that Congress has the authority to extend the ratification period and, in light of the relevant political, social and economic conditions, the responsibility to do so. Further it seems to me clear that Congress may order the time extension through a measure (a bill or a joint or concurrent resolution) adopted by majority vote of both Houses

I. CONGRESS HAS AUTHORITY TO EXTEND THE TIME FOR RATIFICATION OF THE PROPOSED EQUAL RIGHTS AMENDMENT

A proposition beyond debate is the appropriate starting point: Congress, as the director under our constitutional scheme of the amendment process, is not locked into a 7-year time specification; 14, 18, even 20 years would constitute a rational, constitutional time period for ratification of the proposed Equal Rights Amendment. The sole issue worthy of attention in these hearings, therefore, is whether Congress may accomplish in two steps what it might have accomplished in one.

In 1972, without extensive discussion of the matter, Congress placed in the clause that precedes the text of the proposed Equal Rights Amendment a then customary procedural provision:

The following article . . . shall be valid . . . as part of the Constitution when ratified . . . within seven years from the date of its submission. . . .

Has Congress, by that casual, procedural measure, so hobbled itself that it is now disabled from assessing whether the proposed Equal Rights Amendment remains a vital political question, a question on which public debate and state legislative consideration should be allowed to continue? The answer, plainly indicated by the Constitution, precedent and the public interest, is no. For the abnegation involved in a conclusion that Congress is powerless to extend the ratification period would not comport with the constitutional design—the large authority and special responsibility Art. V invests in Congress.

A. Implicit in Article V is the requirement that ratification of a proposed constitutional amendment occur within some reasonable time; the Constitution entrusts to Congress authority to determine 1) what constitutes a reasonable time, and 2) the mode in which timeliness questions shall be addressed.

In 1921, ending a debate whether proposed constitutional amendments ever die, the Supreme Court declared, in *Dillon v. Gloss*, 256 U.S. 368, 375: [T]he fair inference or implication from Article V is that ratification must be within some reasonable time.

Dillon also ruled that "Congress is left free to define" what constitutes a reasonable time in the case of any particular amendment; the timeliness assessment is a matter "of detail" Congress may settle, "incident [to] its power to designate the mode of ratification," in the manner "the public interests and changing conditions may require." 256 U.S. at 371, 376.

In 1939, the Supreme Court further clarified, in *Coleman v. Miller*, 307 U.S. 433, that Congress, not the Court, is the forum entrusted by the Constitution with control of the timeliness question. "Reasonable time" issues in relation to constitutional amendments, the Court said, call for "essentially political" judgments, for they involve "an appraisal of a great variety of relevant conditions, political, social and economic." 307 U.S. at 453-54. An appraisal of that character, *Coleman* held, lies within the province of the House and Senate, and not within the bailiwick of the judiciary.

In *Dillon*, the Court upheld against constitutional challenge the authority of Congress to include a time limitation in the very text of a proposed amendment. In *Coleman*, the Court confirmed the prerogative of Congress to consider and resolve the question of timeliness when "the time arrives for the promulgation of the adoption of the amendment." 307 U.S. at 454. In short, Congress could deal with timeliness as a threshold matter, as *Dillon* held, or as an ultimate question, as *Coleman* declared. There should be little doubt, given the range and breadth of power and responsibility Article V invests in Congress, that a middle course may also be pursued. In lieu of a fixed period set in the text of the proposed amendment, or a total "wait and see" approach with no time frame at all suggested at the onset of the ratification process, Congress could preliminarily establish a time schedule, a schedule subject to extension when necessary and proper, in light of "the public interests" and "relevant conditions." *Dillon v. Gloss, supra*, 256 U.S. at 376; *Coleman v. Miller, supra*, 307 U.S. at 453-54.

B. The mode in which Congress dealt with timeliness in the proposed Equal Rights Amendment indicates a middle course: Congress did not make the time frame a fixed and integral part of the amendment's text; it did not avoid the time question altogether; it did establish an initial, procedural limitation susceptible to extension.

The first seventeen amendments to the Constitution were submitted to the states, and thereafter adopted, without any indication by Congress, at any stage in the process, of a time limit for ratification. From that stance, Congress moved to the opposite pole. In the eighteenth, twentieth, twenty-first and twenty-second amendments, Congress *fixed in the text of the amendment* a definite period for ratification. The time frame was made an integral part of the proposed addition to the Constitution submitted to the states for ratification.

In contrast to these polar approaches, Congress proceeded to a middle course in the four most recent constitutional amendments. The twenty-third and twenty-fourth amendments contain no textual time limitations. Instead, Congress placed in the resolution clause preceding the submitted texts a procedural directive: the proposed amendments were to be valid "only if ratified . . . within seven years." A less rigid formula was employed in the introductory clauses of the resolutions proposing the twenty-fifth and twenty-sixth amendments to the states. The proposed amendments were to be valid "when ratified . . . within seven years. The "when ratified" formula was thereafter repeated by Congress in the resolution clause preceding the submitted text of the Equal Rights Amendment.

In sum, the congressional approach first changed radically from no time stated at all, to reference of the time limit to the states for their ratification as an integral part of the amendment's text. Thereafter, Congress approached the timeliness issue, more appropriately, as a procedural facet of the amendment process. Congress did not place the "reasonable time" determination beyond its further control by fixing the ratification period in the text of the amendment thereby submitting that issue to the states for their approval. Rather, Congress expressed an initial judgment as to time, but it separated that preliminary judgment from the text of the proposed amendment submitted to the states. Congress thereby retained authority to extend the period, should "the public interests" and "relevant conditions" so warrant.

II. THE VOTE REQUIRED TO EXTEND THE RATIFICATION PERIOD

Extension of the ratification period, a procedural decision incident to congressional responsibility for designating the mode of ratification, may be accomplished through a measure (a bill or a joint or concurrent resolution) approved by a simple majority of each House. Article V, consistent with the style in which our Constitution is drafted, "speaks in general terms." *Dillon v. Gloss*, supra, 256 U.S. at 376. However, on the question of supermajorities, Article V is specific; it singles out four instance[s] in which a simple majority will not suffice. (a) Amendments must be proposed by two-thirds of both Houses. (2) Alternatively, on application of the legislators [sic] of two-thirds of the states, Congress shall call a Convention for proposing amendments. (3) Legislatures in three-fourths of the states must ratify. (4) Alternatively, ratification may be effected by conventions in three-fourths of the states. Significantly, no congressional supermajority is commanded by Article V to propose the mode of ratification, or to declare that an amendment submitted to the states has been ratified. *A fortiori*, no supermajority is required to state or extend a time period not incorporated in the text of a proposed amendment.

Congress might have pursued a two-step process in proposing the Equal Rights Amendment: (1) a resolution proposing the "Article of Amendment" adopted by two-thirds vote; (2) a separate measure designating the mode of ratification, including an initial "reasonable time" estimate, for which a simple majority would suffice. A more efficient course was followed. Congress combined the two steps in one resolution. But that joinder did not alter the distinct character of the two elements of the resolution. To propose the "article," a two-thirds vote was necessary. To specify the mode of ratification and a time estimate, no more than a simple majority was needed; the additional votes were superfluous. Similarly, to extend an initial "reasonable time" estimate kept outside the text of a proposed amendment, votes above a simple majority would be superfluous.

III. THE "PUBLIC INTERESTS" AND "RELEVANT CONDITIONS, POLITICAL, SOCIAL AND ECONOMIC," MAKE IT NECESSARY AND PROPER FOR CONGRESS TO EXTEND THE RATIFICATION PERIOD FOR THE PROPOSED EQUAL RIGHTS AMENDMENT

Social and economic conditions in the period 1972 to the present demonstrate the vitality of the issue to which the Equal Rights Amendment responds. Recognition of the equality of men and women before the law, far from diminishing in significance to the Nation, is today an idea attracting widespread and constant attention.

The debate on the Equal Rights Amendment, far more complex than those attending other recent amendments, has not run its course and should be allowed to continue. The proposed amendment remains a matter of urgent public concern. Thus, Congress would be acting responsibly in extending its initial "reasonable time" estimate.

7.9 A Future Supreme Court Justice Re-examines the Political Questions Doctrine*

In this case which involved a question that arose during the unsuccessful attempts to ratify the Equal Rights Amendment, a three-judge U.S. District Court had to decide whether the Illinois legislature had the power to require that it ratify a federal amendment by more than a majority vote. The decision, written by John Paul Stevens who would soon be appointed to the U.S. Supreme Court by President Gerald Ford, suggests that the "political questions" doctrine applied by the Supreme Court in *Coleman v. Miller* (Reading 6-9) might have been seriously eroded in subsequent cases. It also suggests, however,

* *Dyer v. Blair*, 390 F. Supp. 1291 (1975), p. 1294 and 1299-1309.

that the Supreme Court is still likely to defer to state ratification decisions (and, arguably, by logical extension, to decisions of Congress) where constitutional language is not specific. Stevens' distinction in this case between ratification rules adopted by state constitutional provision and by the state legislature is a particularly fascinating one which might also be relevant to future decisions.

John Paul Stevens:

The question presented in each of these cases is whether action taken during the 78th General Assembly of the Illinois legislature constituted "ratification" of the proposed Equal Rights Amendment to the United States Constitution within the meaning of article V of that instrument. That amendment received a favorable vote of more than a majority but less than three-fifths of the members of each house of the Illinois legislature. The question arises because the precise meaning of the term "ratified" has not yet been given a federal definition, but the Illinois State Constitution, as well as a rule adopted by the Illinois House of Representatives and a ruling of the President of the Illinois Senate in the 78th General Assembly, have prescribed a three-fifths majority requirement for amendment to the federal Constitution. . . .

Defendants contend that these cases present a "political question," that is to say, a question which can only be answered by either the executive or the legislative branch of the Federal Government. The contention is supported by alternative arguments: first, that Congress has sole and complete control over the entire amending process, subject to no judicial review; and second, that even if every aspect of the amending process is not controlled by Congress, the specific issue raised in these cases is.

There is force to the first argument since it was expressly accepted by four Justices of the Supreme Court in Coleman v. Miller . . . But since a majority of the Court refused to accept that position in that case, and since the Court has on several occasions decided questions arising under article V, even in the face of "political question" contentions, that argument is not one which a District Court is free to accept. We therefore must consider whether this particular issue is a "political question" under the standards identified in Powell v. McCormack, 395 U.S. 486, 518-519, 89 S.Ct. 1944, 23 L.Ed. 2d 491, and Baker v. Carr, 369 U.S. 186, 217, 82 S.Ct. 691, 7 L.Ed.2d 663, and in Chief Justice Hughes's opinion for the Court in Coleman v. Miller, *supra*.

The text of the Constitution does not expressly direct Congress, rather than the judiciary, to interpret the word "ratified" as it is used in article V, or to decide whether a particular state has taken action which constitutes ratification of a proposed amendment. Rather than relying on the "textual commitment" test for identifying a political question, defendants primarily suggest that the issue is one which may produce an unseemly conflict between coordinate branches of government unless we treat it as nonjusticiable. We are persuaded, however, that this suggestion is foreclosed by the Supreme Court's rejection of a comparable argument in Powell v. McCormack, *supra*. . . .

Such a decision falls squarely within the traditional role of the federal judiciary to construe that document. The possibility that such an adjudication may conflict with the views of Congress cannot justify the courts' avoiding their constitutional responsibility. As the Supreme Court pointedly noted in its citation of McPherson v. Blacker, 146 U.S. 1, 24, 13 S.Ct. 3, 36 L.Ed. 869, the possibility that action might be taken in disregard of a final judicial determination is an "inadmissible suggestion."

The strongest argument for regarding the issue presented by these cases as a "political question" rests on an asserted "lack of judicially discoverable and manageable standards for resolving it." *See* Baker v. Carr, 369 U.S. at 217, 83 S.Ct. at 710. That argument is buttressed by the holding in Coleman v. Miller, 307 U.S. 433. 59 S.Ct. 972, 83 L.Ed. 1385 that the question whether the lapse of 13 years between the proposal of an amendment and the favorable action by the Kansas legislature make the ratification ineffective was a "political question" to be finally determined by Congress.

That holding was based on the absence of any acceptable criteria for making a judicial determination of whether the proposed amendment had lost its vitality through lapse of time. The Court noted that different periods might be reasonable for different proposed amendments and that varying economic or social conditions might support differing conclusions. Such considerations, although entirely acceptable as a predicate for decision by political departments of the government, might be wholly inappropriate as a basis for judicial decision.

Although the issue in these cases is somewhat comparable to the lapse of time issue in *Coleman* in that the criteria for judicial determination are, perhaps, equally hard to find, the answer does not depend on economic, social or political factors that vary from time to time and might well change during the interval between the proposal and ratification. A question that might be answered in different ways for different amendments must surely be controlled by political standards rather than standards easily characterized as judicially manageable.

It is primarily the character of the standards, not merely the difficulty of their application, that differentiates between those which are political and those which are judicial. The mere fact that a court has little or nothing but the language of the Constitution as a guide to its interpretation does not mean that the task of construction is judicially unmanageable. Consider, for example, the Supreme Court's comments in Dillon v. Gloss on the problem of deciding whether or not a ratification was timely:

> It will be seen that this article says nothing about the time within which ratification may be had. . . . Neither the debates in the federal convention which framed the Constitution nor those in the state conventions which ratified it shed any light on the question.
>
> . . . . .
>
> That the Constitution contains no express provision on the subject is not in itself controlling . . . for with the Constitution, as with a statute or other written instrument, what is reasonably implied is as much a part of it as what is expressed. . . .

We are persuaded that the word "ratification" as used in article V of the federal Constitution must be interpreted with the kind of consistency that is characteristic of judicial, as opposed to political, decision making. We conclude, therefore, that whatever the word "ratification" means as it is used in article V, that meaning must be constant for each amendment that Congress may propose. We turn, then, to the problem of ascertaining the meaning of that term.

The power of a state legislature to ratify an amendment to the federal Constitution is derived from that instrument. By virtue of the supremacy clause in article VI, it is clear that the legislature's ratifying function may not be abridged by a state. Mr. Justice Brandeis, speaking for a unanimous court in Leser v. Garnett . . . made this point abundantly clear. . . .

Quite clearly, therefore, if the federal Constitution specifies that ratification shall be accomplished in a particular way, or by a particular vote of a state legislature or a state convention, no state may superimpose a more stringent requirement on that federal specification. The difficulty presented by the cases before us, however, results from the fact that neither the Constitution itself, nor the record of the deliberations of the constitutional convention which drafted it, contains any unambiguous description or definition of what the state legislature must do in order to perform its federal ratifying function.

History teaches us that the framers of the Constitution were dissatisfied with the extraordinary difficulty of amending the Articles of Confederation. Accordingly, there was extensive discussion and debate about article V of the new Constitution, but it is fair to state that such deliberation was concerned almost exclusively with the procedure for initiating proposed amendments, or with the number of states which must express their assent to a proposal in order to make it effective. We have found no evidence of any significant discussion about the procedure which a state legislature or state convention should follow in deciding whether or not to ratify a proposal.

Congress is, of course, given the power to decide whether the ratifying process should be performed by state conventions or by state legislatures, and the Supreme Court has affirmed Congress' power to prescribe a time limit within which the ratifying process must be completed. But the Constitution is totally silent with respect to the procedure which each state convention or each state legislature, as the case may be, should follow in performing its ratifying function.

There can be no doubt about the fact that the Constitution permits many aspects of the ratification procedure to be determined by representatives of the several states. As Professor Dodd has noted:

> It should be remembered, however, that ratification is by state legislatures, and that although the state may not provide any other method of ratification or impose limitations upon the power to ratify, it does seem to be clearly within the power of the state through its constitution or otherwise of the state's representative legislative body, and what shall be the quorum for action by that body. It, of course, also rests within the power of the state itself as to when regular or special sessions of the state's representative body shall meet, and as to how that representative body shall be organized. Dodd, Amending the Federal Constitution, 30 Yale L.J. 321[,] 344-345 (1921).

Arguably, the vote required to effectuate a ratification might be considered a procedural matter, comparable to the determination of a quorum, subject to control by the states. Alternatively, it can be argued with equal force that since the term must have a federal definition, and since the number of votes required to ratify is a matter of critical importance, that number must be set by federal law. Theoretically, the number might be determined by at least five different standards.

First, since the entire ratification process is not effective unless three fourths of the state legislatures have concurred, it might be inferred that a comparable fraction of each body must support a ratifying resolution. Second, it might be thought that a lesser extraordinary majority—such as the Illinois three-fifths requirement—of the legislators elected and eligible to vote would be appropriate. Or, third, an extraordinary majority of the legislators present and voting could be required. Conceivably this latter extraordinary majority might be obtained more easily than the fourth alternative, a vote of 51% of the elected legislators, a constitutional majority. And fifth, as plaintiffs argue in this case, a simple majority, a majority of a quorum—or more precisely of the legislators present when a quorum is present—may suffice.

The vote of the Kansas Legislature, which under the holding in Coleman v. Miller . . . constituted an effective ratification, was 21 to 20. We may take it as decided, therefore, that an extraordinary majority is not *required* by federal law. There is, moreover, some evidence that when article V was drafted the framers assumed that state legislatures would act by majority vote. That evidence, like the text of article V itself, is equally consistent with the view that a majority of a quorum would be sufficient, or with a view that a majority of the elected legislators would be required. And, of course, it is also consistent with the view that the framers did not intend to impose either of those alternatives upon the state legislators, but, instead, intended to leave that choice to the ratifying assemblies.

This last view seems most plausible to us. If the framers had intended to require the state legislatures to act by a simple majority, we think they would have said so explicitly. When the Constitution requires action to be taken by an extraordinary majority, that requirement is plainly stated. While the omission of a comparable requirement in connection with ratification makes it quite clear that a bare majority is permissible, it does not necessarily indicate that either a simple majority or a constitutional majority must be accepted as necessary. We think the omission more reasonably indicates that the framers intended to treat the determination of the vote required to pass a ratifying resolution as an aspect of the process that each state legislature, or state convention, may specify for itself.

This conclusion is consistent with—though by no means compelled by—the underlying philosophy of the framers with regard to the respective roles of the central government and the several state governments. Madison expressed the thought in urging ratification of the Constitution in The Federalist No. 45:

> The powers delegated by the proposed Constitution to the federal government are few and defined. Those which are to remain in the State governments are numerous and indefinite.

The Federalist No. 45, at 303 (Modern Library ed.) (Madison). The ratifying power did not, of course, "remain in the State governments" because it was created by article V of the new Constitution. But the failure to prescribe any particular ratification procedure, or required vote to effectuate a ratification, is certainly consistent with the basic understanding that state legislatures should have the power and the discretion to determine for themselves how they should discharge the responsibilities committed to them by the federal government.

In addition, were we to conclude that article V does mandate a particular majority vote in each state legislature, we would then have to choose among the myriad of possibilities set forth above. The fact that the several states have actually adopted a wide variety of ratification requirements . . . demonstrates that no one voting percentage or procedure is manifestly preferable to all others. Moreover, this history manifests a common understanding that there is no federal objection to the state legislatures' independent determining of their own voting requirements. The absence of criticism of this independent action throughout our history strongly suggests that the common understanding existed when the original Constitution was ratified and that the framers did not intend to prescribe any one of the various alternatives as mandatory.

Plaintiffs in the cases before us have argued that ratification under article V requires the use of a simple majority, or, at most, a majority of those entitled to vote, a constitutional majority. We find no principled reason for holding that either of those procedures, rather than any of the supermajority hybrids that have emerged since article V was adopted, is the one mandated by the Constitution.

Article V identifies the body—either a legislature or a convention—which must ratify a proposed amendment. The act of ratification is an expression of consent to the amendment by that body. By what means that body shall decide to consent or not to consent is a matter for that body to determine for itself. This conclusion is not inconsistent with the premise that the definition of the term "ratified" is a matter of federal law. The term merely requires that the decision to consent or not to consent to a proposed amendment be made by each legislature, or by each convention, in accordance with procedures which each such body shall prescribe.

The Supreme Court has held that a state may not inhibit its legislature's federal power to ratify a proposed amendment to the United States Constitution by requiring approval at a popular referendum; it seems equally clear that a state constitution may not require that a new legislature be elected before the proposal may be considered. The Illinois Attorney General has on three occasions expressed the opinion that a due regard for the federal character of the legislature's ratifying function must invalidate the Illinois constitutional requirement of a favorable vote by a three-fifths majority. . . .

The Attorney General's analysis is consistent with ours. We have concluded that article V delegates to the state legislatures —or the state conventions depending upon the mode of ratification selected by Congress—the power to determine their own voting requirements. The decisions of the Supreme Court, as well as the text of article V, illuminate the critical point that the delegation is not to the states but rather to the designated ratifying bodies. We do not believe that delegated federal power may be inhibited by a state constitutional provision which, in practical effect, determines whether votes of legislators opposing an amendment shall be given greater, lesser, or the same weight as the votes of legislators who favor the proposal.

In the 77th General Assembly the Illinois Senate took the position that, in the performance of its federal function, it was not inhibited by article XIV, 4 of the Illinois Constitution and formally recorded its favorable action on the proposed Equal Rights Amendment notwithstanding the failure to obtain a three-fifths vote. In the 78th General Assembly, however, the House as well as the Senate took a different view. If our analysis of the nature of the delegated power is correct, the Illinois constitutional provision may only be precatory in its effect on the federal process, and those bodies are free to accept or to reject the three-fifths requirement.

They did accept that requirement during the 78th General Assembly. Whether they did so because of a mistaken understanding of the applicable law (notwithstanding the advice of the Attorney General of the state that they were free to disregard the limitation), or because of their decision to respect a policy choice made by the framers of their own constitution in 1970, or simply because they independently determined that the supermajority requirement would be desirable, is of no legal significance. It is clearly not our province to inquire into the individual motives of the legislators who voted in favor of the procedural rules adopted by each branch of the General Assembly to govern its own deliberations, including those relating to ratification of a proposed amendment to the federal Constitution.

In sum, we conclude that the action taken by the 78th Session of the Illinois General Assembly did not constitute an effective ratification because the resolution did not pass by the vote required by the applicable rules of procedure adopted by both houses of the legislature. This conclusion does not reflect disagreement with the contention of the plaintiffs, or the thrice-expressed opinion of the Attorney General of Illinois, that article XIV, 4 of the Illinois Constitution of 1970 does not impose a valid restraint on the power of any session of the Illinois General Assembly to determine for itself the number of affirmative votes which will be required to ratify a proposed amendment to the Constitution of the United States.

7.10 A U.S. District Court Addresses the Ratification of the Equal Rights Amendment*

Few proposed amendments have been more controversial than the one which would have extended equal rights to women. Partisan controversy over what the amendment would mean were it adopted was heightened when, in 1978, just a year before the ratification deadline that Congress had proposed in its authorizing resolution—albeit not in the text of the amendment itself—the House of Representatives accepted the arguments of Professor Ginsburg and others and by a vote of 253 to 189 (followed by a vote in the Senate of 60 to 36) authorized the extension of the ratification deadline for another three years. At the same time, some of the 35 states that had initially ratified the amendment, attempted to rescind their votes. In the opinion below, a U.S. District Court grappled with these issues, in the process casting doubt, as had a

* *Idaho v. Freeman*, 529 F. Supp. 1107 (1981), pp. 1125-9; 1131-39; and 1146-54.

federal court in *Dyer v. Blair* (Reading 7-9) on whether amending issues were any longer considered to be political questions. This decision was mooted when the new ratification deadline passed without any additional state ratifications.

Chief Judge Callister

. . . The defendant argues that the whole of this case is barred from judicial consideration because the Congress is granted exclusive and plenary control over all phases of and questions arising out of the amendatory procedure. A three-judge court in *Dyer v. Blair*, 390 F.Supp. 1291 (1975) addressed this proposition. Judge Stevens (now Justice Stevens) wrote:

> There is force to . . . [this] argument since it was expressly accepted by four Justices of the Supreme Court in Coleman v. Miller, 307 U.S. 433, 59 S.Ct. 972, 83 L.Ed.. 1385. But since a majority of the Court refused to accept that position in that case, and since the Court has on several occasions decided questions arising under article V, even in the face of "political question" contentions, that argument is not one which a District Court is free to accept.

Dyer v. Blair, supra at 1299, 1300 (footnotes omitted). Furthermore, a review of Article V reveals that the judiciary, while only dealing with article V in a handful of cases, has nevertheless dealt with virtually all the significant portions of that article. . . .

Finally, as will be pointed out later, giving plenary power to Congress to control the amendment process runs completely counter to the intentions of the founding fathers in including article V with its particular structure in the Constitution. Therefore, in accordance with the holding in *Dyer* and the overwhelming precedent established in the case law arising under article V, the position taken by the defendant that the Congress is empowered to decide all issues concerning the amendment process is clearly foreclosed, leaving this Court with the more difficult question of determining the various allocations of power under article V and the areas wherein judicial review is precluded. . . .

Regarding the amending body as the repository of legal sovereignty has an interesting impact on the perception of the amendment process and the participants therein. Initially it should be noted that the two participants listed in article V having a part in the amendment process—Congress and the state legislature or state convention—comprise an independent body which solely has the power to alter the fundamental laws of the land. In short, a body which transcends both federal and state authority. When acting as part of the amending body, both participants act pursuant to the power and authority granted by article V and their traditionally defined roles have no bearing on their authority to either limit or expand them . . . Within article V each of the participants are assigned certain powers which appear to be carefully balanced and approximately equally distributed. . . .

Thus it was with a focus on promoting these two essential values—(1) flexibility to respond to pressures; and (2) the importance that the change proposed be supported by a consensus of the people—that the founding fathers sought to balance the amending power between the national and local representatives. . . .

Thus, in promoting the first value of the amendment clause, i.e., providing a means by which the Constitution can remain responsive to change, authority was given to both the states and Congress to propose necessary amendments. The national government was given the power to propose amendments because as Hamilton wrote the state legislatures can "erect barriers" against its encroachment. Since the power to propose is equally divided, the power to create barriers against the national government must flow from the distribution of authority in determining whether or not proper consent for the change is derived from the people.

While the drafters of the Constitution found it appropriate to grant the same power to propose amendments to both the local and national governments, a somewhat different distribution of authority was applied for determining whether there is sufficient consensus or support for the change. Like the power to propose amendments, both the states and Congress were given a part in determining the extent of consent but unlike the power to propose amendments, the authority given each is distinctly different. Article V gives Congress complete and unrestricted control of designating the "Mode of Ratification", the power to propose which of the two local entities, the state legislature or state convention, will act in ratifying the amendment. The essential purpose behind this grant of authority is for Congress to determine which of these entities will best reflect the local sentiment regarding the proposed amendment. The states, on the other hand, acting through the body chosen by Congress, have the responsibility of ascertaining the local sentiment or actual popular consent regarding the amendment. It is clear that in formulating article V the framers found that the states could most accurately reflect the existence *vel non* of consent.

In considering the scope of the power granted to Congress to set the mode of ratification the Court has found that certain natural inferences must be read into that delegation of authority. [The Court cites *Dillon v. Gloss* and *Coleman v. Miller*.] . . .

It is important to note that Congress' part in determining whether or not a consensus has been reached in a reasonable contemporaneous time period is not one where they must initially or ultimately determine the actual existence of consent or consensus, for that determination Congress must look to the expressions of the states in their role of representing the people locally. Rather, the congressional determination is one of timing, i.e., whether the concepts which gave rise to the amendment continue in full force and effect during the period in which the states act in ratifying.

This role of orchestrating the expressions of the states which Congress has under its power to propose the mode of ratification is appropriate for two related reasons. First, in its role as a national legislature the Congress is best suited to act in accumulating the states' expressions of consent to formulate a broad picture of local consensus. Second, Congress, it would appear, is also best suited, because of the basic nature of the question, to determine whether or not the expressions of consent are sufficiently contemporaneous in time with each other and with the proposal of the amendment. For example, at the time of the Constitutional Convention the founding fathers saw the necessity of an amending clause as being predicated on the need for a process to meet and solve unanticipated constitutional crises. As such it was anticipated that the need for changing the Constitution would not arise in a theoretical vacuum but be brought about by socio/political economic forces which would serve as the impetus for the move to amend. An amendment, therefore, would be a reasoned response to the particular pressures and a specific solution to them. It follows that as long as the socio/political, economic pressures continue, and the proposed amendment remains responsive to those pressures, it can be said that the amendment is still viable, and any state's action in ratifying would be considered "contemporaneous" with all other actions on the amendment. If, however, a change occurs in the socio/political economic milieu, or in the proposed amendment's ability to respond, then the amendment cannot be said to be viable nor would a state's action in ratifying the amendment be "contemporaneous" with the spirit of the proposal or with other states which ratified soon after the amendment was proposed. . . .

Therefore, since the essential inquiry regarding the contemporaneousness of the consensus is one in which the socio-political economic underpinnings are monitored, it would appear such an exercise is clearly best suited to the capabilities of Congress.

The states, on the other hand, have complete and exclusive power of the process of determining actual consent. They determine whether or not sufficient local consensus exists and the process by which that consensus is determined. It is this allocation of exclusive control over the actual process of ratification, or determination of actual consensus, that creates the "barrier to national encroachment" that the founding fathers saw as a necessity. The recognition of this local barrier to encroachment has been recognized in two areas, the procedure the states may follow in determining consent, and the actual determination of consent itself. . . .

From the foregoing it becomes clear that the precise questions presented to this Court are not barred from judicial review because of a textual commitment to a coordinate branch of government. First, it is evident from the balance struck between the two participants in the amendment process that the framers did not intend either of those two parties to be the final arbiter of the process. It seems more logical that the courts, as a neutral third party, and having the responsibility of "guardian of the Constitution" decide these questions raised under article V because the amending power was split between Congress and the states. The question of whether or not a rescission of a prior ratification is a proper exercise of a state's power under article V is one that is not committed to Congress, and should not be, but is appropriate for judicial interpretation under the Court's authority to "say what the law is." Furthermore, while the question of the reasonableness of the ratification period is one committed to Congress, such is not the question presented here. Rather, the question presented to the Court is one of procedure under article V and these procedural questions have been held to be ones which the Court must decide. . . .

Recently, in *Goldwater v. Carter* . . . Justice Rehnquist, drawing heavily from *Dyer*, formulated a two-part test in the application of the lack of judicial standard formulation of the political question doctrine. . . .

Thus Justice Rehnquist found that where (1) there is no specific constitutional provision governing the particular question at hand, and (2) where it is found that different answers might be appropriate in different situations, the question is one to be controlled by political standards and resolved by one of the political arms of the government.

Applying Justice Rehnquist's test to the questions presented to this Court, it is certainly evident from the Court's consideration of the structure of article V that the Constitution is silent as to a determination of the issues presented by the plaintiffs' complaint. But, it is equally evident that the question of the state's ability to rescind and the propriety of changing an established time limitation are ones which should not be answered "in different ways for different amendments." Rather, it is clear that these questions are such that they "must be interpreted with the kind of consistency that is characteristic of a judicial as opposed to political, decision making." To subject these questions to a variety of inconsistent interpretations or approaches would create an incurable uncertainty regarding the validity of the acts of the participants, severely crippling the amendment process. Such a result would violate the Supreme Court's articulated purpose for the application of the political question doctrine, "a tool for maintenance of governmental order will not be so applied as to promote only disorder." *Baker v. Carr*. . . .

If the question of the effectiveness of a ratification after a rejection and the effect of a rescission on a prior ratification are treated similarly as "political questions," it would, in effect, mean that Congress would have control over ultimately assessing whether or not there is continued local consent. For example, if Congress could refuse to recognize a state's rescission, it would mean that Congress would supplant the expression of the people's representative with its own assessment of consent by holding that the prior expression of consent is still valid. Such a broad interpretation of congressional powers would destroy the balance created in article V and remove the state's power to create a barrier to encroachment by the national government. Therefore, while it might be conceded that the effectiveness of a ratification in light of a prior rejection is proper for resolution by a political arm of the government, the question of the effect of a rescission in light of a prior ratification does not bring into play the same type of considerations, and thus, because the questions posed by a rescission are not proper for consideration by the political branch, they should be treated differently.

The application of the prudential consideration formulation of the "political question" doctrine to the procedural issues surrounding the problem of the constitutionality of the congressional extension of the ratification deadline is also not warranted. Nothing in the nature of the questions nor in the legislative history of the extension resolution is present which would convince the Court that the congressional enactment of the extension resolution is the type of determination by a political branch which the courts ought to unquestioningly adhere to.

From the Court's review of all the ramifications of the "political question" doctrine, there does not appear to be any compelling reasons for it to withhold its jurisdiction with regard to the questions presented. Furthermore, the Court is persuaded that both the questions of the efficacy of a rescission and the proper procedure for establishing a time period for ratification are the type of questions that must be interpreted with the kind of consistency that is characteristic of judicial rather than political decision making. Whatever the outcome of these questions as they related to the powers vested by article V, they must be interpreted consistently for each amendment that may be proposed. . . .

Rescission

In addressing the question of whether or nor a rescission of a prior ratification is a proper exercise of the state's authority under article V to act on proposed amendments, it must be noted that whatever authority the states have is derived solely from the Constitution itself. The critical portion of article V that the Court must examine provides that an amendment becomes part of the Constitution "when ratified by the Legislatures of three-fourths of the several States, or by Conventions. . . ." With reference to the phrase "when ratified", commentators and courts have explored a variety of interpretations to what can best be termed "subsequent acts," i.e., the subsequent act of ratifying after a rejection or rescinding after a ratification. Three separate approaches have been postulated, which are important to review in this Court's consideration of the question of the state's power to rescind.

The first approach to be considered contends that whatever action is initially taken by the state, whether rejection or ratification, exhausts the state's power under article V making any subsequent act to reverse the prior action a nullity. . . .

The second approach postulated would condone only the act of ratification, and the negative expressions of rejection or rescission would be treated as a nullity. . . .

A third approach which has received support is that both the subsequent acts of ratification after a rejection and rescission after ratification should be recognized. Of course, one clear limitation is evident which is that any subsequent rescission after a prior ratification could not come after three-fourths of the states had ratified, for at that point the amendment automatically becomes part of the Constitution and a state cannot withdraw its consent thereafter. . . .

From the approaches outlined above, in order to decide which should be controlling in the Court's determination of the validity of a state's rescission in light of its powers under article V, it is necessary to understand what a state is doing when it acts on a proposed amendment. First, it must be observed that the drafters of the Constitution considered it important that the power to change the Constitution must in some respect draw on that same power which is the source of the original authority of the Constitution—"the consent of the people." The structure of article V indicates that it is the state that must ascertain the existence of local consent and reflect that sentiment when acting on an amendment. . . .

Considering that an amendment cannot become part of the Constitution until a proper consensus of the people has been reached and it is the exclusive role of the states to determine what the local sentiment is, it logically follows that the subsequent act of rescission would promote the democratic ideal by giving a truer picture of the people's will as of the time three-fourths of the states have acted in affirming the amendment. To allow a situation where either the first act of a state is irrevocable or where a rejection can be changed by a ratification, but not permit rescission, would permit an amendment to be ratified by a technicality—where clearly one is not intended—and not because there is really a considered consensus supporting the amendment which is the avowed purpose of the amendment procedure. Furthermore, an irrevocable ratification prior to the time that three-fourths have acted would completely dissociate the democratic notion of a considered consensus from the ratification procedure and create the very real possibility that an amendment could become part of the Constitution when the people have not been unified in their consent.

The only apparent criticism of the approach which would recognize a rescission after a ratification is that to allow a change after a ratification would create confusion and uncertainty and essentially paralyze the process. This objection has little merit when it is realized that all Congress or its designate must do is count the state's most recent official certification to determine whether or not three-fourths have ratified. . . .

The states are the entity embodied with the power to speak for the people during the period in which the amendment is pending. To make a state's ratification binding with no right to rescind would give ratification a technical significance which would be clearly inappropriate considering that the Constitution through article V gives technical significance to a state's ratification at only one time—when three-fourths of the states have acted to ratify. Until the technical three-fourths has been reached, a rescission of a prior ratification is clearly a proper exercise of a state's power granted by the article V phrase "when ratified" especially when that act would give a true picture of local sentiment regarding the proposed amendment. . . .

Extension

The question of whether it is a proper exercise of congressional authority under article V to alter a previously proposed time limitation for ratification, and if so by what majority, presents for the Court a question of constitutional interpretation of congressional authority, and an inquiry into the procedural aspects of exercising that power. Thus, the Court's inquiry is two-fold: First, does Congress under its power to "propose" the "mode of Ratification" have the power to change its proposal once it has been made and sent to the states; second, if the initial proposal can be subsequently changed, may Congress act by less than a two-thirds majority. One related question that has been raised that should be dealt with at this time is whether or not a state's ratification resolution specifically acknowledging the ratification period set by Congress is impaired if the original time period is extended or whether it is a "conditional" ratification arguably prohibited by the amendment process.

To begin with, the actions of Congress in relation to a proposed amendment must be properly characterized in order to approach the question presented. First, it must be recognized that Congress' power to participate in the amendment process stems solely from Article V. As Justice Stevens noted, "the function of a state Legislature in ratifying a proposed amendment to the federal Constitution, *like* the function of Congress in proposing the amendment, *is a federal function* derived from the federal Constitution. . . ." *Dyer v. Blair* . . . Thus Congress, outside of the authority granted by article V, has no power to act with regard to an amendment, i.e., it does not retain any of its traditional authority vested in it by article I. The power of Congress to set a time period in which ratification must be completed is derived from their function of settling the mode of ratification. See *Dillon v. Gloss* . . . The defendant in this action attempts to create a substance/procedure dichotomy by contending that since the time restriction in this instance is part of the proposing resolution it is proper for reconsideration where if the time period were part of the amendment itself it would not be. The argument follows that a change of a substantive aspect of an amendment is clearly improper once it has been submitted to the states, but a change in the proposing resolution, on the other hand, does not change the essential nature of the amendment and thus is a matter of detail which Congress can change at will. The Supreme Court in *Dillon v. Gloss*, *supra*, had an opportunity to address this substance/procedure dichotomy when the eighteenth amendment was challenged on the grounds that the seven-year ratification period called for in Section 3 of that amendment was unconstitutional. While the *Dillon* court indicated that "[a]n examination of article V discloses that it is intended to invest Congress with a wide range of power in proposing amendments" . . . the court did not recognize the setting of the time limitation as being a function of Congress' power to propose amendments but instead indicated that

> [w]hether a definite period for ratification should be fixed so that all may know what it is and speculation on what is a reasonable time may be avoided, is, in our opinion, a matter of detail which Congress may determine as an *incident of its power to designate the mode of ratification.*

Id. at 376, 41 S.Ct. at 513 (emphasis added). The court did not recognize a substance/procedure dichotomy and thus any authority to limit the time period for consideration must flow from the Congress' power to set the mode of ratification.

Accordingly, the Court's attention is drawn to a consideration of Congress' power to set and change the time period for ratification under its power to set the mode of ratification.

The United States Supreme Court in *United States v. Sprague* . . . recognized that Congress has absolute discretion within its power to propose the mode of ratification to establish which of the two local entities will act as the spokesman for the people. The Supreme Court in the *Dillon* and *Coleman* cases found that as a "subsidiary matter of detail" to this congressional prerogative, Congress must also determine whether or not the local expressions of consent are "sufficiently contemporaneous in that number of States to reflect the will of the people in all sections at relatively the same period. . ." *Dillon* 256 U.S. at 375, . . . In making its determination that the requisite consensus has been reached in a sufficiently contemporaneous period, the Supreme Court in *Coleman, supra*, indicated that if no time restriction is set initially, Congress retains its authority to decide when the requisite number of states have acted. . . . The court in *Dillon* further clarified the scope of Congress' power by indicating that while Congress is not compelled to make a determination of a reasonable time period in advance of the actions of the requisite number of states, it is not precluded from doing so. The *Dillon* court held that Congress may fix a reasonable time in advance. . . . It should be noted that the *Dillon* court did not intimate that the setting of a definite time period was a projection or preliminary assessment of a reasonable time period which would be reevaluated as time passed. Rather, the Court indicated that the exercise of Congress' power to set a time period for ratification is one which is intended to infuse certainty into an area which is inherently vague. Thus the inference that can be drawn from *Dillon* and *Coleman* is that within Congress' role of determining a reasonably contemporaneous consensus, or in other words, determining whether the socio/political, economic forces giving rise to the amendment remain alive and unchanged during the period in which the state act in giving their assent to the proposal, Congress may exercise its function in one of two ways: first, it can leave the question of a reasonable time open until the requisite number of states have acted and thus continually monitor the viability of the amendment; second, where it appears to Congress that the socio/political, economic factors giving rise to the amendment are such that they are unlikely to change for an indefinite period of time, and rather than have the proposed amendment pending perpetually, Congress can set an arbitrary yet reasonable time period in order to establish a termination point for consideration and thus promote prompt action on the amendment by the states.

It, therefore, appears compelling that in order to fulfill the purposes for fixing a time limitation for ratification as outlined in *Dillon*—"so all may know and speculation ... be avoided"—the congressional determination of a reasonable period once made and proposed to the states cannot be altered. If Congress determines that a particular amendment requires ongoing assessment as to its viability or monitoring of the time period, it can do so, not by defeating the certainty implied by the *Dillon* case, but by not setting a time period at the outset and reserving the question until three-fourths of the states have acted.

The Court's conclusion that Congress cannot change the ratification period once it is set also finds support from the form in which it is presented to the states. While the setting of a time period for ratification has been described as a "subsidiary matter of detail," pursuant to Congress' power to propose the mode of ratification, if the Congress chooses to fix a time period by making it part of its proposal to the states, that determination of a time period becomes an integral part of the proposed mode of ratification. Once the proposal has been formulated and sent to the states, the time period could not be changed any more than the entity designated to ratify could be changed from the state legislature to a state convention or vice versa. Once the proposal is made, Congress is not at liberty to change it.

In any event, while the general power of Congress to change its prior proposal may be argued, it is more than clear that in this instance Congress' promulgation of the extension resolution was in violation of the constitutional requirement that Congress act by two-thirds of both Houses when exercising its article V powers. Since Congress can act only within the authority given it by article V, and in none other, when proposing amendments or the mode of ratification, arguments relating to acceptable parliamentary order or procedure have little bearing in determining what voting requirement is necessary for Congress to alter a proposed time limitation on ratification. This is because such an argument presumes Congress is functioning in a legislative capacity when exercising its powers under article V. To determine in what manner Congress must act in utilizing its authority under article V, reference must first be made to the Constitution itself. If it is silent, then the courts can leave Congress to decide its own procedural requirements. . . . Article V grants Congress only one power which can be exercised with regard to two separate considerations. Congress has the power to "propose." It can "propose" the text of the amendment and it can "propose" the mode of ratification. When acting in its function of proposing the amendment itself, article V has given the term "congress" a particular definition. Article V states, "The Congress, *whenever two thirds of both Houses shall deem it necessary*, shall propose Amendments. . . ." U.S. Const., Art. V (emphasis added). Within its powers to propose the mode of ratification, however, no specific reference is made by what concurrence of both Houses, or even if both Houses must act, in order for the mode of ratification to be proposed and sent to the states. Article V only provides that ratification be "by the legislatures of three fourths of the several States, or by Conventions in three fourths thereof, as the one or the other Mode of Ratification may be *proposed by Congress. . . .*" U.S. Const., art V (emphasis added). The defendant argues that this failure of the drafters to designate by what majority the power to propose the mode of ratification indicates that it should be left to Congress to set its own procedure. But the argument overlooks the fact that the word "Congress" has been specifically defined earlier in the same sentence. Rather than give the word "Congress" two different meanings within the same provision, it seems more logical to give it a consistent interpretation throughout. This conclusion seems even more reasonable when it is considered that what is being dealt with is the same power—the congressional power to "propose."

One final observation. Reviewing several of the most recent resolutions proposing amendments to the Constitution and referring particularly to the resolution proposing the Equal Rights Amendment, the mode of ratification has been proposed by the approval of both Houses of Congress, thus indicating by general practice that this is the appropriate measure of approval.

Therefore, the Court is persuaded that the congressional act of extending the time period for ratification was an improper exercise of Congress' authority under article V. While Congress is not required to set a time period in advance of the required number of states acting to ratify, if it chooses to do so to remove uncertainty regarding the question, it cannot thereafter remove that certainty by changing the time period. In addition, since it is clear that Congress must act by a two-thirds concurrence of both Houses when acting pursuant to its authority under article V, and because the extension resolution was enacted by only a simple majority, the extension resolution is an unconstitutional exercise of congressional authority under article V.

Since the Court has determined that the enactment of the extension resolution was an *ultra vires* act, and thus unconstitutional, the question of the effect of the extension of a state's alleged "conditional" ratification is one that the Court does not need to address. However, the Court would point out the irony of the defendant's position in arguing that a state cannot condition its ratification and then contend that the condition can be purged from the ratification leaving the state's adoption of the amendment intact. If the defendant truly maintains that a ratification cannot be conditioned, then it would seem consistent that conditional ratification must be considered a nullity. If a state has acted improperly in exercising its ratification powers, only the states can cure the impropriety and neither Congress nor the courts can exorcise the statements of condition form the ratification. It must either succeed or fail as it is enacted.

7.11 Constitutional Convention Implementation Act Explained*

Probably not since the period surrounding the American Civil War has the unused Article V constitutional convention mechanism been more discussed than in the last twenty-five years. While the movement to call a convention to limit the Supreme Court apportionment decisions failed, there has been a renewed effort to use this mechanism to attempt to solve federal budget deficits.

Despite a number of attempts, first initiated by Senator Sam Ervin of North Carolina, to adopt legislation, none has so far been passed. Agreement is made difficult by questions as to whether a convention could be limited and arguably by fears that if a procedure were spelled out it might be resorted to more frequently. In the speech below, Senator Orrin Hatch of Utah both spells out various questions still surrounding the convention mechanism and explains how his legislation would address various issues that have been raised. While he presents a distinct point of view, readers should be able to identify some of the most important issues which are currently the subject of dispute.

Senator Hatch:
Mr. President, I am pleased to introduce today the Constitutional Convention Implementation Act of 1991. This important proposal was approved by the full Judiciary Committee in both the 98th and 99th Congresses.

Article V of the U.S. Constitution provides that constitutional amendments may be proposed in either of two ways. The first—the means by which every successful amendment to the Constitution has been proposed—requires the agreement of two-thirds of each House of Congress. The second requires the agreement of a convention called by Congress in response to the applications of two-thirds of the State legislatures. Ratification of amendments proposed through either method is to be done either by the legislatures, or by conventions, in three-

* *Congressional Record*, Senate, January 15, 1991, S559-S563.

fourths of the States, depending upon the determination of Congress.

Largely as a result of the fact that the convention method of constitutional revision has never been successfully employed, there are substantial questions that related to it:

What constitutes a valid application to the Congress?

What procedures must a State follow in submitting an application?

Must the precise language of the proposed amendment be included within the application?

How similar must the language be in applications of various States in order to allow them to be aggregated?

How long does an application remain valid? May such applications be rescinded by the States?

What is the extent of congressional power to review applications? What is the extent of congressional power to restrict the deliberations of the convention?

What is the extent of State power to restrict the deliberations of the convention?

How is the convention to be organized? How are the States to be represented at the convention?

May Congress refuse to submit the product of a convention to the States for ratification?

How are constitutional convention-proposed amendments to be ratified by the States?

With respect to most of these questions, there is very little constitutional guidance. The relevant language of article V states simply:

The Congress "on the application of the legislature of two-thirds of the several states, shall call a convention for proposing amendments."

NOR are there useful precedents in view of the fact that there has never been a constitutional convention under article V. Each of the questions involved in this, the alternative means of amending the Constitution, is therefore a threshold question.

Objectives of the Act

Article I, section 8, clause 18 of the Constitution invests authority in Congress to:

Make all laws which shall be necessary and proper for carrying into execution the foregoing powers, and all other powers vested by this Constitution in the Government of the United States.

This provision clearly authorizes the Congress to pass legislation that would give effect to the convention method of constitutional alteration. This would be a direct function of its article V authority to call a convention pursuant to applications of two-thirds of the States.

I am introducing legislation, the Constitutional Convention Implementation Act, which would fill in the interstices of article V. It is similar to legislation which I have introduced during the previous four Congresses, and which was unanimously approved by the Subcommittee on the Constitution during the 97th Congress. It is particularly important that this body act on this, or similar legislation, in view of the fact that numerous State legislatures have already purposed to submit applications to Congress for the convening of a constitution[al] convention on the subject of a balanced budget amendment. I would only hope that this act, however, could be considered separately from the merits of this or any other specific amendment.

The Constitutional Convention Implementation Act is designed to establish what are basically neutral procedures to guide the conduct of constitutional conventions generally. While the imminence of a convention of the matter of a balanced budget has clearly created the urgency for this legislation, the act is designed neither to facilitate nor obstruct the eventual achievement of a balanced budget amendment, or any other constitutional amendment. The purpose of this legislation is primarily to insure that Congress has clear standards and criteria by which to judge convention applications before it, and that any convention that takes place under article V is conducted in an orderly and nonchaotic manner.

One must look to the policy underlying the establishment of the convention form of amendment in order to construct an appropriate procedures bill. Even a cursory analysis of the original Constitutional Convention—convened under the auspices of the Articles of Confederation—makes clear that the final provisions of article V resulted from a compromise between those delegates who sought to invest proposal authority solely in Congress and those who sought to invest it solely in the State legislature. The two modes of initiating amendments were viewed as essentially equivalent alternatives, each of which was to serve as a check upon the intransigence of either the national legislature or the State legislature in the matter of proposing constitutional revision.

In view of this fundamental purpose, I believe that legislation giving effect to the convention method of amendment should be such that resort to its use will not render the Constitution too mutable—the Federalist No. 43—while at the same time insuring that it will not be rendered null and void because it remains too cumbersome a method. The amendment process should never be one that can be successfully employed with great ease, yet neither should it be a process totally incapable of being used to alter the Constitution. The requirement that State convention applications relate to the same general subject or subjects serves to ensure the existence of some real consensus among the States with respect to the need for constitutional revision in some relatively circumscribed area.

Provisions of Act

I would like to briefly discuss the provisions of this act and explain their justification. I should add at the outset my debt to the efforts of our former colleague, Senator Sam Ervin. While my bill differs in a number of respects from legislation that Senator Ervin successfully shephered through the Senate in 1971 and 1973, its basic structure is closely related to that measure. That legislation was approved unanimously on one occasion by this body, and by a voice vote on the other occasion.

Section I of my bill states that its short title is the "constitutional Convention Implementation Act of 1989."

Convention Applications

Section 2 specifies the manner in which States are to make applications for a constitutional convention. It states simply that the legislature shall specify within its application for a convention, the general subject of the amendment or amendments to be proposed. The objective of this standard is to ensure that two-thirds of the States have a sufficiently similar purpose to warrant the aggregation of their applications.

The purpose of the application process is to determine that there exists some form of consensus among the States on the matter of a relatively well-defined area of amendment. This consensus cannot fairly be said to be in evidence if aggregation is to be permitted of applications that are, at best, only incidentally related.

On the other hand, it cannot be reasonably expected that identical, or even nearly identical, language be employed in petitions that ought to be aggregated. Such a requirement is highly unrealistic with respect to 50 diverse State legislative bodies; the imposition of such a rigid rule would effectively render the alternative method of amendment provided in article V useless. Further, to the extent that a petition was required to be precise, either with respect to the specific amendment sought, or the specific language sought, there would be little use for the convention itself. To limit the convention to the consideration of a single, meticulously worded amendment is to make the convention a farce. In order for the convention to be a meaningful part of the article V process, it must have some leeway within which to exercise its legitimate discretion.

Limited Conventions

That this discretion, however, is not without its limits is the subject of section 2 (b), and, indeed, is the basic theme of the Constitutional Convention Implementation Act. This section states that the procedures provided in the act are to be followed only in the case applications for what are commonly referred to as "limited" conventions. Such conventions are defined for the purposes of this act as conventions designed to consider one or more specific predefined areas of amendment to the Constitution of the United States. Implicit in this section is the recognition that the States may call for the convening of either limited or general conventions; it is, however, simply with respect to the former that the terms of this act apply.

A general convention would be one in which the States petitioned for a convention, not with any specific or limited purposes in mind, but for the purpose of making whatever revisions were deemed necessary or desirable by the convention itself. It is this sort of convention that poses such great concerns to most observers, including myself. I am far from confident that a contemporary general convention could do much to improve upon the work of Madison, Hamilton, and Wilson. While there is no way that Congress, through passage of a simple statute, could preclude the States from requesting a general convention—this is their right under Article V—neither is Congress precluded from clarifying that the States are fully within their rights in seeking a limited convention.

There is academic dispute as to the possibilities of a limited constitutional convention. Prof. Charles Black of the Yale Law School, for example, believes that the constitutional convention is a free agent, sovereign and without limitations. According to this theory, the convention represents the premier assembly of the people, and is therefore supreme to all other Government branches and agencies. It cannot be limited in the scope of its deliberations, whatever the limited nature of the grievances that brought the convention into being.

I would disagree with this interpretation. The constitutional convention, while clearly a unique and separate element of the Government—a temporary new branch of the Government—a new branch of the Government, so to speak—is subject to the same limitations and checks and balances as the other, permanent branches of the Government. A constitutional conventions [sic], as its name clearly implies, is a constitutional entity; it is appointed under the terms of the Constitution and subject to all of the express and implied limitations imposed by that document. As observed by Professor Jameson in his classic work on constitutional conventions:

> The convention's principal feature is that it is subaltern—it is evoked by the side and at the call of a Government preexisting and intended to survive it, for the purpose of administering to its special needs. It never governs. Though called to look into and recommend improvement in the fundamental laws, it enacts neither them nor the statute laws; and it performs no act of administration.

The Federal constitutional convention is an instrument of the Government, and acts properly only when it acts in conformity to its authorized powers.

There is nothing in the language of article V to suggest that the convention method of amendment cannot be limited to a single area of amendment. The symmetry between the competing processes of constitutional amendment is emphasized by Madison in the Federalist No. 43 in discussing the objectives of article V: [Hatch quotes passage]

It was clearly contemplated that the article V primarily anticipated specific amendment or amendments, rather than general revisions, and that no distinction was to be drawn between the competing methods of amendment in this respect.

To enable Congress to propose specific constitutional amendments while allowing the States only to propose general constitutional revision is to confer markedly unequal powers of amendment upon these governments, an intention contradicted by the unanimous weight of documentary evidence. If the States are to have no ability to control the actions of a convention in the form of their convention applications, then there will be strong disincentives for them to seek such conventions. In the absence of broad-based dissatisfaction with the existing constitutional system, why should they want to risk the possibility of a convention acting beyond the scope of their application? Why, in seeking to originate the "amendment of errors" described by Madison should the State have to risk total revision of the constitutional system?

It is anomalous that in seeking to correct what might be a narrow defect in the system that the States should have to place the entire system in jeopardy. What better means could there be to perpetuate the discovered faults of the system? What better means could there be to place the convention system of amendment in an unequivalent position to the congressional system of amendment? What better means could there be to completely discourage any and all resort to the convention means of constitutional amendment?

As Prof. William Van Alstyne has remarked:

> I find it perfectly remarkable that some have argued for a construction of article V which not only limits the power of State legislatures to have a convention, but would limit that power to its least expected, least appropriate, most difficult (and yet most dangerous) use.

It is the States, not Congress, that ought to properly have the ability to limit the scope of the convention, through their convention applications. While Congress, under section 7 of the Constitutional Implementational Act, is empowered to specify in its call for the convention the scope of permissible deliberations, it is performing basically an administrative, nondiscretionary function in doing so; it is simply translating the State applications into formal convention call.

Application Procedures

Section 3(a) of the act specified that the procedures to be followed in making a convention application are those adopted by the States themselves. Although a State is free to adopt procedures uniquely applicable to the convention application process—as the State of Illinois, for example, has done with respect to the amendment ratification process—it is anticipated that most States will follow procedures that govern the adoption of simple statutes or resolutions.

Section 3(b) provides further that questions concerning the extent to which States have acted in compliance with their own rules of procedure are also to be determined by the State legislatures themselves. While recognizing that, in pursuit of their authority under Article V, the States are acting in quasi-Federal capacity rather than in a purely State role, *Leser v. Garnett* (158 U.S. 130, 137 (1922)), it would nevertheless be incongruous for anybody to determine whether or not there has been procedural regularity in a State legislative action other than the legislature itself.

In *Field v. Clark* (143 U.S. 649 (1881)), the Supreme Court held that the procedural requirements of the legislative process were presumed to have been satisfied when legislation was formally certified by the appropriate legislative officer. Rather than intruding Congress or the courts into these matters, there is no reason why this traditional rule ought not continue to apply with respect to convention application actions. There is no compelling reason why article V should require sacrifice by State legislatures of their inherent right to regulate their own proceedings.

Whatever the procedures in the State legislatures, such actions are to be considered valid without the assent of the Governor of the State. Thus the term "legislatures" in article V is treated in the same manner, for the purposes of convention applications, as it has traditionally been treated for the purposes of amendment ratification, *Hollingworth v. Virginia* (3 Dall. 376 (1978)); *Hawke v. Smith* (253 U.S. 221 (1920).

Transmission of Applications

Section 4 of the act specifies the means by which the States are to transmit their applications for a convention to Congress. Section 4(a) states that, within 30 days of the adoption by a State of an application, the appropriate official is to transmit copies to the President of the Senate and the Speaker of the House of Representatives.

Section 4(b) directs the States to include within their applications: The title of the resolution, the date of adoption, and an official certification. In addition, States are encouraged, but not required, to list in the application other pending State applications which are felt to relate to substantially the same subject. While such a listing is not to be considered conclusive with respect to Congress, it is nevertheless considered that such a listing will be useful to Congress in carrying out its responsibilities in aggregating applications.

Section 4(c) requires each House to establish a public record of each State application, and to notify each State legislature of the fact of each application. Through internal procedures to be determined by each House, Congress would be charged with making an initial decision on whether or not to aggregate applications within the 10-day period following each new application. The criteria would be whether or not the applications references the same "general subject or subjects."

These initial decisions, however, would not be binding. Under article V, Congress would not be compelled to make its final decision on aggregation of applications until that point at which it was required to make a decision with respect to an actual convention call. The requirement of an ongoing effort at determining the aggregation question is designed primarily to limit opportunities for political manipulation at this point of the application process, as well as to allow States which are not aggregated in what they consider the proper manner to amend their convention applications.

As observed earlier, it is the objective of the "same general subject of subjects" standard to ensure the existence of some real consensus among the States with respect to the need for constitutional revision in some relatively circumscribed area. At the same time, in order not to interfere with the legitimate freedom of action of a convention, there ought not to be the requirement of extreme precision, either in the text or the subject-matter. The language contained in the bill is designed to draw some rough balance between these considerations.

In order to ensure that the consensus for a constitutional amendment remains a relatively contemporaneous one, *Dillion* [sic] *v. Gloss* (256 U.S. 368 (1921)), section 5(a) states that an application shall be effective for no longer than a 7-year period, with shorter effective periods contained within the body of an application to be respected. [Hatch quotes from *Dillon*.]

Similarly, State convention applications and the calling of a constitutional convention are not unrelated acts, but necessary, succeeding steps in a single endeavor. There should be a reasonable relationship in time, between these actions, *Coleman v. Miller*, (307 U.S. 433 (1938). There is the same need to avoid staleness of applications to Congress as there is to avoid staleness of amendment proposals to the States.

In view of the fact that every amendment proposed by Congress, except one, since the 18th amendment, has contained a 7-year time limitation, either in the body or in the enacting clause, it has been decided to use this same period for determining effectiveness [of] applications.

Language has also been included in this section which maintains the effectiveness, for a minimum of 2 years, of those applications which have been submitted to Congress within the previous 16-year period, notwithstanding the expiration of the regular 7-year period. This provision is designed to ensure that those applications, submitted in recent years which have not had the statutory guidance of procedures legislation, are kept temporarily effective for a short transitional period.

Section 5(b) authorizes States to withdraw their applications at any time prior to the time that there are a sufficient number of valid applications before Congress to enable it to call a convention. There would seem to be no valid policy reason for denying them this right. Indeed, in order to ensure that the amendment process reflects the notion of contemporaneous consensus, it is vital that the States should not be dragooned unwillingly into an artificial consensus because of an inability to rethink earlier application decisions.

Calling of the Convention

Section 6 of the Constitution Convention Implementation Act relates to the actual calling by Congress of the convention. It provides that, upon receipt in each House of the application putting two-thirds of the States in agreement on the need for some particular amendment or amendments, it is the duty of that House to call for convening of a Federal constitutional convention on the general subject or subjects. Congress is to designate the time and place of the meeting of the convention, and set forth the general subject of the amendment or amendments for consideration. The convention is to be convened not later than 8 months following the adoption by Congress of its resolutions.

Despite some misconceptions on this point, it is obligatory that Congress call a convention upon the receipt of valid applications by two-thirds of the States. [Hatch quotes Hamilton and Madison to this effect.]

Convention Delegates

Section 7 relates to the selection of delegates to the constitutional convention. The language is taken nearly verbatim form article II, section 1, paragraph 2 of the Constitution concerning the selection of Presidential electors. The great compromise between the larger and the smaller States is carried over into the selection of convention delegates with each State being entitled to that number of delegates equal to the combined number of its Senators and Representatives in Congress. The States are given a free hand in selecting their delegates in whatever—constitutional—manner they deem appropriate.

If the experience of the electoral college is at all relevent [sic]—and I believe that it is—each of the States will no doubt introduce some means of popular election for the delegate positions. I would be personally opposed to any other manner of selection, although I do not believe that it is the business of this body to specify particular procedures for the States.

While there are those who would prefer to see a delegate selection system more precisely based upon population, I see no reason not to extend smaller States that slight disproportionate influence in the proposal of amendments through the convention system that they currently enjoy in the proposal of amendments through the congressional system. The apportionment procedures in section 7 is the method of delegate selection that most closely conforms to the basis for congressional representation and which would most closely aline the alternative systems of proposing amendments.

Section 7 also excludes Members of Congress, the very embodiment of the national influence, from serving as convention delegates and confers the same immunity from arrest upon convention delegates, for the duration of the convention, that article I, section 6 of the Constitution confers upon Members of Congress.

Convening of Convention

Section 8 directs each delegate to the convention to subscribe to an oath by which he commits himself, during the conduct of the convention, to comply with the Constitution of the United States.

Administering the oath of office to the delegates would be the senior chief judge of the highest courts of the States. Rather than having the Vice President or Chief Justice of the United States, fill this function, it is my belief that what is basically a State convention should remain that and not run any unnecessary risks, however remote, of being influenced by national officials. I emphasize again the basic purpose of including the convention method of amendment in article V—the need for the States to be able to amend the Constitution in the face of an intransigent National Government.

Convention Procedures

Section 8 states that the convention itself is to have responsibility for drawing up its own rules of procedures, rather than Congress, except that there is to be no unit-rule voting procedures. No Federal funds may be appropriated specifically for the payment of the expenses of the convention, except that the Administrator of the General Services Administration is authorized to provide facilities for the convention, and incur whatever incidental expenses are necessary related to this provision of facilities. At the request of the convention, the Federal Government is also permitted to provide sundry technical information and assistance to the convention.

Section 9 provides that the convention is to maintain a daily verbatim record of the proceedings, analogous to the CONGRESSIONAL RECORD. All records of official proceedings are to be transmitted by the convention to the National Archives within 30 days following termination of the proceedings of the convention. This section also requires the termination of the convention within 6 months of its convening unless Congress agrees to extent it at the convention's request.

Section 10 again underscores that premise of this act that a limited convention may properly be called. It restates what is already implicit in the act that the convention called under its terms may not propose amendments of a general subject different from that stated in the convention's charter—the resolution approved by Congress. The convention exercises no legitimate governmental authority beyond that granted by the

States through Congress. The convention thus is morally obliged to limit its considerations to the subjects set forth in the State applications; I believe further that it is appropriate for Congress to establish a legal obligation to this same effect.

Submission of Amendments to States

Section 11 concerns the procedures through which the convention product is submitted to the States for ratification. Within 30 days after the completion of the convention, its presiding officer is to transmit the exact text of any proposed amendments to Congress. The officers to [sic] each House within 30 more days of continuous session, are to transmit the amendments to the General Services Administration who, in turn, is to submit the amendments to the States. The amendments are to be accompanied by a congressional resolution specifying, pursuant to article V, the model of ratification—whether it is to be ratified by the State legislatures or by special ratifying conventions within each of the States.

Congress may refuse to transmit an amendment and resolution to the States only if it makes the determination that the amendment relates to or includes a general subject which differs from, or was not included as one of the general subjects within the scope of the convention's authority. The objective is to provide some remedy for a failure by the convention to honor the limitations on its authority to propose amendments to the Constitution. Congress has no power whatsoever to refuse to submit an amendment because of disagreement with its substantive merits. Nor is it empowered to refuse to submit an amendment because of what it perceives as procedural irregularities in the proceedings of the convention. Convention procedure is not within the ambit of congressional concern; checks upon procedural abuse must come from the States themselves in the form of the ratification process. Because this check also exists with respect to conventions acting in an ultra vires manner, it is hoped that Congress will resolve any doubts as to whether or not the convention acted within the scope of its authority in favor of an affirmative finding.

Ratification of Amendments

Section 12 of the act, borrowing language directly from article V, states simply that amendments proposed by "limited" constitutional conventions are to become part of the Constitution when ratified in accordance with the terms of article V—by three-fourths of the States in a timely and proper manner. Certified copies of the ratification documents are to be forwarded by the States to the General Services Administration, although the ratification itself becomes effective once action is completed within the State legislature, *Dillon v. Gloss* (256 U.S. 368, 376 D(1921)).

Section 13 expressly holds that the States are free to reconsider and reverse their ratification decisions, at least until that point at which an amendment has been ratified by three-fourths of the States. Thus, any State may ratify a proposed amendment after having previously rejected it, or may rescind an earlier ratification of a proposed amendment. It is again my view that the most reliable determination of the existence —or lack thereof—of a contemporaneous consensus can be made if the States are free to reconsider and rethink their ratification decisions until that point at which three-fourths of the States are in agreement in support of amendment, or until that point that a reasonable period of time has passed for ratification. . . .

Section 14 imposes upon the General Services Administration the duty to proclaim the final ratification of an amendment once it is in receipt of certifications of ratification from three-fourths of the States. As section 16 clarifies, however, this is an administrative duty of a symbolic nature, not one with an impact upon the actual effectiveness of an amendment. Under article V—and section 16—the amendment becomes part of the Constitution at the moment the final State has ratified, or on any date specified in the body of the amendment itself.

Judicial Review

Finally, Section 15 relates to the role of the judicial branch in the constitutional convention process. It establishes two express situations in which an allegedly aggrieved State may bring a direct action in the Supreme Court, pursuant to article III, section 2 of the Constitution. The first involves cases in which a State disputes any determination or finding by Congress, or the failure of Congress to make a determination or finding, with respect to its section 6 responsibilities. Section 6 requires Congress to "call" a convention upon determining the existence of valid applications for such a convention from two-thirds of the States.

The second situation involves cases in which Congress' actions, with respect to its section 11 responsibilities, are questioned. Section 11 requires Congress to submit amendments proposed by the convention to the States unless it determines that the convention acted on subject matter outside the purview of its authority.

Section 15(c) expressly states that these two actions may not be inclusive with respect to the right to a Supreme Court hearing, and that nothing in the act limits the right to judicial review of any other decision made under the act or such review as is otherwise provided by the Constitution or any other law of the United States. Section 15 further requires suit to be brought within 60 days of a claim against the Secretary of the Senate, the Clerk of the House, the General Service Administrator, or any other party as may be necessary to afford the relief sought.

Thus, the act would reject that version of the so-called political questions doctrine that suggests that all interpretative matters deriving from article V are to be resolved by Congress solely at its discretion. I find it ironic that so many individuals who have been so sympathetic to the advance of judicial activism in recent years are also those who would deny the Federal courts, particularly the Supreme Court, their constitutional obligation to interpret the plain language of that document. . . .

Conclusion

Mr. President, the convention method of constitutional amendment has been defended and described as an essential component of our Constitution by such statesmen as James Madison, Alexander Hamilton, George Washington, Benjamin

Franklin, and Abraham Lincoln. While no amendment has ever been ratified that has been proposed through this method, it has nevertheless exerted its influence in indirect ways. The 17th amendment to the Constitution, for example —providing for the direct election of U.S. Senators—was proposed by Congress in 1912 in response to an effort in the States to call a convention on this subject. Other convention efforts on such matters as Federal tax limitation and State legislative apportionment have also evoked a significant congressional response. It is clear, too, that the present balanced budget movement is having an impact upon national public policy.

It is necessary in order to insure some measure of symmetry in the alternative amendment processes under article V to establish clearcut procedures for resort to the convention method. While the absence of legislation such as the Constitutional Convention Implementation Act will not preclude the States from exercising their right to call a convention, it will insure that the amendment process will become bogged down in constant litigation, partisan political decisions, and constitutional uncertainty. The effect on this can only be to undermine the integrity of our constitutional system. In the process, also, we will erode one of the basic institutions for preserving some semblance of balance between the national and the State governments. [Hatch quotes Hamilton.]

While there is not one who respects more than I do the achievement of the Founding Fathers, nor anyone who would place a greater burden of proof upon those who propose to alter the Constitution, I would nevertheless agree with Prof. Malcolm Eiselen who states:

> To assume, as many apparently do, that a second convention could alter the Constitution only for the worse . . . is an unwarrantable libel upon the creative statesmanship and political sagacity of the American people.

The purpose of the Constitutional Convention Implementation Act is to prevent both Congress and the constitutional convention from acting outside the scope of each of their proper authority. It is designed to insure that the States, in the event that Congress remains intransigent with respect to some issue of constitutional controversy, are able to circumvent Congress and act on their own to remedy such a situation. It is designed also to insure that the States—and Congress—are not forced to surrender totally their sovereignty to the convention. It is designed to insure that the same matrix of constitutional checks and balances is applicable to the constitutional convention as to the other permanent institutions within our governmental system.

There can be no runaway convention unless, ultimately, the dissatisfaction of the people are so broad and pervasive that it is a runaway convention that they expressly desire. The best way that Congress can work to insure that this never becomes the case is to allow the people and the States to work their will under established procedures when their grievances are more narrow and more limited, rather than allowing them to fester as a result of contrived procedural irregularities. It is occasionally sobering to some of my colleagues, yet it is true, that ultimately it is the citizenry, not Congress, that is the responsible party in our political system.

7.12. The Flag Desecration Amendment

In *Texas v. Johnson*, 109 S. Ct. 2533 (1989), the Supreme Court overturned the conviction of a protestor at the Republican National Convention who had burned an American flag. The Court reasoned that he had been convicted not for burning the flag but for the political ideas which he had attempted to express—ideas whose expression is protected by the First Amendment.

An amendment, backed by President Bush and others, was soon proposed which would have provided that, "The Congress and the States shall have the power to prohibit physical desecration of the flag of the United States."

Despite strong pressure, Congress rejected this amendment for a statute designed to do the same thing. When the Supreme Court subsequently overruled this statute in *United States v. Eichman*, 110 S. Ct. 2404 (1990), proponents again pushed for an amendment. They found, however, that support for such a proposal had eroded as many members of Congress began to think about the dangers of altering the Bill of Rights and the precedent that this might set. As a consequence, the amendment failed to get the necessary majorities when voted on in Congress. Congress could, of course, reconsider this measure; with the appointment of new justices, it is also possible that the Supreme Court will reverse these opinions

7.13. The Twenty-Seventh Amendment

In May, 1992, many observers were startled when the thirty-eighth state ratified the Twenty-Seventh Amendment providing that, "No law, varying the compensation for the services of the Senators and Representatives, shall take effect, until an election of Representatives shall have intervened."

Given the rising expressions of concern about perceived congressional abuses of power and opposition to past pay raises, the subject of the amendment was not surprising. What was unusual was the fact that the amendment was first proposed by James Madison as one of twelve amendments (ten of which became the Bill of Rights) back in 1789. Originally ratified by six of the eleven states required, the amendment was given a seventh ratification in 1897 and an eighth in 1978. Subsequent ratifications had been mustered by Gregory Watson, an aide to a Texas state legislator, who had discovered the dormant amendment while doing research on a term paper for a political science class.

Although the amendment had not, like some later ones, been proposed to the state with a ratification deadline, its belated ratification certainly raised doubts among those who believed that amendments should express a contemporary consensus of opinion. Clearly feeling the political heat, Congress quickly voted to accept the amendment, an action which, having occurred only one other time in American history (with the adoption of the Fourteenth Amendment) arguably highlighted still further the bizarre precedent that this amendment seemed to set.

Index